Mythistory

Mythistory

The Making of a Modern Historiography

JOSEPH MALI

THE UNIVERSITY OF CHICAGO PRESS

CHICAGO AND LONDON

Joseph Mali teaches history at Tel Aviv University. He is the author of
The Rehabilitation of Myth: Vico's New Science.

The University of Chicago Press, Chicago 60637
The University of Chicago Press, Ltd., London
© 2003 by The University of Chicago
All rights reserved. Published 2003
Printed in the United States of America

12 11 10 09 08 07 06 05 04 03   1 2 3 4 5

ISBN: 0-226-50262-7 (cloth)

Library of Congress Cataloging-in-Publication Data

Mali, Joseph.
    Mythistory : the making of a modern historiography / Joseph Mali.
        p. cm.
    Includes bibliographical references and index.
    ISBN 0-226-50262-7 (cloth : alk. paper)
        1. History—Historiography.   2. Historiography.   3. Mythology—Historiography.
    4. History, Ancient—Historiography.   5. History, Modern—Historiography.
    I. Title.

    D13 .M268 2003
    907'.2—dc21

                                                                    2002015446

For Maya, Daniella, and Tom

AND HERE STANDS MAN, *stripped of myth, eternally starving, surrounded by every past there has ever been, digging and scrabbling for roots, even if he must dig for them in the most remote antiquities. The tremendous historical need of our unsatisfied modern culture, the accumulation of countless other cultures, the consuming desire for knowledge—what does all this point to, if not to the loss of myth, the loss of the mythical home, the mythical maternal womb?*

FRIEDRICH NIETZSCHE, *The Birth of Tragedy*

Contents

Preface

Although I came upon the notion of "mythistory" rather late in my life, I have known what it means for many years. For life in Jerusalem, around the sites of stories that have permeated the venerable histories of whole religions, nations, and civilizations, has long alerted me to the fact that however modern we might have all become, our life and history are still largely determined by some very ancient myths. How could it otherwise be that the biblical and later historical fictions spun around Mount Moriah in the Old City continue to incite such volatile emotions and actions? Why do so many intelligent people believe in stories that are plainly false? And why would so many others, who don't believe in these or any other stories that consecrate ancient ancestries and territories, still live (and die) in and for this or that Holy Land? How does myth relate to history?

These were the initial questions that set me upon my inquiry into the substance and persistence of myth in history. This inquiry soon proved to be unfathomable, at least for a cultural historian who, much like his master, Burckhardt, is not a *philosophischer Kopf.*" In the present study I still pursue the same initial existential questions that have long preoccupied me, however, even if I now do so indirectly, more reflectively, and by using more practicable measures. For over the years I have redirected and restricted my reflections to the substance and persistence of myth in *historiography.* Having realized that even—and especially—those historians who do not believe mythical history are bound to live it, I began to inquire whether, and to what extent, traditional and professional historians have been aware of the mythical compulsions that motivate all historical actions and creations (including their own). The decision to concentrate on this problem was spurred by the impression that the common terms by which historians have usually sought to account for the origins and functions of myths in history were inadequate. In the long history of historiography, the basic categories of both myth and history have always been defined antithetically, as if myth was all fabrication and pure fiction and therefore a spurious description of what merely appears to have happened, whereas history was a serious and reliable explanation of what actually happened insofar as its empirical sources and discourses were veritable. Assuming thus that myths were utterly primitive and fictive representations of historical reality, critical historians from Thucydides to Ranke, as well as all their modern followers, have commonly failed to account for the psychological and historical conditions under which these archaic modes of historical comprehension and composition were formed, what higher metaphysical truths they served, and, ultimately, why they still persist in the collective imagination and cultural traditions of all religions, nations, and civilizations. Even such great scholars as Karl Marx and Marc Bloch, who were otherwise cognizant of the dominance of certain classical and theological myths in the political history of France, dismissed these myths, respectively, as "self-deception" and "collective error" and thus failed to appreciate their real significance in the creation of French national traditions and institutions. Contemporary historians have likewise tended to dismiss the astounding proliferation of racial and social myths in the last century as an aberration in or as a reaction to the process of modernization, or, to use the fashionable terms of Marxists and other critical theorists, as yet another example of the "invention of tradition."

Against this apparent "modern" historiography that criticizes myth, I propose an alternative historiography that recognizes myth for what it is: a story that has passed into and become history. The critical task of this historiography, or *mythistory*, is to reappraise these stories as inevitable, and ultimately valuable, histories of personal and communal identity. Such, for example, are the myths of common ancestry and territory that define and defend the national community, or, more fundamentally, the primordial myths of birth and death, fertility and purity, damnation and salvation, and so on, that make up the moral and cultural inhibitions of humanity. As the subtitle of the book indicates, mythistory is essential to the making of modern historiography because it consists, like all modern arts and human sciences, in the recognition of myth.

As noted above, I grappled with the topics that make up this book long before I actually wrote it. During those years I was fortunate to discuss its initial notions and plan with two unforgettable mentors, the late Isaiah

Berlin and Amos Funkenstein, whose words of wisdom accompanied me throughout the work. I also wish to thank my former teachers Zvi Yavetz, Saul Friedländer, Michael Confino, and Ernst Schulin, from whom I continue to learn. My friend and colleague Jonathan Price deserves special thanks for the lively conversations we have had during our routine voyage from Tel Aviv to Jerusalem.

My greatest personal and professional debt is to Lionel Gossman. His studies in modern historiography are a source of pleasure and intellectual stimulation—not only because they are marvelously written, but also because they are permeated with profound humanistic convictions. Although our perceptions of modern historiography are quite different, he was most generous with his comments on earlier versions of this book. Mark Lilla read the entire manuscript with his customary critical acuity. I have benefited greatly from his incisive observations, which enabled me to rearrange substantial parts of it into a more "symphonic" composition. Jeffrey Barash read the first chapter and raised some important philosophical questions on the ethical and political implications of mythistory that required me to revisit and refit its foundations. Thanks are also due to an anonymous reader for the University of Chicago Press whose commentary led to a slight yet significant alteration in the subtitle of the book.

I wish to express my deep gratitude to John Tryneski, my editor at the University of Chicago Press, for the firm judgment and encouragement he has shown throughout the process of evaluation, and to his assistant Anne Ford for her meticulous attention at all stages of production. I was fortunate to enjoy the expertise of Lois R. Crum, whose editorial skills were greatly appreciated.

Portions of this book have appeared in different form in the following articles: "Real Narratives: Myth, History, and Mythistory," in *Storia della storiografia* 30 (1996): 3–18; "Ernst Kantorowicz: History as *Mythenschau*," in *History of Political Thought* 18 (1997): 579–603; "The Reconciliation of Myth: Benjamin's Homage to Bachofen," *Journal of the History of Ideas* 60 (1999): 165–87. I am grateful to the respective publishers for permission to reprint passages from these publications.

All quotations from non-English works are my own except where indicated otherwise.

Finally, I would like to express my grateful thanks to my wife, Anya, for having given me the time and energy to bring this work to completion. I dedicate the book to my children, Maya, Daniella, and Tom, who might one day understand what it is all about.

ONE

Where Terms Begin: Myth, History, and Mythistory

Ever since Herodotus declared that the aim of his *History* was to preserve the memory of "the great and wonderful actions of the Greeks and the Barbarians,"[1] the debate on the use and abuse of myths in historiography has never been safely laid to rest. For what Herodotus implied in this assertion was that the task of the historian is not to eliminate but to illuminate historical myths: "For myself, my duty is to report all that is said; but I am not obliged to believe it all alike—a remark which may be understood to apply to my whole *History*."[2] Herodotus was well aware that such fanciful tales about gods and heroes as he had recorded from the Babylonians and the Egyptians might render his *History* more mythological than historical, but he trusted that his audience would know what the stories were all about and deal with them accordingly. Those who realized, as he did, that they were the historical myths of these nations would not ask whether they were true or false, but rather what they meant: "Such as think the tales told by the Egyptians credible are free to accept them for history. For my own part, I propose to myself throughout my whole work faithfully to record the traditions of several nations . . . If this be true, I know not; I write what is said."[3] Herodotus seems to have realized that even though these memories and tales were not proper histories of the nations, they must be preserved for, and in, their histories for further inquiries into their origins and destinies. As Arnaldo Momigliano has noted, we must bear in mind that "when Herodotus took the recording of tradition as his primary duty, he was in fact doing something more than simply saving facts from oblivion. He was guiding historical research towards the exploration of the unknown and the forgotten."[4]

Alas, the problem with Herodotus's mythological historiography was that it could not be critical about its sources. Thucydides saw this when he remarked against his predecessor that because "men accept from one another hearsay reports of former events, neglecting to test them just the same," they were leaving historical truth, and themselves, exposed to all kinds of distortion and manipulation.[5] For Thucydides and his fellow rationalists, the "mythic" signified any story that could not be tested or inquired about, either because it had occurred in too distant times or because it contained too many fantasies.[6] He knew, however, that the charms of the Homeric myths, like those of the Sirens, were too great to resist; he therefore chose, much like the hero of the *Odyssey* himself, to tie his fellow travelers, his "readers," to stricter disciplines, to make sure that they would not submit to the mythological temptation. Thus, whereas Herodotus began his *History* with a long recitation of the Homeric myths about the origins of war (relating them to marital quarrels of gods and heroes) and only then, gradually and hypothetically, developed his own theory about their mere human causes, Thucydides defied this entire oral tradition by deliberately using distinct literal measures: "Of the events of the war . . . I have described nothing but what I either saw myself, or learned from others of whom I made the most careful and particular inquiry . . . And very likely the strictly historical character of my narrative may be disappointing to the ear" of the listener, because it was written for the one who "desires to have before his eyes a true picture of the events which have happened, and of the like events which may be expected to happen hereafter in the order of human things."[7] Along with his fellow citizen Plato, who forbade the recitation of Homeric myths in the Republic, Thucydides sought to overcome the harmful forces of myth by means of a new policy of literacy.[8]

And yet, as later Greek historians like Polybius, Diodorus, or Pausanias realized, the ancient mythical tradition continued to thrive in the poetical creations, rhetorical orations, and political institutions of the nation and hence had to be reworked into its history.[9] Thus, Polybius, who echoes Thucydides in his commitment to "a history of actual events" devoid of any effects, and moreover based on seeing rather than hearing, goes on to characterize the ideal historian by citing the words with which Homer introduces Odysseus: "Tell me, oh Muse, the man of many shifts, who wandered far and wide . . . And towns of many he saw, and learnt their mind, and suffered much in heart by land and sea . . . Passing through wars of men and grievous waves."[10] This evocation of Odysseus, the man of action but also of narration, the protagonist of the myths he relates, is more pertinent to an adventurer and storyteller like Herodotus than to the analytical and critical arbiter Thucydides.

This original controversy between the patriarchs of Western historiography has since been reiterated in various controversies: Tacitus versus Livy, William of Newburgh versus Geoffrey of Monmouth, Valla versus Lactantius, Guicciardini versus Flavio Biondo, Montesquieu versus Machiavelli, Gibbon versus Bossuet and Tillemont, Ranke versus Scott, Mommsen versus Niebuhr and Bachofen, Wilamowitz-Moellendorff versus Burckhardt, Mathiez versus Michelet, Brackmann versus Kantorowicz, the *annalistes* versus all the narrativists. And it continues, implicitly at least, in many modern controversies over the essentiality of myth in and for historiography. On the whole, professional historians have followed Thucydides rather than Herodotus. Longinus's passing description of Herodotus as "the most Homeric" of historians and Plutarch's vicious attack on his credibility echo in Juan Luis Vives's charge that Herodotus was the father not of history but of lies, and such criticism may still be detected among modern classicists doing their *Quellenforschung*. There have been some brief periods when Herodotus seemed to prevail—as, for example, in the age of discoveries in the sixteenth century, when European historians harked back to his anthropological curiosity and virtuosity in the description of alien civilizations[11]—but the establishment of so-called scientific historiography in the early nineteenth century, predicated on exact measures of verification and evaluation of historical sources, signaled Thucydides' triumph. Significantly, Leopold Ranke, the founder of that school, wrote his doctoral dissertation on Thucydides.

During the past two or three decades, however, there has been a remarkable change in the evaluation of both historians. The emergence of "new cultural history" out of the new social sciences of anthropology, psychology, and narratology has shifted the attention of scholars of historiography from scientific to hermeneutic questions. For example, what do historians actually do when they tell a story? How do they thereby participate in the creation of collective memories and identities? Recent studies of Herodotus have been deeply affected by these theories and have done much to recharge them by showing how Herodotus's work may be pertinent to modern discussions on "heterology," "social memory," or "narrative construction of reality." As John Gould remarks, "Thucydidean narrative, in the very rhythms and texture of its language, claims and enacts authority. Herodotean narrative, by the same criteria, is a very different thing: it retains the rhythms and forms of oral tradition, familiar to us in folk-tales and märchen, but at the same time incorporates into the text, as folk narrative never does, its own authorial commentary on the sources and truth-value of the narrative."[12] Above all, however, Herodotus has become "modern" in his employment of historical myths in his *History*. What he intimated has in our day become a major claim in the historical profession: that in order to know who the Egyptians and all other "barbarians" really were, the historian must know who they thought they were, where they came from, and where they went. And the best—perhaps the only—way to get this knowledge is to take their historical myths seriously.

For historical myths are now commonly perceived as "foundational narratives," as stories that purport to explain the present in terms of some momentous event that occurred in the past. Stories like these are in many ways historical—though rarely, if ever, do they refer to an actual past. Rather, they refer to a virtual past, to the fact that historical communities, like religions or nations, consist in the beliefs that their members have about them—more concretely, in the stories they tell about them. As Wendy Doniger O'Flaherty has put it, "a myth is a story that is sacred to and shared by a group of people who find their most important meanings in it; it is a story believed to have been composed in the past about an event in the past, or, more rarely, in the future, an event that continues to have meaning in the present because it is remembered."[13] These stories tend to be about events that occurred in what Mircea Eliade calls *illud tempus*, the primordial mythical time that precedes historical time, and therefore they are likely to remain forever beyond historical verification or refutation. Yet, as Eliade points out, stories like that usually relate "a creation," in which "something *new, strong,* and *significant* was manifested," something that is still very actual even if it is not quite factual. Myths are not strictly historical, then, but since they serve to "reveal that the world, man, and life have a supernatural origin and history, and that this history is significant, precious, and exemplary," they impart meaning to history.[14] However legendary a myth may be, it does not signify fabrication or pure fiction, because it usually contains or refers to certain crucial issues in the history of the community, such as those that concern the common ancestry or territory of the community. These issues require and inspire *historical* myths because they pertain not only to such metaphysical mysteries as the ultimate origins and destinies of the community, but primarily to those practical verities in which the members of the community all believe and live, even though (or precisely because) they are mythical rather than logical or historical deductions. Irad Malkin has shown that this was the main function of Homer's *Odyssey* in the archaic Mediterranean civilization: the myths of return (*nostoi*) involving heroes who fought at Troy were commonly used by the Greek colonists, as well as by the indigenous peoples among whom they settled, to conceptualize and legitimate their ethnic heredity and identity. According to Malkin, "the entire ethnography of the Mediterranean could be explained as originating from the Big Bang of the Trojan War and the consequent *Nostos* diffusion." [15] The *nostoi* myths proved so effective among all the Mediterranean nations because they were universally admired, not only for their poetical superiority, but also, and primarily, for their historical authority: for many centuries they served as the standard measure of communication and mediation in "international" affairs. They would probably not have lasted if they did not contain at least some truths that could not be otherwise known.

This informal definition of historical myths as "foundational," that is to say as stories that retain their original narrative force and essential meaning from generation to generation, is now widely accepted by classicists and social anthropologists. [16] The anthropologist Percy Cohen has pointed out that it is not accidental that the greatest myths of our or any other civilization are concerned with beginnings, with "a moment in time in which a series of events is anchored"; rather, this is the rule of myth: "To locate things in time, even if the exact time is unspecified, creates a far more effective device for legitimization, for example, than simply creating a set of abstract ideas which are timeless." [17] The impersonal style of the mythical narration, aptly characterized by Claude Lévi-Strauss as "anonymous, collective, and objective," [18] serves this purpose by making the messages impervious to any logical or historical refutation: "The original form (provided this notion means anything) is and remains forever elusive. However far we may go, a myth is known only as something that has been heard and repeated." [19] According to Clifford Geertz, myths serve as "symbolic models of emotion"; that is to say they lay out for us basic precedents, rules, and prescriptions for "cultural" reaction against our own "natural" reactions. "In order to make up our minds we must know how we feel about things; and to know how we feel about things we need the public images of sentiment that only ritual, myth, and art can provide." [20]

From a more historical perspective, the anthropologist Victor Turner has rightly pointed out that as stories that purport to impose meaning on social life in contingent critical (i.e., historical) situations, myths are not dogmatic but dramatic stories of tradition. They become significant precisely in moments when common traditional meanings of life and history have become indeterminate, as in wars or revolutions, and their social utility is to sustain the structural tradition of society by some dramatic reactivation of its original motivations. "Where historical life itself fails to make cultural sense in terms that formerly held good, narrative and cultural drama may have the task of *poesis,* that is of remaking cultural sense."[21] Or, to rephrase this notion in Malinowski's well-known terms, historical myths function as "social charters"—the narration of ultimate origins and ends of the most fundamental laws and institutions of the community secures their authority against any rational or historical attack on their validity.[22] Through their commemoration in the religious and national traditions of the historical community, these stories set up its moral norms and social forms of life.[23] And to the extent that the members of that community share and carry out these traditional meanings in their social actions, their historical reality is meaningful only within the narratives that make up their tradition. Historical myths might thus be simply redefined as those stories that are not merely told but actually lived.

Ernest Renan realized as much when he claimed long ago that as historical narrations of successive generations, myths not only are needed to form a national identity, but they also pass into that identity itself, so that in order to understand what it means to be French, for example, the historian has to accept certain common stories that might be "wrong" (e.g., Joan of Arc) as "true," that is, as effective insofar as they are affective.[24] Modern social theorists and historians of nationalism have generally come to accept this assumption.[25] As Anthony Smith has observed, although "civic" elements

> are obviously required to maintain a nation in the modern world with its particular complex of economic and political conditions, ethnic profiles and identities are increasingly sought, if only to stem the tide of rationalisation and disenchantment. It is to their ethnic symbols, values, myths and memories that so many populations turn for inspiration and guidance, not in the everyday, practical business of running a state, but for that sense of fraternity and heroism which will enable them to conduct their affairs successfully.[26]

On these premises Smith seeks to reassess the contribution of past and modern historians to that process. Although he duly recognizes that historians since the nineteenth century have commonly sought to determine national identities by forging a sense of unity and continuity with the past and have thereby served national ideologies, Smith nevertheless points out that historians have also been, and should always remain, those who could best discern, explain, and criticize these social operations for what they are.[27] Smith rightly concludes that whether historians work for or against national myths, they must work on myths; that is to say they must recognize the role of myth in the constitution of national identities.

It seems, however, that most historians still tend to dismiss myths as false histories and, as such, inauthentic sources of national identity. This is evidently true of Pierre Nora and his collaborators on *Realms of Memory*, who seem to accept that the "national identity" of modern France is largely made up of canonical memories and myths and yet assume that the critical task of history is to expose, so as to oppose, the fallacies of mythical memory that abound in the popular traditions and locations of French history.[28] Yet, whereas Nora and like-minded historians at least seek to write national history out of—even if ultimately against—its mythical sources, the more radical historians of the old Marxist or the new postcolonialist schools still tend to denounce myths of the nation as ideological fabrications or "inventions" of the ruling authorities. For these historians, historical myths are just means to masquerade, under the false pretenses of communal unity and continuity, real sociopolitical tensions and conflicts and historical ruptures. Note, for example, Eric Hobsbawm's explanation for "the invention of tradition" in modern political cultures: "It is clear that plenty of political institutions, ideological movements and groups—not least in nationalism—were so unprecedented that even historic continuity had to be invented, for example by creating an ancient past beyond effective historical continuity either by semi-fiction (Boadicea, Vercingetorix, Arminius the Cheruscan) or by forgery (Ossian, the Czech medieval manuscripts)."[29]

Hobsbawm's sociological and psychological explanation of "the invention of tradition" in modern nations is ingenious, and it might be correct on factual grounds. The edification of a continuous Aryan tradition from Arminius the Cheruscan might well be seen as an "invention" of the German nationalists. Yet what do we mean by "invention"? The German nationalists did not invent the historical myth of Arminius, nor did they invent the Germanic tradition that had evolved around him since antiquity. Like their predecessors in the Renaissance, they merely revived and greatly amplified the memorable descriptions of Tacitus.[30] The Aryan myth was not so much an invention of a new German identity as an evocation of a very old one, an identity that was not really imposed on modern Germans; it was revealed to them by new interpretations and creations of that myth. As Benedict Anderson has explained, nations are "imagined communities" that do not merely invent but actually consist in myths of historical unity and continuity.[31] He points out that "if nation states are widely considered to be 'new' and 'historical,' the nation states to which they give political expression always loom out of an immemorial past and . . . glide into a limitless future," so that nationalism must be aligned not with "self-consciously held political ideologies" but rather with the much larger "cultural systems that preceded it, out of which—as well as against which—it came into being"; such systems are what I have called historical myths: the narratives that express and explain the beliefs in the common origins and destinies that alone turn the new "imagined communities" into real, because very old, ones.[32] Anderson's attempt to expose the more archaic psychological motivations and mythical associations of the seemingly "new" political-historical traditions, namely, the beliefs that preceded and enabled their modern "invention," may thus deprive the very notion of "invention" of its fashionable critical and rather mechanical connotations. It reminds us that any "invention of tradition" is a reactivation of the historical recollection that makes up and sustains the nation throughout history.

Modern historians of Germany must therefore take the historical myth of Arminius seriously because it makes sense of German history, especially since the Germans themselves have always taken it seriously. Long before the modern nationalists, they cherished their *Sagen* as authentic lessons, or *Weisungen,* of their history, and precisely because they were myths—truly objective and collective creations of *das Volk*—rather than official histories of their nation. Throughout their history they have consistently, consciously, and explicitly defined themselves as mythmakers. The origins of this self-identity lie in the classical work that defined and projected that image, Tacitus's *Germania.* Tacitus noted that the Germans grounded their ancestral and territorial claims "in their ancient songs [*carminibus antiquis*]," which were "their only way of remembering or recording their history [*quod unum apud illos memoriae et annalium genus est*]." This was a clue for Tacitus, as it is for all modern historians of Germany, that in order to know who the Germans really were, it is necessary to begin "in their ancient songs." Those are the "real narratives" that not only the people but also their historians actually have, and their task, therefore, should be to illuminate, not to eliminate, these narratives, by showing their extension or configuration of historical reality.

This "recognition of myth" defines the task of *mythistory.* Although the term itself is a neologism, it carries certain connotations and functions from older historiographical traditions, which may be traced back to Herodotus, Livy, and their followers in early modern historiography, the most notable of whom are Machiavelli and Vico. The first (and only) attempt to revive the notion and tradition of mythistory in modern historiography was made by Donald R. Kelley in his important essay "Mythistory in the Age of Ranke."[33] Kelley presents mythistory as a revisionist movement in modern historiography, opposed to the dominant Rankean School on both ideological and methodological grounds. Yet Kelley applies the term, and confines his study, to the romantic historiography of the late eighteenth and early nineteenth centuries. According to Kelley, *mythistory* was until then a common, albeit pejorative, term among historians in the Enlightenment. In his *Dictionarium Brittanicum* (1730), Nathan Bailey defined mythistory as "an history mingled with false fables and tales." However, the romantic reaction to the excessive rationalism of the Enlightenment enabled historical scholars such as Herder, Schleiermacher, Creuzer, Savigny, Grimm, Bachofen, and, above all, Michelet to reassess these "false fables and tales" as historical sources and eventually as historical truths. They did not define their works as mythistory, but they practiced it. Kelley shows that their "attempt to recreate the life and thought of the remote past through a new combination of human faculties" that were not normally appreciated, let alone used, by modern historians—faculties such as imagination, fabulation, memorization—was a decisive stage in the development of cultural history. For as the romantic historians came to realize that history is made up of myths, they duly concluded that it must be interpreted—and eventually even written—in terms of those myths. As Kelley adds elsewhere, mythistory reminds us that "the study of history, like the human condition it affects to portray, cannot entirely disengage itself from the irrational and the subconscious; as a form of human memory, it cannot entirely escape its own primitive heritage."[34] This, *in nuce*, is what mythistory is all about.

The romantic fashion of mythistory did not last. It is nowadays known, if at all, mainly through the caricature of Mr. Casaubon in George Eliot's novel *Middlemarch* (1872). Eliot describes Mr. Casaubon as a typical romantic historian who, infatuated by the belief that "all the mythical fragments in the world were corruptions of a tradition originally revealed," wastes his whole life and nearly destroys the life of his young wife, Dorothea, in a futile search for "the key to all mythologies." After his death the sensible Dorothea dismisses the whole project as pathetic and unscientific, considering its mythologies just "shattered mummies, and fragments of a tradition which was itself a mosaic wrought from crushed ruins."[35]

Fifty years after George Eliot's renunciation of mythistory, her namesake, the poet T. S. Eliot, came to recognize the quest for the "mythical" for what it is: a sign of modernity. The romantic reversion to myth is distinctly modern insofar as it signifies disenchantment with the very notion of modernity. It marks a new phase in the process of reaction to the alienation or (to use Eliot's phrase) "dissociation of sensibility" that emerged in the scientific revolution of the seventeenth century and intensified during the first decades of the nineteenth century, as the shocks and ruptures of the age of revolution seemed to destroy the very notion of a durable and usable "tradition." As Richard Terdiman has argued, in that period the "people experienced the insecurity of their culture's involvement with its past, the perturbation of the link to their own inheritance," and were thus forced to grapple with what he calls a "memory crisis: a sense that their past had somehow evaded memory, that recollection had ceased to integrate with consciousness."[36] The romantics sought to overcome this critical realization of modernity by radical valorization of its deeper historicity. Their energetic efforts to repair the disruption of memorial tradition by means of artificial commemoration, to fashion the nation through narration, signify, for Terdiman, a new, self-conscious, and hence very modern attempt at recollection. Because the romantics sought to reveal alternative, more imaginative patterns of continuation between the past and the present, to expose, as Baudelaire did, the network of sensual associations, or *correspondances,* that renders the experience of urbanity compatible with that of primitive antiquity, they were distinctly modernistic, as were all those who have since come to share this view. Benjamin characterized Kafka as an author who had lost the "significance [*Bedeutung*]" of tradition; he claimed that that was why Kafka became so acutely aware of its "predominance [*Geltung*]" in his life and in history. In general, the same could be said of all the great modernists. For only those who accept the inevitability and indispensability of tradition, those who, in other words, do not believe in the very possibility of modernity, are truly modern. This is how T. S. Eliot defined modernism in his poetry and theory.

According to Eliot, the composition of poetry, like that of history itself, is essentially traditional; that is to say it consists in the transmission of those ancient images that have made up and sustain the network of language, symbol, and institutions that we call civilization. Already in his review of Wyndham Lewis's novel *Tarr* (1916), Eliot defined the modern artist as being "more *primitive,* as well as more civilized, than his contemporaries[;] his experience is deeper than civilization, and he only uses the phenomena of civilization in expressing it."[37] This is also the main message of his classic essay "Tradition and the Individual Talent" (1919), where he defines the task of modern poetry in mythical-historical rather than radical terms, claiming that the modern poet must have a sense of history that "involves a perception, not only of the pastness of the past, but also of its presence" and "compels a man to write not merely with his own generation in his bones, but with a feeling that the whole of the literature of Europe from Homer and within it the whole of the literature of his own country has a simultaneous existence and composes a simultaneous order."[38] Eliot accomplished this task in *The Waste Land*.

Because *modernism* is one of those "essentially contested terms" that defy common definition, I would like to make clear that I thoroughly endorse Eliot's conception. As becomes clear below and throughout this study, "modern" historiography, as I perceive it, consists in the "recognition of myth." This may not be the explicit meaning that many modernists have expounded in their numerous "manifestos" of the movement. Pound's exclamation—"Make it New!"—is probably still the most pervasive idea of modernism.[39] And yet, as Paul de Man has shown in his famous essay on Nietzsche and the genealogy of modernism, if "being modern" is defined by the "desire to wipe out whatever came earlier, in the hope of reaching at last a point that could be called a true present, a point of origin that marks a new departure," then Nietzsche's recognition of the deep historicity, or "mythicity," of all our human actions and institutions defies his own attempt to undo this predicament. "It becomes impossible to overcome history in the name of life or to forget the past in the name of modernity, because both are linked by a temporal chain that gives them a common destiny."[40] Nietzsche, like all true modernists, became a modernist only by failing to be one, or, as I would put it, once he had come to the "recognition of myth."

Following on this astute conception of the modern, I redefine *mythistory* accordingly. My main argument is that this classic-romantic historiographical tradition initiated a certain movement *in* modern historiography that *is* modern historiography in the original and full sense of the term. As proponents of the "modern," from Baudelaire (who first gave the term its current connotations) through Nietzsche (who first defined thereby a new kind of historiography) to all their many followers, have claimed in their artistic and theoretical works, the "modern" consists in the recognition of myth as the primal "order" in human life and history. Eliot's famous characterization of Joyce's *Ulysses* in these terms has long been the canonical definition of modernism:

> In using the myth, in manipulating a continuous parallel between contemporaneity and antiquity, Mr. Joyce is pursuing a method which others must pursue after him. They will not be imitators, any more than the scientist who uses the discoveries of an Einstein in pursuing his own, independent, further investigations. It is simply a way of controlling, of

ordering, of giving a shape and significance to the immense panorama of futility and anarchy which is contemporary history. It is a method . . . for which the horoscope is auspicious. Psychology (such as it is, and whether our reaction to it be comic or serious), ethnology, and *The Golden Bough* have concurred to make possible what was impossible even a few years ago. Instead of narrative method, we may now use the mythical method. It is, I seriously believe, a step toward making the modern world possible for art.[41]

When Eliot wrote these words, he had already worked out this "mythical method" to perfection in his own great poem *The Waste Land*. The apparent parody in the "continuous parallel" treatment of ancient myths in both works—the representation of Leopold Bloom as a modern Odysseus in *Ulysses* and of the chaotic scenes on London Bridge as modern Punic Wars in *The Waste Land*—has often been taken to mean that the "mythical method" in question and modernism at large consist in the ironic exploitation and desecration of these myths, as if the whole point of their evocation were to liberate the modern self from these and all other honorific traditions and ultimately from history itself.[42] This is the common interpretation of Stephen Dedalus's famous cry that history is the nightmare from which he is trying to awake. However, as many critical commentators have seen, the ironical allusions to myth in *Ulysses* and in *The Waste Land* do not necessarily convey an ironical conception of myth as such. Rather, they attest to the acute critical and historical perception of the potency and relevancy of myths, even in an age that cannot live up to their classical "heroic" order and standards. For even in the most ironical descriptions of common men like Leopold Bloom or Stetson as pathetic modern "heroes," and however accidental or superficial their relationship to the prototypical mythical figures may appear, the human experiences and problems they confront are like those that the mythical heroes, and indeed all men, must deal with: mortality, liberty, sexuality, and other eternal insoluble riddles.[43] Thomas Mann writes in his own "mythical novel" *Joseph and His Brothers:* "For it *is*, always *is*, however much we say it was. Thus speaks the myth, which is only the garment of mystery."[44] It is this sense of repetition and integration of the self in the larger forces of life and history, of the continuity between ancient civilizations and our own, and of the unity of all human experiences that the "mythical method" reveals. A passage from Eliot's *Use of Poetry and the Use of Criticism* shows what he meant by this method: "Why, for all of us, out of all that we have heard, seen, felt in a lifetime, do certain images recur, charged with emotion rather than others?" He then singles out five images, some of which have reappeared in his own poetry, and concludes: "Such memories may have symbolic value, but of what we cannot tell, for they come to represent the depths of feeling into which we cannot peer."[45] The realization of the continuity and the simultaneity of these images in history defies the liberal conception of advancement and development in history. It is above all this recognition of myth that renders the "mythical method" more appropriate than the "narrative method" to express and to explain modern history. Eliot thus adds that the employment of myth in *Ulysses* "has the importance of a scientific discovery," apparently not only for literature but also for all the humanities, whose practitioners must likewise discover behind "the immense panorama of futility and anarchy which is contemporary history" those permanent mythological images and narratives that impart some orientation to contingent human reality.[46]

As I noted above, it seems to me that, unlike their fellow artists and human scientists, historians have not yet come to realize the full potential of the "mythical method" and therefore have failed to produce a historiography that is really and clearly "modern" in the same way that "modern literature" or "modern art" are. Moreover, inattention to the "mythical method" has affected not only historians but also scholars of historiography who have otherwise called for the creation of "modern historiography" along the guidelines of the modern arts and sciences. Thus, in his classic essay "The Burden of History" (1965), Hayden White argues that a modernistic turn in historiography is both possible and indispensable if historians wish to make their works relevant to contemporary readers. Following the path of scientists like Einstein, Freud, and Weber, or artists such as Joyce or Kafka, the modern historian must likewise overcome the positivistic modes of exploration and representation that prevailed in the "realistic" arts and sciences of the nineteenth century and "come to terms with the techniques of analysis and representation that *modern* science and *modern* art have offered for understanding the operations of consciousness and social process."[47] But White's notion of the "modern" in the arts and sciences is much too formal; it pertains only to the "techniques" by which the modernists evoke their perceptions of reality, assuming, it seems, that the employment of such modes of representation as juxtaposition, involution, reduction, and distortion betrays a deeper ironic and even nihilistic perception of a reality devoid of all objective order, laws, and truths and thus open, as White would have it, to all sorts of new subjective interpretations and artistic creations. Like Eliot, White equates modernism with the renunciation of the conventional "narrative method" that dominated the sciences and the arts in the nineteenth century, from natural history to the novel and to Rankean historiography.

Significantly, the only historian whom White regards as "modern" in that sense is Jacob Burckhardt, whose *Civilization of the Renaissance in Italy* White deems an "impressionistic historiography," similar to what contemporary artists like Baudelaire or Cézanne were aiming at. Although I generally concur with this judgment of Burckhardt as modernist in this (and only in this!) specific artistic sense, I would like to add—and I explain in chapter 3, on Burckhardt—that he was modern because he pursued the "mythical method." His initial perception of history as "mystery and poetry" set him apart from those who saw in history "a source of knowledge, a science,"[48] and, moreover, turned his historiography into a contemplation of the poetic means, the myths, that poets and artists, as well as all other humanists, have always used to perceive the "mystery" of human life and history. Having thus recognized the mythical constitution of the human condition, Burckhardt inveighed against those "who regard the past as a contrast to and preliminary stage of our own time as the full development" and concluded: "We shall study the *recurrent, constant* and *typical* as echoing in us and intelligible through us"[49]—words that clearly align him with the mythistorical tradition. Although Kelley does not count Burckhardt among the mythistorians, he rightly notes that Burckhardt was "sympathetic to certain kinds of mythistory and to imaginative interpretation."[50] Burckhardt was attentive to this tradition from the time of his early theological studies and thereafter in his historical studies in Ranke's *Historisches Seminar* at the University of Berlin, where some of his teachers—such as Schelling, Savigny, and Grimm—propagated the messages of mythistory.

Thus, as in ancient historiography, so too in modern historiography, the predicament of mythistory in historiography might best be exemplified by the apparent opposition between its two patriarchs, Leopold von Ranke and Jacob Burckhardt. Whereas Ranke believed that history was (or at least had to be) a system of *Wissenschaft,* a science based on factual sources and laws, Burckhardt saw history as primarily a process of *Bildung.* As the term implies, *Bildung* grows out of *das Bild:* in the German tradition, it was generally conceived as education through instruction in the classical cultural tradition, literally by emulation (*Nachbildung*) of a concrete archetypical model (*Vorbild*) from its lore of figures and cases. *Bildung,* in other words, consists in the transmission of *Bilder,* mythological images, in the cultural tradition of any nation and civilization. In his great work *The Civilization of the Renaissance of Italy,* Burckhardt elaborated this process in modern history and, moreover, composed his own work accordingly, using the mythical images and tales of the Renaissance in order to illuminate his historical representation (*Darstellung*) of its civilization.

The scholar who made this "recognition of myth" essential to modern historiography was, notably, Friedrich Nietzsche, Burckhardt's colleague at the University of Basel, who, till his very last sane moment, admired Burckhardt as his "great teacher." In his *Birth of Tragedy* Nietzsche declared:

> Without myth every culture loses the healthy natural power of its creativity: only a horizon defined by myths completes and unifies a whole cultural movement . . . The images of myth have to be the unnoticed omnipresent demonic guardians, under whose care the young soul grows to maturity and whose signs help the man to interpret his life and struggles. Even the state knows no more powerful unwritten laws than the mythical foundation that guarantees its connection with religion and its growth from mythical notions.[51]

In their influential study on the origins and various meanings of the "modern" in European arts and letters, Malcolm Bradbury and James McFarland point out that the notion of myth acquired its "modernistic" connotations around the end of the nineteenth century, as both the old and the new orders and theories of European society, above all the very notion of civilization, collapsed, and thinkers and artists began to look for a new kind of "order." It should be not merely "objective," like that of the old mechanistic and other naturalistic theories, which have by now been disproved by the new discoveries in biological and physical sciences, but a more "subjective" order, "made" rather than "given," a rational reconciliation of the irrational.

> Within this situation of growing fluidity, "myth" (as Sorel was soon to argue) commended itself as a highly effective device for imposing order of a symbolic, even poetic, kind on the chaos of quotidian event . . . Born of the irrational, and obeying a logic much closer to the subjective and associative promptings of the unconscious mind than to the formal progression of scientific inquiry, myth offered a new kind of insight into the wayward realities of social phenomena.[52]

The German sociologist Ferdinand Tönnies defined modern society similarly: in his famous study of 1887, he juxtaposed premodern community (*Gemeinschaft*), based on organic life, and modern society (*Gesellschaft*), which had lost and sought to retrieve these myths of unity and continuity.[53]

This was also the tacit message of Sir James Frazer's *Golden Bough,* first published in 1890, the work that has had the most decisive effect on modern literature.[54] Although Frazer himself was not a modernist (and as a mythologist, he was rather like Mr. Casaubon), he managed to captivate a whole generation of scholars and common readers by artfully evoking the ancient myths of gods dying and being reborn, of killing and eating divine animals or men in order to acquire the powers of the god they incarnate, of totems and scapegoats, of rites of purity and fertility. His conclusion that all "these spring and harvest customs are based on the same ancient modes of thought, and form parts of the same primitive heathendom, which was doubtless practiced by our forefathers long before the dawn of history, as it is practiced to this day by many of their descendants,"[55] proved particularly effective when encountered by a generation that had lost, and sought to regain, its belief in the greatest story of resurrection of all. As Lionel Trilling has noted, "Scientific though his purpose was, Frazer had the effect of validating those old modes of experiencing the world which modern men, beginning with the Romantics, have sought to revive in order to escape from positivism and common sense."[56] Nonetheless, the primal energies and passions that Frazer exposed in the "dark pages of *The Golden Bough*" inspired the modernists to use them against Frazer's own beliefs in reason and civilization: "Nothing is more characteristic of modern literature than its discovery and canonization of the primal nonethical energies."[57]

These energies are evident in such early modernistic masterpieces as Mahler's three *Wunderhorn* symphonies (1887–1900), Conrad's *Heart of Darkness* (1899), Picasso's *Les demoiselles d'Avignon* (1907), and Nijinsky's *Le sacre du printemps* (1913), as well as in some of the major works of modern human sciences, including those of Weber, Durkheim, and Freud, which commonly exposed the vital primitive compulsions in modernity. Conrad's narrator in *Heart of Darkness,* Marlowe, reenacts the entire modernistic movement when he remarks that his journey up the river Congo to find the ivory hunter Kurtz at the Inner Station "was like travelling back to the earliest beginnings of the world."[58] The tragic fate of Kurtz, who had "gone native" and attained "knowledge" only to discover what lies in the heart of darkness—"The horror! The horror!"—seems to affirm George Steiner's observation that Conrad's novels around 1900 are the ones that, more than any other literary or philosophical work of the era, reveal "the impulses towards disintegration, the cracks in the wall of European stability."[59] But Conrad's novel may also show why and how he and his fellow modernists sought to overcome that nihilistic predicament by reversion to myth. For Marlowe's decision to follow Kurtz, the good European who was "an emissary of pity and science, and progress," was motivated by his desire to discover why Kurtz had failed to accomplish his mission of civilization. Marlowe thus defines his mission as aiming "to know what he [Kurtz] belonged to, how many powers of darkness claimed him for their own."[60] His attempt to find in primitive reality and mentality the powerful compulsions that have always defied the attempts of all good Europeans to attain those noble ideals of civilization—pity, science, progress—is redolent of what other modernists at the time were also looking for.[61]

As intellectual historians like H. Stuart Hughes, Fritz Stern, and Zeev Sternhell have pointed out, the employment of myth as a useful category by which artists and scientists have chosen to account for the vicissitudes of modern reality betrays a more pervasive tendency toward the *Kulturpessimismus* that affected many European intellectuals around the turn of the century.[62] The numerous biological, psychological, and historical theories that exposed the evolutionary and hereditary aspects of human life and history imparted scientific credibility to the notion of myth. Radical opponents of liberal democracy from both the right and the left used the new science of mythology to undermine the facile bourgeois ideology of progressive amelioration and liberation from ancient traditions and institutions.

This dialectical pattern of "recognition of myth" emerges most clearly in Carl Schorske's magisterial study of the phenomenal modernistic movement in fin-de-siècle Vienna.[63] Schorske shows that underlying the works of Schnitzler and Hofmannsthal, Klimt and Kokoschka, Mahler and Schoenberg, Musil and Kraus, Mach and Freud was a common political conviction that Austrian liberalism, like that of most European nations, had failed to recognize the irrational forces in human life and history. They saw that political reactionaries like Schönerer and Lueger were so successful because each "in his own way utilized aristocratic style, gesture, or pretension to mobilize a mass of followers still hungry for a leadership that based its authority on something older and deeper than the power of rational argument and empirical evidence."[64] As Hofmannsthal concluded, "[p]olitics is magic. He who knows how to summon the forces from the deep, him they will follow."[65] Schorske further shows that as these modernists turned away and retreated from the public political arena into their own psychical sphere, they were particularly likely to expose the mythic forces they had previously experienced in the new artistic and scientific terms of modernism. Freud's metapsychological speculations on the archaic events that still determine modernity, such as those that invoke "the father of the primal horde," were, in his own terms, "scientific myths," devised, as it were, as metaphorical or hypothetical reflections on the psychic forces— drives and energies—that, much like physical entities in natural occur- rences, incite human actions.[66] Yet, since these "scientific myths" were based on and presented as anthropological and historical reconstruction of actual case studies that had been recorded in biblical or classical sources— for such were Freud's interpretations of Moses and Romulus—they also served to expose the historicity of myths, to reveal their continuity and ac- tuality in modernity, and thus to show that even if such mythological cases are likely to remain hypothetical, they have become historical.

In any case, Freud's ultimate question to Albert Einstein—"Does not every science come in the end to a kind of mythology?"[67]—indicates that the quest for a deeper and different kind of order, more poetical than po- litical, which lies, as it were, beyond the common world of regular appear- ances and laws, affected not only artists and social theorists but also natu- ral scientists. Gillian Beer points out that in the late nineteenth century, scientists and artists came to share the same modernistic conviction that the classical mechanical representations of reality had become inadequate to account for the dynamic forces that empowered it.[68] Once they realized that classical geometric and mechanistic terms were inadequate to account for the unpredictable reality exposed by the new natural sciences, they harked back to myth, precisely because it was so clearly a poetic creation of order that could be used to "save the appearances" in a way that both imposed and exposed the artificiality of all scientific conventions.[69] As Michael Bell writes, "[t]he anthropological study of 'primitive' myths in the nineteenth century eventually produced a cultural reflector by which Europeans could recognise their own world view as having an ultimately similar status. As science sought to understand myth, it increasingly found itself *as* myth."[70]

Hence, I define modernism as a cultural movement that consists in the "recognition of myth," and I define modern historiography in those terms as well. Recalling the famous words of Claude Lévi-Strauss—that his aim was "to show not how men think in myths, but how myths operate in men's minds [*les mythes se pensent dans les hommes*] without their being aware of the fact"[71]—I argue that modern historians ought to be (and ought to make us) more aware of the mythical patterns of thought and action that reside in all historical events and narratives (including their own). Or, to put this notion in the original terms of this discussion, they must revise the positivistic theories and works of Thucydides and his followers to the more hermeneutic theories and works of Herodotus and his fellow mythistorians (in all but name).

Francis Cornford did so, of course, long ago in his classic *Thucydides Mythistoricus,* the work that literally reinvented the term *mythistory* in modern historiography.[72] Cornford belonged to a group of classicists, the so-called Cambridge Ritualists (William Robertson Smith, Jane Ellen Harrison, Gilbert Murray, and A. B. Cook), who were closely associated with James Frazer. They readily employed his theory of agricultural fertility to explore the origins of Greek tragedy and, more generally, pursued his assumption that myths arise out of chthonic rites yet continue to animate religion, art, literature, and various symbolic forms long after the original primitive rites have died out. In his interpretation of Thucydides and Greek historiography, Cornford attempted to expose the various myths that lurk in Thucydides' *Peloponnesian Wars.* Thucydides, of course, did not know and would not have accepted that he was a "mythistorian." Cornford's presentation of him as such is critical and deliberately ironical, aimed at Thucydides' claim—and, by implication, the claims of all his followers in modern historiography—to have purged the historical profession of all mythological fallacies. Cornford tacitly rebukes this claim by showing that Thucydides could not be as antimythical as he claimed to be, and, of course, he should not have been so. According to Cornford, certain truths about human nature that the Greek historian held to and presented in the scientific jargon of Hippocratic medicine had in fact been derived from the mythological sources in the histories of Herodotus and the tragedies of Aeschylus; they are truths that were revealed and became meaningful in Thucydides' narration of the historical events. For Thucydides held to an agnostic conception of history: he did not believe in any supernatural or merely natural forces in it; rather, he conceived history—in overtly dramatic terms—to be a test of character, an ongoing attempt of men to assert themselves in, and over against, reality that they could not fully understand nor really change.[73] And as he sought to account for human actions in real terms (i.e., their own terms), he eschewed the theological and other later theoretical modes of explanation and concentrated instead on what the agents had said and done, their ideal expressions (hence the proliferation of "speeches" in his history) and innermost impressions—a tendency that, Cornford argues, led him to imbue his history with mythical patterns of thought and action that prevailed in history. Cornford rightly calls this kind of historical composition "infiguration," not invention, because Thucydides did not really impose his own narrative on the events so much as he used a narrative pattern that was well known in his culture, a narrative, moreover, that the historical agents of whom he writes must have not only known but also enacted in the events.[74]

Cornford's attempt to regain mythistory for modern historiography failed. The term itself, not merely the historiographical tradition it designates, sank into irrelevance. Some historians were attentive to the recognition of myth in the modern arts and sciences of the early twentieth century and explored its actual manifestations in historical reality, but even they continued to perceive myth itself in the common pejorative terms of positivistic historical scholarship, dismissing its images and tales as ephemeral expressions of more fundamental conditions in social reality, which alone, they thought, deserved serious consideration. This is most obvious in the case of Marc Bloch, the great originator of modern scientific historiography, whose book *Les rois thamaturges* (1924) is widely regarded as one of the most important studies in historical mythology.[75] In that work Bloch explores the origins and transformations of the "royal touch," the belief in the miraculous power of the king to heal by touch the scrofula (a tuberculous inflammation of the neck glands). The fact that this rite survived for more than eight hundred years, mainly in the royal courts in France and England, indicated to Bloch that it was primarily a political fabrication, conceived by the medieval kings who wished to consecrate their own power in competition with the ecclesiastical authorities. "The royal miracle stands out above all as the expression of a certain concept of supreme political power. From this point of view, to explain it would be to link it with the whole body of ideas and beliefs of which it was one of the most characteristic expressions."[76] Conceived as a "contribution to the political history of Europe in the widest and truest sense of the word," the study demonstrates how ancient Christian beliefs in a messianic redeemer and more recent popular reverence for the legitimate ruler coalesced in the folklore of the wonder-working kings. Along with other modernists, Bloch was deeply inspired by the "splendid works by Sir James Frazer, which have long taught us how to see links, which long remained unknown, between certain ancient concepts of the nature of things and the earliest political institutions of the human race." He rejects Frazer's comparative anthropological methodology, however, for a stricter historical one, such as would determine not only the "deep causes" of this specific rite but also the "exact occasion" that brought it into actual being in certain times and places.[77] Consequently, for all its original observations on the formation of royal authority through magical beliefs and rites, *Les rois thaumaturges* charts a rather conventional political history of one particular rite—how it was forged by the medieval kings and their courtiers; when and where it was used; and why it eventually died out in the Enlightenment, when the collective ideas of the masses and the individual ambitions of the kings who had always sustained it crumbled under the attacks of the rationalists.

Based on novel sources and modes of interpretation, Bloch's book was, and remains, one of the most innovative studies of the new methodology that has become synonymous with modern historiography, the *Annales* school, an early model of what came to be known as the history of *mentalités*.[78] Yet, as Lucien Febvre, Bloch's colleague and the cofounder of this methodology, observed, Bloch's study fails to convince that he had really solved the mystery of this rite, primarily, Febvre intimates, because as an atheist and a rationalist historian, Bloch did not take the rite as seriously as he should have, which means as seriously as the masses who had actually performed the rite had taken it.[79] The main problem in this case is not how the kings had used this myth but rather why so many people had become so susceptible to it. Bloch's final judgment on that rite—that "it is difficult to see faith in the royal miracle as anything but the result of collective error"[80]—betrays his liberal assumption, common to contemporary social scientists such as Frazer, Durkheim, and Lévy-Bruhl, that the myth underlying this rite (the divinity of the king) was primitive, irrational, and false.[81] The fact that the myths of royalty are still effective, albeit in different forms, implies that modern historiography, in order to be really modern, must overcome the positivistic fallacy that still prevailed in the human sciences of the early decades of the twentieth century when Bloch conducted his study, namely the belief that we can fully explain subjective human creations like mythology by the more objective terms or "scientific laws" of historical sociology, anthropology, or psychology.[82] Mythology, in the strict meaning of the term, operates and becomes meaningful by its own "logic of myth." The meaning of a historical myth like that of the "royal touch" is essentially mythological rather than historical: it requires a deeper "recognition of myth" as a permanent factor in human life and history. On these assumptions, Bloch's attempt to explain historical mythology by the new historical sciences of his times failed because it was more historical than really mythological, or, to put it in my terms, because it was not properly mythistorical.

Ludwig Wittgenstein saw the historical fallacy in the study of mythology when he pointed out that the historical methodology of Frazer in *The Golden Bough* had misled Frazer to conceive of ancient rituals as primitive or prelogical phases of our fully human mentality. In Wittgenstein's view,

"the deep and sinister" impression that we derive from observing these rituals is a sensation that arises not from external knowledge of their "history" but rather "from an experience in our own inner selves."[83] What we
discover in the study of myth and ritual is that man is, by nature and history, a "ceremonious animal": a being who has always devised different,
yet equivalent, formal systems of meaning over against an unbearably contingent reality (16). In his later works, Wittgenstein sought to show how
all our thoughts and actions occur, and must be understood, as beliefs, customs, traditions, institutions, agreements, and similar habitual performances that we commonly practice in social life. These performances, which
make up our "networks of tradition," are, as Wittgenstein saw, "mythological" in the sense that they are artificial representations, which constitute our "world-picture" as a "graphic illustration" or "perspicuous form
of representation [übersichtliche Darstellungsform]" (9). What he meant by
this formal definition of mythology is that the human representations
that make up our world-picture are poetic models, which, much like
Nietzsche's "timeless allegories," allow us to apply a certain pattern to
what we want to represent but also to invent new patterns in a way that
makes us more aware of our means of representation and of the objects or
states of affair represented. Having thus understood that in our language
we intermingle, yet keep apart, the descriptions we make of the world and
the stories we make up to illustrate how things in the world appear to
us and what we feel about them, Wittgenstein concluded that "a whole
mythology is deposited in our language" (10).

According to Wittgenstein, a myth should thus be thought of primarily not as an explanation of the world but as an expression of how the
people perceive it, a representation of the world in terms of their fears,
wishes, and so on. "The difficulty," he acknowledged, "is to realize [einzu-
sehen] the groundlessness of our believing"—the fact, namely, that, for example, "very intelligent and well-educated people believe in the story of
creation in the Bible, while others hold it as proven false, and the grounds
of the latter are well known to the former."[84] What saved these world-
pictures (and, according to Wittgenstein, any other foundational world-
pictures) from becoming "superstitions" was precisely their "mythological" form, the fact that as clearly defined narratives they were "perspicuous
forms of representation": they enabled the believers to perceive in and
through them the essential pictorial dimensions of their form of life. His
remarks on the formation of Christianity might be taken as a prime example of his interpretive theory and, moreover, of mythistory as the practice of that theory:

Christianity is not based on a historical truth; rather, it offers us a (histori-cal) narrative and says: now believe! But not, believe this narrative with the belief appropriate to a historical narrative, rather: believe, through thick and thin, which you can do only as the result of life . . . The historical ac-counts in the Gospels might, historically speaking, be demonstrably false and yet belief would lose nothing by this: not, however, because historical proof (the historical proof-game) is irrelevant to belief. This message (the Gospels) is seized on by men believingly (i.e. lovingly). That is the certainty characterizing this particular acceptance-as-true, not something else.[85]

Such claims for the primacy of beliefs over reasons, images over ideas, nar-ratives over arguments and explanations, and myths over theories have in recent years become most prevalent in the so-called interpretive theories in the humanities and social sciences: for example, "revisionism" in moral philosophy, "communitarianism" in social philosophy, and "historical re-alism" in the philosophy and history of science.[86] Common to them all is the postulation of the "narrative construction of reality," of the fact that the explanation of human actions in history must always include—and perhaps even take the form of—an attempt to recover and interpret the subjective meanings of these actions from the point of view of the agents performing them, even if, and especially when, these meanings are imme-morial and largely impersonal.[87] Believing, with Plato, that people inherit their basic psychological and social capabilities through the tales of their mothers and nurses, the proponents of the "narrative turn" in modern so-cial sciences claim that people organize their experience and memory of human happenings mainly according to stories of past actions and events. This awareness of the narrative patterns of historical reality inspires their actions and therewith all historical events and processes. As David Carr explains, "[h]istorical narrative is an extension by other means, and to some extent with different attitudes, of historical existence itself. To tell the story of a community . . . is simply to continue, at a somewhat more reflective and usually more retrospective level the story-telling process through which the community constitutes itself and its actions."[88]

In order to explain historical events, it is thus imperative to grasp those ultimate narratives of the agents performing them, their myths. I would add that this *modernistic* recognition of myth might also enable contem-porary historians to overcome the fashionable *postmodernistic* renunciation of myth along with all other "grand narratives" as a fiction that, like any other aesthetic representation without foundation in historical reality, is li-able to be disciplinarian and totalitarian. For, as mythistorians, they would readily admit that the Christian theory of history, with its grand narrative of Creation to Salvation, is a myth, the "greatest story" of transcendental history indeed—yet not one that has been devised as such in order to conceal from the ignorant masses the awful truth of their accidental predicament, as postmodernists (quoting Nietzsche) would have it, but rather one that has grown over many centuries out of the popular impressions and interpretations of historical reality. This perception of the objective and collective formation of historical myths defies Lyotard's stark distinction between the two forms of narrative discourses in society—the actual "stories" that communities and individuals tell themselves about their local life and history and the universal "histories" of civilization, the nation, or the revolution that subsume (in Hegelian *aufheben*) these and all other heterogeneous diversions under one law or theory—by showing how both narrative creations derive from the same dramatic resources.[89]

The first, albeit also the last, serious attempt to revive the very notion and tradition of mythistory in modern historiography along the new hermeneutical guidelines was made by William McNeill in his presidential address to the American Historical Association in 1985: "Mythistory, or Truth, Myth, History, and Historians."[90] The title indicates its message, that the principal question for the historian is not "What is Truth?" for (in McNeill's words) this "unalterable and eternal truth remains like the Kingdom of Heaven, an eschatological hope," but rather, What have groups of people known and believed about their past and found necessary to preserve as essential for their entire social existence, namely their "truths" (8). The task of the historians is not to explain these truths away by reducing them to some more basic and universal Truth comprised of such crude naturalistic categories as physical causes, biological impulses, economic needs, or social functions, but rather to adopt more hermeneutical methods, which will enable them to interpret these truths as the symbolic means by which people react to "the natural world and to one another." What they must realize, in other words, is that once "ideas and ideals thus become self-validating within remarkably elastic limits," all human beings, including the historians themselves, become immersed in a new reality of "extraordinary behavioral motility," in which the connection between external reality and human responses has been loosened up, thereby "freeing us from instinct by setting us adrift on a sea of uncertainty"—that of myths and similar symbolic representations of natural and social reality (2). McNeill concludes that since "mythistory is what we actually have," then "to be a truth seeking mythographer is therefore a high and serious calling, for what a group of people knows and believes about the past channels expectations and affects the decisions on which their lives, their fortunes, and their sacred honor all depend" (10).

During the last three decades, more and more historians seem to have figured out, though in their own words and ways, this new kind of historiography. In his famous essay "The Revival of Narrative," which deals with modern historiography, Lawrence Stone has discerned the professional and ideological reasons for the demise of the previously dominant socioeconomic and other positivist methodologies among the so-called new historians, who, having come to distrust the Marxist and other "a priori statistical models of human behavior" that flourished in the 1950s and early 1960s, rediscovered the alternative Weberian methodology of "understanding based on observation, experience, judgment and intuition." [91] Stone thus demonstrates how these "new historians" have opted, as a rule, to deal with the lower classes and their habitual patterns of thought and action; to use such informal historical sources as court records, folk tales, or iconography; to rely on those psychological, anthropological, and literary theories that interpret human behavior in symbolic, rather than in naturalistic, terms; to write in the descriptive, rather than the analytic, modes of presentations; to account for whole societies and cultures by unique episodic narratives rather than by general comprehensive theories; to articulate, in short, the various narrative means by which the common people have produced their meaningful experiences of reality.[92]

I take just two examples of many. In her book *Fiction in the Archives: Pardon Tales and Their Tellers in Sixteenth-Century France,* Natalie Zemon Davis takes the "fictional" aspect of the letters of pardon seriously; that is, she considers them to be first and foremost literary texts and only then and thereby social documents. When taken in and on their distinctly literary terms, as primarily tales, these letters open up new historical perspectives, revealing "how sixteenth-century people told stories . . . what they thought a good story was, how they accounted for motive, and how through narrative they made sense of the unexpected and built coherence into immediate experience."[93] In the same vein, Carlo Ginzburg's *Ecstasies: Deciphering the Witches' Sabbath* purports to study the European witch craze during the sixteenth and seventeenth centuries from the new interpretive and narrative perspectives outlined above.[94] Ginzburg argues that traditional historians (principally Norman Cohn and Hugh Trevor-Roper), by conceiving this case as essentially "ideological," failed to see its deeper subjective meanings and wider universal implications. These historians explained the whole affair as merely a fabrication of the political and theological authorities against their social enemies (the peasants, the Jews, and other minorities); as a result they all but ignored the beliefs and practices of the witches themselves and thus, according to Ginzburg, failed to perceive that the witches' confessions, though forced and distorted, nevertheless disclosed some authentic historical perceptions and experiences of human reality. Accordingly, Ginzburg is not content with merely discovering "the meanings attributed by the actors to the myths they relived in ecstasy": he seeks to decipher in the witches' accounts of nocturnal flights, animal metamorphoses, and similar fantasies a certain "lived experience" that is still meaningful today, a living myth.[95] He literally "follows" these myths beyond their formal summaries and explanations (those of Hellenistic mythographers, medieval penitentials, nineteenth-century folklorists, and twentieth-century structuralists) to where they led their makers, to the "unfathomable experience that humanity has symbolically expressed for millennia," which "remains one of the hidden centers of our culture, of the way we exist in this world"—to the myth of "the journey of the living into the world of the dead." This myth, he says, is "not one narrative among many, but the matrix of all possible narratives"—most notably that of history: "The attempt to attain knowledge of the past is also a journey into the world of the dead."[96] Thus, since Ginzburg offers not only a historical interpretation of one particular myth but also a mythical interpretation of "history" itself, which is, in Ginzburg's account, yet another manifestation of that myth, his book may serve to remind historians that they must always work on myth. As Hans Blumenberg once put it, "Only work *on* myth, even if it is the work of finally reducing it—makes the work *of* myth manifest."[97]

And yet, significantly enough, none of the "new historians," not even those who otherwise display many of the characteristics of mythistory, have so far employed, let alone applied, the term in their works. McNeill seems to have been right in predicting that mythistory would probably not catch on in professional circles.[98] Why has mythistory failed among these and other historians? It appears that, though many historians might admit that in one way or other all history is inevitably mythological, they do not go so far as to accept the more extreme claim—which postmodernists commonly evoke—that there is no such thing as "historical truth" to be found out there and rescued from beyond the many layers of mythical fabulation. A historiography of that kind, which deals exclusively with the cognitive and aesthetic modes by which men account for their social reality, ignores the concrete structure of that reality—such as the geographic, climatic, and demographic conditions and the technological and political changes. A historical study that is concerned with collective experiences and deep impressions of historical events, and not with the events themselves, does not and cannot answer the main historical question of what actually happened in those events.

Yet this is precisely the problem that mythistorians since Burckhardt have had with Ranke's famous dictum: What exactly actually happened? Assuming that human reality is so permeated by its foundational myths that it cannot be reduced by scientific-historical research to presumably more elemental explanations, they would urge modern historians to consider the narratives and other symbolic interpretations of historical reality in which the people believe to be as real as the conditions and events in which they actually live. On their premises, modern historiography must deal not only with what actually happened (that is, in common terms, history), nor with what people merely imagine to have actually happened (myth), but rather with the process in which both affect the production and reproduction of historical meaning (mythistory). The efficacy of this general theoretical method can best be demonstrated by applying it to a concrete historical event that was long perceived as more mythological than historical, the taking of the Bastille on 14 July 1789. The three main narrative modes by which historians have dealt with this event are the mythical, the historical, and the mythistorical.

Jules Michelet's *History of the French Revolution* (1847) is the obvious example of the mythical option.[99] His whole work is mythological, and quite consciously so, for he conceived the Revolution to be a new and higher revelation—the French fulfillment of the Christian messianic message of redemption—and his own role in it as its evangelist. And like the original evangelists, he too came late, when the believers seemed to have lost hope in the fulfillment of the message; and yet he managed, as they did, to revive and save that message by the miracle of communion, his historical narration being a new and higher form of a ritual association and spiritual identification with the dead. Michelet recounts the fabulous events of the Revolution in a ceremonial fashion, using all the rhetorical means of a sermonizer in a Christian Mass who seeks to move his followers to participate in the events, not just to recollect the Passion but also to reenact it. As in his earlier work on Joan of Arc, whom he described in the mythical idioms of the evangelists as a messianic agent, her appearance and very human actions, like those of Jesus, being a miraculous divine intervention in our dull human affairs, a sudden irruption of sacred history into profane history, so too in his *History of the French Revolution* he chose to describe the momentous historical event as a theophany, another, and greater, moment of revelation in the long human progression from Creation to Resurrection. The taking of the Bastille assumes in that story the meanings of deliverance: "The Bastille was known and detested by the whole world. Bastille and tyranny were, in every language synonymous terms. Every nation, at the news of its destruction, believed it had recovered its liberty." The description is fittingly biblical: "The attack on the Bastille was by no means reasonable. It was an act of faith. Nobody proposed; but all believed, and all acted. Along the streets, the quays, and the boulevards, the crowd shouted to the crowd: 'To the Bastille! The Bastille!'"[100] And when Thuriot and his comrades conquered the fortress ("the Monster"), they appeared, like Saint George, to have defeated the dragon.

Albert Soboul's *French Revolution, 1789–1799* (1975) is a massive study of 613 pages; the taking of the Bastille takes up hardly half a page in it.[101] Soboul, who for many years held the prestigious chair of Professor of the History of the French Revolution at the Sorbonne, acknowledges that this event became a "symbol of popular insurrection," what Georges Sorel called a "political myth." But the modern historian regards the event as a rather negligible episode, because it did not have any real political or military significance for the Revolution: "The Bastille was defended by no more than 80 disabled soldiers officered by 30 Swiss Guards; yet with its hundred-foot-high walls and its moat over eighty feet wide it withstood the attacks which the people mounted against it."[102] Soboul does not go beyond this factual architectonic description of the Bastille: he pays no attention, let alone homage, to what the people of Paris—indeed "the whole world"—imagined and believed it to be, a monster. His positivistic history ignores this and all other mythical images, meanings, and implications of the event.

Simon Schama's *Citizens* (1989) is subtitled *A Chronicle of the French Revolution*.[103] As Schama points out, it aims to be just that, a simple narrative of the events along natural (chronological) and personal guidelines, "allowing different issues and interests to shape the flow of the story as they arise, year after year, month after month" (xv). The issues and interests are primarily those of the "citizens" themselves: what they felt and thought and recorded in their own chronicles as they went along (and as they fell). What renders his work mythistorical is his concrete observation that, contrary to what Marx thought, when the French revolutionaries "performed the task of their time in Roman costume and with Roman phrases," they were not just acting but were actually acting up to what they really believed in. "Cato, Cicero and Junius Brutus stood at the shoulders of

Mirabeau, Vergniaud and Robespierre," serving as their role models in everything they thought and did (xvi). Against the Marxists and fellow critical theorists, he could argue, with Sorel and other revisionists in modern historiography, that any revolution requires and generates such mythical evocations, which are not feats of pathetic "self deception" (as Marx thought) but rather of dramatic self-realization. And so, when Schama deals with the taking of the Bastille, he does not inflate its myths (as Michelet did), nor does he reduce them to realities (as Soboul did), but he considers the "myths and realities" of this monument—principally those of "buried alive"—as equally significant in its actual construction and destruction (369–425). He recounts the legendary stories of prisoners such as Linguet, Latude, or de Sade, which created the myths, as well as the prosaic reports of contemporary and modern experts, which describe its realities, and goes on to describe not only what actually happened in the Bastille on 14 July 1789 but also what happened to it afterward, in the commemorative festivals and other mythical forms of historical consciousness. Schama, then, does not indulge solely in myth nor (for that matter) strictly in history but rather practices what I have called mythistory.

The "crucial test" of mythistory, indeed of any form of modern historiography, is whether it offers a new explanation for what is really "modern" in contemporary history, to wit, the devastation of Western civilization in the totalitarian revolutions and wars of the twentieth century. A full explanation of these momentous events would be possible (if at all) only by some kind of "total history," but we may nevertheless ask whether mythistory, with its methodical "recognition of myth," could be useful in the illumination of that singular event that so typifies this history and yet defies all the conventional categories of traditional historiography: the Holocaust. The attainment of this "recognition of myth" by the historian Saul Friedländer may show how this notion has become vital to modern historiography of Nazism and the Final Solution.

After his attempt in the 1960s to analyze the anti-Semitic policy of Nazi Germany with the conventional categories of real-political historiography[104] and then, in the early 1970s, with the more problematic categories of psychoanalytical historiography, which he then rejected, Friedländer eventually came to realize that the deeper motivations and further fluctuations of the Nazi ideology (to this day) stem from Germanic mythology.[105] He first raised this consideration in his autobiographical meditation *When Memory Comes* (1979), where he acknowledged "the importance of myths in our societies," and then, more pointedly, in his *Reflections of Nazism: An Essay on Kitsch and Death* (1984).[106] In that essay Friedländer analyzed the imagery of some popular representations of Hitler and Nazi Germany that came out during the 1970s, among them films like Visconti's *Damned*, Syberberg's *Hitler, a Film from Germany*, and Fassbinder's *Lily Marleen* and novels like Tournier's *Ogre* and Steiner's *Portage to San Cristóbal*, so as to show that these aesthetic reflections *on* Nazism are as much reflections *of* Nazism and as such are particularly useful in the historical interpretation of this ideology. For the new works re-evoke, inadvertently and therefore potently, the mythic visions that Hitler produced in Nazi Germany, above all the "apocalyptic reveries of total destruction," which other modern ideologies (e.g., Marxism) have also inherited from ancient theologies; the artistic works may therefore help us to perceive in that powerful myth of salvation the deep sources of fascination that captivated the Nazi masses and—as the new films and novels on Nazism manifest— are still so attractive in modern society.

The recognition of this particular myth as the major catalyst in the historical development and predicament of modern societies enabled Friedländer in his major study *Nazi Germany and the Jews* to trace the ideological origins of the Nazi Final Solution to the mythological doctrines of Richard Wagner and the Bayreuth Circle, who, ridden by "fear of racial degeneration and belief in redemption," reinstated the Jew as the eternal enemy that must be eliminated and thus created a new mythology that Friedländer terms "redemptive anti-Semitism."[107] Friedländer rightly observes that the later Nazi ideology acquired credibility and popularity because it was cast in the form of this apocalyptic mythology, as in Hitler's *Mein Kampf* and in Alfred Rosenberg's *Der Mythus des zwanzigsten Jahrhunderts;* Hitler and Rosenberg used all sorts of new biological or geopolitical theories to retell the same old mythological stories of Holy War against the eternal Jew. The phenomenal heuristic cogency of Friedländer's study proves that, as Eliot saw, the *methodical* recognition of myth has "the importance of a scientific discovery," not only for literature but also for all the humanities, above all for modern historiography, whose practitioners must likewise reveal the myths that lurk behind "the immense panorama of futility and anarchy which is contemporary history."

What is required, then, is that modern historians, who have already taken several "turns" in their profession—linguistic, narrative, interpretive—now take the "mythic turn," as Giambattista Vico, the great initiator of these turns in modern human sciences, prescribed long ago:

It follows that the first science to be learned should be mythology or the interpretation of fables; for, as we shall see, all the histories of the nations have their beginnings in fables, which were their first histories. By such a method the beginnings of the sciences as well as of the nations are to be discovered, for they . . . had their beginnings in the public needs or utilities of the peoples and were later perfected as acute individuals applied their reflection to them.[108]

Vico's *New Science* is the most original and still the most seminal contribution to mythistory and therefore to what I call, in the subtitle of this study, "the making of a modern historiography," where the term *making* should be understood in the specific Greek connotations that Vico gave it, as *poeiein*, or "poetic creation" of historical societies and their historians.[109] His attempt to decipher the mythology of history, to reveal what he called the "poetic logic" by which men have made and written their own history, should be critically important to modern historiography, as were David Friedrich Strauss's *Life of Jesus* to theology, Friedrich Nietzsche's *Birth of Tragedy* to classical philology, Max Weber's *Protestant Ethic and the Spirit of Capitalism* to sociology, Sigmund Freud's *Totem and Taboo* to psychology, Wittgenstein's *Philosophical Investigations* to philosophy, Claude Lévi-Strauss's *Mythologiques* to anthropology, and Northrop Frye's *Anatomy of Criticism* to literary theory. These are all works that recognized the myths underlying the main truths in their respective fields of knowledge and thereby made their professions truly modern.

"The Vico road goes round and round to meet where terms begin." James Joyce's words allude to Vico's basic conception of history as a recurrent process of *corsi e ricorsi*, a movement that is neither progressive nor regressive but essentially concentric, leading away from but always back to the mythical origin, whether that is Vico's "Great Thunder" (which both Joyce and Eliot evoked) or any other occasion in the archaic history of the nation or civilization that is still memorable in their traditions.[110] According to Vico, this is the road that all nations must traverse, and their historians ought to do so, too, as should, I would add, the historian of those historians. In this introductory chapter, I have been concerned mainly with the conceptual question of "where terms begin"; in subsequent chapters I move on to "the Vico road" itself. Here is a brief guide to the itinerary.

Chapter 2, "The Vico Road," covers the long journey from the distant beginnings of mythistory in Roman antiquity up to modernity. The movement concurs with the basic pattern of the "Vico road": first a *corso* "From Myth to History" and then a *ricorso* "From History to Myth." The first two sections concentrate on Livy and his most famous commentator, Machiavelli, both of whom sought to recover true history from uncertain myth. The third and fourth reverse this direction and show how Vico and his first rediscoverer and admirer, Michelet, sought to recover a deeper and truer myth from uncertain history.

As noted above, I regard Burckhardt's *Civilization of the Renaissance in Italy* as the pivotal moment in the history of mythistory and thereby of modern historiography. In chapter 3, on Burckhardt, I explain why he deserves to be considered the first—and still the greatest—mythistorian, the real maker of modern historiography. In that book he managed to produce, over against Michelet's mythological history, a study in historical mythology. His acute attention to the mythical "perceptions [*Anschauungen*]" by which the makers of the Renaissance accounted for their history is still vital to Renaissance historiography, indeed to modern historiography as such, to the extent that modern historiographers have become aware of the linguistic and poetic means by which all societies construe a story in history, how they describe historical transition by such narrative structures as that of the Renaissance.

Among the historians who were attentive to Burckhardt's legacy in German historiography were Aby Warburg and Ernst Kantorowicz, as well as, in his own critical and dialectical way, Walter Benjamin. Chapters 4, 5, and 6 are devoted to their works. There were other historians, in Germany and elsewhere, who were also affected by Burckhardt's new historiography, and even more so. Most notably, the Dutch historian Johan Huizinga's book *The Autumn of the Middle Ages* (1919), with its brilliant notion and execution of historiography as an evocation of images (*verbeelden*), is the finest example of what mythistory could be.[111] I nevertheless decided to concentrate on the three German scholars mentioned above, because the recognition of myth in modern historiography was particularly significant in and to Germany during the fateful decades when these scholars lived and worked there, roughly from 1890 to 1940. Though radically different from each other in their ideological and methodological evaluations of myth, they all worked within—even if also against—the same German tradition that had long recognized myth as the most significant source of historical identity. As Ernst Cassirer (quoting Schelling) has put it, "[i]n the relation between myth and history myth proves to be the primary, history the secondary and derived factor. It is not by its history that the mythology of a nation is determined but, conversely, its history is determined by its mythology—or rather, the mythology of a people does not *determine* but *is* its fate, its destiny as decreed from the very beginning."[112]

This conviction inspired the entire German intellectual tradition in the nineteenth and early twentieth centuries and is evident in the lives and works of the three scholars whom I single out as the masters of mythistory.

The fact that they were all Jews and had all become alien to their religion and their cultural tradition may explain their peculiar attraction to the classical mythological tradition with its distinct Christian and German manifestations.[113] More generally, the engagement of these and other German Jews in the various philosophical schools, cultural movements, and political ideologies of myth in the early decades of the twentieth century (and since) betrays their close affinity with these darker aspects of German cultural history. As Peter Gay points out, the assumption that all or even most German Jews adhered to the liberal political forces that opposed the neomythical tendencies in Wilhelmine Germany is false: "German Jews thought and acted like Germans . . . Far fewer cultural revolutionaries and far more cultural reactionaries were Jews than historians have recognized."[114] The absorption of Jews into Christian and German mythology might best be exemplified by the fact that the most mythological of all cultural movements in modern Germany, the *George-Kreis,* was so heavily dominated by Jewish members.[115] As Stefan George himself pointed out, Jews were particularly disposed to his conception of Germany as primarily a mythical—rather than a political—Reich because as such it was open and equal to all Germans, regardless of their ethnic and civic categorization. The phenomenal contribution of German Jewish scholars to the recognition of myth in and for modern cultural history is evident in the works of the philosophers Hermann Cohen, Ernst Cassirer, and Ernst Bloch, the social theorists Max Horkheimer, Erich Fromm, and Herbert Marcuse, and authors and artists such as Franz Kafka, Else Lasker-Schüler, Hermann Broch, and Arnold Schoenberg. Moreover, it is precisely this recognition of myth as so essential to every religion and cultural tradition that prompted the most prominent scholars of Judaism in Germany—notably Martin Buber, Franz Rosenzweig, and Gershom Scholem—to rediscover the Jewish mythology of the Kabbalah and the Hasidic movement and thereby to redefine the "essence of Judaism" accordingly.

Although Warburg, Kantorowicz, and Benjamin were not concerned with these (or any other) studies of their own Jewish history, they shared this very German Jewish sensation: that myth was, or rather has become again, a major factor in the configuration of social reality.[116] As George Mosse observed, the attention to "modern" myths in social life and history was peculiar to scholars like Warburg, Freud, and Cassirer, whom he characterizes as "German Jews beyond Judaism." Mosse argues that because these German Jews were secular and largely cosmopolitan intellectuals, they were estranged not only from their own parochial tradition but also, and more crucially, from the *völkisch* alliances of their fellow German mythologists. Thus they could examine the very notion and the various manifestations of myth from more critical perspectives: "Their confrontation with the irrational forces of the age was destined to reinvigorate whole fields of study and to extend the boundaries of traditional disciplines, founding a new kind of cultural history. Scholarship of this type rediscovered the importance of myth as determining the actions of men and societies . . . Myth was no longer confined to the thought of primitive man but was treated as a present concern, an enemy to be defeated and exorcised."[117]

Although Mosse's explanation for the peculiar fascination of German Jewish scholars with myth is ingenious, his conclusion—that they commonly regarded myth as "an enemy to be defeated and exorcised"—is inaccurate. In fact, of the three prime examples mentioned by Mosse, only one, the philosopher Ernst Cassirer, came to regard myth in such negative terms. Even in his case, this was a very late conclusion. In his major philosophical works of the 1920s, Cassirer dealt with the various notions, theories, and manifestations of myth in rather objective and quite positive terms. Only after his emigration from Nazi Germany did Cassirer come to revise his all-too-theoretical evaluation of myth by more practical, and primarily political, considerations. Most other German Jewish scholars of mythology, and quite clearly the three historical scholars with whom I deal in this study, were not essentially "estranged" from German mythology but rather intimately attracted and committed to it, even if, as in the case of Benjamin, also very critical of it. As Steven Aschheim points out, the German Jewish intellectuals who came of age during World War I shared with their fellow German and other European intellectuals a keen appreciation of the mythical as essential to their own new radical and apocalyptical ideologies of redemption—whether anarchism, communism, or Zionism—which they forged out of and against the older German-Jewish tradition of Bildung.[118]

The concentration on Warburg, Kantorowicz, and Benjamin also enables me to elaborate the dialectical motion and main configurations by which the new recognition of myth, or mythistory, entered and shaped modern historiography. Warburg's inquiries into the magical origins of pictorial images in art history, his "iconology," informed his perception of "history as ancient mythology." Kantorowicz's inquiries into the theological origins of the imperial ideology in medieval political history allowed him to expose the basic mythopoeic motivations of all modern nations and states, as well as of their historians, and thus to reinaugurate (after Nietzsche) "history as new mythology." Reflecting on the proliferation of such old and new mythologies in modern poetry and theory of history, Walter Benjamin remarked: "But precisely the modern, *la modernité*, is always citing primal history [*Urgeschichte*]."[119] By that he meant to suggest that what we call the modern is precisely the apparition of the new as very old and its eventual acceptance as such, which amounts to what I have called throughout this chapter the recognition of myth.

In chapter 7 I return to James Joyce's *Ulysses*, the great modern novel that, as noted above, exemplifies the "mythical method" that I recommend for modern historiography. Concentrating on the second chapter (the "Nestor" episode) of that novel, I propose to read it as a story that explores the moral deliberations of the mythistorian. For this is how one might characterize its young hero, Stephen Dedalus, a teacher of history at a private school for boys in Dalkey, near Dublin. In the course of one lesson of history, and thereafter through a day of wandering and wondering about Dublin, Dedalus comes to a critical recognition of the myths that dominate his life and history.

C⁀ T W O ⁀Ɔ

The Vico Road: From Livy to Michelet

I

Such traditions as belong to the time before the city was founded, or rather was presently to be founded, and are rather adorned with poetic legends than based on trustworthy historical proofs, I propose neither to affirm nor to refute. It is the privilege of antiquity to mingle divine things with human, and so to add dignity to the beginnings of cities; and if any people ought to be allowed to consecrate their origins and refer them to a divine source, so great is the military glory of the Roman People that when they profess that their Father and the Father of their Founder was none other than Mars, the nations of the earth may well submit to this also with as good a grace as they submit to Rome's dominion. But to such legends as these, however they shall be regarded and judged, I shall, for my own part, attach no great importance. Here are the questions to which I would have every reader give his close attention—what life and morals were like; through what men and by what policies, in peace and in war, empire was established and enlarged; then let him note how, with the gradual relaxation of discipline, morals first gave way, as it were, then sank lower and lower, and finally began the downward plunge which has brought us to the present time, when we can endure neither our vices not their cure.[1]

Livy's famous pronouncement in the preface to his *History of Rome* has always incited historians to further inquiries and debates on the mythological origins and destinies of nations. It still reverberates in modern discussions on the use and abuse of myth in history.[2] For although modern historians have long ago turned the old positivistic controversies on the historicity of Roman myths into a new hermeneutic comprehension, they remain, as Livy apparently was, deeply ambivalent about the significance of

36

"such traditions": Are they merely "poetic legends [*poeticae fabulae*]"? Are they really devoid of any "trustworthy historical facts [*incorrupta rerum gestarum monumenta*]"? Or perhaps, as Livy himself surely believed, there is, or at least ought to be, a historical connection between the old cultural tradition and the new moral condition of the Roman nation. The causal construction of his preface implies that the issue he deems truly important for the attentive reader of his *History*—the gradual disintegration of morality in Roman society—evolves, both rhetorically and historically, from prior examples: "what life and morals were like; through what men and by what policies, in peace and in war, empire was established and enlarged." The title of his lifework, *Ab urbe condita* (From the foundation of the city), attests to his neostoic convictions, above all to his belief that the entire history of Rome was determined by *fatum:* "Fate, by whose law the unchangeable order of human affairs is arranged."[3] Nevertheless, in his *History of Rome,* Livy was able to transform this mythical notion of *fatum* into a historical conception, showing how certain events that occurred in the early ages of the city had become exemplary to its citizens and thereby "fateful" to its subsequent history. Livy knew and explained to the reader that in Roman life and history, such *exempla,* especially those that pertained to the most crucial period of the foundation of the city, were inevitably historical myths, *fabulae* rather than *monumenta,* and thus, by his own account, untrustworthy (*corrupta*) for historical reconstruction. And yet, the fact that he went on to recount these myths indicates that he found them in some way "trustworthy"—if not for historical *reconstruction,* then at least for historical *interpretation* of "what life and morals were like" in ancient times. Note, for example, how Livy recounts the death of Romulus:

> When these deathless deeds had been done, as the king was holding a muster near the swamp of Capra, for the purpose of reviewing the army, suddenly a storm came up, with loud claps of thunder, and enveloped him in a cloud so thick as to hide him from the sight of the assembly; and from that moment Romulus was no more on earth. The Roman soldiers at length recovered from their panic, when this hour of wild confusion had been succeeded by a sunny calm; but when they saw that the royal seat was empty, although they readily believed the assertion of the senators, who had been standing next to Romulus, that he had been caught up on high in the blast, they nevertheless remained for some time sorrowful and silent, as if filled with the fear of orphanhood. Then when a few men had taken the initiative, they all with one accord hailed Romulus as a god and god's son, the King and Father of the Roman City, and with prayers besought his favor that he would graciously be pleased forever to protect his children. There

were some, I believe, even then who secretly asserted that the king had been rent in pieces by the hand of the senators, for this rumor, too, got abroad, but in very obscure terms; the other version obtained currency, owing to men's admiration for the hero and the intensity of their panic.[4]

Livy is obviously skeptical of the official story of Romulus's disappearance. But, whereas a modern historian would seek to refute this story, Livy chooses to repeat it. Moreover, as we read further in the account we realize that Livy is not really concerned with a historical reconstruction of the event as much as with a historical reconstruction of the story. Leaving aside, and unresolved, the question of what really happened to Romulus then and there, whether he vanished by the storm or by the hands of the senators, Livy concentrates on what happened to him ever after: his deification "as a god and god's son, the King and Father of the Roman City." Livy duly notes that this common, semiofficial "version" of Roman tradition prevailed over the "rumor" of assassination by the senators, not because it is more credible but rather because it is more credulous: "owing to men's admiration for the hero and the intensity of their panic." And these experiential and memorial impressions surrounding the event were, for him, more significant than the actual circumstances in which it occurred, because they initiated a tradition of deification down to his own time. His seemingly innocuous comment that the rumor of Romulus's assassination was rife "even then" tacitly refers to the more recent case of Julius Caesar, in which, in a similar fashion, a ruler who "had been rent in pieces by the hands of the senators" was transfigured into a god.[5] He goes on to describe how this story "gained new credit" through the "shrewd device [*consilio*]" of Proculus Julius, whose testimony before the assembly on Romulus's godlike reappearance (*apotheosis*) from heaven with this message to the Romans—"let them cherish the art of war, and let them know and teach their children that no human strength can resist Roman arms"— proved decisive for the moment and for a whole new movement in Roman history. Livy concludes: "It is wonderful what credence the people placed in that man's tale, and how the grief for the loss of Romulus, which the plebeians and the army felt, was quieted by the assurance of his immortality."[6]

Such comments imply that Livy was well aware of what is now called "the invention of tradition," in this instance that the deification of Romulus was initially a political manipulation of the masses, a fabrication perpetrated by the ruling authorities to masquerade their own deed (the assassination of the king) through symbolic rites of unity and continuity.

But Livy was equally, and more acutely, aware of the historicity of tradition, of the fact that traditional beliefs and stories like those concerning
Romulus's apotheosis had long passed into and made up Roman history.[7]
The opening sentences of Livy's work make it clear that although he knew
that the sources on the foundation of the city were fallible, he nonetheless
found pleasure in having managed, to the best of his ability, to use them to
nurture "the memories of the great deeds [rerum gestarum memoriae]" of the
greatest people on earth. As G. P. Walsh has shown, the preface is crucial
for Livy and his readers because it not only reveals what Livy sought to do
in his work: to demonstrate "to posterity that national greatness cannot be
achieved without the possession, especially by the leading men of the state,
of the attributes which promote a healthy morality and sagacity in the execution of external or domestic policies." It also shows how he actually did
it, by a careful representation, more artful than truthful, of cases in which
attributes like dignitas and gravitas, "pietas towards the gods and fides towards
men," clementia and disciplina, and pudicitia (in women) and virtus (in men)
had been achieved by the ancient Romans.[8]

Because Livy sought to reconstruct the historical foundation by this
kind of narration, he deserved indeed the Ciceronian title of the "founder
of histories [historiae conditor]" in the literal sense of the term. He assumed
and attempted to prove that even though the events themselves (res gestae)
defied historical verification, the alleged consequences of these events—
their memories—were historical facts. And he deemed it his task, as historian of Rome, to take into account such facts. Thus, when explaining his
reason for recounting improbable stories about gods and heroes that were
recorded by Roman priests, Livy writes: "I am well aware that, because of
the religious indifference [neglegentia] today inspiring the general belief that
the gods foretell nothing, no prodigies are publicly reported or listed in
historical works. But as I write of ancient days my mind somehow becomes
old-fashioned [antiquus], and a kind of religious awe prevents me from regarding as unworthy of my history the events which those famous and far
sighted men decreed should be dealt with by the state."[9] His solution to
this predicament was to preserve the historical myths and yet expose them
as such. Following Cicero, he judged the myths by stoic, rather than skeptic, categories, seeking to counter any supernatural narration by a very
rational explanation.[10] Thus, right at the beginning of the well-known tale
of Romulus and Remus, he recounts how their mother, a vestal girl, was
raped and then, "having given birth to twin sons, named Mars as the father of her doubtful offspring, whether actually so believing, or because it

seemed less wrong if a god were the author of her fault."[11] The consequent episode of the she-wolf and the twins receives the same skeptic treatment. Livy remarks that this "marvelous story" arose because the woman who actually fed the boys, Larentia, "having been free with her favors," was nicknamed "she-wolf [*lupa*]," which was then the common vulgar term for women of her kind.[12]

As this observation reveals, and as modern commentators on his work have pointed out, Livy was much more sophisticated in his treatment of historical myths than scholars of historiography have commonly presumed. Among the latter was R. G. Collingwood, who argued that Livy "makes no attempt to discover how the tradition has grown up and through what various distorting media it has reached him; he therefore cannot reinterpret a tradition, that is, explain it as meaning something other than it explicitly says. He has to take it or leave it, and, on the whole, Livy's tendency is to accept his tradition and repeat it in good faith."[13] Contemporary Livian scholars such as Luce, Miles, and Feldherr dispute this judgment and seek to discover the deeper reasons for Livy's apparent complicity with tradition. They maintain that Livy was more concerned with "Roman tradition" than with "Roman history," believing that this tradition was the true history of the Romans, having formed their identity through the ages. According to Luce, Livy was primarily interested in the historical formation of the "Roman national character": "For him it was the people who counted most: not simply what they did but in what frame of mind they did it . . . Livy preferred concrete stories exemplifying Roman virtues and their opposites."[14] He argues that Livy's "nationalistic" beliefs were not detrimental to his historiography, even if they certainly affected the selection and interpretation of its material sources. Whereas the doyen of modern Livian scholarship, G. P. Walsh, still sought to show how Livy's declaration of moral and cultural principles in the preface consequently led him to the "Distortion of History," modern readers of Livy tend to regard this apparent fallacy as an inevitable, and moreover valuable, precondition for the "composition" of his—or any other—history. On these hermeneutic premises, Livy's claim in the preface that the Romans were right to "profess that their Father and the Father of their Founder was none other than Mars" has a certain kind of validity. Miles states:

> It expresses something about how the Romans choose to view and represent themselves; something, moreover, that is in some sense both true and verifiable in the present, namely Rome's overwhelming superiority in warfare . . . The *claim* of divine ancestry is justified here not because of its

literal truth but rather because it appropriately symbolizes the martial ac-
complishments of the Romans, who, whatever the reality of their origins,
have the ability to compel others to accede to that claim.[15]

Livy's further injunction that "the nations of the earth may well submit to
this [myth] also with as good a grace as they submit to Rome's dominion"
may thus not be as crass as it seems: it betrays Livy's assumption that myths
like this have brought about and still sustain "Rome's dominion."[16] As
Feldherr remarks, in his narration of tradition Livy consciously assumed
"the role of *imperator.*" Because he attempted to augment national authority by historical means, his work complemented what Roman rulers did by
political means. "The tales about divine parentage may be pure fictions,
from a historian's point of view, but even fictional gods can be *auctores* in
the sense that they contribute to the city's cumulative *auctoritas.*"[17] It is for
this reason that Livy, in his turn, strives to sustain these myths within his
narrative history, precisely because it is a narrative history, namely a history that recognizes and records the dialectical process whereby action and
fiction work up the process of tradition. Miles argues that in so doing Livy
contributed "to a redefinition of history and its characteristic usefulness.
History in this version remains useful not because it represents accurate
reconstructions of past events that can serve as analogies in the present
but rather because it perpetuates and interprets the collective memory on
which the identity and character of the Roman people depend."[18]

Alas, for all his insightful appropriation of Roman myths for his *History,*
Livy did not elaborate on the more general philosophical meanings and
political implications of historical myth. Commentators on his work have
often noted that Livy was primarily a patriotic historian, who not merely
composed but actually believed in "Roman History" as a divinely ordained
and providentially guided mission; he was thus much too immersed in its
myths to analyze them in critical philosophical or historical terms. His devotion to Roman tradition prevented him from more radical reflections on
its formation and narration. And yet, his critical comments on such venerable stories as the ones about the she-wolf and the twins and Romulus's
apotheosis demonstrate that in his treatment of historical myths, Livy was
a patriotic but not a dogmatic historian. He was indeed a traditionalist, but
one who was fully aware and proud of this fact and therefore exposed himself and his historiography to further, more critical, reflections on the use
and abuse of myth in history. His candid admission in the preface that "to
such legends as these, however they shall be regarded and judged, I shall,
for my own part, attach no great importance" was not a sign of indecision

and historiographical confusion. Rather, it signaled his recognition, as a historian with his own limitations, of tradition's predicament with regard to myth and history. This predicament was particularly problematic for Livy because he lived at a time when historical myths became extremely intensive and authoritative in Roman society. As Paul Zanker has shown, during that period the Augustan regime consciously sought to build up the imperial identity of Rome by a massive production of popular images and spectacles that celebrated its heroic achievements.[19] Feldherr shows that, much like the imperial authorities, who were intent on public and dramatic exhibitions of their messages, Livy sought to impress his readers by a very theatrical description of historical events and actions. His moving depictions of Lucretia's fate is full of melodramatic gestures and speeches that turn his readers into spectators in a classic tragedy and thereby, as Aristotle taught, make it possible for them to identify with the patriotic emotions and actions of its protagonists.[20] This reader response is especially pronounced when they encounter historical stories that defy commonsensical reception, like that of the capture of Veii, which Livy finds hard to accept and yet retains with the admission that "in matters of so great antiquity, I should be content if things probable . . . were to be received *as true*," even if they are not, because this is how they were actually received in Roman history—as exhibitions of Roman virtuosity in warfare. The duty of the historian in the implausible yet "probable" case in the cave near Veii is akin to that of the dramatist—to cause the readers or hearers to suspend disbelief in order to enhance their comprehension of human affairs beyond its common logical and historical boundaries. Livy thus reiterates his fundamental premise that "this story, more fit to be displayed on the stage, that delights in wonders, than to be believed, it is worth while neither to affirm nor to refute."[21]

To sum up: Livy may not have believed the ancient Roman myths, but he still believed *in* them, knowing that these stories had animated the ethical and political beliefs of the ancient Romans and were therefore both *fabulae* and *monumenta*, equally mythical and historical, or, as I would call them, mythistorical. The protagonists of this course in modern historiography were those historians who, for *their part*, could not ignore the question that Livy had posed but then all too easily waved off: how "such legends as these . . . shall be regarded and judged." Assuming, with Livy, that the Romans indeed considered Mars to be the founder of their nation, these modern historians, unlike Livy, have resolved to attach to this and other myths "great importance." First and foremost among them was Livy's greatest mediator into modern times, Niccolò Machiavelli.

II

In October 1504 Niccolò Machiavelli completed a poem in 550 lines, known as the *First Decennale*, in which he described the tumultuous events of the past ten years in Italy. The French invasion of 1494 ushered in an era of fierce internal wars and political intricacies that ravaged the city-states and nearly enslaved them to foreign mercenaries and other "barbarians." Having witnessed, as a secretary and ambassador of the republican government of Florence, the calamities wrought on his country and city by inept princes, kings, and popes, Machiavelli turns his attention and hopes from the leaders to the common people of Italy. He recalls the words of Petrarch "that the ancient valor is not yet dead in Italian hearts" and appeals in the very last lines of his poem to his fellow Florentine citizens, beseeching them not to despair and to support his plan for the formation of a republican army (*militia*): "but the road would be short and easy, if you would reopen the temple of Mars."[22]

When Machiavelli wrote these lines, he must have borne in mind that according to a well-known Florentine tradition, the Church of Saint John the Baptist in the city stood on the ruins of what was once a temple erected in honor of Mars. His plea to "reopen the temple of Mars" might thus be interpreted as a call for the reassertion of pagan mythology as against Christian theology. He truly believed that in order to revive *l'antico valor* in the hearts of the moderns, it was necessary to turn them into ancients, in the same way that Livy had made himself *antiquus* and Machiavelli was also going to do:

> When evening comes I return home and go into my study, and at the door I take off my daytime dress covered in mud and dirt, and put on royal and curial robes; and then decently attired I enter the courts of the ancients, where affectionately greeted by them, I partake of that food which is mine alone and for which I was born; where I am not ashamed to talk with them and inquire the reasons of their actions; and they out of their human kindness answer me, and for four hours at a stretch I feel no worry of any kind; I forget all my troubles, I am not afraid of poverty or of death. I give myself entirely to them.[23]

When Machiavelli wrote these famous words in a letter of 10 December 1513 to his friend Francesco Vettori, the Florentine ambassador in Rome, he was about to begin work on the book that records his most essential lessons from this conversation with the ancients, the *Discourses on the First Ten Books of Livy*.[24] Having just finished "a short work *de Principatibus*," now known as *The Prince*, in which he delivered his lessons on and for "new princes" (as were the Medici rulers in Florence and in the Vatican), he now sought to derive a different kind of lessons, more philosophical-historical than strictly political, for his fellow Florentine citizens, who at that time must have had no faith in their republican government and ideals. When he completed the work around 1517, he dedicated it to his friends Zanobi Buondelmonti and Cosimo Rucellai, with whom he used to meet in the learned gatherings of Florentine intellectuals in the Orti Oricellari, the garden of the Rucellai family, where he had first presented and discussed his *Discourses*.[25]

His main aim in that work was to demonstrate to his republican comrades how Roman society had attained its political power through the consolidation of some ethical qualities, generally connoted by the term *virtus* (virtue, *virtù* in Italian), that had become imperative for all its citizens. Machiavelli's main contention was that these virtues were established in antiquity and could be regained in modernity, primarily through a "proper appreciation of history." What he meant thereby, however, was not a new kind of historical methodology but rather an old kind of historical ideology: he learned from the Roman historians, above all from Livy, how to turn ancient history into a modern mythology. In the *Discourses* he used Livy's mythological history of Rome to create his own historical mythology of "Rome," which, in his presentation, became the model—not the ideal—republic. As such it was worthy of meditation and imitation. Machiavelli makes his intention clear in the introduction to the first book of his work, where he notes, critically, that although "antiquity" is generally venerated by the moderns, "what history has to say about the highly virtuous actions performed by ancient kingdoms and republics, by their kings, their generals, their citizens, their legislators, and by others who have worn themselves out in their country's service, is rather admired than imitated."[26] Against this idleness Machiavelli commends the usefulness of history in Roman society, where the ruling classes, especially the senators, knew how to draw the right "practical lessons" from their history. He was particularly impressed by their ability to render even the most horrible cases "highly virtuous" by making them reasonable and memorable. And again we may recall the case of Romulus's disappearance, which the senators, with their dutiful historian, were able to transform into a myth replete with important "lessons" for the Roman people. Compared with this astute historical policy, the lighthearted treatment of history by its modern producers and consumers was liable to cause only damage: "The erroneous views, based on ill-chosen examples, which have been introduced by our corrupt age, prevent men from considering whether to depart from the customary methods."[27] Machiavelli sought to rectify this predicament by a new presentation of some well-chosen examples from Livy's *History*. He trusted that his interpretation of these sources would reveal in them new historical meanings, actual rather than merely factual, so that those who read his work might come to virtuous views and actions.[28]

In so doing Machiavelli did not abuse history, but rather, much as Nietzsche was to recommend later, he used it "for life." Already in *The Prince* he argues that history is a practical, more precisely a "medical," art, which, by examining human affairs as they "really happen" rather than "theories and speculations" about them, could cure its practitioners (and above all, the rulers) of all sorts of theological, philosophical, and other metaphysical follies. "For many have imagined republics and principalities that had never been seen or known to exist. However, how men live is so different from how they should live that a ruler who does not do what is generally done, but persists in doing what ought to be done, will undermine his power rather than maintain it."[29] In the *Discourses* Machiavelli turned his attention from the politics of singular rulers to the politics of entire peoples, and there he inverted his main philosophical-political teaching: whereas in *The Prince* he argued that an individual ruler could only survive without *virtù*, in the *Discourses* he argued that a community could only survive with *virtù*, which he now redefined in more holistic and classic terms as *communal* rather than as *personal* qualities. Felix Gilbert has noted that Machiavelli's new conception of *virtù* "contains the suggestion that in every well-organized society a spiritual element pervades all its members and institutions tying them together in a dynamic unit which is more than a summation of its consistent parts."[30] And as Machiavelli began to inquire how these qualities are formed and sustained in the whole way of life (*modo del vivere*) of communities, finding that they inhered in the memorial tales and rites that animated their historical institutions, he came to reflect on the wider meanings and implications of historical edification. He saw that its "lessons" were often more emotional than rational, mythical rather than practical.[31] He concluded that real political authority (*auctoritas*), as distinct from actual power (*potestas*), in the state resides only in the mythical-historical "modes and orders" of government. And though his declared aim in the opening sentence of the *Discourses* was to offer "*new* modes and orders,"[32] he subsequently showed that these new modes and orders ought to be, or at least appear to be, very *old* ones.

He who desires or proposes to change the form of a government in a state and wishes it to be acceptable and to be able to maintain it to everyone's satisfaction, must needs retain at least the shadow of its ancient customs, so that institutions may not appear to its people to have been changed, though in point of fact the new institution may be radically different from the old ones. This he must do because men in general are more affected by what a thing appears to be than by what it is, and are frequently influenced more by appearances than by reality.[33]

As this passage reveals, there is a tacit affinity and continuity between the different perceptions of *virtù* in *The Prince* and in the *Discourses:* in both books Machiavelli asserts that *virtù* ought to be exemplified to the masses by their singular leaders, who should know how to enchant their political actions or institutions by historical and mythical associations.

More generally, Machiavelli induced that since the political world is ruled by "appearances," "false impressions," "rumors," and other popular deceptions, the masters of this world are those who know how to manipulate these human fallacies, like the prince who "must be a great feigner and dissembler" so as to be able "to seem"—but never really to be—merciful and trustworthy to his subjects.[34] In his famous illustration of this recommendation, Machiavelli likens all rulers to "foxes" and "lions"; Hanna Pitkin has shown that he generally tended to identify with the foxes and foxlike characters, those who know the truth (*la verità*) about human reality yet do not tell it, seeking rather to expose it in the various discourses of "truth"—or myths—by which it operates.[35] Historians, like politicians, must pay attention to such myths, not because a myth is a better (i.e., truer) history than the official one (this was Vico's argument against Livy), but rather because it records more faithfully the popular beliefs, memories, and all other delusions that make up social-political reality. This attention to the rhetorical and political functions of ancient historiography affected Machiavelli's own historical work, most notably his *Florentine Histories,* where he consciously rehearsed Florentine myths that had proved indispensable for the memorial tradition (*la memoria*) of the commonwealth. This tradition was so deeply rooted in the minds of the citizens that "even if their fathers have not recalled it, the public buildings, the offices of the magistrates, the insignia of the free organizations recall it. Of a certainty the citizens will perceive the meaning of these things with the utmost longing."[36]

This explains his predilection for Livy over all other Roman historians: Machiavelli did not regard Livy as the best historian—he clearly favored Polybius and was by temperament much more akin to Tacitus—but he trusted Livy as a "good historian" and constantly referred to him as "our historian," terms that betray his affection for Livy's *History*. As far as Machiavelli was concerned, the fact that Livy composed his *History* in order to prove the superiority and exemplarity of Roman history over all other histories did not diminish but rather established its superiority and exemplarity over all other histories. In any case, as Leo Strauss points out, even when Machiavelli is critical of Livy, he is not really concerned with Livy himself but only with his stories, which have become so influential. He therefore prefers to comment on Livy rather than to quote him.[37] But above all Machiavelli adhered to Livy because he was the most republican of all Roman historians.[38] His admiration for Livy's work may be traced back to his childhood, for we know that his father possessed a fine edition of this work that young Niccolò himself collected from the binder. Indeed, as his modern biographer opines, Machiavelli may well have started his commentaries on Livy by writing notes in the margins of that copy.[39] These biographical and bibliographical trivia enhance the impression we get while reading Machiavelli's *Discourses,* that he preferred Livy's work precisely because its author was so naive, even superficial, in his treatment of Roman historical tradition. From Machiavelli's perspectives, Livy's apparent weaknesses—his credulity, simplicity, and above all fidelity to authority—were the very qualities that enabled him to record and transmit the ancient virtuous traditions. Moreover, as Machiavelli notes in the preface, he decided to comment "on all those books of Titus Livy which have not by the malignity of time had their continuity broken," namely on the first ten *decades,* because only a very long history, such as Livy had managed to compose, could manifest the forceful durability of the original Roman virtues throughout all subsequent political transformations.[40] Livy's *History,* for all its professional deficiencies, proved superior to all other histories in its faithful, and therefore truthful, evocation of this classical *Romanità.* Livy was a "good historian" of his nation because he did not seek to disprove the historical factuality of its foundational traditions, or myths, but rather to approve their political actuality.

Above all, Livy was a historian of action, whose greatest achievement as a narrative historian was the description of collective events and movements, especially those that showed the Roman masses gripped by strong emotions of grief, joy, excitement, or terror.[41] Machiavelli duly saw that Livy wrote these descriptions of action in order to evoke action. On these pragmatic premises, he also commended Cato against his fellow republican Cicero, because as a political rhetorician Cato knew that words were less important than deeds and moreover could corrupt them—as, in Cato's view, did the deliberations of the "foreign philosophy" to the Roman operations of *virtù*.[42] In the preface to book 2 of the *Discourses*, where he criticizes the modern tendency to rely on old theories, histories, and memories, Machiavelli asks himself whether in his discourses he too has been prey to this human folly.

> Indeed, if the virtue that then prevailed and the vices which are prevalent today were not as clear as the sun, I should be more reserved in my statements lest I should fall into the very fault for which I am blaming others. But as the facts are there for anyone to see, I shall make so bold as to declare plainly what I think of those days and of our own, so that the minds of the young men who read what I have written may turn from the one and prepare to imitate the other whenever fortune provides them with occasion for so doing.[43]

From such thoughts arose his decision to concentrate and comment only on Livy's stories, not on his theories, on what the Roman historian described rather than on what he prescribed. According to Lisa Jardine and Anthony Grafton, Livy's readers in the sixteenth century indeed read him as Machiavelli had taught, as a historian of and for action.[44]

Yet, as much as he tried to emulate Livy as a "virtuous" historian, Machiavelli knew that as a modern historian his duty was much more difficult than that of the ancient historian. For Livy lived in a world suffused with historical tradition, where the *mos maiorum,* the ancient customs of the ancestors, set the standards and models for the moderns; Machiavelli lived in a world devoid of such time-honored authority. Most importantly, Roman society saw to it that this tradition was sanctified by the wise old men of the senate, who served as its official protectors and interpreters throughout the ages. As he reflected on the sorry state of affairs in the Florentine republic, Machiavelli often bemoaned Florence's lack of such senators, men like himself, who would know how to preserve its mythical and historical traditions. Machiavelli elaborates on and celebrates the senatorial achievement in his discourse on the riotous class struggles between the Roman populace and the upper class, in which he makes the most controversial assertion in his entire *Discourses:* "That Discord between the Plebs and the Senate of Rome made this Republic both free and Powerful." He chides those historians who, because they "pay more attention to the noise and clamour resulting from such commotions than to what resulted from them, i.e. to the good effects which they produced," do not see that these clashes brought about "all legislation favourable to liberty."[45]

As Machiavelli would have it, the Roman authorities knew how to transform these popular tumults, which occur "in every republic," into "striking examples of virtue" by a careful policy of retaliation that "seldom led to banishment, and still more seldom to bloodshed," examples that they then used in the education of the masses and in the edification of "laws and institutions whereby the liberties of the public benefited." Moreover, they also knew "that every city should provide ways and means whereby the ambitions of the populace may find an outlet, especially a city which proposes to avail itself of the populace in important undertakings" such as military mobilization and colonization. The officials of such cities should allow the popular protest movements to run their course, certain that their deep motivations and ambitions "are very seldom harmful to liberty." All the masses need is a man of authority, a senator, who will explain to them that this is what they really want. Machiavelli concurs with Cicero's conclusion that although "the populace may be ignorant, it is capable of grasping the truth and readily yields when a man, worthy of confidence, lays the truth before it" (1.4.4–5). Recalling the wonderful story of how Pacuvius dealt with the citizens who attacked their local senators, Machiavelli concludes that even if particular members of the senate were always liable to err, the institution itself was right, as the Roman citizens themselves had realized on this and many other occasions (1.47.2–3).

Throughout his *Discourses,* Machiavelli repeatedly refers to the fact that the Roman republic managed to secure its political stability not by forceful imposition of laws but rather by magical and mythological, or what we would call psychological, evocations of the historical occasions in which those laws came into being.[46] Right from the start, he states that what made Rome so great was its republican history rather than any theory (1.2.1). This is how Hans Baron sums up this creed: "Political *virtù* among a healthy people must continuously be renewed in all groups and classes. Even the political and military greatness of Rome was not the product of an ideal, perfect constitution but rested on an order permitting the constant regeneration of civic energy, through free rivalry, even through civil strife among Roman classes and elites."[47] After Baron, modern scholars have come to appraise Machiavelli as a champion of political liberty; they hardly deal with his specific observations on how the Romans actually exercised it, why they needed a "constant regeneration of civic energy," and by what measures they induced it. In their efforts to align Machiavelli with the liberal ideology of "civic humanism," they have not paid due attention to his "Machiavellism," namely to the fact that the liberty he espoused, like the other republican virtues, was predetermined for the citizens by strong political traditions and institutions, created by the manipulative means of indoctrination and propagation rather than by education.

For, as much as Machiavelli admired the rhetorical-political achievements of the Roman authorities in the education of the masses, he conceded that they were able to perpetuate their policy under the auspices of Roman religion. "It was a religion that facilitated whatever enterprise the senate and the great men of Rome designed to undertake."[48] Machiavelli did not believe in any particular religion, but he believed in religion as a tool, most definitely so when religion "helped in the control of the armies, in encouraging the plebs, in producing good men, and in shaming the bad" (1.11.3). In his famous discourse titled "The Religion of the Romans," he shows that the Romans' religion was more useful in political affairs than Christianity was, because its "spirit" (la quale religione) was primarily historical rather than metaphysical, inspired by mythical rather than mystical epiphanies, and could thus be applied in states of emergency (such as that which arose after Romulus's disappearance) or, more commonly, in occasional ceremonies, as, for example, in the taking of the auspices before battles, where, as a rule, the priests evoked suitable deities to inspire confidence in the troops (1.12.2, 1.14, 3.33.2). According to Machiavelli, the Romans were particularly susceptible to all these beliefs and rites because they "were more afraid of breaking an oath than of breaking the law, since they held in higher esteem the power of God than the power of man" (1.11.2). Under pagan direction of awe-inspiring rites and sacrifices, these basic human sentiments galvanized into strong ethical and political commitments, for the citizens came to regard their laws and historical traditions as sacred. Machiavelli's conclusion was that "[t]hose princes and those republics which desire to remain free from corruption, should above all else maintain incorrupt the ceremonies of their religion and should hold them always in veneration; for there can be no surer indication of the decline of a country than to see divine worship neglected" (1.12.1).

Machiavelli thought that basic human qualities like credulity and fidelity were conducive to republican governments, whose leaders should know how to foster and use the pervasive "fear of God" against the "fear of a prince" and, moreover, should know how to use it in order to enhance their own authority. Referring to the ancient example of Numa, who "pretended to have private conferences with a nymph who advised him about the advice he should give to the people," and to the recent example of Friar Savonarola, who likewise claimed to have conversed with God, Machiavelli commends both for their artful exploitation of divination

(1.11.3, 11). On this matter Machiavelli highly praises Livy, who seems to have understood the significance of auguries for Roman society, even if he himself, like his modern commentator, must have found them "quite fallacious." Moreover, Machiavelli insists that this ability to solidify popular religious beliefs in patriotic historical myths is a virtuous task of the "wise men" in the republic (1.12.2). He thus observes that even if Livy's description of the miraculous events that occurred in the Temple of Juno in Veii (where the statue of the goddess appeared to nod to the Roman soldiers who asked it, "with all due respect," whether it wished to come to Rome) is "foolish," he was right to recount it, because this is an exemplary case that proves how myths of this kind empowered the Roman troops in their task, all the more so when so ably magnified by Camillus and all the other senators (1.12.3). Elsewhere Machiavelli cites "the words that Livy put into the mouth of Appius Claudius . . . 'Nowadays they are allowed to mock at religious rites; what does it matter if the chickens don't eat, if they are too slow in coming out of their pens, or if one of the birds clucks? They are small things, but it was by not despising small things that our ancestors made this republic as great as it is.'"[49] According to Machiavelli, these are the words and works that made Rome "conspicuous alike for virtue, religion, and orderly conduct."[50] He reiterates the lesson of Roman history:

> The rulers of a republic or of a kingdom, therefore, should uphold the basic principles of the religion which sustains them in being, and, if this be done, it will be easy for them to keep their commonwealth religious, and, in consequence, good and united. They should also foster and encourage everything likely to be of help to this end, even though they be convinced that it is quite fallacious. And the more they should do this the greater their prudence and the more they know of natural laws.[51]

Underlying all these considerations was a radical reevaluation of "the masses." Like his Roman heroes and Florentine fellows, Machiavelli regarded la moltitudine as utterly "useless" in itself, and he commonly employed the Aristotelian terminology according to which the people were the "matter" that received its "form" from the leaders. And yet, at the same time, he was mindful of Livy's acute characterization of the Roman masses: "As a crowd they were a fierce lot, but, as individuals each was so afraid that he obeyed."[52] In his reflections on this passage, Machiavelli displays all his ironical skills, and under the guise of polite agreement with this judgment, he tacitly inverts its intentions and contentions. Amid concessions that indeed "in criticizing the decisions of their rulers the masses are often bold" or "that scant attention should be paid to what the populace says about its own good," Machiavelli reveals that the apparently irrational opinions and actions of the masses are motivated by some deep and true republican convictions of which they are only dimly aware. Although Machiavelli does not define these primordial convictions as myths, I would maintain that, in our parlance, this is what they are.

Machiavelli's contention against Livy becomes clear in the consequent discourse on the political competence of "the masses," in which he openly argues that as political agents they were much more prudent than was commonly assumed. He reexamines the historical cases that so repelled Livy and "all other historians" and shows that the popular reactions that these intellectuals found so capricious and atrocious were in fact "highly virtuous." His interpretation of the apparent hypocrisy of the Roman masses in the case of Manlius Capitolinus is revealing. According to Livy, when this popular hero of the war against the Gauls was cited by the tribunes of the people to appear before the Roman people as a result of the tumults he raised against the senate and the laws of the country, his plebeian followers turned against him and eventually condemned him to death, only to realize, after he had been executed, that they wished him back.[53] Machiavelli would not accept that this emotional reaction was "irrational." He argues that the Roman people wanted Manlius Capitolinus back when he was dead precisely and only because he was dead, "for what they wanted was his virtue, which had been such that his *memory* evoked everyone's sympathy," and he adds that "had Manlius, in response to this desire, been raised from the dead, the Roman people would have passed on him the same sentence as it did, have had him arrested and, shortly after, have condemned him to death."[54] What motivated the masses were not some spiritual reveries but actual memories of virtuous actions in their history, in this case of Manlius Capitolinus's heroic deeds in the war against the Gauls in 390 B.C., when, aroused by the geese, he had called enough men together to save the Capitol. Such actions became fundamental to the Roman ideology only after they were purified from all that was nonessential or accidental, in short, once the historical had been rendered mythological.

Myth, for Machiavelli, was the enchantment of political memory. And since he perceived all political traditions and institutions as primarily memorial, that is to say as human constructions that required the creation, preservation, and reactivation of original historical memories, he accepted the mythological augmentation of these memories as integral to any historical formation and education. The proliferation of such myths and other memorial traditions in the official ceremonies, constitutions, and institutions enhanced the republican convictions of the masses. Their reactions (as well as those of the nobles) in the case of Manlius Capitolinus proved the efficacy of this poetical-political education; that can be gauged from

> the fact that not a soul in that city was disposed to defend a citizen who was replete with virtue of every kind and alike in public and in private had done very many things worthy of commendation. For with all of them love of country [*patria*] weighed more than any other consideration, and they looked upon the present dangers for which he was responsible as of much greater importance than his former merits; with the result that they chose he should die in order that they might remain free.[55]

In his letters and works, Machiavelli repeatedly pointed out that "love of country [*lo amore della patria*]" is the paramount republican virtue. Following on the classical tradition that defined the "good citizen" as the one who pursues communal rather than his own personal interests, Machiavelli concluded that such a man must feel and act as lovers do—with compassion, commitment, and self-abnegation. Machiavelli distinguishes between the natural "love of country," which is sentimental and common to all men insofar as they feel affection for local people, customs, and surroundings, and the cultural mode that prevailed in Rome, which is more fundamental: it is edified by mythological, historical, and political instructions. In his discourses on the Roman examples of "love of country," Machiavelli accentuated the different mentalities of subjects of monarchies and of citizens of republics: "The former, like the latter, are attached to places, to memories, and to a culture, but lack the spirit of equality, solidarity, and responsibility which grows only among individuals which have shared as equal citizens the pains and the joys of republican liberty and self-government."[56]

He further observes that the origins of this fervent republican ideology, and principally the popular opposition to royal government, lie in some primordial memories of traumatic experiences in Roman history: "If we consider the Roman populace it will be found that for four hundred years they were enemies to the *very name* of king and lovers of the common good of their country."[57] Machiavelli summed it up in *The Prince*: "Anyone who becomes master of a city accustomed to a free way of life, and does not destroy it, may expect to be destroyed by it himself, because when it rebels, it will always be able to appeal to the spirit of freedom and its ancient institutions, which are never forgotten, despite the passage of time and any benefits bestowed by the new ruler." Republican historical myths impart to their adherents "greater vitality, more hatred, and a stronger desire for revenge; they do not forget, indeed cannot forget, their lost liberties."[58]

Although Machiavelli devoted hundreds of pages to the philosophical and historical repudiation of royal government, he must have been aware that Roman tradition accomplished this task by some memorable stories about the horrible deeds of the Tarquins. The tragic tale of Lucretia resonated throughout Roman history and evoked the horror of tyrannical rulers even under popular leaders like Julius Caesar. On the whole, Machiavelli praises Roman historiography for its contribution to this narrative indoctrination. He claims that whoever reads Roman history and the records of ancient deeds to which it calls attention will prefer "to conduct himself in his fatherland rather as Scipio did than as Caesar did." And with regard to those Roman historians who extolled Caesar, Machiavelli dismisses them as having been corrupted or overawed by his power; he trusts that had these historians been free, they would have revealed their republican sentiments, as in fact they still managed to do by bestowing praise on Marcus Junius Brutus.[59]

Assuming thus that republics are based on a deep and long *memoria* of epochal actions like the foundation of cities, the liberation of states, or victories in wars, which manifest for all generations the virtuous origins and traditions of the polity, Machiavelli sought to reconcile this remembrance of history with the reverence for its myths. He reasoned that it cannot be otherwise, because "the whole truth about olden times is not grasped, since what redounds to their discredit is often passed over in silence, whereas what is likely to make them appear glorious is pompously recounted in all its details."[60] As noted above, Machiavelli knew that this critical judgment on the mythic structure of ancient historiography applied also, and primarily, to Livy's *History,* yet he trusted that modern readers like himself, who perceived the deeper political reasons that motivated the Roman historian to shape his *History* in that mythic fashion, could overcome this "malignant" predicament and thereby attain a "true understanding of histories [*vera cognizione delle storie*]." In any event, the memories and stories of ancient chroniclers, however "fabulous" they surely are, may suffice to testify on the general conditions that prevailed in prehistorical times, as, for example, on what happened in Rome after the expulsion of the Tarquin kings.[61] Able historians like Livy knew how to use such sources, and modern readers should know how to use them, too. Machiavelli's admiration for some great leaders from classical or biblical antiquity, such as Moses and Theseus, Romulus and Cyrus, indicates that he did not care who they really were or what they actually did as long as they—or rather their historians—set the right examples for posterity. He said in *The Prince:*

> As for mental exercise, a ruler should read historical works, especially for the light they shed on the actions of eminent men: to find out how they waged war, to discover the reasons for their victories and defeats, in order to avoid reverses and achieve conquests; and above all, to imitate some eminent man, who himself set out to imitate some predecessor of his who was considered worthy of praise and glory, always taking his deeds and actions as a model for himself, as it is said that Alexander the great imitated Achilles, Caesar imitated Alexander, and Scipio imitated Cyrus.[62]

Machiavelli regarded Xenophon as a great historian because his *Education of Cyrus* molded the education of Scipio, and he admired Xenophon all the more because this "education" was largely the historian's own creation.[63]

His fascination with this kind of historiography may explain the curious fact, noted by Hugh Trevor-Roper and cited by Isaiah Berlin, that "the heroes of this supreme realist are all, wholly or in part, mythical."[64] Machiavelli must simply have realized that since there is no history without myth, the best historians are those who recognize and utilize this fact, as he did in his employment of Livy's mythological history of Rome for the creation of historical mythology for Florence. Unfortunately for him, modern historians still fail to accept this predicament and therefore tend to dismiss his own historical works as "mythical." Mark Hulliung summed it all up most poignantly:

> Historians can destroy Machiavelli, of course, by saying that his reading of Rome was inaccurate, but then they destroy Livy's Rome, too, which was equally mythical; worse, the historians, if they attack Machiavelli on historical grounds, will be destroying myth itself, the storehouse of those images and symbols without which there is no "great tradition" transmitted from generation to generation. Machiavelli can indeed be destroyed by the kind of history that, failing to appreciate how deeply an intellectual tradition rests on historical myths, leaves us with books "of historical interest only."[65]

Judged by the modern standards of historical scholarship, Machiavelli was a "biased" historian.[66] His treatment of Livy in the *Discourses* is typical: he is not really concerned with questions of historical authenticity and objectivity of his sources, only with their applicability to his rhetorical and political purposes. In his subsequent works, primarily in his own *Florentine Histories,* Machiavelli not only used but also produced historical myths; much like Livy, he freely invented "speeches." And yet, it ought to be clear that what prompted Machiavelli to indulge in all kinds of historical manipulation was not some cynical or immoral political desire for power. His treatment of history grew out of his conviction that the ethical notions so essential to any political association were so deeply and inseparably embedded in mythical narration because, in themselves, they could not be grounded in any other rhetorical, political, or historical demonstration. Consider again Machiavelli's dealing with the notion of "love of country," or what we would call patriotism. As noted above, Machiavelli was keenly aware that this *virtù* defied not only commonsensical or historical argumentation but also, more deeply, some very human, even prehuman, propensities: the instinctual obligations to self-preservation, blood relation, affiliation with family and clan, and the like. Roman tradition solved this problem by the consecration and continuous narration of certain historical myths that merely told and showed simply and clearly how some virtuous Romans had actually performed the ultimate patriotic actions—for example, Romulus, who killed his brother Remus; Horatius, who killed his sister; or Brutus, who executed his sons.

In his discourses on these cases, Machiavelli endorses the official Roman version and its representation by Livy, who largely condoned them. Commentators on Machiavelli have often argued that his apology for these horrible deeds proves that Machiavelli was as immoral in the *Discourses* as he was in *The Prince* and that his advocacy of the apparent "virtuosity" in these and other political affairs is not a sign of true liberality but of crass utility. Yet this interpretation misses Machiavelli's practical intention in his discourses on these cases, which, in his view, was also that of their Roman makers (in history and in historiography alike), namely to work out behavioral rather than moral precedents. He rebukes the classical humanistic and modern moralistic judgments on these cases as inadequate interpretations of their true historical meanings, which, for him, were not really ethical but mythical. Thus, on the question of the original fratricide, he takes issue with Cicero and his humanistic followers, who opined that it was "a bad precedent that the founder of the state, such as Romulus, should first have killed his brother, and then have acquiesced in the death of Titus Tatius, the Sabine, whom he had taken as his colleague in the kingdom. They will urge if such actions be justifiable, ambitious citizens who are eager to govern, may follow the example of their prince and use violence against those who are opposed to their authority."[67] In Machiavelli's reformulation of the humanistic position, the questions concerning Romulus's deed turn out to be very pragmatic—Was it a "bad precedent"? Is it "justifiable" (rather than "just" in itself)?—and he answers them in a similar casuistic manner. Assuming that Romulus acted in order to secure the "sole authority" of the "founder," which he (and Machiavelli) deemed crucial to the polity in this early stage, Machiavelli retorts that never will

> any reasonable man blame any ruler for taking any action, however extraordinary, which may be of service in the organizing of a kingdom or the constituting of a republic. It is a sound maxim that reprehensible actions may be justified by their effects, and that when the effect is good, as it was in the case of Romulus, it always justifies the action. For it is the man who uses violence to spoil things, not the man who uses it to mend them, that is blameworthy. (1.9.2)

On these premises he then concludes "that Romulus's action in regard to the death of Remus and Titus Tatius is excusable, not blameworthy" (1.9.6). As this typical discussion reveals, Machiavelli's main consideration in this case is whether it has become "blameworthy" or not, as if to affirm that as in ancient history, so too in modern historiography, such cases, whether acted or narrated, ought to be considered as rhetorical and political exercises in the political education of the masses.

Machiavelli amplifies this position in his discourses on the killing of the sons of Brutus by their father. In this case the deed has become proverbial in Roman history, in Florentine politics, and in Machiavelli's discourses: "He who establishes a tyranny and does not kill 'Brutus,' and he who establishes a democratic regime and does not kill 'the sons of Brutus,' will not last long" (3.3.1–2). Again, as in the case of Romulus's fratricide, Machiavelli is not concerned with the deed itself but rather with its lasting impression, principally on the Roman masses, for whom this case must have entailed certain tacit messages that have eluded the humanists and the educated classes because they were mythical rather than logical. In Machiavelli's view, the horrible actions of Romulus and Brutus proved to be the most memorable and credible manifestations of the Roman *virtù* of patriotism because both showed, very literally, how loyalty to the *Patria* could prevail over the loyalty to or of the *Pater*. Bruce James Smith has observed, in his discourses on these most difficult cases in Livy's *History,* that Machiavelli inverts the common meaning of "patriotism," which in its basic literal and traditional connotations implied a servile "reverence for the fathers," and gives it a new, distinctly republican, meaning: "love of that which belonged to the fathers," that is, their virtues.[68] In the same vein,

Machiavelli's silence over some important cases in early Roman history, most notably the apparent assassination of Romulus by the senators, implies that he did not regard this action as virtuous.[69] Yet even here, we may add, Machiavelli would have approved the consequent actions of the senators, who knew how to transform this hideous historical action into the stupendous mythical fiction of "the apotheosis."

The remarkable achievement of Roman tradition in this and similar cases was that it knew how to conceal but also to preserve the dreadful truth of the event. Livy maintained this tradition. Machiavelli noted and elaborated these contentions in Livy's work. In Machiavelli's discourse on the eternal enmity of the Roman masses to "the very name of king," his psycho-historical conclusion that "when the populace begins to have a horror of something it remains of the same mind for many centuries" betrays his deeper conviction that underlying all our political traditions and institutions are some primordial existential horrors—of violent death, of oblivion, of abandonment, of enslavement—which these traditions and institutions retain, forever animated but suspended, by making them *felt* in myths and rites rather than fully *known*. According to Leo Strauss, "The *Discourses* do speak of things which make shudder him who reads them, to say nothing of him who is faced by them, provided those horrible things are not well known; the *Discourses* deal with the terrors inherent in the ultimate causes or with the initial terror."[70]

Having considered these stark observations, we may now reassess Machiavelli's decision to devote his entire work only to the first ten "decades" of Livy's. For in the earliest parts of his *History*, Livy recounted the most horrible deeds *ab urbe condita* in mythical terms that concealed yet preserved their true historical reality. In so doing he did not expose, nor did he disguise, the awful truth about the beginnings of the *patria;* he merely intimated it in a way that enabled the readers to perceive its deeper meanings, or, to use Machiavelli's terms, to draw its "practical lessons." As such these paradigmatic cases could be—and had to be—repeatedly evoked and experienced by the moderns in their own lives. Machiavelli believed that in order to overcome moral and cultural stagnation, human beings must confront some difficult truths about their beginnings, recognizing their own depravity; and this, he knew, could not be accomplished by purposeful historical memories but through frightful mythical evocations of primordial experiences. He intended his *Discourses* to teach them this lesson about their "lessons."

Machiavelli's intentions are fully revealed in his famous recommendation in book 3 of the *Discourses* that all social-historical bodies such as religions or states should conduct a policy of "frequent renovations" through reactivation of their foundational experiences. Setting out from the assumption that such bodies are organic entities liable to degenerate, Machiavelli proposes to revitalize their original and seminal traditions: "The way to renovate them . . . is to return them to their beginnings. For at the beginning religious institutions, republics and kingdoms have in all cases some good in them, to which their early reputation and progress is due. But since in process of time this goodness is corrupted, such a body must of necessity die unless something happens which brings it up to the mark."[71] Machiavelli suggests two possible ways by which this process could be accomplished: either accidentally, by "some external event," such as a defeat in war, which is likely to shake these "bodies" to the ground, or by their "own intrinsic good sense," that is, intentionally and methodically, by ritual and cultural festivities that revive in their modern performers the original memories and myths of their virtuous founders. Although both remedies proved effective in Roman history, Machiavelli prescribes the "internal" treatment as more careful and useful. From Roman history he cites seven memorable examples of the use of this drastic policy; five of them involved public executions. "Such events," he says, "because of their unwonted severity and their notoriety, brought men to the mark every time one of them happened" (3.1.5).

The Romans conducted their religious policy accordingly: "Their ceremonies lacked neither pomp nor magnificence, but, conjoined with this, were sacrificial acts in which there was much shedding of blood and much ferocity . . . Such spectacles, because terrible, caused men to become like them" (2.2.6). Considering the case of religious institutions (sette), Machiavelli allows that the measures might be less drastic but equally dramatic and mythic. Such were the works and words of Saint Francis and Saint Dominic, who "by their poverty and exemplification of the life of Christ revived religion in the minds of men in whom it was quite dead." But even in this case, Machiavelli implies that the achievements of both reformers owed much to their rhetorical skills as "confessors and preachers," whereas those who did not heed their exhortations "behave[d] as badly as they [could], because they [were] not afraid of punishments which they [did] not see and in which they [did] not believe" (3.1.8).

Machiavelli's arguments for "cultural primitivism" are not very original; they rehearse the classical arguments of Livy and his ilk. What makes his notion of renovation unique is the accentuation of the dramatic, or what we would nowadays call the traumatic, aspects in this process, namely his recommendation for a "shock of recognition" whereby the patients come to terms with their "critical condition." John Pocock would call this acute recognition of the fragility of all human institutions the "Machiavellian Moment" in the history of republican communities, the moment when the members of the community become conscious of the precarious conditions of its foundation and commit themselves to its protection.[72] In conceiving of the "returning toward the beginnings" as an attempt to regain the historical myths of the community, Machiavelli may seem to have come to that "recognition of myth" that, according to my definition, marks the "modern" conception of history.

And yet, for all his acute observations on the origins and functions of historical mythology, Machiavelli remained curiously alien to it. He studied the social and political operations of myth but not these operations as they actually occurred, how atavistic impressions evolved into artistic expressions, why certain images acquired tales, and so on. Machiavelli, in short, was interested only in the politics and not in the poetics of myth. He completely ignored the great classical theories and interpretations of mythology—Plato's "psychology," Aristotle's "physiology," Lucretius's "anthropology," Pausanias's "archaeology," Varro's "philology," and many other works that might have enabled him to extend his mythological inquiries beyond the rather narrow boundaries of political actuality. Consequently, the "practical lessons" that he derives from ancient mythology seem rather simplistic and all too often casuistic, as, for example, in his attempt to present the founders of religion (Moses, Numa) and their provisions as primarily political rather than theological. He does not believe that they really believed in what they said and did. In his discourses on Roman religion, he does not deal with Roman religiosity, as if its rites and institutions could be studied without the beliefs of the agents performing them. Isaiah Berlin has rightly noted that Machiavelli's "sociological and psychological imagination" is "excessively primitive."[73] I argue, by way of conclusion, that this fallacy hampered his historical and political interpretations of Livy's History, indeed of any history, because, to repeat my words, in order to know who the Romans really were, the historian must know who they thought they really were, where they came from and where they went. And the best—perhaps the only—way to get this knowledge is to take their historical myths seriously.

Machiavelli did not do so. In his discourses on Roman myths, he asked what these fictions ultimately meant in the construction of society and history but not what they actually meant to those who made them up. Thus, for example, Mark Hulliung points out that "Machiavelli did not understand that to Livy fortuna meant destiny, not chance or accident."[74] This is

a crucial misapprehension if we recall that for Livy this mythological goddess represented a divine agency (*fatum*) "by whose law the unchangeable
order of human affairs is arranged";[75] Machiavelli describes her as the mis-
tress of chance and accident, who interferes in human affairs capriciously
and arbitrarily: "This unstable goddess and fickle deity . . . disposes of time
as suits her; she raises up, she puts us down without pity, without law or
reason."[76] Machiavelli's inattention to Livy's mythical word betrays his total alienation from Livy's mythical world. Beyond that, it attests to a deeper
and more fundamental problem in Machiavelli's life as well as in his work,
that he lacked true historical sensibility, which had already come to be
defined by his contemporaries as awareness of the mental difference between the present age and the past. Machiavelli conducted his historical investigations on the opposite assumption. In his famous letter to Francesco
Vettori, he referred to the great ancient authors as his friends and guests.
In the *Discourses* he justified this emotional attachment on rational grounds.
He directed this work against those who believed that imitation of the ancients was impossible, "as if the heaven, the sun, the elements, and man had
in their motion, their order, and their potency, become different from
what they used to be."[77] Rather, he says, "If the present be compared with
the remote past, it is easily seen that in all cities and in all peoples there are
the same desires and the same passions as there always were."[78]

Modern historiography began with the recognition of this hermeneutical fallacy, as scholars in various fields of knowledge realized that the
norms and forms of life in classical antiquity were more primitive than, and
therefore inadequate to, those of their own modern times. Historians of
historiography have traced this discovery back to various sources: Italian
humanists in the fifteenth century, French jurists in the sixteenth century,
English political theorists in the seventeenth century, and German philologists in the eighteenth century. From our perspectives, however, which
identify modern historiography with mythistory, the first, or at least the
foremost, discoverer of historical mythology was Giambattista Vico. As I
now argue, Vico's radical redefinition of myth as a "true narration [*vera
narratio*]" of human life and history marks the real turning point in the
modern scholarship of myth, history, and mythistory.

III

In 1686, at the age of eighteen, Giambattista Vico left his native town of
Naples to work as a private tutor to the sons of Don Domenico Rocca in
his estate at Vatolla. In his *Autobiography* Vico recalls the nine years he spent
in the Roccas' castle of the Cilento as a blissful time. During those years

he "made the greatest progress in his studies" and also completed his first metaphysical and poetical compositions.[79] In 1695 he returned to Naples to find out that the vast "learning and erudition" he had acquired in Vatolla made him "a stranger in his own land," because in his absence the entire intellectual community of Naples had become thoroughly infatuated by the "physics of Descartes." The new Cartesian philosophy made the old Aristotelian philosophy a "laughingstock" and consigned the Platonic philosophy of Renaissance men such as Marsilio Ficino, Pico della Mirandola, or Alessandro Piccolomini to "being shut up in the cloisters." And as for Plato himself, "an occasional passage was turned to poetic use, or quoted to parade an erudite memory, and that was all."[80] Reflecting on these early misfortunes in his intellectual life, Vico writes that "he felt most grateful for those woods in which, guided by his good genius, he had followed the main course of his studies untroubled by sectarian prejudices." While "in the city taste in letters changed every two or three years like styles in dress," Vico prides himself on having remained loyal to the ancient classical tradition of *litterae humaniores:* "For these reasons Vico lived in his native city not only a stranger but quite unknown."[81]

Modern scholars have long suspected that this melodramatic description of the lonely genius, with its topical classical jargon of authenticity— a forlorn "disperato" against all the cohorts of "Renato"[82]—is inaccurate, "a myth."[83] They point out that Vico moved in the most prominent intellectual circles of Naples and was a member of various academies that must have acquainted him with the major modern discoveries and theories in the European Republic of Letters.[84] According to Max Harold Fisch, Vico exaggerates his isolation from the new philosophy during the Vatolla years and, moreover, hides the fact that he himself was a Cartesian until about the age of forty, thereby creating the false impression that already in his early years he had attained the position of his later work.[85] Nonetheless, recalling Croce's asseveration that Vico's *Autobiography* ought to be read as "the application of the *New Science* to the life of the author,"[86] we may read Vico's "myth" of his own life in the same way that Vico read myths in the *New Science:* as a "poetic history" of what had really happened, which, since it conveys the innermost impressions of the original and most seminal confrontations with reality, amounts to a "true narration [*vera narratio*]" of human life and history.

In 1699 Vico managed to secure for himself a modest position as a professor of eloquence at the University of Naples, but this occupation, which Vico held throughout his professional life and which confined him to the classical humanistic tradition, seems only to have enhanced his sense of alienation from the dominant intellectual fashion of the times. His early pedagogical and philosophical works, primarily the tracts *On the Study Methods of Our Time* (1708) and *On the Most Ancient Wisdom of the Ancients* (1710), attest to his acute dialectical engagement with the Cartesian philosophy. Already in these works he sensed that the denigration of history and other venerable humanistic *artes* under the hegemony of the new Cartesian *méthode* had a pernicious effect on the very constitution of social life: "Our young men, because of their training, which is based on these [Cartesian] studies, are unable to engage in the life of the community, to conduct themselves with sufficient wisdom and prudence," which, he argued, consist in the courses and discourses of "tradition."[87] His initial notion of a *scienza nuova*, a New Science, of humanity that consists in the recognition of myth as the origin of all our human institutions and traditions (*cose umane*) grew out of these early attempts to defend the classical *litterae humaniores* against Descartes's attack on their validity. For in his *Discourse on Method*, Descartes claimed:

> Then, too, the mythical stories represent, as having happened, many things which are in no wise possible. Even the most trustworthy of the histories, if they do not change or exaggerate the import of things, in order to make them seem more worthy of perusal, at least omit almost all the more commonplace and less striking of the background circumstances, and the account they give of them is to that extent misleading. Those who regulate their conduct by examples drawn from these sources are all too likely to be betrayed into romantic extravagances, forming projects that exceed their powers.[88]

These assertions defined for Vico his "new scientific" task. His greatest achievement in the creation of a new science of humanity was, on his own testimony, the deciphering of the "poetic characters" by which the ancient mythmakers had made up their—our—human institutions: "This discovery, which is the master key of this Science, has cost us the persistent research of almost all our literary life, because with our civilized natures we [moderns] cannot at all imagine and can understand only by great toil the poetic nature of these first men."[89] In the *Autobiography* he describes the publication of the first edition of the *New Science* in 1725 accordingly:

> In this work he [Vico] finally discovers in its full extent the principle which in his previous works he had as yet understood only in a confused and indistinct way . . . He discovers this new science by means of a new critical method for sifting the truth as to the founders of the pagan nations from

the popular traditions of the nations they founded. Whereas the writers to whose works criticism is usually applied came thousands of years after these founders. By the light of this new critical method the origins of almost all the disciplines, whether sciences or arts, which are necessary if we are to discuss with clarity of ideas and propriety of language the natural law of nations, are discovered to be quite different from those that have previously been imagined.[90]

In *The New Science* Vico summed up this "new scientific" methodology in this incisive axiomatic formulation: "Theories must start from the point where the matter of which they treat first began."[91] On these methodological premises, Vico himself sought to discover the origins of human history in some fundamental "institutions," or, to use the terms he had used in the title of the first edition of his major work, to set up a *New Science concerning the Principles of Humanity*.[92] The key terms in this original title, as well as in the title of the last edition (*Principles of a New Science concerning the Nature of the Nations, by which are found the Principles of Another System of the Natural Law of the Gentes*), allude to the greatest scientific work of these and all times: Sir Isaac Newton's *Mathematical Principles of Natural Philosophy*, which, since its publication in 1687, has become universally known as the *Principia*.

Newton's revolution consists in the very definition of his *Principia*. "These Principles," Newton wrote, are not some "occult qualities" that cannot be observed and tested, like metaphysical entities, but are those physical properties and forces—such as cohesion of bodies, inertia, and gravity—which form and govern the movements of all natural things in the world and might therefore be rightly called the "general Laws of Nature."[93] Few people had actually read, and fewer had understood, Newton's work, but his empirical method and worldview were soon accepted by all as valid—in the natural as well as in the human sciences.[94] In order to know anything human—a word, an idea, a custom, a whole society or civilization—it was necessary to discover its "principles," which, as the term *pre-incipium* (that which precedes birth) implies, are those primal elements that have generated it. Vico was alert to this new scientific methodology.[95] Already in his preliminary study *On Universal Law* of 1720, he observed: "History does not yet have its principles."[96] In *The New Science* he wished to establish these principles. Setting out from the assumption that "the nature of institutions is nothing but their coming into being at certain times and in certain guises," Vico thus sought to discover "in the deplorable obscurity of the beginnings of the nations and in the innumerable variety of their customs" the "principles of humanity," that is, those primal capacities of human beings that, much like Newton's "principles of nature," have formed and govern their social life and history.[97]

Vico's debt to Newton is evident. He even sent his book to Newton, but Newton, by then very old, probably never read it.[98] However, even though Vico molded his work on Newton's scientific methodology, he eventually inverted its premises: he came to realize that his new science of humanity was not only more "certain" than the science of nature—because it relied on a more intimate knowledge of its object—but that it was also more "true," because it processed a better kind of knowledge: that of the one who has made the very object of knowledge.[99] This seems to be the new message of *The New Science,* a message that is coded already in Vico's early works, most clearly in the phrase that has become Vico's trademark: *verum et factum convertuntur sunt.*[100] Vico took this classical-theological formulation, which literally means "The true [*verum*] and the made [*factum*] are the same," to mean that we can know as true only that which has been made by us or ("with great effort") by other human beings. Yet, whereas in his earlier writings Vico had argued that such "true knowledge" through conventions was possible only in mathematics, where we deal with definitions, axioms, and postulates—all artificial objects that we have made—in *The New Science* he transposed the notion of *verum* as *factum* from pure conventions (such as geometrical figures) to "more real" cultural and social conventions (myths, laws, states, and the like). Not until that last work of his life did he come to realize that practically all our "civil institutions" are as artificial and conventional as geometrical forms are and that consequently our knowledge of the human world results from what is equally an essentially constructive activity: we know this world because, and only to the extent that, we still make or share its constitutive ideal fictions, its myths. Vico celebrated this seminal illumination in some memorable words:

> But in the night of thick darkness enveloping the earliest antiquity, so remote from ourselves, there shines the eternal and never failing light of a truth beyond all question: that the world of civil society has certainly been made by men, and that its principles are therefore to be found within the modifications of our own human mind. Whoever reflects on this cannot but marvel that the philosophers should have bent all their energies to the study of the world of nature, which, since God made it, He alone knows; and that they should have neglected the study of the world of nations, or civil world, which, since men had made it, men could come to know.[101]

This passage has often been quoted and discussed by theorists of the human sciences, who rightly regard it as one of the most significant contributions to the formation of their methodology.[102] Yet very few of them, if any, have realized that the actual method of inquiry that Vico had in mind pertains to "historical mythology." In other words, Vico believed that the archaic narratives of "fabulous beginnings," in which the peoples of ancient civilization preserved "the memories of the laws and institutions that bind them in their societies," were the earliest, and therefore the best, sources of the "principles of humanity."[103] Moreover, these sacred narratives were, he claimed, the means by which we could study other human beings and societies that are "so remote from ourselves," because we could use them to "descend from these human and refined natures of ours to those quite wild and savage natures, which we cannot at all imagine and can comprehend only with great effort."[104] Isaiah Berlin elaborates on the idea: "Myths, according to Vico, are systematic ways of seeing, understanding, and reacting to the world, intelligible fully perhaps only to their creators and users, the early generations of men"; but at the same time, they are also "for modern critics the richest of all sources of knowledge of the physical and mental habits and the social ways of life of their creators."[105] This, indeed, was Vico's greatest achievement as the "founder of modern human sciences": he was able to show in practical and historical terms how men in "earliest antiquity" had actually made *their* world by certain "modifications" that still prevailed in *our* world of "modernity." For Vico indicates quite clearly that he has discovered the "truth" about the "civil world [*mondo civile*]"—how men made it and why, therefore, men could come to know it—in some archaic "human creations [*cose umane*]" that made up and still sustain this "civil world," being thus "its principles"; these creations, the ones that are still verifiable to us, "are to be found within the modifications of our own human mind." In order to accomplish this difficult hermeneutical task, we must indeed "enter," as Berlin likes to paraphrase Vico, into the "minds" of the historical agents whom we study, yet not by any mystical feats of intuitive "empathy" or speculative identification with "those quite wild and savage" brutes, whom indeed "we cannot at all imagine," but rather by methodical investigation of those mental expressions which we "can comprehend if only with great effort," precisely as modern psychologists or anthropologists do when they interpret dreams or myths.

As a philologist of "earliest antiquity," Vico was particularly privileged—and obliged—to observe the various ways in which its poetic tradition still inspired the age of Enlightenment: "The poetic speech which our poetic logic has helped us to understand continued for a long time into the historical period, much as great and rapid rivers continue far into the sea, keeping sweet the water borne by the force of their flow."[106] His main task was to show that, as in the case of linguistic metaphors, the archaic mythopoeic "modifications" continue to "flow into" all our "human institutions." Vico accomplished this task, above all, in the second book of *The New Science,* "On Poetic Wisdom [*Della sapienza poetica*]," which constitutes about half of the whole work and is largely concerned with the mythological origins of all our "human institutions."

Modern scholars of classical mythology are now likely to dismiss as mere speculations most of the etymological and historical interpretations put forth by Vico. They may even use the terms by which Vico himself dismissed Francis Bacon's mythological interpretations: he said they were "more ingenious and learned than true."[107] Nevertheless, Vico's "great effort" in conjuring all these interpretations demonstrates that he had indeed arrived, for the first time in modern historiography, at a full recognition of myth. Ernst Cassirer was therefore right to praise Vico as "the true discoverer of myth."[108] By that he meant to suggest that Vico was the first theorist who conceived of myth as a new kind of knowledge, literally a *scienza nuova,* replete with its own epistemic, aesthetic, and linguistic configurations. Although this observation is certainly correct, it obscures the fact that for Vico the investigation of mythology was primarily historical rather than philosophical, intensely anthropological rather than merely philological. Gianfranco Cantelli has observed:

> The common tendency of the majority of Vico's interpreters has been to approach the problem [of myth] from a point of view too exclusively aesthetic and linguistic, which has left obscure the perhaps decisive fact that, for Vico, the investigation of the origins of poetry grew out of a predominantly historical inquiry and that his true intention was less to establish the manner in which poetic language was born than to examine the function of myths, to clarify the origins of religion, and to determine its role in the civil development of mankind.[109]

Assuming that the ancient myths encode the innermost motivations that drove man to constitute, and still sustain, those "human institutions" that have proved crucial for "the preservation of the human race," Vico sought to decipher in their images and tales the deep reasons of the "principles of humanity": "Our mythologies agree with the institutions under consideration, not by force and distortion, but directly, easily, and naturally. They will be seen to be civil histories of the first peoples, who were everywhere poets."[110] These poets could not possibly have known all the sublime meanings that later mythographers ascribed to their myths: "In their fables the nations have in a rough way, and in the language of the human senses, described the beginning of the world of the sciences, which the specialized studies of the scholars have since clarified for us by reasoning and generalization."[111] He concludes, on that basis:

> It follows that the first science to be learned should be mythology or the interpretation of fables; for, as we shall see, all the histories of the gentiles have their beginnings in fables, which were the first histories of the nations. By such a method the beginnings of the sciences as well as of the nations are to be discovered, for they . . . had their beginnings in the public needs or utilities of the peoples and were later perfected as acute individuals applied their reflection to them.[112]

"Mythology, or the interpretation of fables" was, then, the "first science [la prima scienza]" of Vico's New Science. And he duly turned it into a new science by grounding the classical myths in the actual norms and forms of life of archaic civilization, which was, according to his account, utterly primitive and imaginative. "To complete the establishment of the principles which have been adopted for this Science," he declares, we "must begin where its subject matter began," namely in the mythology of pagan antiquity: "We must therefore go back with the philologians and fetch it from the stones of Deucalion and Pyrrha, from the rocks of Ampion, from the men who sprang from the furrows of Cadmus or the hard oak of Vergil. With the philosophers we must fetch it from the frogs of Epicurus, from the cicadas of Hobbes, from the simpletons of Grotius; from the men cast into this world without care or aid of God."[113]

Vico's careful limitation of his New Science to the postdiluvian "gentes [genti]" attests to his deep Catholic conviction that the biblical historia sacra of the Hebrews was prior and superior to pagan mythology.[114] He may also have chosen to concentrate on the gentile historia profana, however, because it enabled him to exemplify his deep humanistic conviction that "the world of civil society has certainly been made by men, and that its principles are therefore to be found within the modifications of our own human mind." For it was principally through pagan history that he could prove how men have really made their own history, by their own natural mythopoeic capacities: imagination (fantasia), memory (memoria), and innovation (ingenium).[115] Note, for example, his tacit rehabilitation of divination, a "science" that was forbidden among the Hebrews and the Christians but widely and wisely exercised by the pagans. According to

Vico, the ancient theological poets, having learned that *"divinari,* to divine, is to understand what is hidden *from* men — the future — or what is hidden *in* them — their consciousness," used their power as diviners of auguries and oracles in much the same way as the biblical prophets used their power when they performed miracles: in order to impress on their beholders the message of divinity.[116] Vergil's expression "All things are full of Jove [*Iovis omnia plena*]" characterizes, for Vico, the essential pagan impression of reality: "For the heavens were observed as the aspect of Jove by all the gentile nations the world over, to receive therefrom their laws in the auspices which they considered to be his divine admonishments or commandments. And this shows that all the nations were born in persuasion of divine providence."[117] Modern scholars who wish to know what the people in pagan antiquity really were like, how they actually lived and believed, must regain their sensual "poetic theology," and they can do so, Vico implies, because it betrays the same religious conviction in "divine providence" that inspires their own "Christian theology."[118] The word *religion* itself retains its original mythological associations, for *religando* means "binding, with reference to those fetters with which Tityus and Prometheus were bound on the mountain crags to have their hearts and entrails devoured by the eagle; that is, by the frightful religion of the auspices of Jove. Hence came the eternal property among all nations, that piety is instilled in children by the fear of some divinity."[119]

The detection of the same religious motivations and institutions among "all nations [*tutte le nazioni*]" indicates that as much as Vico insisted on the distinction between the two histories of pagans and Christians, his *New Science* pertained to both, or, to put it differently, he assumed, against his own Catholic convictions, that all nations, Christian as well pagan, had made their history by the same mythopoeic faculties that we still possess "within the modifications of our own human mind." Vico thus concludes:

> From these first men, stupid, insensate, and horrible beasts, all the philosophers and philologists should have begun their investigations of the wisdom of the ancient gentiles . . . And they should have begun with metaphysics, which seeks its proofs not in the external world but within the modifications of the mind of him who meditates it. For since this world of nations has certainly been made by men, it is within these modifications that its principles should have been sought.[120]

Clearly, Vico was well aware of the radical meanings and implications of his realistic, even naturalistic, conception of mythology. Recalling the famous passage in which Tacitus refers to the "ancient songs" by which the

Germans preserve "the beginning of their history" and some recent observations on similar practices among the American Indians, as well as
among the Persians and the Chinese, Vico concludes that "if the peoples
were established by laws, and if among all these peoples the laws were
given in verse, and if the first institutions of these peoples were likewise
preserved in verse, it necessarily follows that all the first peoples were poets," namely men whose "poetical" creations were primarily "political,"
their mythologies referring only to physical, not to any metaphysical, reality.[121] The assertion that the ancient myths were practical expressions of
the "public needs or utilities of the peoples" deprived them of all the metaphysical, allegorical, and other all-too-theoretical meanings that they acquired over the centuries while "acute individuals applied their reflection
to them." Vico was particularly critical of two of his "four major authors,"[122] Plato and Bacon, who were, respectively, the first and the last
great masters of the allegorical tradition in mythological interpretation.[123]

Plato's notorious attack in book 10 of *The Republic* on the Homeric tradition and its followers—including the mothers and nurses who recited
the Homeric myths to their children—has obscured the fact that Plato
himself was not altogether hostile to mythmaking. Although he taught that
"the myth is, as a whole, false," he also admitted that "there is truth in it
too," a truth pertaining to certain ultimate questions of life and death, origins and ends of nations, fate and character, and similar metaphysical
dilemmas.[124] Plato therefore went on to interpret—and invent—myths as
"golden lies," as stories that were and could still be so designed as to make
certain ethical and political "truths," which could not be demonstrated by
logical or historical proofs, accessible and palatable.[125] Vico approved some
of Plato's political and historical interpretations of Greek mythology,[126]
but he resolutely rejected his philosophical interpretations, arguing that its
makers, the theological poets, were incapable of any ratiocination. Vico
nevertheless assumed that these archaic mythmakers must have sensed and
expressed certain divine truths, which enabled them to transcend their
very physical predicament. On some "occasions"—Vico was well aware of
Malebranche's theory—the gentile nations enjoyed a certain "revelation,"
as, for example, when they imagined the thunder in the primeval forest to
be the commandment of Jove that forbade them to act like "wild beasts."

> Hence poetic wisdom, the first wisdom of the gentile world, must have
> begun with metaphysics not rational and abstract like that of learned men
> now, but felt and imagined as that of these first men must have been,
> who, without power of ratiocination, were all robust sense and vigorous
> imagination. This metaphysics was their poetry, a faculty born . . . of their

ignorance of causes, for ignorance, the mother of wonder, made everything wonderful to men who were ignorant of everything.[127]

As for Bacon, Vico was deeply impressed by his book *The Wisdom of the Ancients* and tried to emulate it in his own work *The Most Ancient Wisdom of the Italians*.[128] Alas, as already noted, he ultimately found Bacon's work "more ingenious and learned than true." Vico duly saw that Bacon had failed because he presumed to have rediscovered in ancient mythology the modern methodology of the scientific revolution and many of its discoveries. This indeed was Bacon's position. He claimed that "beneath no small number of these fables of the ancient poets there lay from the very beginning a mystery and allegory . . . in some of these fables, as well as in the very frame and texture of the story as in the propriety of the names . . . I find a conformity and connexion with the thing signified, so close and so evident, that one cannot help believing such signification to have been designed and meditated from the first, and purposely shadowed out."[129] Vico dismissed this kind of reasoning as "conceit of the scholars, who will have it that what they know is as old as the world."[130] He trusted that his own "discovery of the [primitive] origins of poetry [did] away with the opinion of the matchless wisdom of the ancients, so ardently sought after from Plato to Bacon's *Wisdom of the Ancients*. For the wisdom of the ancients was the vulgar wisdom of the lawgivers who founded the human race, not the esoteric wisdom of great and rare philosophers" (par. 384).

According to Vico, then, Bacon imputed too much and the wrong kind of "wisdom" to the ancients. He failed because he sought, as did all the allegorists, to save the "beautiful" forms of classical mythology by rationalistic (and therefore anachronistic) interpretations of their "ugly" norms. Vico insisted on the original unity of the aesthetical and the ethical in myth, for these were the very qualities that enabled it to fulfill its moral function in the process of civilization: the sublimation of desire. For Vico, and for the eighteenth century at large, this moral test was still the most common criterion by which to evaluate myth (and any other work of art):

In such fashion the first men of the gentile nations, children of the nascent mankind, created things according to their own ideas. But this creation was infinitely different from that of God. For God, in his purest intelligence, knows things, and, by knowing them, creates them; but they, in their robust ignorance, did it by virtue of a wholly corporeal imagination. And because it was quite corporeal, they did it with marvelous sublimity; a sublimity such and so great that it excessively perturbed the very persons who by imagining did the creating, for which they were called "poets," which is Greek for "creators." For this is the threefold labor of great poetry: (1) to invent sublime fables suited to the popular understanding; (2) to perturb to excess, with a view to the end proposed; (3) to teach the vulgar to act virtuously, as the poets have taught themselves. (par. 376)

This was the great achievement of the ancient mythmakers in the age of heroes, whom Vico calls "theological poets." Thus Orpheus "came forth so skilled in the Greek language that he composed in it verses of marvelous poetry, with which he tamed the barbarians through their ears; for although organized in nations they were not restrained by their eyes from setting fire to cities full of marvels" (par. 79). Vico insists, however, that these Orphic myths were much more severe as well as more sincere than the later Homeric myths. For if we read the Homeric myths literally, as Plato and generations of Christian moralists did, we find in them awful stories like those of "an adulterous Jove, a Juno who is the mortal enemy of the virtues of the Herculeses, a chaste Diana who solicits the sleeping Endimions at night," and "a Mars who, as if it were not enough for the gods to commit adultery on earth, carries it even into the sea with Venus." Vico adds, sarcastically, "[M]any of the gods and goddesses in heaven do not contract matrimony at all. One marriage there is, that of Jove and Juno, and it is sterile; and not only sterile but full of atrocious wrangling. Jove indeed fixes in the air his chaste and jealous wife and he himself gives birth to Minerva, who springs from his head. And finally Saturn, if he begets children, devours them" (par. 80).

What, then, were the "verses of marvelous poetry" used by Orpheus to educate the barbarian Greek peoples? Clearly they could not have been the amorous myths as we now know them, for "such examples, powerful divine examples as they are (though such fables may contain all the recondite wisdom desired by Plato and in our time by Bacon of Verulam in his *Wisdom of the Ancients*), if taken at face value would corrupt the most civilized peoples and would incite them to become as bestial as the very beast of Orpheus; so apt and efficacious they are to transform men from the state of beasts to that of humanity!" (par. 80). Vico's answer to that problem was simple: the myths must not be taken at face value; their "severe poetry" must be historicized and understood as befitting the rough mentality of the primitive giants and their clients in the first societies. Both Plato and Bacon failed to do so. Vico notes, for example, that Plato's Socrates should not have been so horrified to find in the myths of Tityus and Prometheus brutal scenes like those that depicted both heroes as "chained to a high rock with their hearts being devoured by an eagle," if he had known how to decipher their historical political lesson: they taught men how to respect divine authority and, subsequently, human authority. "Their being rendered immobile by fear was expressed by the Latins in the heroic phrase *terrore defixi,* and the artists depict them chained hand and foot with such links upon the mountains. Of these links was formed the great chain that Longinus admires as the most sublime of all Homeric fables" (par. 387). This was the "marvelous sublimity" by which Orpheus "through the fables, in their first meaning, first founded and then confirmed the humanity of Greece" (par. 81). Vico trusted that his "new science of mythology" would restore these myths to their original meaning as *vera narratio* (true narration), by which he meant what we would nowadays call "performative stories"—not stories that merely tell how the first "human institutions" were made, but stories that actually made them, and still keep them intact, by the sheer power of their poetry, through very physical imagery that has since been camouflaged by metaphysical sophistry (par. 400).

> But these treacherous reefs of mythology will be avoided by the principles of this Science, which will show that such fables in their beginning were all true and severe and worthy of the founders of the nations, and only later (when the long passage of years had obscured their beginnings, and customs had changed from austere to dissolute, and because men to console their consciences wanted to sin with the authority of the gods) came to have the obscene meanings with which they have come down to us.[131]

Whereas his contemporaries, the *philosophes* of the Enlightenment and other libertines, regarded the "humanization" of myths as a sign of "civilization" and human progression, Vico deplored it as regression of certain human qualities—primarily of the mythopoeic and heroic capabilities— to *sublimità.*[132] The preservation of the Homeric myths, even in the age of the great philosophers and playmakers, was the greatest educational achievement of the Greek nation, comparable, in modern times, to the achievement of the French, who likewise managed to preserve "in the midst of the barbarism of the twelfth century . . . all those fables of the heroes of France called paladins which were later to fill so many romances and poems," thereby ensuring that "French remained a language of the greatest refinement."[133] Vico thus concluded that both Plato and Bacon had failed to discover the truth of myth because they looked for it through and behind its figurative language, not in that language itself.[134] For Vico, in contrast, all myths were creations in and of this language. This was, on his own testimony, his greatest discovery, "the master-key" of his science:

We find that the principle of these origins both of languages and of letters lies in the fact that the first gentile peoples, by a demonstrated necessity of nature, were poets who spoke in poetic characters. This discovery, which is the master key of this Science, has cost the persistent research of almost all our literary life, because with our civilized natures we [moderns] cannot at all imagine and can understand only by great toil the poetic nature of these first men. The characters of which we speak were certain imaginative genera (images for the most part of animate substances, of gods and heroes, formed by their imagination) to which they reduced all the species or all the particulars appertaining to each genus . . . These divine or heroic characters were true fables or myths, and their allegories are found to contain meanings not analogical but univocal, not philosophical but historical, of the peoples of Greece of those times.[135]

This "key" passage has received much attention. In his classic essay "Vico and Aesthetic Historicism," the great literary historian Erich Auerbach notes that Vico's notion of the "poetic" was antiromantic, in fact antiaesthetic, because he conceived of poetry in practical and anthropological categories: it was a primarily a song, a ritualistic incantation, that served to impose the "magic formalism" of the word upon the world.[136] Modern scholars have likewise called attention to Vico's vocation and his commitment to the classical rhetorical tradition, which has always accentuated the moral and cultural functions of linguistic performances.[137] Vico's original conception of "poetic characters," his explanation of the epistemic and linguistic potentialities that render them "imaginative universals," and, more generally, his epochal recognition of the metaphorical constitution of all our "human institutions" are contributions now commonly hailed as novel and important to modern cultural sciences.[138] Yet, as in the case of the *verum et factum* principle, and contrary to Vico's methodological instructions to his readers, his "discovery" of the "poetic characters" has generally received more "philosophical contemplation" than "philological observation." In his fundamental distinction between the two disciplines ("Philosophy contemplates reason, whence comes knowledge of the true; philology observes that of which human choice is author, whence comes consciousness of the certain"),[139] Vico assigned the general "study of the languages and deeds of peoples" to philology[140] and, in the specific case of "the first gentile peoples" and their "poetic characters," to "historical mythology." What Vico actually meant by New Science was in fact philology—an old art that traditionally entailed the formal interpretation of words in classical books, but which Vico transformed into a new science of understanding human beings in past or foreign cultures through their symbolic figures and myths.[141]

Throughout his work Vico, the royal professor of eloquence at the University of Naples, used his considerable knowledge of rhetoric to point out that the linguistic categories by which we order and define the distinct forms of speech—the master tropes of metaphor, metonymy, synecdoche, and irony—are generally descriptive of the mental growth through which all peoples and nations must go in their *nasciemento,* their becoming human.[142] Setting out from the observation that "[t]he human mind is naturally inclined by the senses to see itself externally in the body, and only with great difficulty does it come to understand itself by means of reflection," Vico draws this "universal principle of etymology in all languages: words are carried over from bodies and from the properties of bodies to signify the institutions of the mind and spirit."[143] Because that kind of "metaphor makes up the great body of the language among all nations" (par. 444), the new etymology, which "tells us the histories of the institutions signified by words, beginning with their original and proper meanings and pursuing the natural progress of their metaphors according to the order of ideas" (par. 354), might enable us to trace the evolution of human ideas and institutions in social history: "first the forests, after that the huts, then the villages, next the cities, and finally the academies" (pars. 238–40).

These observations on the common social conditions underlying all human languages enabled Vico to perceive that the forms of signification in the various languages are commensurable because they all pertain to the same human predicament, which has produced the same basic emotional reactions and prudential or, in Vico's term, "common-sensible" lessons: "Human choice, by its nature most uncertain, is made certain and determined by the common sense of men with respect to human needs or utilities, which are the two sources of the natural law of the gentes. Common sense is judgment without reflection, shared by an entire class, an entire people, an entire nation, or the entire human race" (pars. 141–42). On these premises, the mythologies are different, yet equivalent, linguistic expressions of the same "judgment without reflection" on social life and history and thus make up, and might be compared to and analyzed by, what Vico called a "mental dictionary":

There must in the nature of human institutions be a mental language common to all nations, which uniformly grasps the substance of things feasible

in human social life and expresses it with as many diverse modifications
as these same things may have diverse aspects. A proof of this is afforded
by proverbs or maxims of vulgar wisdom, in which substantially the same
meanings find as many diverse expressions as there are nations ancient and
modern. (par. 161)

Vico's "discovery" of the deep historicity of language is akin to what modern cultural theorists have eventually come to proclaim as their own discovery; To use Wittgenstein's words, "a whole mythology is deposited in
our language."[144] Vico notes it, for example, in "the usage that that has
come down in the languages of many Christian nations of taking heaven
for God" and duly relates it to the pagan antiquity and mentality of all these
nations.[145] On a more fundamental level, this discovery suggests that Vico
could establish his *New Science* only after he had taken a linguistic turn:
he saw that the world in which we live is a world of institutions based
on language and that therefore the task the human sciences most resemble
and must be modeled on is the interpretation of texts. He correctly saw
that language creates a distinctly human domain, an elaborate framework
of rules and norms and concepts without which it is impossible to construct, let alone to understand, the realities of the *mondo civile*. "To sum up,
a man is properly only mind, body and speech, and speech stands as it were
midway between mind and body" (par. 1045).

Ultimately, and most importantly for this study of mythistory, Vico
used his linguistic discoveries and theories to explore specific historical
texts and cases, such as Roman law, which was, in his peculiar interpretation, a kind of "severe poetry" (par. 1037). Assuming that "the poems of
Homer are civil histories of ancient Greek customs" (par. 156), he arrived
at a new conception of this work, his "Discovery of the True Homer,"
which, though virtually unknown in his lifetime, remains radical even today. He boldly argued that the Homeric epic belonged to a heroic yet utterly primitive phase in Greek history; that its heroes, such as Achilles,
were only "poetic characters," reflecting the barbarous moral and social
norms of the Greek peoples; and ultimately that Homer himself was not
a real person, let alone the singular author of the *Iliad* and the *Odyssey*.
Rather, "the Greek peoples were themselves Homer . . . our Homer truly
lived on the lips and in the memories of the peoples of Greece throughout
the whole period from the Trojan War down to the time of Numa, a span
of 460 years" (pars. 875–76).

All these "discoveries" or (as we would call them) "linguistic turns" ultimately enabled Vico to devise a whole new interpretation and reconstruction of Roman history based on its mythology. Long before Barthold

Georg Niebuhr, he seized upon "vulgar traditions" as the most authentic testimonies of and about Roman history, especially because he deemed these popular and largely plebeian traditions to be less biased by nationalistic and academic conceits than were the official patrician versions of Livy and his ilk. "Vulgar traditions must have had public grounds of truth, by virtue of which they came into being and were preserved by entire peoples over long periods of time. It will be another great labor of this Science to recover these grounds of truth—truth which, with the passage of the years and the changes in languages and customs, has come down to us enveloped in falsehood" (pars. 149–50). In order to overcome this fallacy, Vico devised a "new art of criticism" to "serve as a torch by which to discern what is true in obscure and fabulous history."[146] He firmly believed that the bountiful tales of gods and heroes contained the most valuable information on the actual origins and transformations of Roman society: "The fables in their origin were true and severe narrations, whence *mythos,* fable, was defined as *vera narratio.* But because they were originally for the most part gross, they gradually lost their individual meanings, were then altered, and subsequently became improbable, after that obscure, then scandalous, and finally incredible."[147] The restoration of the original meanings of these stories and the deciphering of their "poetic truth" were to reveal the "historic truth" about their makers, how they had initially imagined and then fashioned their world. For "poetic truth is metaphysical truth, and physical truth which is not in conformity with it should be considered false. Thence springs this important consideration in poetic theory: the true war chief, for example, is the Godfrey that Torquato Tasso imagines; and all the chiefs who do not conform throughout to Godfrey are not true chiefs of war."[148]

Spurred by this "major discovery" of the historicity of "poetic characters," Vico devotes the entire second book of *The New Science* to a reconstruction of Roman history according to its mythological sources. Its main contention is that this history was much more primitive and combative than Livy led us to believe. For Livy and his followers—above all Machiavelli—conveniently ignored the harsh physical and physiological conditions of the early Romans, who, like all other *primi uomini,* "were all robust sense and vigorous imagination" and as such could not have had all the virtuous qualities that their admirers imputed to them. Vico's sarcastic commentaries on Livy's work must be read as a direct refutation of Machiavelli's *Discourses.* Vico's Roman historian, let us recall, was not Livy but Tacitus, the only historian among "his four authors" and the most political of them all.[149] Unlike Livy and his modern republican followers who glorified the "virtuous" policy and achievements of Roman society, Vico perceived it as much more agonistic or "heroic," in the specific connotations he assigned to this term, that is, more barbarous than chivalrous.[150] Whereas Livy depicted the time of the war against Pyrrhus as a glorious and virtuous period ("there was never an age more productive of virtues [*nulla aetas virtutum feracior*]"), Vico denounced it as an age in which the patricians oppressed the plebeians with "intolerable pride, profound avarice and pitiless cruelty."[151] He charges:

> What did any of them [the patricians] do for the poor and unhappy Roman plebs? Assuredly they did not increase their burdens by war, plunge them deeper in the sea of usury, in order to bury them to a greater depth in the private prisons of the nobles . . . Precisely because the nobles of the first peoples considered themselves heroes and of a nature superior to that of their plebeians, they were capable of such misgovernment of the poor masses of the nations. For certainly Roman history will puzzle any intelligent reader who tries to find in it any evidence of Roman virtue where there was so much arrogance, or of moderation in the midst of such avarice, or of justice or mercy where so much inequality and cruelty prevailed. (par. 668)

Livy consistently obscured this truth, even when he knew it, mainly because of his loyalty to the patrician republican tradition but also because he was not really conversant with the mythopoeic sources and structures of that tradition. Thus, whereas Livy accepted the Roman myth about the Greek origins and philosophical meanings of the Twelve Tables, Vico exposes and accentuates its Roman origins and poetical meanings: he calls this oldest law a "serious poem" because it was made up and chanted by primitive people who were all "poets who spoke in poetic characters" (pars. 154, 284, 319, 566). Or, to cite another example, whereas Livy had dismissed traditional stories of the early Romans who claimed to be "sons of the earth," Vico discerned in these stories a "poetic truth" about the way in which early men tied themselves to their land through burial and cultivation.[152] Stories like this were more credible than Livy's stories about the foundation of monarchy, a senate, and asylum, by the "fathers" of the nation, which Vico dismissed as anachronistic fictions. Against these artificial myths of the late Roman historian he posits the actual myths of the Roman people, primarily their accounts of "natural theogony." He postulates that the division of Roman gods into those of the *gentes maiores* and those of the *gentes minores* mirrored the political evolution of Roman society from aristocracy to democracy.[153] The twelve "major" Olympian gods were collective representations of the *maiores,* and they attest to the main stages in the process of Roman (or any other) civilization. Thus, the myths of Jove and Juno signify the formation of religion and family life, and the myths of Diana and Actaeon, Apollo and Daphne, and Hercules' labors signify the consecration of springs, families, and fields, respectively (pars. 533–36, 541–43). Vico fits the foundation of Rome into this mythological order. He ignores the common myths of foundation and radically reinterprets others, so as to show that this city began as an asylum for wanderers. Mars is a "poetic character" of the patrician landlords, the heroes (*eroi*) who defended their fields against the plebeian interlopers. Eventually these foreigners were allowed in as slaves and serfs (*famuli*), and they adopted Mars as their protector (par. 562). Vico then describes the long strife between the classes as a mythological war, in which the two classes fought against each other through and over myths. Some of his most original interpretations pertain to cases of "double fables or characters," in which the plebeian mythmakers challenged the patrician monopoly over Roman tradition by appropriation of distinctly patrician gods (pars. 579–81). This is how he recounts the political history in the myth of Minerva: "Vulcan, it was said, split with an ax the forehead of Jove, whence sprang Minerva. By this they meant to signify that the multitude of *famuli* practicing servile arts (which came under the poetic genus of the plebeian Vulcan) broke (in the sense of weakening or diminishing) the rule of Jove . . . For Jove's rule in the family-state had been monarchic, and they changed it to aristocratic in the city-state" (par. 589). The plebeians were able to form a class-consciousness by the creation of their own countermythology. Vico cites these famous lines from Phaedrus's *Liber Fabularum* 3.34–38, which sum up his own theory most poignantly:

> Attend me briefly while I now disclose
> How art of fable telling first arose.
> Unhappy slaves, in servitude confined,
> Dared not to their harsh masters show their mind,
> But under veiling of the fable's dress
> Contrived their thoughts and feelings to express,
> Escaping still their lords' affronted wrath,
> So Aesop did; I widen out his path. (par. 425)

According to Vico, each major event in this history—the plebeian achievement of the right to limited ownership of land in exchange for military service (*lex poetelia*), the attainment of the right to full ownership of the land (set forth in the Twelve Tables), and the ratification of the right to lawful marriage and inheritance (the law of *Connubium*)—is better recorded in Roman myths than in its histories, for the latter preserve only one (the patrician) version. He even claims to have derived the entire political history of Roman society from four basic "heroic characters" in classical mythology: the lyre of Orpheus or Apollo, the head of Medusa, the Roman faces, and the struggle of Hercules with Antaeus! (pars. 614–18). Vico discerns historical episodes from the class struggle in the myths of Apollo (signifying the patricians), who engages in a contest with the satyr Marsyas (the plebeians); of Atalanta (a patrician deity), who throws away golden apples (fields) to fend off the suitors (plebeians); and of many others.[154] The image of Pegasus soaring over Mount Parnassus might be taken to represent the invention of riding, but as Vico interprets it, Pegasus's wings allude to the birds whose flight lent meaning to the auspices. Pegasus must therefore be seen as a symbol of the horse-riding nobility, which held the right of taking auspices and with it the *auctoritas* over all major decisions in ancient society.[155] The myth of Mercury, the messenger of the gods, encapsulates in his dress and comportment the entire story of negotiations and legal agreements between the patrician and the plebeian classes.

> It is Mercury who carries the law to the mutinous *famuli* in his divine rod (a real word for the auspices), the same rod with which, as Vergil tells, he brings back souls from Orcus . . . The rod is described for us as having one or two serpents wound about it. (These were serpent skins, one signifying the bonitary ownership granted to the *famuli* by the heroes, the other the quiritary ownership they reserved for themselves). There are two wings at the top of the rod (signifying the eminent domain of the orders), and the cap worn by Mercury is also winged (to confirm their high and free sovereign constitution, as the cap remained a hieroglyph of liberty). In addition, Mercury has wings on his heels (signifying that ownership of the fields resided in the reigning senates). He is otherwise naked (because the ownership he carried to the *famuli* was stripped of all civil solemnity and based entirely on the honor of the heroes).[156]

What Vico perceived in and through ancient mythology was, then, a new materialistic, but not a deterministic, theory of social life and history. Vico acknowledged the primacy of material necessities over spiritual aspirations, but he did not reduce these latter creations of the imagination to conditions of production, as his later, more vulgar, Marxist admirers have all too easily done.[157] He realized that these myths were essentially distorted forms of reality that appeared at an early stage of historical development. As such "forms," however, they were real enough; that is, they could not be conscious distortions of reality, as old and new Euhemerists like Machiavelli, Hobbes, and Feuerbach all too simply implied when they explained myths as political fabrications, which have always been made up and sustained by the ruling authorities in order to control and manipulate the ignorant masses. Rather, as more sensitive interpreters of Vico such as Max Horkheimer have seen, Vico saw myths as naive but intensive "reflections" of—and on—actual natural and social predicaments, for example, the class structure in ancient society.[158] Roman mythology, in other words, was not just an arbitrary assemblage of separate gods and heroes, invented and stockpiled at random by the Romans as they went along. Vico reasoned that Roman mythology was a careful, even if unconscious, composition of some permanent and many chthonic deities, an elaborate network of figures and events set up alongside and over against each other in a meaningful pattern. The mutual relations between gods and heroes in this mythological society reflected and illuminated class relations in historical society. For Vico, then, mythology is not only a description of reality but also, as the term literally implies, an interpretation thereof. As such, it opens up "methodological," not just "ideological," perspectives for social research.

I trust that these insightful notions make it clear why Vico has been considered "the true discoverer of myth." But, as I argue at the beginning of this chapter, his prime aim in his investigation of mythology was to find therein the "principles of humanity." How did mythology, the "first science" of *The New Science,* help Vico to establish its principles, and what are they? As we recall, Vico sought to discover them "by a severe analysis of human thoughts about the human necessities or utilities of social life," such as might be shown to inhere in those "human institutions" that have proved to be crucial for "the preservation of the human race."[159] Here is his conclusion:

> Now since this world of nations has been made by men, let us see in what institutions all men agree and always have agreed. For these institutions will be able to give us the universal and eternal principles (such as every science must have) on which all nations were founded and still preserve themselves. We observe that all nations, barbarous as well as civilized, though separately founded because remote from each other in time and space, keep these three human customs: all have some religion, all contract solemn marriages, all bury their dead. And in no nation, however savage and crude, are any human actions performed with more elaborate ceremonies and more sacred

solemnity than the rites of religion, marriage, and burial. For, by the axiom that "uniform ideas, born among peoples unknown to each other, must have a common ground of truth," it must have been dictated to all nations that from these three institutions humanity began among them all, so that the world should not again become a bestial wilderness . . . These must be the bounds of human reason. And let him who would transgress them beware lest he transgress all humanity.[160]

Now the validity of Vico's concrete "principles" may be—and has been—contested on empirical grounds. Vico himself cites the counterarguments of Arnauld, Bayle, and Spinoza, and modern readers could certainly produce even better empirical refutations.[161] But such claims miss the essential point in Vico's argument. For what is really novel and important in his notion of the "principles of humanity" is the hermeneutical, not the empirical, claim, namely his assertion that if any cross-cultural understanding is possible at all, it must assume and pursue certain absolute norms or, to use a modern phrase, "limiting notions" of morality, which determine the range within which various forms of life can be exercised and can be recognized as human.[162] Vico explains that he opted for these three "civil institutions" because they are, or rather have become, "natural customs" among all the peoples.[163] The moment when certain customs become natural marks the beginning of humanity, as well as the starting point of all human sciences, because the appearance of certain rule-governed routines, which are manifestly morally principled, suggests that the human creatures who behave in that way no longer obey their natural instincts but instead submit themselves to their own rules and can thus be followed by us. This, however, is feasible only if we can relate their rule-governed or "principled" behavior to our own experience, however different that may be. For example, in order to understand an alien religious belief or rite, we must have some kind of religious experience or knowledge. This, then, is Vico's contention: that since the world in which people live is a world of cultural meaning that they themselves have created, in order to understand it we must grasp this meaning for them and in ourselves. And the best, indeed the only, way to get this meaning properly is to attend closely to the mythological dimensions of these rites, which are, or at least can be, known to us from our own lives. Or, to quote Wittgenstein again, the myths have such forceful meanings for us because they pertain to something "deep and sinister" in us.[164]

This becomes clear when we note that the decisive proof that Vico offers for the peculiar status of religion, marriage, and burial as "principles of humanity" is that they are and have always been "performed with more elaborate ceremonies and more sacred solemnity" than any other "human actions" in all known societies—a proof that the demarcation of the human from the inhuman, of the cultural from the natural, in human life and history is not and could never be sufficiently grounded in or guaranteed by rational convictions; there are no compelling reasons to perform these rites at all, other than those that human life and history have taught us: that without them no human society could possibly survive.[165] They must always be guarded by mythological images and tales, which are continuously recalled in "elaborate ceremonies and sacred solemnity." Vico shows, for example, that many mythological deities in ancient society served to impose the morality of the *Eroi* on *Eros* and that many of their matrimonial solemnities, including those which require that "women be veiled in token of that sense of shame that gave rise to the first marriages in the world" or "a certain show of force in taking a wife, recalling the real violence with which the giants dragged the first wives into their caves," have been preserved by all nations, evoking in us, unconsciously, the deep reasons for their observation. On a higher level of sophistication, they affirm yet again that "the nature of institutions is nothing but their coming into being at certain times and in certain guises" (502—18).

Vico sums up his argument poignantly: "Truth is sifted from falsehood in everything that has been preserved for us through long centuries by those vulgar traditions which, since they have been preserved for so long a time and by entire peoples, must have had a public ground of truth. The great fragments of antiquity, hitherto useless to science because they lay begrimed, broken, and scattered, shed great light when cleaned, pieced together, and restored" (pars. 356—57). What is that truth? Presumably that to which Plato referred when he said that "the myth is false, but there is truth in it also." The truth about truth is that ultimately all our moral and social theories are (or at least should be rendered) mythological: they grow out of and express "the public grounds of truth" of specific historical communities and civilizations. For "the public grounds of truth," the English translation does not convey the exact meaning of the Italian original, *publici motivi del vero*, which indicates more clearly what Vico regards as the main force in the social construction of reality: the popular impressions and interpretations of reality that, being the essential lessons of the collective historical experience, are continuously recorded, reassessed, reaffirmed, and transmitted by the various "vulgar traditions" in which we all believe and live.

Our Science therefore comes to describe at the same time an ideal eternal history traversed in time by the history of every nation in its rise, development, maturity, decline, and fall. Indeed, we make bold to affirm that he who meditates this Science narrates to himself this ideal eternal history so far as he himself makes it for himself by that proof "it had, has, and will have to be." For the first indubitable principle posited above is that this world of nations has certainly been made by men, and its guise must therefore be found within the modifications of our own human mind. And history cannot be more certain than when he who creates the things also narrates them. (par. 349)

Vico thus came to redefine myth as "true narration [*vera narratio*]" of human life and history, because he saw that in our (or any other) civilization, the fictions of mythology illuminate the "real world" by constituting or "prefiguring" all its human actions and institutions: unlike natural occurrences, which display lawlike, repetitive regularities that are unknowable to us because they are totally alien to our form of life, human occurrences throughout history display forms of moral action that are knowable to us, because we can recognize in them the coherent narrative patterns of the mythical stories with their archetypal characters and plots. Mythology thus fully deserved to be called the "first science" of *The New Science,* because ultimately it was more than just the "interpretation of fables." It was really the explanation of history.

IV

The first real reception of Vico's *New Science* occurred exactly a hundred years after its first publication: in 1824 the young French historian Jules Michelet discovered Vico's book and immediately set out to translate it into French. For the rest of his life, Michelet recalled that discovery as the most decisive moment in his intellectual development. In 1869, in a new preface to his monumental *L'histoire de France,* he looked back on its inception and confessed: "I had no other master than Vico. His principle of living force, of humanity creating itself, made both my book and my teaching." [166] In his notebook he could still evoke his first impressions in some memorable words: "1824. Vico. Effort, infernal shades, grandeur, the Golden Bough"—terms abounding with mythical connotations. From that moment on, he added, he "was seized by a frenzy caught from Vico, an incredible intoxication with his great historical principle." [167] The "great historical principle" that Michelet found in Vico and employed in his own works was the notion quoted in the last lines above: "that this world of nations has certainly been made by men, and its guise must therefore be found within the modifications of our own human mind. And history cannot be more certain than when he who creates the things also narrates them." Michelet understood and duly applied this notion in his work.[168]

Already in an early lecture in 1825, Michelet cited Vico's pragmatic definition of truth as "a judgment without reflection, shared by an entire class, an entire people, an entire nation, or the entire human race," in order to argue that for those who seek to attain truth, Vico's notion of "common sense" or myth is superior to Descartes's reason, because truths in social life and history are productions of "la pensée commune."[169] In his own historical works, Michelet thus resolved to rely on the most common and communal forms of expression by which those who actually made history also narrated their actions and achievements. In his early reflections on Roman history, Michelet used Vico's theory to argue that the uncertainty of archaic times might be clarified by the "essential truths" contained within myth and popular poetry.

> The myths and the poetry of barbarian peoples present the traditions of this time; they are ordinarily the true national history of a people, such as its genius has made it. It is irrelevant whether it accords with the facts. The story of Wilhelm Tell has for centuries aroused the enthusiasm of the Swiss . . . The story itself may well not be real, but it is eminently true, that is to say, perfectly conformable to the character of the people which has taken it for history.[170]

Michelet readily admitted that he had found this notion in Vico's *New Science*.[171] The great achievement of Vico's work, in Michelet's famous formulation, was the assertion of the principles that "[h]umanity is its own creation [*l'humanité est son oeuvre à elle-même*]" and, more crucially, that this creation was essentially mythical. Assuming, with Vico, that the real makers of history are not individual heroes but social groups, he concluded that the great heroes of antiquity were not real historical persons but rather ideal mythological embodiments of what the masses—*le peuple*—had collectively experienced. Nonetheless, as a liberal historian committed to modernity and rationality, Michelet thought that these primitive myths must now be recognized as such, and this, in his view, was precisely what Vico had done:

> The heroes of myth—Hercules who thrusts mountains aside, Lycurgus and Romulus, swift legislators who accomplish in a lifetime the work of centuries—are creations of the people's thought. God alone is great. When man

desired to have men-gods, he had to condense whole generations into one person; to combine in a single hero the conceptions of a whole poetic cycle. Thus it was that he fashioned his historical idols—a Romulus, a Numa. The peoples remained prostrate before these gigantic phantoms. Philosophy raises them up and says to them: "That which you adore is yourselves, your own conceptions."[172]

The Revolution of July 1830, which Michelet enthusiastically endorsed, alerted him to the deeper historical truths in Vico's mythological theory. In 1854 he was still thrilled: "My Vico, my July, my heroic principle."[173] What he actually discovered in Vico's historical mythology was a whole new conception of mythological history; that is to say he now realized that myths were crucial to "heroic" actions in history like those performed during the July Revolution. "During those memorable days," he wrote in 1869, "a great light appeared, and I perceived France."[174] He had a new vision of France within world history, as well as an illumination of his own vocation as its historian. He now fathomed that the entire historical process of civilization consisted in the notion and various manifestations of human liberation, which had moved from the Eastern regions and religions through Christianity toward its final culmination in the French Revolution. This was the "great light" in Michelet's *Introduction à l'histoire universelle,* composed "on the burning pavements of Paris" in the summer of 1830 and promptly published in 1831: "With the world began a war which will end only with the world: the war of man against nature, of spirit against matter, of liberty against fatality. History is nothing other than the record of this interminable struggle."[175] He assumed that the great myths of classical antiquity and Christianity were the early imaginative and still the most effective expressions of this momentous process of civilization, attesting to the material necessities and spiritual aspirations that initially impelled and enabled their makers to transcend by their own human faculties the harsh physical conditions into which they were born.[176] France was the nation that had preserved and carried on this great tradition of creation and liberation through popular narration. The task of the historian was to regain this message of liberation from and for the popular tradition of the nation through historical reconstruction and critical interpretation of its myths.[177] In his great historical project, *L'histoire de France,* which began to appear in 1833, Michelet thus concentrated on those historical sources that were most mythical, because these, rather than any official documents, were the authentic testimonies of how the French people had really made up their history by popular narration, how, long before the Revolution, they had already invoked the great ideals of liberty, equality, and fraternity in their collective memories and imagination. He writes in his *Journal* in 1843: "See, in the Middle Ages, how the popular or pacific legend of the saints, the popular and noble legend of the gallant knights led to noble and chivalric ideal. Reciprocal education which re-descended and ennobled all the people."[178]

His famous chapters on Joan of Arc in *L'histoire de France* attest to this belief in the great metaphysical truth that emanates from and through historical myth. Michelet knew that the wonderful stories about the miraculous deeds of this "belle et brave fille" were largely fictitious, a "legend," but he nevertheless insisted that the legend was an "incontestable histoire," and not merely because it was believed to be so by the people. More fundamentally for Michelet, because Joan herself was in some deep sense the creation of French history, an embodiment of its "national morality," her very appearance and actions as a virgin warrior were, to the simple folk who saw themselves in her, a realization of "la grande image du peuple"— an image that the historian must recognize as true.[179] As Paul Viallaneix has shown, Michelet failed to produce a real historical reconstruction of this affair because, as much as he tried to combine narration with critical interpretation of this myth, he also sought, quite consciously, to regenerate it.[180] In his narration Michelet deliberately accentuates the mythical rather than the historical aspects of the events: the hours of Joan's voyages become more important than the exact dates, the seasons of her wars more important than the years, the landscapes of her trials more important than actual circumstances. The whole story assumes the familiar pattern of the Passion, ending, like the original myth on which it is modeled, not with Joan's death, but with her resurrection—in the popular tradition of French history and, ultimately and most magnificently, in Michelet's apostolic *L'histoire de France.*

According to Michelet, Vico was not fully conscious of these ethical and political implications of his theory of myth: "The basic idea" of *The New Science,* Michelet writes, "is bold; bolder perhaps than the author himself suspected."[181] Michelet repeatedly praised Vico's notion of the evolution of humanity through successive stages of mental configuration—the ages of gods, heroes, and men—and all but ignored Vico's atavistic tendencies and pessimistic auguries. He assumed that Vico's cyclical theory of history, with its catastrophic prognostications, was an expression of a devout Catholic who could not yet liberate himself from his Augustinian convictions.[182] In 1842 he noted in his *Journal:* "With a twist of the compass [Vico] traces a center, a cycle, a circular movement. But on the second round, his strength failed him, he did not perceive the eternal process."[183] Vico discovered the truth *about* historical myths but failed to discover the truth *of* these myths, the essential message of all the epic stories of the nations, above all those of France—the message of liberty—which thus becomes for Michelet the myth of history itself. As Michelet pursued this kind of mythological history, he moved further and further away from Vico's historical mythology, which had initially set him on his historical studies. His work ultimately became more mythical than historical and therefore remains a romantic—and most definitely not a modernistic—mythistory.

However we judge Michelet's legacy in modern historiography, his contribution to the rehabilitation of myths as authentic sources of national history is immense. His notions inspired contemporary historians to probe the deeper mythical origins and constitutions of nations, states, and nation-states. Thus, to note just one classic work in this genre, Fustel de Coulanges's study of the Greek polis, *La cité antique,* which appeared in 1864, identified the function of religion and myth as the cement that binds together any society or political community. His conservative theory of the state as an organic community that consists in a shared system of beliefs and myths, in a "tradition" rather than in a "constitution," exercised a profound impression on later sociological and anthropological studies of history.[184] The profusion of ancient mythologies in the new national ideologies forced many critical and radical scholars of history to reassess the function of historical myths in modernity. Karl Marx's famous attack in the opening lines of his essay *The Eighteenth Brumaire of Louis Bonaparte,* on the mythological follies of the French revolutionaries—"In the classically austere traditions of the Roman republic its gladiators found the ideals and the art forms, the self-deception that they needed in order to conceal from themselves the bourgeois limitations of the content of their struggles and to keep their enthusiasm on the high plane of great historical tragedy"—attests to the fact that after 1848 mythology had become a political, not just a historical, problem.[185]

In his polemical study "The Creation of Mythology," Marcel Detienne has argued that from around 1860 to 1890 the term *myth* acquired some new pejorative meanings that it largely still retains. Whereas the romantics still admired myth as a classic and artistic form of expression and used it to valorize their own ancient traditions, the new scientists of man—scholars like Max Müller, E. B. Tylor, and Andrew Lang—perceived myth as an ancient and primitive form of knowledge, a "disease of language" (as Müller defined it) that was typical of savage mentality and could well be cured by a dose of rationality.[186] Using these rationalistic categories, they duly redefined mythology as a "science of myth." As Detienne (following Foucault) would have it, mythology, like other disciplines in modern human sciences, was an "invention" that enabled the Victorian champions of reason to impose law and order on what they deemed most dangerous to their authority—the desires, rumors, and fantasies that rage in the archaic and anarchic myths. What Detienne overlooks is that precisely this new conception of myth as so aboriginal and prerational endeared it to modernists like Baudelaire and Nietzsche, who found both the old romantic and the new scientific categorical definitions of myth equally inadequate to account for the phenomenal reactivation of myth in modernity. Whether myth was defined as true or false, transcendental or elemental, virtuous or atrocious, the problem was not so much what myth is but rather what it does, why it still matters at all in this age of rationality and modernity. As that most philosophical of all historians, Edward Gibbon, admitted: "The deities of Olympus, as they are painted by the immortal bard, imprint themselves on the minds which are the least addicted to superstitious credulity." [187] Karl Marx raised the crucial question:

> Where does Vulcan come in as against Roberts & Co.; Jupiter, as against the lightning rod; and Hermes as against the Crédit Mobilier? . . . Is Achilles possible side by side with powder and lead? Or is the *Iliad* at all compatible with the printing press and steam press? Do not singing and reciting and the muses necessarily go out of existence with the appearance of the printer's bar, and do not, therefore, the prerequisites of epic poetry disappear? . . . The real difficulty is not in grasping the idea that Greek art and epos are bound up with certain forms of social development. It rather lies in understanding why they still constitute a source of enjoyment with us, and in certain aspects prevail as a standard and model beyond attainment. [188]

This indeed was the "real difficulty" for the postromantic historians. [189] They properly learned what their fellow scholars in the classical, philological, and anthropological studies of myth had taught about its origination in ancient and primitive societies, but they used these discoveries and theories in order to explore the regeneration of myth in modern society. The notion that captured the historical imagination of this age was that of the *Renaissance* of classical antiquity in modernity. Michelet's famous definition of *La Renaissance*—"the discovery of the world and the discovery of man"—appeared in the seventh volume of his *L'histoire de France,* which he published in 1855 and which was largely confined to the new intellectual developments in sixteenth-century France, above all to the secular tendencies that he detected in the writings of Cujas, Rabelais, and

Montaigne.[190] As a champion of the democratic and anti-ecclesiastic revolution of 1848, he came to denounce the Christian spirituality he had so glorified in the earlier volumes of the work ("the miracle of the Middle Ages")[191] as a mere "spiritualization" of natural human norms and forms of life, and he was thus particularly attentive to those realistic artists and scientists who had rediscovered the naturalistic dimensions of reality. This, in his view, was the great achievement of Brunelleschi, Jan van Eyck, and Leonardo, of Columbus and Copernicus, but also of Luther and Calvin, whose conception of man was more realistic, even if much too fatalistic. Michelet rightly points out that they all turned to antiquity, whether classical or biblical, in order to overcome medieval Catholic Christianity, and must therefore be considered as precursors of modernity. However, their singular achievements were not yet sufficient to produce a general way of life, a new society, a whole civilization: this happened only in France, where the new intellectual movement turned into a new social philosophy of liberation and progression, an early manifestation or prophetic prefiguration of the eventual Revolution. Michelet's interpretation of the *Renaissance* thus becomes yet another chapter in his mythological history rather than a study in historical mythology. The real discoverer of the *Renaissance,* the historian who enabled us to see what ancient mythology really meant to those who rediscovered it and what it still means to us, was Jacob Burckhardt.

THREE

Jacob Burckhardt: Mythistorian

I

On 24 July 1889, Jacob Burckhardt wrote a letter to Friedrich von Preen from his vacation in Baden im Aargau: "There I bought Rochholz, *Legend of the Aargau,* and must on this occasion confess that myths attract me more and more, and draw me away from history. It was not for nothing that the only book I took with me from Basel was the Greek Pausanias. Bit by bit I am acquiring really mythical eyes, perhaps they are those of an old man once again approaching childhood?"[1] *Die rechten mythischen Augen:* what were they for Burckhardt, and how did he perceive reality through them? These are the questions I probe in this chapter. Taking my cue from Burckhardt's intimation that the "mythical eyes" were initially those of a "child," apparently Burckhardt himself, I first seek to show that the transformation in Burckhardt's perception—from the historical to the mythological—began in his early life. I then elaborate on the wider meanings of this perception for his mature historical views and works. Throughout, I reflect on its potential implications for modern historical scholarship, principally for the new art of mythistory, which, as Burckhardt implies, could well be as old as Pausanias's *Description of Greece.*

What did Burckhardt mean by saying that his "mythical eyes" were those of "an old man once again approaching childhood"? Around the same time that he wrote this letter, Burckhardt composed his final summation of his life (*Lebensbericht*), which was to be read at his funeral. In this composition Burckhardt noted that the death of his mother when he was twelve years old had left him with a sense of the "great caducity and uncertainty of all earthly things" and probably had instilled in him for the rest of his life a most serene temperament.[2] This early impression pervades all his works and, I would argue, is the core of his entire historical vocation. For Burckhardt's acute awareness of the precarious nature of this world led him to look for stability in a history above and beyond this history, to deal with what he sometimes called "eternal affairs [*Ewigungen*]" rather than with momentary ones (*Zeitungen*).[3] That explains his regression from the anarchic and transient in history toward the more archaic and permanent in it, from the fleeting events to their lasting images and myths. In Burckhardt's early years, there was one crucial period, a time of personal and vocational crisis, in which he recognized the verity of this predilection.

As befitted the son of the vicar of the Minster of Basel, the young Burckhardt chose to study theology. During the years in which he studied at the University of Basel, from 1835 to 1838, modern theology was rocked by the most turbulent controversy of the century—the so-called mythical interpretation of the Bible as put forth by David Friedrich Strauss in his *Life of Jesus*. Strauss's main thesis was that the stories of the Gospels are so incredible and full of difficulties and contradictions that the only way to make them seem reasonable to modern believers is by reassessing them as "myths," as popular stories that refer not to specific events but rather to the general cultural conditions and collective consciousness. Strauss was careful not to dismiss the Gospels as mere legendary tales, however improbable and incredible they may seem to us. Rather, since they were grounded in concrete historical reality, they belonged to the category that Strauss called "historical myth." He included under that label the stories in the New Testament that could be traced back to some actual events but would now defy any historical verification because of having since "been seized upon by religious enthusiasm, and twined around with mythical conceptions culled from the idea of Christ."[4] The mythological interpretation could resolve the problem of theologians who were concerned with the historical verity of these Gospel stories. According to Strauss, these stories were veritable "historical" sources inasmuch as they recorded how the original Christian community had actually responded to the actions and teachings of Jesus. An improbable story like that of the temptation could not have come from Jesus himself but was nevertheless understandable and acceptable as "historical" if it was viewed as a story that had been "spun around him" by people who were still thoroughly immersed in the "oriental mythology" of the Jewish tradition. Strauss insists that a story like this ought to be considered a "historical myth" rather than "a parable" that could have been delivered by Jesus himself or made by some other individual concerning Jesus, because "the narrative in question is formed less out of instructive thoughts and their poetical clothing, as is the case with a parable, than out of Old Testament passages and types" that were common among Jews and early Christians. It must therefore be "traced solely to thoughts, to Jewish and primitive Christian representations," namely to the biblical conceptions and messianic expectations that empowered all kinds of myths about Satan.[5]

Strauss sought to defend himself against critics who claimed he had turned the whole story of Jesus into myth. At the end of the introduction to the second edition of his book, he states: "The boundary line between the mythical and the historical . . . will ever remain fluctuating and unsusceptible of precise attainment. Least of all can it be expected that the first comprehensive attempt [Strauss's own work] to treat these records from a critical point of view should be successful in drawing a sharply defined line of demarcation." Above all he wished "to guard himself in those places where he declares he knows not what happened, from the imputation of asserting that he knows that nothing happened."[6] But these fine distinctions were largely lost on common readers. As far as they could understand, Strauss's message was clear and devastating—that what we actually have in the Bible are only myths, which do not refer to specific historical events but to general historical conditions and to a collective consciousness that was still replete with spirits, gods, and demons. More crucially, for these readers the mythological interpretation had made the Gospels more understandable as "historical" stories but had thereby rendered them much too reasonable as "mythological" stories, so much so that they all but lost their essential religious power to invoke faith.

Burckhardt's teacher of theology at Basel, Wilhelm Dewette, developed his own mythological theories prior to the publication of Strauss's work and was all too willing to propagate them in the new radical version of Strauss during those turbulent years.[7] The good old liberal tradition of Basel, which had guarded heretic scholars since Erasmus and Paracelsus, enabled him to preach the Straussian theory while the master himself was denied the right of teaching in Zurich (where his appointment to the chair of theology provoked an armed popular uprising—the so-called *Straussenputsch*—and led to the collapse of the liberal government in 1839). Burckhardt was soon won over to its cause.[8] In a letter to a friend in the summer of 1838 he wrote:

In my eyes, Dewette's system grows in stature every day; one simply has to follow him, there is no alternative; but every day a part of our traditional

Doctrine melts away under his hand. Today, finally, I realized that he regards the birth of Christ simply as myth—and that I do too. And I shuddered as a number of reasons struck me why this almost had to be so . . . For the moment I cannot look the ruins of my convictions in the face.[9]

Burckhardt's conclusion in that letter was that from then on he would be an "honest heretic [*ehrlicher Ketzer*]": heretic, because he did not believe anymore in these truths; honest, because he thought that these truths, which have constituted our Western civilization, were still crucial to it, and that whoever was so acutely aware of the "great uncertainty of all earthly things" as he was must uphold them. Burckhardt's "honest heresy" further convinced him that the original and indispensable core of Christianity was and had to remain a mythical image, one of such magnitude (he might have added with his friend Franz Overbeck) that it could not be, and should never have been, translated, and thereby literally disciplined, into the doctrines of theology. This new conviction guided him throughout his life, in his pedagogical activities and in his historical investigations. Burckhardt's notion of "worldliness [*Weltlichkeit*]," by which he defined the peculiar secularity of the Italian Renaissance and which was quite clearly his own, is the ultimate expression of his initial "honest heresy":

This worldliness was not frivolous, but earnest, and was ennobled by art and poetry. It is a lofty necessity of the human spirit that this attitude, once gained, can never again be lost, that an irresistible impulse forces us to the investigation of men and things, and that we must hold this inquiry to be our proper end and work. How soon and by what paths this search will lead us back to God, and in what ways the religious temper of the individual will be affected by it, are questions which cannot be met by any general answer.[10]

The intellectual origins of Burckhardt's *Weltlichkeit* lie in his fateful confrontation with Dewette's theories and eventual recognition of myth as fundamental to Christianity. For Burckhardt, however, this recognition did not mean the invalidation of religion but rather its reevaluation by new "higher critical" categories, which were neither theological nor strictly historical but rather "mythistorical." This was the main methodological lesson that Burckhardt had learned from Dewette—to reconcile history ("Jesus") and myth ("Christ") so as to show how both produced a new powerful historical myth ("Jesus Christ"). In the summer of 1938, Burckhardt lost his faith in the historical validity of the events but discovered the historical validity of their impressions and images. This history of images, he then came to see, is the true history, that which exists even above and beyond the history of the events. Accordingly, from that crucial moment on, throughout his life, Burckhardt's aim was not to prove that this or that "mythical" source was true or false but rather to explore what it meant: to explain under what psychological and historical conditions certain modes of comprehension were necessarily created, what higher metaphysical truths they served, and, ultimately, why they still persisted in our collective imagination. His decision to terminate his studies of theology in Basel and to embark on a study of history in Berlin was the logical conclusion of a student who came to realize that the truths of Christianity were to be found not in the original Gospels but in their historical tradition.

A year later, around Christmas 1840, when Burckhardt was already a student of history in Berlin, he was still shaken by the turmoil of his religious crisis; but at the same time, he was confident that he had found the way to overcome it: "And now here I am grubbing about in the ruins of my former view of life, trying to discover what is still usable in the old foundations, though in a different way"—the way of history.[11] Moreover, as Burckhardt points out in the same letter, the study of history enabled him to overcome not only the religious crisis but also the new, in many ways worse, crises that this loss of faith entailed—the maladies of "skepticism" and of "fatalism." He writes: "Abyss after abyss opens at my feet," and "other demons" arise from them, threatening him with a "complete worldliness in the manner of seeing and doing everything. One remedy [*Rettung*] against this I have found in my main subject, *History*, which was the first shock that unseated my fatalism and the view of life I had based upon it."[12] By 1844 he admitted that his historical studies had indeed destroyed his denominational Christianity but not his emotional religiosity: "With every breath of fresh air, learning lays bare the disintegration of the Church as an inner fact, and hastens it as an external one . . . the most prudent thing a negative theologian can do is to change over to another faculty."[13] Several months later, in a letter of 1845, he could already conclude that history was indeed the one and only salvation—for this is the real meaning of *Rettung*—for the "honest heretic": "That Christianity has its great ages behind it is as evident to me as is the fact that twice two is four; in what ways its eternal content [*ewiger Gehalt*] is to be saved in new forms, history will teach us in due course."[14] Eventually Burckhardt defined this history of the "new forms" of spirituality as *historia altera*.[15] As noted above, the tacit confession in *The Civilization of the Renaissance in Italy* on the vicissitudes of his secular vocation—"How soon and by what paths this search will lead us back to God, and in what ways the religious temper of the individual will be affected by it, are questions which cannot be met by any general answer"—indicates that even though Burckhardt himself had not found in this *historia altera* the path back to God, he was certain that this was the right search for it. In order to see how the young Burckhardt came to this new conception of history, what it really meant in practical terms, and how it determined his vocation as a mythistorian, we must turn our attention to his life and studies in the *Historisches Seminar* in Berlin.

II

Burckhardt was a student in that famous institution between 1839 and 1842. His teachers there included the most illustrious historians of the generation: Johann Gustav Droysen, August Böckh, Jacob Grimm, and above all Leopold von Ranke, who, in Burckhardt's words, presented the "science of history [*Geschichtswissenschaft*]" in all its "gigantische Grösse." Burckhardt admired his teacher for his "colossal learning" but found him "utterly bereft of character."[16] In any case, he never became Ranke's disciple or colleague, and later in his life he refused to be nominated for Ranke's chair of history in Berlin. This detachment was as much professional as personal.[17] Since Ranke and Burckhardt are (in Friedrich Meinecke's words) "the two greatest historical thinkers" of the nineteenth century,[18] it might be appropriate to consider briefly Ranke's judgment on the issue under discussion, namely, the essentiality of myth in and for modern historiography, and then compare it with Burckhardt's. It might be useful to start with Ranke's initiation into historical scholarship, as we have done for Burckhardt.

In a famous autobiographical passage, Leopold von Ranke recalled his first steps toward the historical profession in his early youth. Upon reading the historical novels of Walter Scott on the age of chivalry, he turned to the historical works of Commines on the period and discovered, to his astonishment, that the romantic pictures of medieval life and of figures such as Charles of Burgundy and Louis XI in *Quentin Durwald* were utterly fictitious. "I found by comparison that the truth was more interesting and beautiful than the romance. I turned away from it and resolved to avoid all invention and imagination in my works and to stick to facts."[19] From then on, Ranke sought to discredit any mythical accounts of historical reality.[20] His dedication to authentic sources has become canonical among historians. The problem was that many myths were authentic sources for the earliest histories of ethnic communities, religious movements, political associations, and so on. As a young historian, Ranke still nourished some romantic notions on the significance of such myths for the nations as well as for their historians. In his first sketch for a universal history, written in the 1830s, he stated:

> As for myths, I do not want to deny categorically that they contain perhaps an occasional historical element. But the most important thing is that they express the view of a people of itself, its attitude toward the world, etc. They are important insofar as the subjective character of a people or its thoughts may have been expressed in them, not because of any objective facts they may contain. In the former respect they possess a firm foundation and are very reliable for historical research, but not in the latter.[21]

Yet, it is clear already here that Ranke had a firm view regarding what were and what were not valid "facts" in and for history; he believed that myths were not to be treated as such, even if, as he himself rightly noted, they informed and formed the collective consciousness of the people. His mature reflections on universal history, written in the 1880s, show how far he had distanced himself from his early romantic notions on the efficacy of national mythologies, let alone from the actual attempts to redeem those mythologies by—and for—history: "History cannot discuss the origin of society, for the art of writing, which is the basis of historical knowledge, is a comparatively late invention . . . The province of history is limited by the means at her command, and the historian would be overbold who should venture to unveil the mystery of the primeval world, the relation of mankind to God and nature. The solution to such problems must be entrusted to the joined efforts of Theology and Science."[22] Accordingly, in his histories of the great European nations, Ranke did not take their historical myths into account. For he saw that because these myths continued to persist in the cultural traditions of the nations, they distorted people's perceptions and narrations of their histories. This was one of the main messages of his celebrated claim that the vocation of the historian is to show how things actually happened—a claim that he exemplified by exposing all the "mythical" prejudices that had contorted Francesco Guicciardini's *History of Italy*. His infatuation with diplomatic documents like the Venetian *Realzioni, Dispazzi,* and *Acti* grew out of his assumption that these official summaries, which were written up in seemingly factual and neutral terms, were largely devoid of rhetorical and mythical figurations. His *History of the Popes* was modeled on these sources—Ranke used the ambassadors' news as well as their views on the papal church and state and managed to produce an account that was impersonal, impartial, and imperial, that is, supremely objective on all the most subjective issues.[23] Alas, as a modern authority on the matter pointed out, these sources "are highly filtered, deeply pondered texts, and they are not in the least spontaneous"; the ambassadors did not merely report on political affairs *wie sie eigentlich gewesen sind* but rather composed them in artful formulations that conveyed all sorts of other messages.[24] Using the cultural codes of the Renaissance, they evoked in their letters a whole mythological lore, which Ranke, who read them as political, not cultural, documents, either ignored or dismissed. This led him to a rather narrow conception of political life and history. As Anthony Grafton has pointed out, "in his reliance on central archives and great families' papers, Ranke had accepted, without reflecting hard enough, a certain interpretation of history itself: one in which the story of nations and monarchies took precedence over that of peoples or cultures, which had initially won his interest in the past."[25]

Obviously, then, Ranke could not yet conceive of the possibility that between myth and history there was a third alternative, mythistory, which, as Donald Kelley has shown in his important essay on the origins of mythistory, other historians in his time were well aware of.[26] As noted above, Burckhardt must have been attentive to this tradition from his early theological studies. His early recognition of the efficacy of the so-called higher critical methodology in theological studies set him apart from Ranke's "critical" methodology in historical studies. His reflections on his historical vocation indicate that he sought in it "satisfaction" for the aesthetic and ecstatic revelations he had once hoped to find in theological studies. In March 1840 he wrote to his friend von Tschudi that his religious doubts abated because of the "exceptionally distracting character of my work." Burckhardt also noted that "the philosophy of history is daily, if only incidentally, in my thoughts"; he made clear, however, his misgivings about the abstract formulations and speculations that emanated from Hegel's works into the lectures of the post-Hegelian *Dozenten,* "whom I do not understand."[27] He was nevertheless quite willing to infuse their new philosophical teachings and his old poetical musings into a new historical work. He explained to his friend: "My poetry, for which you prophesied fair weather, is in great danger of being sent packing now that I have found the height of poetry in history itself. There was a time when I looked upon the play of fantasy as the highest requirement of poetry; but since I must esteem the development of spiritual states, or, quite simply, inner states as such, higher still, I now find my satisfaction in history itself."[28] And so he did. His historical studies in Ranke's *Historisches Seminar* at the University of Berlin transformed this initial "poetic" notion of history into a more substantial conception of mythistory. He became acquainted with its main doctrines while studying with Schelling, Savigny, and Grimm. Burckhardt himself singled out Jacob Grimm's seminar on Tacitus's *Germania* as the most important of his entire studies in Berlin. In this work Tacitus reasoned that the "ancient hymns" of the Germans were "the only style of record or history which they possess"—a fact that rendered these myths indispensable for the reconstruction of the early Germans' life and history. In his notebook Burckhardt summed up the lesson of this course: "History rises up like the sun from the dawn of legend [*Sage*]. Myth and history depend on each other . . . Our knowledge [of primordial history] does not yet suffice to philosophical reflection." [29] A few months later Burckhardt reiterated this early mythistorical conviction in a letter, which remains the most revealing statement on his entire historical work:

> A man like me, who is altogether incapable of speculation, and who does not apply himself to abstract thought for a single minute in the whole year, does best to try and clarify the most important questions of his life and studies in the way that comes naturally to him. My surrogate is contemplation [*Anschauung*], daily clearer and directed more and more upon essentials. I cling by nature to the concrete, to visible nature, and to history . . . You would not believe me how, little by little, as a result of this possibly one-sided effort, the *facta* of history, works of art, the monuments of all ages gradually acquire significance as witnesses to a past stage in the development of the spirit. Believe me, when I see the present lying quite clearly in the past, I feel moved by a shudder of profound respect . . . This is where I stand on the shore of the world—stretching out my arms towards the *fons* and *origo* of all things, and that is why history to me is sheer poetry, that can be mastered through contemplation. You philosophers go further, your system penetrates into the depths of the secrets of the world, and to you history is a source of knowledge, a science, because you see, or think you see, the *primum agens* where I only see mystery and poetry. [30]

"Mystery and poetry"—for Burckhardt, this is what history is all about: the interpretation of how men have created their own human world out of and against chaotic reality by means of their meaningful fictions.

The predicament of the "honest heretic" thus became the vocation of the modern historian. For in this process of creation and interpretation, Burckhardt saw, we are not dealing with the same kind of knowledge that scientists, philosophers, and theologians have always been concerned with—knowledge of the ultimate reasons and truths—but rather with the concrete reasons and truths that men themselves have made and lived by, namely the poetic images, beliefs, and practices by which they have sought to solve the mysteries of life, their myths. And so, as he realized that these fanciful images and tales—rather than any seemingly more real causes or events—are the *fons* and *origo* of all historical creations, the spiritual roots of all modern things, that in them indeed he could see "the present lying quite clearly in the past," he was "moved by a shudder of profound respect." It is for this reason that history is to be "poetry on the grandest scale," because it is a work both of and on myth.

Many years later, in the public lectures that he gave in Basel during the 1860s, which are now known as his *Reflections on History,* Burckhardt reiterated this conviction. In the chapter "On the Historical Consideration of Poetry," he maintains that "history finds in poetry not only one of its most important, but also one of its purest and finest sources . . . Poetry, for the historical observer, is the image of the eternal in its temporal and national expression; hence, instructive in all its aspects and, moreover, often the best or only thing to survive."[31] More concretely, Burckhardt assumed that mythology was a "poetic representation [*poetische Darstellung*]" of the history of every religion, nation, or civilization. As he stated in his *Griechische Kulturgeschichte,* myth is the fateful image (*Schicksalbild*) of the nation, the initial perception that determines its entire life and history. He thus defined and conducted his "classisch-humanistisches Bildungsprogramm" in cultural history as an attempt to understand a nation through its definitive myths. Note, for example, how he perceived Goethe's *Faust,* according to a letter that he wrote in 1855 to a young student:

> What you are destined to discover in *Faust,* you will have to discover intuitively . . . *Faust* is a genuine myth, i.e. a great and ancient image, in which everyman has to discover his own being and destiny in his own way . . . Let me make a comparison: whatever would the Greeks have said if a commentator had planted himself between them and the Oedipus saga? There was an Oedipus fever in every Greek which needed to be stirred and to tremble after its own fashion without intermediary, immediately. The same is true of *Faust* and the German nation.[32]

The soulful Faust is as typical to the German nation as the resourceful Till Eulenspiegl is typical to the Flemish nation.[33] Whereas Ranke regarded such myths as having a pernicious effect on the study of history, Burckhardt saw that they might be the best means for such study. This would be all the more true if they still persisted in the historian's own mind and culture. "Our intellect, no matter how independent of the past it may feel in matters of science and technology, is ever renewed and consecrated by the consciousness of its connection with the mind of the remotest times and civilizations."[34] Hence arises his contention against the Hegelian and all other "philosophers of history who regard the past as a contrast to and preliminary stage of our own time as the full development. We shall study the *recurrent, constant* and *typical* as echoing in us and intelligible through us."[35] Burckhardt thus sought to discern certain permanent modes of thought and action in human affairs, yet he did so in his own "poetic" way. He completely ignored the systematic methods of the new inductive social sciences of biology, psychology, and sociology that were becoming fashionable at the time; he concentrated instead on intuitive elucidation of what he called the "grosses geistiges Kontinuum" of Western civilization, whereby some primordial mythological images and traditions—those of Christianity, for example—that have made it up still sustain it.

This was the main argument in his first major historical work, *The Age of Constantine the Great*, which he published in 1852. As the title of the book indicates, and as Burckhardt states in the preface, the book was not so much about Constantine himself as about his "Age."[36] What was important in this age, as in any historical age, were primarily spiritual rather than material conditions. He generally believed that "every event has a spiritual aspect by which it partakes of immortality."[37] The first and most notable factor in the age of Constantine was the general degeneration (*Veraltung*) of late Roman society, which, as Burckhardt describes it, had lost its spiritual vitality to the vibrant new religion of Christianity.[38] Contrary to the fashionable Enlightenment tradition of interpretation, he attributes the rise and success of Christianity not to clerical or political manipulations of power, certainly not to Constantine himself, whom he dismisses as "essentially unreligious, even if he pictures himself standing in the midst of a churchly community" (292), but rather to the sincere redemptive aspirations and efforts of the common people at the time, as revealed, for example, in Hieronymus's stories on saints and martyrs. Already in this early work, Burckhardt reveals his predilection for folk stories over histories, a tendency that may have caused him to accept all too willingly the literary fabrications of the *Historia Augusta* as a reliable historical source (31–35). He trusted that such popular stories, however legendary they appeared to be, revealed more about the true religiosity of the age than did the histories of the church fathers. He thus criticizes the "odious hypocrisy" of Constantine's official biographer, Eusebius of Caesarea, who portrayed his hero as a singular pious Christian among his pagan barbarian troops; Burckhardt prefers to rely on "a reasonable pagan like Ammianus," an *ehrlicher Ketzer* like himself who knew how to depict Constantine's personality in and against his age, as a man who held to, and concealed, his pagan and Christian and many other beliefs, as was common and required at such a time of crisis, when the old classical civilization was already dying out and a new Christian civilization was just emerging (261).

Burckhardt's "honest heresy" thus shaped not only his religious identity but also his historical vocation. From the beginning of his historical studies, it set him apart from the liberal Hegelian and against the radical Marxian critics of religion, who commonly thought that modern man should finally overcome (*aufheben*) his primitive mythical beliefs, either (as Hegel recommended) by turning them into more refined philosophical notions or (as Marx commanded) by totally erasing them. Whereas Marx believed that "[m]an makes religion, religion does not make man," Burckhardt came to believe in the mythical-religious construction of reality. Later in his life, he developed against these radical theorists of history his own conservative theory: they regarded the rational and historical criticism of religion as its complete deconstruction and sought to reduce religious sentiments to their mere psychological, sociological, political, or any other human (all-too-human) causes, but he would present religion as a main historical "force [*Potenz*]" in any constitution of social reality, one that is as crucial to it as the other forces of the polity and the culture.[39]

Clearly, then, Burckhardt's essential mythological conception of reality defined his entire historical work. He realized that the vocation of history was not really *Wissenschaft*, as Ranke had taught him, but rather *Bildung*, which literally means a configuration or realization of images in life and history.[40] Hans-Georg Gadamer has pointed out that "*Bildung* calls rather on the ancient mystical tradition, according to which man carries in his soul the image of God after whom he is fashioned and [which he] must cultivate in himself."[41] Burckhardt molded his own life on such *Vorbilder*, mostly scholars like himself—the Greek opponents of totalitarian democracy and autocracy Socrates, Pythagoras, and Demosthenes; the first Christian anchoritic monks and the last pagan scholars in the Roman empire; and Saint Severin, Dante, and Fra Urbano Valeriano of Belluno. All of these defied the political events and authorities of their times by adhering to the cultural tradition of Western civilization.[42] Reflecting on the anchorites, those "crushed spirits" and "towering personalities" driven by "spiritual forces" into the desert, where they "waged their struggles with God apart from the world," Burckhardt writes:

> It is in the nature of man, when he feels lost in the large and busy external world, that he should seek to find his proper self in solitude. And the more deeply he has felt the inward cleavage and rending, the more absolute is the solitude required . . . Every earthly consideration vanishes and the recluse

becomes an ascetic, partly to do penance, partly to owe the world with nothing more than the barest existence, but partly also to keep the soul capable of constant intercourse with the sublime.[43]

This is what Burckhardt himself had done in the early months of 1846. This was a period of intense political struggles between radicalists and traditionalists both at home and all over Europe. Burckhardt perceived the entire struggle over the restoration as futile, because he realized that the restoration of the legitimate dynasties could not, in itself, reassert the efficacy of their ancient values, customs, and institutions in the minds of the people. They, Burckhardt claimed, had been liberated from these once and forever and were now living and believing in a liberal world—indeed, in Burckhardt's view, in a world that had become much too liberal.[44] For he saw nothing valuable in liberalism that consisted in secular humanism and other modern doctrines that destroyed all metaphysical commitments and duties and, moreover, encouraged men to pursue only their physical desires and interests.[45] In his letters to his liberal friends in Germany, he ridiculed their populist sympathies: "I know too much history to expect anything from the despotism of the masses but a future tyranny, which will mean the end of history."[46]

Burckhardt's disenchantment with the liberal ideology in history eventually set him against its equivalent methodology in historiography. During the mid-1840s he became increasingly hostile to Ranke's historical teachings. Twenty years later the Wars of Unification confirmed his early suspicions about the affinities between Ranke's historical methodology and the new German political ideology. In 1874 Burckhardt summed up his opposition to Ranke's historical philosophy in a letter to Nietzsche: "As teacher and professor I can, however, maintain that I have never taught history for the sake of what goes under the high-falutin' name of 'world history,' but essentially as a propaedeutic study: my task has been to put people in possession of the scaffolding which is indispensable if their further studies of whatever kind were not to be aimless. I have done everything I possibly could to lead them on to acquire personal possession of the past—in whatever shape and form—and at least not to sicken them of it."[47]

These late reflections refer back to the conditions and considerations that determined Burckhardt's decision in 1846 to devote his life to the study and teaching of "cultural history [*Kulturgeschichte*]." For it was there and then that Burckhardt, "so tired of the present," decided to "strike up new relations with life and poetry." His famous letter to his friend

Hermann Schauenburg from 5 March 1846 is still thrilling: "Good heavens, I can't after all alter things, and before universal barbarism breaks in . . . I want to help to save things, as far as my humble station allows . . . We may all perish; but at least I want to discover the interest for which I am to perish, namely, the culture of Old Europe [*die Bildung Alteuropas*]."[48] "The culture of Old Europe": from that moment on, this was the main motive in Burckhardt's life and works. And if, as Henri Bergson once said, any great thinker conjures up one, and only one, momentous idea, which he then spends his whole life trying to work out,[49] then, in Burckhardt's case, this must have been that idea. He realized in March 1846 that what was needed was not a political restoration but a cultural renaissance. He concludes in the letter quoted above: "Out of the storm a new existence will arise, formed, that is, upon old and new foundations; that is your place and not in the forefront of irresponsible action. Our destiny is to help build anew when the crisis is over."[50] In his *Reflections on History,* Burckhardt expressed this notion in more general terms: "A peculiarity of higher cultures is their susceptibility to renaissances. Either one and the same or a later people partially adopts a past culture into its own by a kind of hereditary right or by right of admiration." A "pure renaissance" like the Italian and European movement of the fifteenth and sixteenth centuries, he says, must be distinguished from "politico-religious restorations" like those of Judaism after the Exile or of Persia by the Sassanidae, because "its specific characteristics were its spontaneity, the evidential vitality through which it triumphed, its extension, to a greater or less degree, to every possible domain of life, e.g. the idea of the State, and finally, its European character."[51] Burckhardt firmly believed that as in Italy of the fifteenth century, the good state ought to be formed and governed by culture, not the other way round, for only in that way is it always "susceptible" to renaissance.

How does a renaissance like this occur? And what is the specific duty of the historian in the process? These are the two crucial problems that Burckhardt set out to solve, in his work and in his life, when he turned away from the "ancient regime" of Europe—which, he knew, had been lost forever—toward "die Bildung Alteuropas," which, he believed, was still vital in its original myths and all their later cultural manifestations. In a poem that he wrote in Rome in 1847, "Asyl," Burckhardt indicates that his vocation was to save these myths.[52] From then on, and to the very last day of his professional life, he held on to this vocational conviction, both as a lecturer and as a writer on cultural history.

Burckhardt's three major works form, or at least can be read as, a history of Western civilization out of its mythological sources: *Griechische Kulturgeschichte* narrates its origination in Greek mythology; *The Age of Constantine the Great*, the transformation of this mythology into Christian theology; and *The Civilization of the Renaissance in Italy*, the regeneration of this mythology in modern culture. In all these works, Burckhardt generally reserved his greatest admiration for those conservative-minded scholars and artists who kept this classical-humanist tradition of *Bildung* going through all kinds of iconoclastic controversies and revolutionary innovations. In classical Greece they were primarily those poets and dramatists who defied philosophical and political strictures on their mythological creations; in late antiquity they were the anchorites as well as the few Roman pagans who retained in their different ways the classical spiritual virtues against both the barbarians and the Christians; and in the Italian Renaissance, they were those thinkers and artists who were strictly "classical" in their works—and therefore truly "humanistic."

This is also the main contention in *The Cicerone*, Burckhardt's major study in art history, published in 1855.[53] Although Burckhardt disguised the theoretical and polemical intentions of this book by writing it in the conventional form of a *Bildungsreise* guide to Italy, intended for common tourists who look for "the enjoyment [*Genuß*]" of its great "works of art," he argued that a full enjoyment of these *Kunstwerke* required some ethical, and not just aesthetical, *Bildung*, that in order to have a real *Anschauung* of their beauty, the viewer must attain the whole vision of reality, the *Weltanschauung*, of their makers, in short a classical education. Concentrating on the great *Kunstwerke* of the Italian Renaissance, Burckhardt thus sought to show how they acquired their "classical" distinction—which for him was still defined by Johann Winckelmann's standards of *edle Einfalt und stille Größe*—by the representation of our miserable human reality from the higher perspectives of universality and immortality. Along with Schiller he believed in the "aesthetic education" of man, trusting that the contemplation of the chaotic scenes of human reality through the beautiful forms that they assume in the great works of art might enable man to perceive the ideal in the real, to subsume the contingent occurrences (*Zeitungen*) of his life under the permanent experiences (*Ewigungen*) of history and thus to reconcile his individual ambition with tradition. Thus, he attempted in *The Cicerone* to reassert the notion of artistic "traditionality" as opposed to "originality," a motion that was amplified by his antipathy to the neoromantic and other fashionable positions in the *Geniestreich*.[54] He loathed the very German conception of the "genius [*Genie*]" as a Faustian artist (or scientist) whose mysterious and precarious powers of creation defy common standards of comprehension and all other conventions of tradition. In that controversy, as in so many others where he sought to counter the liberal equation of modernity with individuality, Burckhardt drew his moral inspiration from the basic conviction that he had carried from his religious crisis of 1838—that "the end which Providence has set before mankind is the conquest of selfishness and the sacrifice of the individual for the sake of the universal."[55]

This was the critical standard by which he sought to evaluate the great Italian artists in *The Cicerone*. As he examined their works, he asked, implicitly, whether they had fulfilled this "providential" task and sacrificed their individuality for the sake of universality. To succeed at that task would mean, in artistic terms, that they were able to retain in their new artistic creations the mythical and the historical images of the classical tradition. According to Burckhardt, a cultural renaissance was possible only by virtue of such a conservative commitment to the cultural tradition, or *Bildung*, of Old Europe, with all its mythical-historical associations. Raphael exemplified that commitment, and Michelangelo did not.

For Burckhardt, the personal struggle between the traditional artist Raphael and the individual artist Michelangelo epitomized the main cultural conflict in the Italian Renaissance, as well as in modern Europe. Of all Renaissance painters, Burckhardt considered Raphael to be the greatest "historical painter," for he knew how to imbue his historical scenes with authentic spiritual impressions and meanings.[56] In his paintings in the Camera della Segnatura in the Vatican, Raphael managed to present scenes like *The Battle of Constantine* and *The School of Athens* in a form that was true both to the historical details and to the moral and aesthetic impressions that they evoked in later generations, and thus he captured "an ideal historical moment" in its full significance (151–52). Michelangelo, in contrast, was not really concerned with such classic-humanist themes or, for that matter, with the contents of any of his paintings as much as with their forms. His *Last Judgment* is a gigantic yet utterly arbitrary exhibition of his own "Promethean pleasure of calling into existence all capabilities of movement, position, foreshortening, grouping of the pure human form," a fact that renders him, in Burckhardt's view, a "mannerist" (126). Michelangelo was "the first modern artist," which means that he was the first one to break the classical tradition and to free himself from all its conventional themes and myths. And because there was no "time-honored myth to guard and limit his fantasy," his paintings, magnificent as they are, seem to the beholder rather eccentric and, all too often, just egocentric, lacking, as it were, the mythical associations that are so crucial to our cultural norms. The dissociation of the historic and the artistic in Michelangelo proved catastrophic for Italian painting: "After his death, all principle in all the different arts was overthrown; everyone strove to reach the absolute, because they did not understand that what in him appeared uncontrolled, in fact, took shape from his innermost personality" (128). The degeneration into mediocrity and vulgarity is most visible in the art of the baroque. Burckhardt dismisses Caravaggio's paintings of mythic scenes, such as *Medusa*, as overtly dramatic, much too ecstatic, and thus unable to arouse sincere emotion, only repulsion (242–52). The realistic depiction of sacred subjects from biblical history is likewise prosaic, in fact "naturalistic," and as such devoid of subtle mythical and historical sensibilities, which are essential to the evocation of compassion.

Burckhardt reiterated this judgment in his lecture "On Narrative Painting" (1884), in which he considered the state of "historical painting [*Historienmalerei*]" in the modern era. He observed that since 1830 this old genre had gone the same way as historical scholarship and had become strictly "documentary" and much too political. Whereas the Burgundian or Venetian historical painters in the Renaissance had focused on the "glorification of dynasties and corporations . . . with the sublimation of power into allegory and mythology," the modern historical painters appealed directly and strictly to their own *Volk:* the realistic depiction of heroic historical moments in the history of the nation provided "instant gratification" to the masses. In that way the factual accuracy of the new "historical painting" diminished the essential quality of all great works of art and history—the ability to tell a beautiful and meaningful story. Reflecting on some modern German historical painters, Burckhardt observed that their pictorial descriptions of the battles of the last wars indeed demonstrated exactitude in the depiction of military details but lacked those optic and aesthetic qualities that transform the concrete historical moment into an eternal moment. Without this harmonic fusion of idealism and realism, or myth and history, these and all other aesthetic representations of reality were bound to be "mere photography."

> For any work of art aspires above all to become a grand beautiful and powerful revelation [*Erscheinung*], such that may inspire imitations and thus keep the work alive even if its original copy is lost . . . And here one must be aware that a work of that kind does not revel in the factual, if this is no

more than just that, but strives for that high world-of-images [*Bilderwelt*] which the peoples and their prolocutors, the poets, have created out of their religions, myths, primal histories, legends, and fairytales.[57]

Burckhardt's predilection for the mythical in art has often been interpreted as antihistorical. Following the recent studies of Sitt, Gossman, and others, I argue that Burckhardt's apparent "asceticism" and "aestheticism"—or "mythicism"—should rather be seen as an application of his new historical conception, or mythistory, to the study of art.[58] The origins of this aesthetic conception of history lie in his early mythopoeic impressions and inclinations. Its principles are clear in a letter that he wrote while still a student in Berlin: "I have never yet thought philosophically, and never had any thought at all that was not connected with something external. I can do nothing unless I start out from contemplation . . . My historical work will perhaps become readable in time, but where there is no inner picture [*ein Bild*] to be set down on paper it is bound to be insolvent."[59] From then on Burckhardt aspired to be, and he became, a "historical painter." In his greatest historical work, *The Civilization of the Renaissance in Italy*, he accomplished this task to perfection.

III

The Civilization of the Renaissance in Italy is one of those rare historical works that are truly classic. Since its publication in 1860, it has been the foundational work in that field. Paul Kristeller pronounced on the centenary of its publication: "After a hundred years, this book still dominates the debate on the Renaissance, and although it has been criticized and supplemented in a variety of ways, it has hardly been replaced."[60] During the last decades, the application of new methodologies such as cultural anthropology, psychology, and narratology in historical studies has of course extended Renaissance scholarship well beyond the conventional categories and boundaries of Burckhardt's study.[61] And yet, as Denys Hay observed in the early 1980s, these innovative studies have not really overturned Burckhardt's general conception and characterizations of the Renaissance: "Anyone surveying the problem of the Renaissance in the last twenty or thirty years must be astonished at the tenacity with which the categories established by Jacob Burckhardt have survived criticism . . . Indeed it is probably true to say that the basic tenets of the Burckhardtian position are more dominant, more unchallenged, today than they were before the two world wars."[62] This judgment is still intact, even though some of

Burckhardt's central notions about the apparent "individualism" or "secularism" of the age have lost their original cogency.[63]

Burckhardt's book deals with the formation of a new, distinctly "modern" civilization, which developed in Italy during the fourteenth and fifteenth centuries, a cultural transformation that, according to Burckhardt, grew out of and consisted in the tension—or rather in the resolution of the tension—between the classical tradition and the spontaneous creative individuals in Italy. In historiographical terms the work was new not only in its subject matter—Burckhardt practically invented the term *Renaissance* and the field of Renaissance study—but also in its style, which, in Burckhardt's words, was "an essay in the strictest sense of the word," namely an informal presentation in figurative rather than in argumentative terms. Its main themes and claims were not so much stated in theoretical generalizations as shown in concrete examples—in precise descriptions of scenes, characters, towns, monuments, works of arts, and so forth. The fact that in his *Civilization of the Renaissance in Italy,* Burckhardt did not deal separately and directly with the art of the Renaissance and (as he himself noted in the preface to the second edition) was unable to repair this "damage" in his discussion of architecture and decorative arts in the *Geschichte der Renaissance in Italien* of 1867 only enhances the impression that Burckhardt did not really need to do so, because he had already thought the art of the Renaissance into his work, or rather because he had in fact construed his book upon it. As Johan Huizinga has put it, "[t]he structure of this matchless example of cultural-historical synthesis is as sturdy and harmonic as any Renaissance work of art."[64] One can continue this line of thought and say that Burckhardt created his work in much the same manner as the Renaissance artists created their most typical work of art; the mural. Like the fresco painter, Burckhardt built up a portrait of the age by minute details here and there, distinct and quite meaningless in themselves but, when viewed from a distance, cohering to reveal a magnificent vision of reality. In what follows I show that this similarity in vision was not merely formal; rather, Burckhardt himself conceived of reality in the same way as did the Renaissance artists: for like the latter, who commonly presented their modern subjects in classical features, costumes, and situations and against a mythological Christian background, Burckhardt viewed modernity from the deep perspectives of mythistory.

Burckhardt could well have found this mythistorical perception in the life and works of Leon Battista Alberti, the great Florentine master of the arts, whom he repeatedly hailed as the complete *uomo universale.*[65]

According to Eugenio Garin, Alberti's picture of the world was permeated by the Neoplatonic sensation that the world as it appeared to him was not real, that he was only dreaming, or rather living in a dream that mankind had created for itself, its civilization. Garin quotes Alberti as saying: "There was a time . . . when I was in the habit of basing my views on truth, my zeal on considerations of utility, my words and expressions on my innermost thoughts . . . But I have learnt now to adopt my views to the prevailing superstitions, my zeal to caprices, and to frame all my words so as to be capable of deception." For Alberti, then, myths were all one had, and the noble task of the artist in this chaotic world was to overcome melancholic exasperation through their reactivation. "These myths console us and create the illusions and seductions of our daily life." [66]

Such notions were particularly dear to a historian who was deeply immersed in the philosophy of Arthur Schopenhauer, as Burckhardt had been throughout his life. In his conversations with Nietzsche, he called Schopenhauer "our philosopher" and elsewhere referred to him as the philosopher who had finally settled the rivalry between poetry and history.[67] As Erich Heller points out, Burckhardt's famous pronouncement in the introduction to *Reflections on History* that he had no "philosophy of history" cannot disguise the fact that he too thought philosophically about history and did so according to certain metaphysical assumptions that he had culled from Schopenhauer.[68] Although Schopenhauer did not develop a systematic philosophy of history, he deduced from his general aesthetic-idealistic conception of human reality that history was "the long, difficult and confused dream of mankind." [69] In his major philosophical work, *The World as Will and Idea,* he grounds the human condition in the basic necessity and capacity for fiction, that is, in the purposeful and artful imagination (*Vorstellung*), which enables people to transcend the world in which they know they must die so as to believe in a world where they can live as free agents—a world that they themselves have made and continue to remake in their artistic creations. In his attempt to deny any materiality to history, Schopenhauer goes on to dismiss the great events of the revolutions and wars that ravaged European society in the early decades of the nineteenth century as mere "fantasies" of liberation, which required ideal philosophical "contemplation" rather than real political "action." As such, his putative philosophy of history, with its playful aesthetic-ascetic preoccupations, was indeed (as Hayden White dubbed it) "perfectly narcissistic" and ultimately conservative;[70] and yet, for historians like Burckhardt, it was also very constructive: it alerted him to the mythic modes by which men had actually made their histories, most visibly so in the civilization of the Renaissance in Italy.[71]

A careful reading of *The Civilization of the Renaissance in Italy* along these lines reveals how Burckhardt incorporated Schopenhauer's philosophy into his historiography. It is evident already in the title of the first part of the book, "The State as a Work of Art," as well as in its concrete investigations and interpretations of the political history of Renaissance Italy, where Burckhardt presents the Italian city-states as artful "creations," forged by "reflection and careful adaptation" and sustained by mythical traditions and fabrications rather than by any ethical or political constitutions.[72] Thus, in the opening discussion of the political conditions in the thirteenth century, Burckhardt accentuates the primacy of myths over theories in the political history of Italy, as well as of superficial sources over official ones in its modern historiography:

It was in vain at such a time that St. Thomas Aquinas, a born subject of Frederick, set up the theory of constitutional monarchy, in which the prince was to be supported by an upper house named by himself, and a representative body elected by the people. Such theories found no echo outside the lecture-room, and Frederick and Ezzelino were and remain for Italy the great political phenomena of the thirteenth century. Their personality, already half legendary, forms the most important subject of "The Hundred Old Tales," whose original composition falls certainly within this century.[73]

Later on, in the discussion on the problematic relationships between the citizens and their hired military commanders, the notorious *condotierri,* Burckhardt introduces this "old story—one of those which are true and not true, everywhere and nowhere":

The citizens of a certain town (Siena seems to be meant) had once an officer in their service who had freed them from foreign aggression; daily they took counsel how to recompense him, and concluded that no reward in their power was great enough, not even if they made him lord of the city. At last one of them rose and said, "Let us kill him and then worship him as our patron saint." And so they did, following the example set by the Roman senate with Romulus.[74]

Now this is pure mythistory. Burckhardt knows, and lets the reader know, that this incident never actually happened in historical reality. Even the town where it presumably occurred is not known, nor in fact is it relevant, because as far as Burckhardt is concerned, the case may well be "true and not true, everywhere and nowhere." Why, then, did he include it in his history? The obvious explanation would be that this anecdote is important because it reflects the political folklore of the Italian towns at the time and thereby reveals its "local truth." Felix Gilbert writes: "The cultural historian does not want to learn from his sources the 'facts' of the past; he studies the sources because they express the spirit of former times. It does not matter, therefore, whether they are factually correct, whether they lie or indulge in exaggeration or inventions. Even misleading statements may tell us something about the mind of a former age."[75] Assuming that Burckhardt indeed conducted his *Quellenforschung* along these new hermeneutical lines, a source like the "old story" quoted above, one "that could happen and be true everywhere," is important for the historian precisely because it reveals the mythical rather than the historical "mind of a former age." Burckhardt, in other words, is interested in this story because it attests to the mythical mentality of the Renaissance and, beyond that, to "the *recurrent, constant* and *typical* as echoing in us and intelligible through us." For Burckhardt, stories like this were the cultural core of the Renaissance and the cultural code for its historian.

Another example is Burckhardt's description of the civil war between the two rival clans in Perugia—the Baglioni and the Oddi—in which he draws heavily on the "admirable historical narratives" of the local chroniclers Graziani and Matarazzo. He relates how, after the Baglioni victory in 1487, the Oddi withdrew to the valley between Perugia and Assisi, where they continued their skirmishes for several years. In 1494 the Oddi attacked the town again and nearly conquered it; alas, writes Burckhardt, "the personal heroism of the Baglioni won them the victory":

> It was then that Simonetto Baglione, a lad of scarcely eighteen, fought in the square with a handful of followers against hundreds of the enemy: he fell at last with more than twenty wounds, but recovered himself when Astorre Baglione came to his help, and mounting on horseback in gilded armour with a falcon on his helmet, "like Mars in bearing and in deeds, plunged into the struggle." At that time Raphael, a boy of twelve years of age, was at school under Pietro Perugino. The impressions of these days are perhaps immortalized in the small, early pictures of St. Michael and St. George: something of them, it may be, lives eternally in the great paintings of St. Michael: and if Astorre Baglione has anywhere found his apotheosis, it is in the figure of the heavenly horseman in the Heliodorus.[76]

Burckhardt knew that his main source, Matarazzo, was a courtier of the Baglioni and wrote his chronicle for them, but he nevertheless was intent on quoting him extensively and, it might seem, uncritically. He did so because he was not so interested in what had actually happened, in the event itself, as in its popular impressions and interpretations, those that Matarazzo faithfully related when he likened his heroes to the figures of classical and Christian mythologies. Drawing on both the narrative descriptions of Matarazzo's chronicles and the figurative descriptions of Raphael's paintings, Burckhardt sought to regain the mythical meanings of the historical affairs in Perugia, for he knew that the classical images and tales by which they were commemorated in the virtual fictions of Matarazzo and Raphael had also inspired the virtuous actions of the Baglioni. As Burckhardt follows Matarazzo to narrate the tragic consequences of this story, this transition from myth to history and ultimately to mythistory becomes clear. He relates how the Oddi and their treacherous collaborators in Perugia continued for several years to conspire against the virtuous Baglioni until their plot "ripened suddenly on the occasion of the marriage of Astorre with Lavinia Colonna, at Midsummer 1500." On the night of 15 July 1500 they broke into town and murdered both Simonetto and Astorre:

> As the corpse of Astorre lay by that of Simonetto in the street, the spectators, "and especially the foreign students," compared him to an ancient Roman, so great and imposing did he seem. In the features of Simonetto could still be traced the audacity and defiance which death itself had not tamed . . . The cathedral, in the immediate neighbourhood of which the greater part of this tragedy had been enacted, was washed with wine and consecrated afresh. The triumphal arch, erected for the wedding, still remained standing, painted with the deeds of Astorre and with the laudatory verses of the narrator of these events, the worthy Matarazzo.[77]

For this reason, because he knew that in the eyes of Matarazzo, Raphael, and their fellow Perugians, Astorre Baglione had really appeared as a mythical hero, Burckhardt saw fit to relate Matarazzo's "legendary history [*ganz sagenhafte Vorgeschichte*]" as it had been written, to quote his words on the hero who "like Mars in bearing and in deeds, plunged into the struggle" as if they expressed factual truth. He rightly assumed that this appearance was in a deep sense what had actually happened in the town square of Perugia. In any case, his artful combination of historical action and fiction in one description of this incident affirms the general observation of Eugenio Garin, that Burckhardt was not so much interested in the history of the Italian Renaissance as in its myth, because in the myth he found the true sources of its collective unconsciousness.[78]

Burckhardt's acute attention to the mythic configuration of the Italian

Renaissance is still vital to Renaissance historiography, indeed to modern historiography as such. Historiography has nowadays become much concerned with the linguistic and other poetic means by which historians construe a story in history, how they describe historical transition by such narrative structures as that of the Renaissance.[79] One of the great masters of Renaissance historiography in our time, William Bouwsma, explained in his presidential address to the American Historical Association in 1979: "A myth is, for the historian, the dynamic equivalent of a model in the social sciences, and we can hardly do without it. The crucial transition from chronicle to history depended on the application of some principle of mythical organization to previously discrete data: the myth of the hero, the myth of the collective advance, the myth of decline."[80] And just as the model in the social sciences—for example, Hobbes's "State of Nature" or Weber's "Ideal Type"—is a theoretical abstraction or reconstruction of empirical qualities intrinsic to the object of study, so too must the myth be in historical studies: it must be exposed in the motivations and actions of the historical agents before it can be imposed on them. In order to understand the myth of the Renaissance, the historian must therefore regain, as Burckhardt taught, the intuitive and imaginative historical "perceptions [*Anschauungen*]" of its makers, their own myths of renaissance. Burckhardt, in fact, seems to have found this methodology in Renaissance historiography itself.

In *The Civilization of the Renaissance in Italy*, Burckhardt repeatedly refers to the fact that this age of historical discovery was also, and primarily, the age that discovered history itself. Florentine humanists and artists made their city "alone and above all other states in the world, the home of historical representation [*geschichtliche Darstellung*] in the modern sense of the term."[81] Since we have seen already what "historical representation" means for Burckhardt, it is interesting to note that he is much more favorable toward the popular compositions of Matarazzo of Perugia or Paolo Giovio of Como than to the official histories of Florentine Leonardo Aretino and Poggio. Regarding Giovio he writes: "It is easy to prove by a hundred passages how superficial and even dishonest he was; not from a man like him can any high and serious purpose be expected. But the breath of the age moves in his pages, and his Leo, his Alfonso, his Pompeo Colonna, live and act before us with such perfect truth and reality, that we seem admitted to the deepest recesses of their nature."[82] Eventually, Burckhardt came to regard this kind of cultural history as the one and only history worth doing. He said as much in a letter to von Preen, written in 1870, during the war between Prussia and France: "To me, as a teacher of history, a very curious phenomenon has become clear: the sudden devaluation of all mere 'events' in the past. From now on in my lectures, I shall only emphasize cultural history [*Kulturgeschichte*], and retain nothing but the quite indispensable external scaffolding."[83] From then on Burckhardt indeed concentrated on "cultural history" and developed it into a major new kind of historiography. In his lectures on Greek cultural history, which he prepared around that time, he elucidates the basic methodological principles of his *Kulturgeschichte:*

> This kind of history aims at the inner core of bygone humanity, and at describing what manner of people these [the Greeks] were, what they wished for, thought, perceived and were capable of. In the process it arrives at what is constant, and finally this constant comes to seem greater and more important than the ephemeral, and qualities greater and more instructive than actions; for actions are only particular expressions of the relevant inner capacity, which can always reproduce such acts. Desires and assumptions are, then, as important as events, the attitude as important as anything done . . . But even where a reported act did not really occur, or not in the way it is said to have occurred, the attitude that assumes it to have occurred, and in that manner, retains its value by virtue of the typicality of the statement.[84]

Turning his attention from singular events to singular individuals in Greek history, Burckhardt declares that instead of "telling their full life stories," he intends to present them "rather as illustration and witness to the things of spirit."[85] Similarly, in the lectures titled "The Great Men of History," which he delivered in 1870, he pays tribute to "those who either never existed, or whose existence was quite different from that described to us, the men, ideal or idealized, who either stand as the founders or leaders of the various peoples, or, as the most beloved figures of popular imagination" and declares that as historians "we cannot leave them out of account, if only because this whole question of the non-existent figure is the strongest proof that a nation has need of great men to represent it . . . their biography contains in symbolic form a part of the history of their people, and especially of its more important institutions."[86] These words were immensely important for at least one of Burckhardt's listeners in that lecture—Friedrich Nietzsche.

IV

In November 1870, after he had heard one of Burckhardt's three public "Great Men of History" lectures, Friedrich Nietzsche wrote a famous letter to his friend von Geersdorff in which he conveyed his impressions:

Yesterday evening I had the pleasure which I would have liked you above all people to have shared, of hearing Jacob Burckhardt lecture. He gave a lecture without notes on Historical Greatness which lay entirely within the orbit of our thoughts and feelings. This very unusual middle-aged man does not, indeed, tend to falsify the truth, but to conceal it . . . I am attending his weekly lectures at the University on the study of history, and believe I am the only one of his sixty hearers who understands his profound train of thought with all its strange circumlocutions and abrupt breaks wherever the subject fringes on the problematical.[87]

What was that "problematical" issue in Burckhardt's lectures that he sought to avoid by all those "strange circumlocutions and abrupt breaks"? And what was his reason for doing so, which Nietzsche claimed to be the only one to have understood? These queries have been much debated by scholars and biographers, most perceptively by Karl Löwith, Edgar Salin, and Erich Heller.[88] They commonly point out that although Burckhardt and Nietzsche were divided on all the most important religious, moral, and cultural matters, the ultimate reason for their uneasy relationship must have been their disagreement on the meaning of history itself, more precisely, on its conception as a process of civilization, or *Bildung*. According to Heller, Nietzsche believed that "Burckhardt knew the desperate truth which he believed himself to have discovered and exposed":[89] that, for example, "God is dead," that all morality is only "Will to Power," that there is no historical progress but only "Eternal Return," that, in sum, history displays no *Bildung* at all and should not be studied and taught as such. Nietzsche's aim was to expose the fallacy of "that rule of chance and accident that has hitherto been called 'History,'" and inevitably, much as he admired Burckhardt, he was bound to turn against him.

Although I generally concur with this interpretation, I would add that this essential controversy between Burckhardt and Nietzsche over the very conception of history occurred, and may even have begun, in their initial antithetical conceptions of classical myth and its functions in the process of European civilization. Although both scholars admired Greek mythology as one of the greatest cultural creations of our civilization, Burckhardt considered it to be the source of the *grosses geistiges Kontinuum*, which constitutes our modern historical culture, whereas Nietzsche regarded the Greek mythic consciousness as utterly opposed—and by far superior— to the "historical sense" of contemporary man. Burckhardt believed that "we see with the eyes of the Greeks and speak with their idioms,"[90] and therefore he looked for historical continuity and development, or *Bildung*, between the mythical and the logical, the primitive and the modern;

Nietzsche rejected such historicistic delusions and called for a total immersion in mythical consciousness, either by returning to Greek mythology or, as he gradually came to prefer, by creating a new myth. The controversy was, quite simply, over the utility and liability of mythistory.

As is well known, till his very last sane day, Nietzsche admired Burckhardt as his "great teacher" and singled him out as the one and only credible historian of the age, because, in his view, Burckhardt was the only contemporary historian who could "survey things and events without being humbugged by stupid theories [of progress]."[91] Yet, in his well-known essay *On the Utility and Liability of History for Life* (1874), Nietzsche directed his attack at some of Burckhardt's deepest convictions about historical *Bildung*. Whereas Burckhardt argued that modern man needs historical knowledge in order to be civil, for "only the study of the past can provide us with a standard by which to measure the rapidity and strength of the particular movement in which we live," and generally believed that "Geschichtslosigkeit ist Barbarei," Nietzsche sought to prove the opposite. In his essay he describes the fateful condition of modern man who "braces himself against the great and ever-greater burden of the past; it weighs him down or bends him over, hampers his gait as an invisible and obscure load that he can pretend to disown," but in fact he cannot do so, because so much of his life has become dependent on historical traditions and institutions.[92] Above all Nietzsche opposed all forms of "historical education," and he portrayed its practitioners, the "historical artists," as manipulators. His main task was to expose their historical methodologies—which he termed the "monumental," the "antiquarian," and the "critical"—as political ideologies, which were liable to tie man to the lessons of the past rather than liberate him from them.[93]

Although Nietzsche does not specify what kind of "historical artist" Burckhardt was, it is significant that his only reference to him occurs in the discussion of the "antiquarian," whom he describes as "the person who preserves and venerates" bygone times, who "looks back with loyalty and love on the origins through which he became what he is" and seeks to "preserve for those who will come after him the conditions under which he himself has come into being—and by doing so serves life." Nietzsche goes on to describe this scholar as the one who "looks beyond his own transient, curious, individual existence and senses himself to be the spirit of his house, his lineage, and his city" and whose "gifts and virtues" are "the ability to empathize with things and divine their greater significance, to detect traces that are almost extinguished, to instinctively read correctly a past frequently overwritten." He then concludes: "It was just such a sensibility and impulse that guided the Italians of the Renaissance and re-awakened in their poets the ancient Italian genius to 'a marvelous new re-sounding of the lyre,' as Jacob Burckhardt has expressed it."[94]

Clearly, then, Nietzsche associated Burckhardt's vocation with a certain kind of conservative policy that instructed him "not to falsify the truth, but to conceal it." Thus, for example, Nietzsche knew that Burckhardt, like himself, had lost his religious faith but refused to do what he himself had done—to declare it boldly and publicly. It was, Nietzsche suspected, Burckhardt's commitment to *Bildung* that required him to preserve the im-age of Christ alive, for educational reasons, although he knew that this im-age was hollow. This educational policy was, as Nietzsche saw, the "classi-cal" conservative ideology of mythology first spelled out by Plato in his *Republic*. Burckhardt defended this tradition already in *The Age of Constan-tine*, where he devoted a whole chapter to the fate of pagan mythology un-der Christian domination.[95] He was particularly eager to show how pagan mythology prevailed under, and ultimately over against, Christian theol-ogy so as to produce a new Christian mythology. Burckhardt, who liked to confide—so as to confound—that he was no "philosophischer Kopf," relishes the opportunity to expose the inadequacy of the Neoplatonic doc-trine of the "absolute One" and similar new conceptual formulations to repose the existential anxieties of an age that has lost its old pagan deities. He argues that the proliferation of such mystical philosophies was a sign of a spiritual degeneration rather than of regeneration: "The need for super-stition was grown the more desperate in the degree that the natural energy with which the individual confronts fate had disappeared."[96] What was needed, and what actually happened, was the creation of a new mytho-logical deity that could accommodate the old pagan to the new Christian sensibilities. Burckhardt further shows how in that process of transforma-tion, "the ancient gods thus became superfluous, unless they were daimo-nized and included in the ranks of lesser powers," such as those of astro-logical deities, where they survive to this day.[97] Burckhardt's conclusion received its definite affirmation from Jean Seznec: "Pagan mythology, far from experiencing a 'rebirth' in fifteenth-century Italy, had remained alive within the culture and art of the Middle Ages. Even the gods were not re-stored to life, for they had never disappeared from the memory or imagi-nation of man."[98]

According to Burckhardt, the main reason for this remarkable dura-bility of pagan mythology was the basic human need for *Anschauung*, for pictorial contemplation and representation of reality through actual "im-ages of the eternal" rather than through conceptual ideas about it. He thus shows how—during the rapid Christianization of classical civilization, as literature began to smack "too plainly of the air of the schools," and "figured poems, when carefully written out," took "the form of an altar, a pan-pipe, and organ, or the like," amid "other such aberrations"—it was ancient myth that remained malleable and so "with poetry and through it could serve as a continuous revelation of the beautiful."[99] The process of Christian civilization consists in this "continuous revelation" of pagan mythology. Whereas Nietzsche saw in all academic renditions of Greek mythology a deceitful inversion of its elemental truths, Burckhardt acknowledged the vital role of academic writers and other practitioners of "rhetoric and its collateral sciences" in the preservation of certain aesthetic norms of classical antiquity: "If all the productions of the fourth century betray decline by labored and tortured form, by heaping up of *sententiae,* by the misuse of metaphor for the simple and the commonplace, by modern turgidity and artificial archaic aridity, still a peculiar reflection of the classical period rests upon many of these writers. They still show the requirement of stylistic style, which is normally alien to us."[100]

Therefore, even though Burckhardt ended his *Age of Constantine* with some drastic pronouncements on the "essential devolution" of classical antiquity, he nevertheless assumed, and in *The Civilization of the Renaissance in Italy* eventually came to affirm, that its legacy of "beauty and freedom" could still live on and be reborn in modernity.[101] Nietzsche must also have noticed that Burckhardt affirmed this ideological tradition in the very last lines of *The Civilization of the Renaissance in Italy,* where he describes the Platonic Academy in Florence as a medium wherein "echoes of mediaeval mysticism here flow into one current with Platonic doctrines, and with a characteristically modern spirit." Burckhardt pays homage to those scholars in the academy who created that "great spiritual continuity" between the classical, Christian, and modern times; they also leave a message to all modern scholars to do the same—as Burckhardt himself did in his work.[102]

Nietzsche vehemently opposed these views, in which, he rightly saw, a conservative conception of the historical vocation necessarily led to a conservative view of the historical interpretation and reconstruction of the past. The Italian Renaissance is a case in point, for where Burckhardt sought and found and celebrated a great cultural continuity, Nietzsche saw only discontinuity and occasional revolutions: "Does anybody at last understand, will anybody understand what the renaissance was? The transvaluation of Christian values, the attempt undertaken with all means, all instincts and all genius to make the opposite values, the noble values triumph."[103] His most powerful conviction throughout his life was that as in classical Athens, so too in the modern city, a true enlightenment was possible only through radical liberation. This could be achieved by means of authentic mythology, a truly archaic and anarchic one like Homer's, and not by an artificial and synthetic one like Plato's "golden lie," which, Nietzsche was sure, was bound to fail. Only a true mythology could destroy, by the sheer power of its images and tales, the facile theories of theology, philosophy, history, and the natural sciences. This, in his view, was the great achievement of Richard Wagner, and he duly celebrated it in *The Birth of Tragedy.*

According to Nietzsche, Burckhardt was initially impressed by these notions. In a letter to Erwin Rohde from mid-February 1872, he claims that Burckhardt approves of his investigations into Greek mentality and of their importance for his own *Kulturphilosophie.*[104] And although Nietzsche must have realized that Burckhardt had gradually distanced himself from the radical implications of these investigations, he continued to claim, till his very last publication, *Twilight of the Idols,* of 1889, that "that profoundest student [of Greek civilization] now living, Jacob Burckhardt of Basel," agreed with his major discovery of the Apollonian and Dionysian as the dominant forces in Greek cultural history.[105] Late in his life, Burckhardt came to detest the "publicity stunt" that Nietzsche had become, and he sought to tone down his earlier association with him.[106] Yet in his "Greek Cultural History," the series of lectures that Burckhardt prepared during the years of his close association with Nietzsche, roughly between 1869 and 1872 (when he gave the first lectures), he seems to have been more receptive to Nietzsche than he later admitted. Much like Nietzsche—and probably influenced by reading *The Birth of Tragedy* upon its publication in 1871—Burckhardt came to believe that Greek civilization was formed and sustained by its mythology, which gave it its "form and meaning [*Gestalt und Deutung*]" and determined its entire historical development. He further argued that as long as the Greeks adhered to their myths, they were vital and creative, though, unlike Nietzsche, he did not regard the intellectual revolutions of the sixth and fifth centuries B.C., during which the Greeks created philosophy, history, and science, as catastrophic. Rather, he sought to show how even in those enlightened times, and in spite of consistent efforts of the philosophers and other "enemies of myth" to eradicate "Homer and his world of gods,"[107] the Greek people retained their mythical traditions and were sustained by them. Burckhardt reiterated this conclusion in a special public lecture in October 1884, in which he dealt again with the question of "Bruch mit dem Mythus" in Hellenic civilization. He chose to concentrate on Pythagoras and showed that even though this free thinker did not believe anymore in the ancient myths, he did not repudiate them. He shied away from them but still reserved some deep veneration for them, as can be seen in his prayers and hymns.

Werner Kaegi points out that Burckhardt may have used this case to reflect on his own religious crisis of 1838.[108] I would add that Burckhardt might also have used it to rebut Nietzsche's attempt to create a new mythology. For Burckhardt, modern myths were impossible, a contradiction in terms: as he put it in his letter of 1855, a "genuine myth" could only be that "great and ancient image, in which everyman has to discover his own being and destiny in his own way." And Burckhardt held that this observation meant also that the only true myths were the old "classic" myths, not the new "romantic" ones.[109] The former were spontaneous cultural creations that evolved out of historical reality and were kept alive by oral and memorial traditions, but the "romantic" myths in modern Germany were artificial fabrications of artists like Richard Wagner, whom Burckhardt detested as a "ruthless" manipulator of the mythological (and more material) resources of the nation for his own egotistical ambition.[110] Nietzsche was rather slow to realize this. In his *Birth of Tragedy*, he hailed Wagner's musical and ideological fabrications of a new German mythology. Eventually he came to renounce Wagner's mythology, but then he invented his own new one in *Zarathustra* (1883).

What saved Burckhardt from this romantic quest for a new mythology was his "great historical hunger," which Nietzsche so loathed. Burckhardt believed in historical continuity and rejected all radical attempts to break it, or break out of it—whether in Nietzsche's return to the myths of primitive paganism or in Kirkegaard's return to the myths of primitive Christianity—as unreasonable and infeasible delusions. In his treatment of modern romantic mythology, Burckhardt seems to have adopted the same critical attitude that he ascribed to the Italian humanists. Although they despised the romantic myths of the Middle Ages, they were required to deal with them, if only because "the people kept them in memory . . . but they could not without hypocrisy treat these myths with any respect."[111] "The special duty of the educated," he believed, was "to perfect and complete, as well as they can, the picture of the continuity of the world and mankind from the beginning. This marks off conscious beings from the unconscious barbarian."[112] Nietzsche was unable, or unwilling, to acknowledge this inevitable continuity, which separates—though it does not necessarily alienate—us from the past; he was therefore, in Burckhardt's terms, "barbarian."

"The hour when our culture does not see any longer beauty in the great images of the Greek gods will be the beginning of barbarism." These words of Burckhardt's in *The Cicerone* sum up his mythistorical theory of art. Assuming that the "great images" of classical mythology define our modern idea and ideal of beauty (*das Schöne*), he concluded that the great modern artists are those who are mindful not merely of the "historicity" of their cultural tradition but also, and more fundamentally, of its "mythicity." In his last work, *Recollections of Rubens* (published posthumously in 1898), he reiterates this view through personal impressions and reflections on a painter who personified, for Burckhardt, the art of mythistory. According to Burckhardt, Rubens's art represents a society that was still very traditional.

> The Bible, vision, legend, mythology, allegory, pastoral, history, and even a piece of everyday world, figures as well as scenes, still formed a whole, and even a mighty naturalist, inspired by his own fullness of life, undertook to maintain all these things at the right temperature. Rubens never really broke through this horizon . . . He was no willful dreamer of strange fantasies, but only the mightiest herald and witness of that great tradition. His vast power of invention was essentially occupied in an ever-fresh response to it and ever-new expression of it.[113]

As in the case of Raphael and Michelangelo, Burckhardt contrasts Rubens with his contemporary rival Rembrandt, who came to personify in the last decades of the nineteenth century the arch-modernist artist, the painter of the darker *Innerlichkeit* of the modern self, symbolizing for German romantic nationalists like Julius Langbehn the cultural rebel against the dominant liberal bourgeois conventions and institutions of European society.[114] Burckhardt's conservative convictions aligned him with Rubens, the loyal burgher of Catholic Antwerp and painter of the old royal dynasties and aristocratic families, with all their ancient mythical and classical associations. Burckhardt admired Rubens as a public artist because in his works he remained loyal to the social institutions, to the artistic tradition, and to himself. Rubens managed to do so because he recognized and expressed the common classical myths that inspired and united all the European nations into one cultural community. He accomplished this task in the great series of allegorical paintings commissioned by Marie de' Medici for the gallery of the Luxembourg Palace: "The brilliant moments of time here depicted are, spiritually and materially, clearly self-sufficient in the theme and details of each picture; they move us in themselves, without suggesting to the spectator that reading-matter on the subject is awaiting him outside. Whatever his response may be today to the factual content of the series, art has still remained art, even in this kind of royal servitude."[115] As the aged Burckhardt recalled and described Rubens's painting *Ulysses and Nausica,* he added: "And so they meet, the Ionian and the Flemish, the two greatest story-tellers our earth has ever borne—Homer and Rubens."[116] Burckhardt might well have added that his own work continued that mythistorical tradition.

"Historia scribitur ad narrandum, non ad probandum"—so wrote Burckhardt in 1863, quoting Quintilian, and then added: "But if, by the truth of representation [*Wahrheit der Drastellung*], it also proves something, so much greater is its worth."[117] What did Burckhardt mean by "truth of representation"? As I suggested, for Burckhardt historical representation was true not only when it pertained to actual events *wie sie eigentlich gewesen sind,* but also, and primarily, when it conveyed the lasting impressions, images, and tales of these events in the cultural tradition, or *Bildung,* of later generations. Burckhardt admired the historians who accomplished this task. In *The Age of Constantine,* they were storytellers like Hieronymus, whose fabulous descriptions of saints and martyrs proved much more truthful than Eusebius's fatuous dictations of "truths";[118] in *The Civilization of the Renaissance in Italy,* he preferred the anonymous authors of "The Hundred Old Tales" as better representatives of their age than Thomas Aquinas,[119] just as biased chroniclers like Matarazzo were more valuable witnesses to the *Zeitgeist* than the ambassadors and other official reporters whom Ranke so admired for their apparent objectivity and historical neutrality. In a veiled attack on the new historical scholarship of his time, he bemoans the degeneration of the mythological tradition in Renaissance historiography into theological and political doctrines: "A superficial comparison of the histories of this period with the earlier chronicles, especially with works so full of life, color, and brilliancy as those of Villani, will lead us loudly to deplore the change . . . Our mistrust is increased when we hear that Livy, the pattern of this school of writers, was copied just where he is least worthy of imitation—on the grounds, namely, 'that he turned a dry and naked tradition into grace and richness.'"[120]

Against this antimythical historiography, Burckhardt posits the most notable follower of Livy in Renaissance historiography. He praises Machiavelli's *Florentine Histories* precisely because the author knew that his "wonderful story" of the virtuous republic of Florence was too wonderful to be really true but was true nonetheless:

> We might find something to say against every line of the 'Storie Fiorentine,' and yet the great and unique value of the whole would remain

unaffected . . . The voluminous record of the collapse of the highest and
most original life which the world could then show may appear to one but
as a collection of curiosities, may awaken in another a devilish delight at the
shipwreck of so much nobility and grandeur, to a third may seem like a
great historical assize; for all it will be an object of thought and study to the
end of time.[121]

What Burckhardt said of Machiavelli might well be said of his own work,
and indeed it has been said. When his *Griechische Kulturgeschichte* was published, Theodor Mommsen is reported to have said that even though
"these Greeks never existed," Burckhardt's book was valuable for general
historiography, and he predicted that it would still be read and still be true
even if every sentence in it came to be corrected by more accurate research.

Burckhardt knew that because he based his book solely upon his own
readings in the sources, without any attention to all the new discoveries
and theories of classical scholarship, it was bound to raise the anger of those
experts whom he used to mock as "*viri eruditissimi* in their professional
chairs,"[122] whose factual knowledge of the ancient world far surpassed that
of Burckhardt, as well as—Burckhardt loved to add—that of the Greeks
themselves. He nevertheless believed in the cogency of his historical work.
In 1871 he confided to a friend: "My consolation is that I have gradually
wrung a goodly portion of independent knowledge of antiquity directly
from the sources, and that I shall be able to present by far the greater part
of all I have to say as my own."[123] His close attention to what the ancient
Greeks said, rather than to what modern scholars said about them, enabled
him to see their world as they saw it, to know them as they knew themselves in the self-perceptions of their myths, and moreover to recognize
ourselves in them. In the introduction to this work, he states:

> One great advantage of studying cultural history is the certainty of the
> more important facts compared with those of history in the ordinary sense
> of narrated events—these are frequently uncertain, controversial, colored,
> or, given the Greek talent for lying, entirely the invention of imagination
> or of self-interest. Cultural history by contrast possesses a primary degree
> of certainty, as it consists for the most part of material conveyed in an un-
> intentional, disinterested or even involuntary way by sources and monu-
> ments; they betray their secrets unconsciously and even, paradoxically,
> through fictitious elaborations, quite apart from the material details they
> may set out to record and glorify, and are thus doubly instructive for the
> cultural historian.[124]

Of all his works, this is the most mythistorical: Burckhardt presents the entire cultural history of Greece as an extension of its Homeric mythology. In the opening chapter, "The Greeks and Their Mythology," he writes: "However questionable their actual knowledge of ancient times may have been, myth was a powerful force dominating Greek life and hovering over it all like a wonderful vision, close at hand. It illuminated the whole of the present for the Greeks, everywhere and until a very late date, as though it belonged to a quite recent past; and essentially it presented a sublime reflection of the perceptions and the life of the nation itself" (22–23). The ancient myths informed the Greeks not only on their earliest times, on their migrations and their founding of city-states, but also on all current moral and cultural issues. "Myth is the underlying given factor in Greek existence. The whole culture, in everything that was done, remained what it had always been, developing only slowly" (25). Burckhardt notes how mythical conceptions permeated and determined all political deliberations over the legitimacy of rulers, the location of temples and palaces, the destination of navigators in search of new colonies, the declaration of wars, and the efficacy of laws and institutions even in later, "historical," times. Although Burckhardt believed that "the world of the Greeks and Romans was entirely secular," he points out that beliefs in theophany were still prevalent in Athens in the sixth and fifth centuries B.C., as can be gauged from the story that tells how the magistrate Peisistratus dwelled with the gods or from the reported facts that at the time of the battle of Marathon, an Athenian messenger's meeting with Pan near Tega was officially accepted, and a shrine to Pan was erected on the spot (34).

Whereas in other national traditions, myth was habitually deprived of its original authority by the rise of philosophical, theological, or historical sciences, "Hellenic myth, having come into being in a wholly unsophisticated period, yet survived in its full richness into a literate, indeed a highly literate age, and was consequently recorded in astonishing completeness" (23). Myth was the *Existenzbild* of the Greeks. In the section "The General Characteristics of Greek Life," Burckhardt shows how the Greeks drew their basic meanings of life and death, fate and human dignity, from their mythology (87–96). And even when myth later "became the subject of erudition and controversy," the Greeks continued to perceive it as an original image of reality that could not be fully analyzed, allegorized, or rationalized into "higher" truths, as was the case, for example, in Christianity. Recalling how liberal theologians like his teacher Dewette reduced the original Christian myths to popular beliefs, stories, and traditions that could not be retained as such in systematic theology, Burckhardt admired the resistance of the Greeks to such modes of modernization: "At the height of their powers, the Greeks did not want to interpret their myths but to preserve and glorify them." [125]

The Greeks managed to save their myths from critical scholars like Heraclitus (who "did not conceal his hatred of Homer and his world of gods") [126] and Thucydides because they were primarily a nation of artists and poets, "the enemies of exact knowledge," whose works "consistently give expression to myth and always regenerate it." [127] In his own work on Greek mythology, Burckhardt assumed the same countercritical position. Note his judgment of the scientific explanations and other pedantic renditions of myth in his time:

> Nowadays we are often told that many of the legends are based on mere natural phenomena, mainly astronomic and meteoric. Bellerophon's madness and misfortune signify apparent disturbances in the courses of the sun and moon, or the story of Phaedra and Hippolitus refers to the sea in which the morning star goes down. But even if such interpretations were irresistible, the elaboration of these terrible human stories from such origins would only be more strikingly and peculiarly characteristic of the Greeks. Who but they, listening to the nightingale's plaint, would have associated it with the behavior of three other birds to form the horrifying myth of Philomela, Procne, Tereus and Itys? . . . Our interest here is not in anatomizing the legends into their primary elements, but, precisely, in the drift of the amplification they received. [128]

Moreover, and crucially for Burckhardt (as well as for the entire tradition of mythistory), it was Greek historiography that preserved the mythological tradition—most notably in Herodotus's composition of oral stories into his *History*. Burckhardt elaborates and justifies the Herodotean methodology of mythistory against the Thucydidean opposition, in terms that clearly assert the primacy of his own "cultural history" over Ranke's "political history."

> Those who have once come to know this typical-mythical form of narrative usually do not seek to recount what literally happened . . . But the scorn with which critical erudition in our time dismisses the anecdotal— which it declares to be utterly worthless for scholarship and incompatible with its duty to deliver only valuable exact information—seems to us not very appropriate. For we are obliged, whether we want to or not, to scrutinize the anecdotal stuff, and may ultimately even conclude that the facts too are rather precarious. Are all those histories, which are often all we have

from a particular time, no longer to be considered as history? Surely they are not history in the usual sense, if only because we cannot learn from them what happened at a particular time, in a particular place, as a result of the action of a particular person. But they certainly constitute to a certain extent a *historia altera,* an imagined history that tells us what human beings were capable of doing and what they most often did. We seem to be so rigidly instructed by our education to value only the exact that we no longer can see any salvation beyond it; the Greeks, on the other hand, seek the typical and they find it in the anecdote, which is always true in general and yet never was true on any particular occasion. Seen in that way, the first book of Herodotus, for instance, remains essentially true, even though not much of it would be left if one discarded all that is typical from it.[129]

Burckhardt's reflections on the moral and cultural virtues of Greek *historia altera* betray his deep affinity with Nietzsche's theories on the primacy of myth in any national history. Nietzsche's epochal statement in *The Birth of Tragedy*—"Without myth every culture loses the healthy power of its creativity: only a horizon defined by myths completes and unifies a whole cultural movement"—echoes in Burckhardt's final judgment on Greek cultural history: "Here, then, was a nation which vigorously defended its myth as the ideal basis of its existence, and tried at all costs to make connections between that myth and practical life."[130] Indeed, so strong was this myth in Greek civilization that it hindered the development of more realistic and rationalistic conceptions of reality. Burckhardt was critical of this mythical tendency and its cultural policy ("this people tolerated no historical drama on its stage and paid little attention to historical epic"), but he nevertheless accepted this predicament as essential to the Greek "tragic" experience of life. For he saw that underlying the Greek *Weltanschauung* were some deep pessimistic, almost nihilistic, perceptions of reality that rendered human life utterly meaningless in itself.

Already in his earlier writings, most notably in the concluding paragraphs of *The Civilization of the Renaissance in Italy,* Burckhardt had criticized the facile attitudes toward human fate and toward the questions of death and afterlife that prevailed in the major theological and philosophical doctrines of Western civilization.[131] Whereas the Romans and the Christians disguised the tragic conception of death by the notions of "immortality" and the "World to come," Homer and his followers "had not sweetened and humanized the conception." Rather, in their myths they expressed the acute realization that they lived in a secular world, and yet they concealed it under beautiful images and tales and thereby made it both memorable and bearable. Burckhardt cites Achilles' answer to

Odysseus—"So much I tell you and aver to thee, that we who are parted from earthly life have the strongest desire to return to it again"—as a prime manifestation of this truth.[132] He saw that because Greek myths encode these self-perceptions of what it is to be human, they endure in the collective remembrance of our civilization, forever teaching us how to cope with this quintessential modern predicament. "We see with their eyes and use their phrases when we speak."[133] Burckhardt thus concludes:

> This, then was the spiritual disposition of the Greek people; and on them the greatest destiny in the history of the world was to evolve. Caught in the toils of their mythical past, only slowly becoming capable of history in any true sense, attaining their full stature in imaginative poetry, they were destined in the course of time to be pioneers in the understanding of all nations, and in communicating this understanding to others . . . At the same time they were to secure for us, through the survival of their culture, continuity in the development of the world; for it is only through the Greeks that different epochs, and our interest in them, are linked and strung together. Without them we would have no knowledge of early times, and what we *might* know without them, we would feel no desire to know.[134]

It was during those long years of work on *Griechische Kulturgeschichte,* while he was sailing in "the real spiritual ocean of that world,"[135] that Burckhardt immersed himself in Pausanias. We recall that Pausanias's *Description of Greece* was the only book that Burckhardt carried with him from Basel on his vacation in Baden im Aargau in the summer of 1889. In this book Burckhardt found much that resembled his own world and works. For when Pausanias toured Greece in the second century A.D., he became acutely aware that the places of worship and many of the other great monuments of classical antiquity had begun to fall into ruin, and he resolved to save for posterity their last visible vestiges of glory, the images of their legendary past, their myths.[136] Pausanias did not believe the ancient myths anymore, but he still believed *in* them, having realized that they imbued Greek life and history with meaning. Thus, when he visits a site in Arcadia that tradition has associated with Cronus, the Titan who devoured his children, Pausanias declares: "When I began this work I used to look on Greek stories like this as little better than foolishness; but now that I have got as far as Arcadia . . . I conjecture that this story about Cronus is a bit of Greek philosophy. In matters of religion I shall follow tradition."[137] What he ultimately perceives in this myth of Cronus, which in his time was already Chronus, the god of time, becomes clear when he arrives in Megalopolis:

I am astounded that Megalopolis which the Arcadians founded in all ea-
gerness, and for which Greece had the highest hopes, should have lost its
beauty and ancient prosperity, or that most of it should be ruins nowadays,
because I know that the daemonic powers love to turn things continually
upside down, and I know that fortune alters everything, strong and weak,
things at their beginning and things at their ending, and drives everything
with a strong necessity and according to her whim. Mycenae which led the
Greeks in their Trojan War, and Nineveh, seat of the Assyrian Kingdom are
deserted and demolished . . . This is how temporary and completely inse-
cure human things are.[138]

We can imagine Burckhardt reading these lines in July 1889 and realizing
that, like the ancient traveler, he too had at last acquired the "rechten
mythischen Augen": those of the historian who has always been acutely
aware of the contingency of all human affairs and yet has managed to discern in the anarchic and transient events of history some more archaic and
permanent structures of meaning, the myths that transform all *Zeitungen*
into *Ewigungen*.

V

Burckhardt's initial perception of history as "mystery and poetry" has always set him apart from those who saw in history "a source of knowledge,
a science,"[139] and it still renders his work, his mythistory, dubious and
unwissenschaftlich to Ranke's modern followers, the "*viri eruditissimi* in their
professional chairs." As Burckhardt himself predicted, the reaction of the
professional guild to his *Griechische Kulturgeschichte* when it was eventually
published after his death was very negative. The harsh judgment of the
eminent classical philologist Ulrich von Wilamowitz-Moellendorf—
"Dies Buch existiert nicht für die Wissenschaft"—is notorious, especially
because Wilamowitz-Moellendorf had already used the same terms some
twenty-seven years earlier to denounce Nietzsche's *Birth of Tragedy* as *unwissenschaftlich*. Yet, as it had in the case of Nietzsche's book, the academic
German historiography eventually came around to recognize the new historical perceptions in *Griechische Kulturgeschichte* and, more generally, in
Burckhardt's conception of *Kulturgeschichte*.[140]

   The decisive moment in this rehabilitation was Friedrich Meinecke's
lecture "Ranke and Burckhardt," which he delivered to the German Academy of Science in Berlin on 22 May 1947.[141] Meinecke's remarkable address has since been widely perceived as the "last testament" of the grand
old man of the German historical profession to his fellows and followers, and it still resounds in current discussions on the vocation of modern

historiography.[142] Underlying Meinecke's reflections on Ranke and Burckhardt was the tacit assumption that their different philosophical conceptions of human life and history determined not only their own lives and works but also those of their followers. This was most certainly Meinecke's own case: "Since my student days, Ranke has been my guiding star, my pole star. Only later for me did Burckhardt begin to shed his luminescence."[143] He was attracted to Ranke because, like most German historians of the Second Reich, Meinecke admired the imperial historian who conceived of his age and the entire world history as moving up to the "political restoration" of the new European order. He could not quite attune himself to Burckhardt's skeptic and aesthetic conception of history, which led to mere "contemplation" rather than to "action" in historical affairs. In an early review essay on Burckhardt's *Reflections on History,* Meinecke dismissed Burckhardt's predilection for the "subjective" aspects of the great "collective" struggles for state and nation as a "romantic" indulgence, unworthy of those historians who had actually lived through these struggles.[144]

The crises and catastrophes of the twentieth century forced Meinecke to revise this judgment on Burckhardt's world and works. The publication of Burckhardt's letters and *Historische Fragmente* in the late 1920s was, as Meinecke admits, crucial for his reevaluation of the two historians and their historiographical legacies during the times of *die deutsche Katastrophe.*[145] In his book on that subject, *The German Catastrophe,* of 1946, Meinecke finally came to the same conclusion that Burckhardt had reached a hundred years before: that the only remedy for modern European civilization, and above all for the German nation, would be a "cultural renaissance" rather than a "political restoration."[146] Meinecke reiterated this conviction in his lecture of May 1947. As much as he admired his teacher Ranke, he now urged his listeners to ask, with him, "whether, in the end, Burckhardt will not have greater importance than Ranke for us as well as for later historians."[147] He conceded that Burckhardt "saw more deeply and acutely into the essential historical character of his own time" and was therefore "able to see the future, too, more definitely and certainly than Ranke could."[148]

Meinecke duly notes that although both historians were conservative, they differed from each other in their philosophical and historical worldviews: whereas Ranke's essentially "political" conception of human life and history aligned him, both personally and professionally, with the "great powers" of religion and state in Germany and the European *Mächte,* Burckhardt's "cultural" conception attracted him to the elusive agents, sects, and communities—from Socrates and Diogenes in antiquity, through the early Christian anchorites and the last pagan sages in the Middle Ages, to the Florentine Academy in the Renaissance and, ultimately, to his own fellow comrades at Basel—who commonly sought to preserve the humanistic tradition of Western civilization over against their respective powerful authorities. Setting out from such different philosophical and political conceptions of what human life and history are all about, Ranke and Burckhardt eventually came to perceive their vocation as historians in entirely different ways: Ranke concentrated on the "great" epochs, events, institutions, and ideas that made and moved world history and largely ignored its individual aspects (avoiding, on the whole, any personal impressions and interpretations as to what actually happened); Burckhardt, in contrast, concentrated on the personal subjects of history, on what Meinecke (echoing Nietzsche) calls "the human—all-too-human—in history."

Ultimately, Meinecke writes, "the two men put different queries to history." Ranke's was "What does man mean for history?" and Burckhardt's was "What does history mean for man?" [149] The first query consists in a providential conception of history, where the *Weltgeschichte* appears *as*—not *in*—the *Weltgericht,* as if revealing the objective judgments *of* history; the second query consists in a human conception of history, where everything that has ever happened appears as utterly contingent and thus open to all kinds of subjective reflections and judgments *on* history. Whereas Ranke (and Meinecke) sought in history the permanent *ideas* that emanated from great men and nations and evolved in all their historical motions, Burckhardt attended to the *myths* that men and nations have forged in order to bestow meaning on their historical motions. It was this mythistorical perception of human reality, of the actual forces that have always motivated human beings to action, that enabled Burckhardt to see so "deeply and acutely into the essential historical character of his own time" and thereby, as Meinecke acknowledged, of our time as well.

Yet this was a late, too late, appreciation. When Burckhardt died in 1897, there were very few German historians who shared his mythistorical convictions. Among them was the young Jewish scholar of art history Aby Warburg. In 1892 Warburg wrote his doctoral dissertation, "Sandro Botticelli's *Birth of Venus* and *Spring:* An Examination of Concepts of Antiquity in the Italian Early Renaissance." [150] According to Warburg's own testimony, he conducted this study of Botticelli's mythologies under the profound influence of Burckhardt's famous description "Society and Festivals" in the fifth section of *The Civilization of the Renaissance in Italy,* and he was above all inspired by Burckhardt's assumption that Renaissance artists could actually see the mythological deities as "living, moving beings" in festive performances: "As Jacob Burckhardt—anticipating future discoveries in one of his unerring intuitive generalizations—once said: 'Italian festive pageantry, in its higher form, is a true transition from life to art.'"[151] The main aim of Warburg's dissertation was to reverse this "transition from life to art" so as to regain life from art, to see what the "renaissance of antiquity" really meant for Botticelli and his contemporaries.

When Warburg completed his dissertation, he sent a copy to Burckhardt, who commended the author on his original perceptions and achievement. Burckhardt advised Warburg to do some more research on "Botticelli, the mystical theologian," a sign, perhaps, that the old Burckhardt was still reluctant to admit that Botticelli was (as Warburg thought) primarily susceptible to ancient pagan mythology.[152] Warburg may have realized as much when he remarked that "Burckhardt was content to do his immediate duty, which was to examine Renaissance man in his most perfectly developed type, and art in its finest manifestations"[153]—leaving it to Warburg, as it were, to complete the task and examine Renaissance man in his imperfect type and art in its crudest materialistic and atavistic manifestations, so as to redefine history as ancient mythology.

FOUR

Aby Warburg: History as Ancient Mythology

I

In October 1918, upon hearing news of the final collapse of Germany in World War I, Aby Warburg, a private scholar and benefactor of art history in Hamburg, went mad. After years of desperate attempts to unravel the tactical and ideological maneuvers of that war, Warburg suddenly came to believe that the war was about himself: he imagined that being a German, a Jew, and a scion of a very wealthy family made him the common target of all the enemies—the Allies' agents, the German anti-Semites, and the Bolshevik revolutionists—who were finally closing in on him from all sides. When he held his wife and children at gunpoint and threatened to finish them off before the enemies could get them, he was taken for psychiatric treatment.[1] In 1921 he was transferred to the famous Bellevue Sanatorium in Kreuzlingen on Lake Constance in Switzerland, where he came under the care of the director, Dr. Ludwig Binswanger. A student of Eugen Bleuler and a colleague of both Freud and Jung, Binswanger developed his own "existential" school of psychology, which was much more attuned to the intellectual and spiritual obsessions of his patients. He reasoned that his patients, like all other human beings, aspired to "self-realization" of personal ambitions, which they could best achieve through creative and communicative work. According to Binswanger, this activity ensured that they would not merely express their innermost desires but also expand and transform them into what Paul de Man has called the "sublimation of self."[2]

By spring 1923, when Binswanger realized that the condition of his patient had improved, he struck a deal with Warburg's assistant Fritz Saxl that if Warburg could prepare and deliver a coherent lecture, he would be allowed to leave the sanatorium and return home. And so it was. On 21 April 1923 Warburg presented to an audience of staff and inmates at Bellevue his lecture "Images from the Region of the Pueblo Indians of North America."[3] Warburg's performance proved that he had overcome his fears and delusions. Warburg did much more than that, however: he showed not only that he had overcome his fears but also *how* he had done so, through his brilliant observations on the Indians' beliefs and rites, which, according to Warburg's interpretation, were concerned with precisely that problem. For although Warburg ostensibly dealt with the ceremonial rites by which the Pueblo Indians sought to secure rainfalls for their lands, he used that case to probe and reflect on the cultural-historical ramifications of his personal predicament: how to overcome primal fear by turning it into thought. His main assumption was that the human ability to transmute primal emotions and reactions into normal notions and reflections originated and still consists in the mythopoeic imagination that imposes *cultural creations* upon *natural reactions*. The transformation of the stars into astral deities was the elemental and still the most monumental achievement of the mythopoeic imagination: "Contemplation of the sky is the grace and curse of humanity."[4] The formation of constellations in the firmament rendered the unstable and unbearable experience of natural reality more endurable and understandable and thereby enabled mankind, as Hans Blumenberg has put it, to reduce the "absolutism of reality" to the "absolutism of humanity."[5]

In the notes that Warburg jotted down during the weeks he spent preparing the lecture, he reflected on its potential contribution to the *Kulturwissenschaft* he had practiced in Hamburg: "I envisage as a description of my library the formulation: a collection of documents relating to the psychology of human expression. The question is: how did human and pictorial expressions originate; what are the feelings or points of view, conscious or unconscious, under which they are stored in the archives of memory? Are there laws to govern their formation or re-emergence?"[6] Warburg realized that in order to answer these questions, he needed all the material sources of his cultural-historical library, but he also needed a better psychological conception of historical collective memory (*Gedächtnis*) and its function in the evolution of "modern" humanity out of—but never entirely away from—"primitive" bestiality. He resolved, therefore,

> [t]o make use of the psychology of primitive man—that is the type of man whose reactions are immediate reflexes rather than literary responses—and also take account of the psychology of civilized man who consciously recalls the stratified formation of his ancestral and his personal memories.

With primitive man the memory image results in a religious embodiment of causes, with civilized man in detachment through naming. All mankind is eternally and at all times schizophrenic. Ontogenetically, however, we may perhaps describe one type of response to memory images as prior and primitive, though it continues on the sidelines. At the later stage the memory no longer arouses an immediate, purposeful reflex movement—be it one of a combative or a religious nature—but the memory images are now consciously stored in pictures and signs. Between these two stages we find a treatment of the impression that may be described as the symbolic mode of thought.[7]

The assertion that "mankind is eternally and at all times schizophrenic" meant that the primal fears and obsessions of our primitive ancestry have never been really and completely eliminated, only abated by apparent rational explanations and other scientific solutions. They live on in all kinds and forms of memorial traditions that have evolved from the earliest confrontations of man with natural reality and still retain the original impressions thereof.

Warburg decided, on this basis, to concentrate in his lecture on the serpent, the primal occasion of fear, whose threat is inborn in all people and has been inscribed in the religions and cultural traditions of all civilizations, most vividly so in Warburg's own fertile mind. Some of the central images of the serpent that Warburg invokes in his lecture—in the biblical tales of Paradise and of the idols of the brazen serpent, in the Dionysian orgy of the Maenads, in the sculpture of Laocoon and his sons—had captivated him since his first inquiries into art history. Common to these archaic representations of the serpent in Western civilization is the sensation that "the serpent is the spirit of evil and of temptation," epitomizing "the hopeless, tragic pessimism of antiquity." The war against the cult of the brazen serpent that King Hezekiah carried out under the influence of the prophet Isaiah and the miracle of Paul in Malta, when he hurled a viper that had bitten him into the fire and was found to be immune to its poison, merely ingrained the most basic and common phobic reaction into a long tradition of destruction. And yet, throughout that long history of repression and superstition, the serpent returned again and again into the same religions and cultural traditions that punished and banished it—as the agent of healing for the very killing it has wrought upon mankind, most notably in the deity of Asclepius, but even in some medieval figurations of the Christian Savior.[8] "In the end," Warburg writes, "the serpent is an international symbolic answer to the question whence come elementary destruction, death, and suffering into the world? . . . We might say that where helpless human suffering searches for redemption, the serpent as an image and explanation of causality cannot be far away. The serpent deserves its own chapter in the philosophy of 'as if' " (50).

Against this long European tradition of repression and tenuous rational resolution of the primal tensions occasioned by the serpent, Warburg used the Indian image and treatment of the serpent in order to expose the deeper psychological and anthropological motivations underpinning—and, as Freud has argued, constantly undermining—our uneasy civilization. He also sought to point out, through the peculiar Indian transformation of the serpent from a diabolical to a symbolic creature, how a different, distinctly mythopoeic civilization could still retain the "experience of the boundless communicability between man and environment" that our civilization lacks, or rather has lost (2). The main question he posed to his audience was this: "To what extent does this pagan worldview, as it persists among the Indians, give us a yardstick for the development from primitive paganism, through the paganism of classical antiquity, to modern man?" (4). He assumed, and sought to prove, that the evolution of the serpent in the Indian civilization from its primitive, presymbolic perception as coeval with lightning (and therefore with life-giving rain and corn) through its mythic transformations into an animal of totemic identification and then into ever more symbolic configurations marked the process of human apperception of reality from "natural objects to signs." That evoluion attests to the peculiar dialectical process of enlightenment in which any intellectual advancement, whether in Warburg's own life or in historical civilization, consists in the creation of myths and in their recognition as such. "The relation of the seeker of redemption to the serpent develops, in the cycle of cultic devotion, from coarse, sense-based interaction to its transcendence" (52). And yet he maintained that this process of rationalization or spiritualization is never complete, nor should it be, for even the most abstract signs of the serpent, in order to be affective and effective, ought to retain a certain naturalistic and even ritualistic "symbolic connection" to the animal that lurks outside as well as inside man.[9] "The poisonous reptile symbolizes the inner and outer demoniac forces that humanity must overcome."[10]

The lecture itself was based on notes and photographs that Warburg had taken in 1896 when he traveled among the Pueblo Indian peoples of Arizona and New Mexico.[11] Already on his first visit to the villages Laguna and Acoma, he noted that in the decoration of pottery, tapestry, and architecture, the serpent appeared as a symbol of lightning and a harbinger of rainfalls. At the end of his journey, he reached the region of Oraibi, where he attended some of the seasonal festivities of the *humaniskachina,* in which the Pueblo Indians danced with live poisonous serpents—rattlesnakes—in their mouths while chanting "You live and do me no harm!" and then set the snakes free. Although Warburg did not actually observe this ceremonial dance, he was profoundly impressed by the way the Indians transformed the "most dangerous of all animals, the rattlesnake," from a "natural object" that generated phobic reaction and retaliation into a "cultural object" that required observation: "In this snake dance the serpent is therefore not sacrificed but rather, through consecration and suggestive dance mimicry, transformed into a messenger and dispatched, so that, returned to the souls of the dead, it may in the form of lightning produce storms from the heavens. We have here an insight into the pervasiveness of myth and magical practice among primitive humanity." [12] Having thus shown how the Indians managed to render the poisonous serpent conducive to life by turning it into a *symbol* of lightning and rain, a mere poetic-artistic *image* of reality and as such suitable to be reflected upon, Warburg then sought to show how the employment of images and myths like this might enable all men to come to terms with fearful experiences through suspension and mediation, sublimation and reflection.

Warburg's choice of topic and general performance in this lecture closely resembled what he observed and learned from the Pueblo Indians: for just as they did not seek to "kill the serpent" but rather to live with and through it, he sought not to suppress his fears and obsessions but rather to elaborate them. Warburg deemed this specific lesson crucial not only for his own life but also for humanity at large. It is essential to his entire theory of mythistory—again, of course, in all but name—where, I argue, "ancient mythology" assumed the meaning and role of "serpentine" vitality in mundane historical reality, signifying both killing and healing and, in any case, indispensable to the process of enlightenment. That process, as Warburg would have it, does not consist in liberation *from* myth but rather in liberation *through* myth. As he reflected on the Indians' dance, he sensed that their mythopoeic elaboration of the diabolical snake into a symbolic serpent implied certain important messages to modern Western civilization, which had long before come to deal with its natural causes of fear and obsession in the more drastic measures of suppression and annihilation.

> Our own technological age has no need of the serpent in order to understand and control lightning. Lightning no longer terrifies the city dweller, who no longer craves a benign storm as the only source of water. He has his water supply, and the lightning serpent is diverted straight to the ground

by a lightning conductor. Scientific explanation has disposed of mythological causation . . . Whether this liberation from the mythological view is of
genuine help in providing adequate answers to the enigmas of existence is
quite another matter. (50)

This "matter" was, however, the real issue underlying Warburg's lecture,
and more generally it was the main issue of his entire life and studies. He
acknowledged that "the American government, like the Catholic Church
before it, has brought modern schooling to the Indians with remarkable
energy," so that "the Indian children now go to school in comely suits and
pinafores and no longer believe in pagan demons." This ironical description reveals what Warburg really thought about this whole process of apparent rationalization and civilization: "It may well denote progress. But
I would be loath to assert that it does justice to the Indians who think in
images and to their, let us say, mythologically anchored souls." Warburg
then relates how he sought to prove this critical suspicion by a genial test
he had devised for the Indian children: he told them a German fairy tale
about a storm and asked them to draw a picture of it. Of the fourteen
drawings, twelve depicted the lightning realistically, but two still illustrated
it symbolically in the form of the arrow-tongued serpent—a proof, Warburg thought, that the mythological language, rites, and arts of the tribe
were still visible and viable in organic societies like that of the Pueblo Indians. "We, however, do not want our imagination to fall under the spell
of the primitive beings of the underworld. We want to ascend to the roof
of the worldhouse," to emerge from the "nocturnal depths" to the light of
the sun. Referring to one of his pictures showing "children stand[ing] before a cave," Warburg recalls these famous words and images of the Platonic fable in order to remind us, as did Plato, that the process of liberation from myth must always be through myth (50–51).

During the lecture Warburg pointed out that the "masked dances are
not child's play, but rather the primary pagan mode of answering the largest and most pressing questions of the Why of things" (48). Modern science and technology may answer only questions of the How of things.
The essential Why question of the serpent myths—"Whence come elementary destruction, death, and suffering into the world?"—seems to have
become irrelevant to an age that does not see or seek any symbolic meanings in the world. Warburg's last reflections turn to this new reality:

The American of today is no longer afraid of the rattlesnake. He kills it; in
any case, he does not worship it. It now faces extermination. The lightning

imprisoned in wire—captured electricity—has produced a culture with no use of paganism. What has replaced it? Natural forces are no longer seen in anthropomorphic or biomorphic guise, but rather as infinite waves obedient to the human touch. With these waves, the culture of the machine destroys what the natural sciences, born of myth, so arduously achieved: the space for devotion, which evolved in turn into the space required for reflection. The modern Prometheus and the modern Icarus, Franklin and the Wright brothers, who invented the dirigible airplane, are precisely those ominous destroyers of the sense of distance, who threaten to lead the planet back into chaos. Telegram and telephone destroy the cosmos. Mythical and symbolic thinking strive to form spiritual bonds between humanity and the surrounding world, shaping distance into the space required for devotion and reflection: the distance undone by the instantaneous electric connection. (54)

"The space required for devotion and reflection" lies between the original association of primitive man with natural reality—which Warburg calls *magic*—and the final dissociation of modern man from that reality through *logic*. In the notes that Warburg appended to the draft of the lecture, he wrote: "These images and words are intended as a help for those who come after me in their attempt to achieve insight and thus to dispel the tragic tension between instinctive magic and analytic logic." [13]

Warburg perceived that the apparent opposition between magic and logic in our civilization has created a "tragic tension" that could be, and occasionally has already been, resolved in the *mythic* form of thought, and this understanding informed all his investigations in cultural history, from his doctoral dissertation on Sandro Botticelli's *Birth of Venus* and *Primavera* (published in 1893) to his last published essay before his mental breakdown, *Pagan-Antique Prophecy in Words and Images in the Age of Luther,* which was published in 1920. In that last work, he clarified the basic terms of his perception: "Logic sets a mental space between man and object by applying a conceptual label; magic destroys that space by creating a superstitious—theoretical or practical—association between man and object." [14] Yet in the age of Reformation, as in previous cultural-historical circumstances that Warburg had probed in the age of Renaissance, this distinction seemed to dissolve so as to produce new syntheses—best exemplified in Dürer's *Melancolia I*—of a "mixed constitution," similar to the one that Warburg himself experienced at Bellevue, where both forms of thought prevailed most vividly. "That age [the German Reformation] when logic and magic blossomed, like trope and metaphor, in Jean Paul's words, 'grafted to a single stem,' is inherently timeless: by showing such a polarity in action, the historian of civilization furnishes new grounds for a more profoundly positive critique of a historiography that rests on a purely chronological theory of development."[15]

Warburg's objection to "a historiography that rests on a purely chronological theory of development" aligns him with Nietzsche and other radical *Kulturkritiker* in Germany, from both left and right, who commonly exposed and rejected the liberal assumptions of this progressive ideology of society and civilization. Along with "modernist" reactionaries like Oswald Spengler and Ludwig Klages and revolutionaries like Ernst Bloch or Walter Benjamin, Warburg had come to realize that the process of civilization was both progressive and regressive, that its cultural ages did not display stages in a diachronic motion from "magical" to ever more "logical" forms of life but were rather synchronic combinations—or, in Warburg's term, "schizophrenic conditions"—of both the magical and the logical as they merged in the "mythical." His colleague Ernst Cassirer regarded the mythic as a necessary but temporary and transitory stage in the "chronological development" of man from magic to logic and was therefore utterly shocked to encounter its resurgence in the political ideologies of the twentieth century, but Warburg was ready and willing to find the mythic everywhere. In his last, unfinished project, *Mnemosyne-Atlas*, he sought to exhibit on large screens the evolution and profusion of certain *Urbilder*, the primal mythic images of passion and other human expressions, from the most primitive and ancient sources to modern representations such as daily newspapers. He trusted that these images were powerful enough to evoke the correct impressions and connections. He made the same point in the opening words of his lecture at Bellevue, where he emphasized that in his lecture, as in his original journey to the Indians, he relied on the transparency of experiential impressions, images, and visual memories.[16]

In the notes to the lecture, Warburg wrote: "I did not yet realize that, as a result of my American journey, the organic connection between the art and the religion of 'primitive' peoples would become so clear to me, so that I could see so clearly the identity, or rather the indestructibility of primitive man—who remains the same in all times, so that I could draw him out as an organic entity precisely in the culture of early Renaissance Florence and, later, in the German Reformation."[17] This acute realization of the essential "primitive" identity of man in all times, and the recognition of these "primitive" features in the great cultural creations of early "modern" European civilization to which he had devoted his entire professional (as well as very personal) life, implied that the mythical compulsions he had observed among the Pueblo Indians were still vital in—and to—that civilization. As Fritz Saxl observed, in America "Warburg learned to see European history through the eyes of an anthropologist"[18]—a real and very modern anthropologist indeed, insofar as he did not yield to the delusion of "primitivism" he had encountered in the sentimental fiction of Karl May (of which, as a boy, he was very fond) or among fashionable theorists of archaic authentic *Gemeinschaft* such as Ferdinand Tönnies. He generally dismissed the presumption that the more archaic was more authentic, and in the case of Oraibi society he even dismissed the notion that it was really archaic—for by the time he arrived in the region of the Pueblo Indians, its "Native American foundation" was thoroughly "contaminated" by Spanish Catholic and North American intrusions. "They are clearly no longer primitives dependent on their senses, for whom no action directed toward the future can exist; but neither are they technologically secure Europeans, for whom future events are expected to be organically or mechanically determined. They stand on the middle ground between magic and logic, and their instrument of orientation is the symbol. Between a culture of touch and a culture of thought is the culture of symbolic connection."[19]

As Edgar Wind has shown, Warburg's conception of "symbolic connection" owes much to Theodor Friedrich Vischer's article "The Symbol," which he first read upon its publication in 1887 and continued to read and reflect on again and again.[20] In that essay Vischer defines the symbol as the connection of image and meaning through a point of comparison. He goes on to distinguish between three kinds or levels of symbolic figuration. The first and most basic one is that of magical association, where, as in the case of the Indian identification of the snake with lightning, image and meaning become one and the same thing. The second form of symbolic figuration is that of conceptual signification, wherein the meaning is not perceived directly and naturally from the image but is rather ascribed to or even imposed on it by allegorical or any other logical interpretation. Yet, crucially for Vischer, between these two extremes, which correspond to Warburg's distinction between magic and logic, lies a third type of connection, which Vischer calls a "connection with reservation" and Warburg would redefine as "symbolic connection," the form that constitutes what he really means by mythic. In this case the symbol is understood as a sign and yet remains a living image. Wind explains: "It occurs when the beholder does not really believe in the magical animation of the image, but is nevertheless compelled by it—for instance, when the poet speaks of the 'ominous' light of the setting sun."[21] Since we do not really believe that this metaphorical description is inimical, actually "ominous," it may arouse us to contemplation but not to action, to aesthetic illusion, which occupies the intermediate position between magical excitation and logical examination and, as Nietzsche had shown, is typical—and crucial—to any mythical creation and thereafter to any other artistic representation: "Even the image of the angry Achilles is *only an image* to him whose angry expression he enjoys with the dreamer's pleasure in illusion. Thus, by this mirror of illusion, he is protected against becoming one and fused with his figure." [22] The creation of such "mirrors of illusion" is crucial for the formation of "human reality" over against "natural reality." The employment of symbolic forms such as images, words, myths, or theories that mediate between impression and expression enables human beings to overcome their propensity to instinctual reaction, to construe that inner *Denkraum der Besonnenheit* wherein they can exercise contemplation before—and for—any reasonable action in the world. As Warburg writes in his final reflections on this matter in the introduction to *Mnemosyne-Atlas,* "[t]he conscious creation of distance between the self and the external world may be called the fundamental act of civilization. Where this gap conditions artistic creativity, this awareness of distance can achieve a lasting social function." [23]

Warburg's ability in his Kreuzlingen lecture to perceive his own personal predicament through the general mythical and historical conditions in which men everywhere have always lived implies that Kurt Forster is only half right in his observation that Warburg "wanted to discover the motor forces of historical life, but he could only perceive them in terms of the psychological conflicts that drove him on." [24] It would be more accurate to invert this assertion and say that Warburg came to perceive "the psychological conflicts that drove him on" as motivated by the "motor forces of historical life." Warburg said as much in a statement that he made shortly before his death in April 1929. His comment has all too often been taken to mean exactly the opposite of what he actually said: "Sometimes it looks to me as if, in my role as psycho-historian, I tried to diagnose the schizophrenia of Western civilization from its images in an autobiographical reflex." [25] Warburg admits indeed that his interpretation of Western civilization may have been affected by personal motivations and preoccupations, as any honest historian should say; he makes clear, however, that he diagnosed it "from its images"—a clear indication that he did not impose his own personal vision on history. Throughout his life he was acutely aware of the priority and atrocity of these images in his life, and he always sought to counter them through comprehension of their deepest psychological and historical origins.

More generally, the confrontation between these two forces—that of collective memorial tradition and that of individual self-assertion, which he connoted by the respective Greek terms *mnemosyne* and *sophrosyne*—was for him the most crucial confrontation in his life and in his works. In one way or another, Warburg's major studies all deal with this confrontation—or, to use his term, *Auseinandersetzung*—of individuals with their collective memorial traditions, above all with the mythological tradition of classical antiquity.

This was also the topic of another special lecture, which Warburg delivered on 27 July 1927, this time at his own *Kulturwissenschaftliche Bibliothek* in Hamburg, in the final session of a seminar on Jacob Burckhardt that he conducted at Hamburg University during the summer semester of that year.[26] Unlike the Kreuzlingen lecture, this one has hardly been studied by scholars. And yet, it is my contention that it was in this brief and informal lecture, rather than in any of his major publications, that Warburg revealed his final and most complete judgment on his vocation as a cultural historian of Western civilization. He did so by some bold observations on the lives and achievements of Jacob Burckhardt and Friedrich Nietzsche. I discuss Warburg's story and theory of this *Sternfreundschaft* in greater detail in the final section and conclusion of this chapter. At the moment I am focusing on Warburg's imagery of the two colleagues from Basel. Starting with the assertion that "we must learn to see Burckhardt and Nietzsche as the receivers of mnemic waves and realize that the consciousness of the world affects the two in a very different way," Warburg goes on to describe how both acted as "very sensitive seismographs whose foundations tremble when they must receive and transmit the waves."[27] The key images here reflect Warburg's conviction that the "dialectical engagement" of the modern cultural historian with the mythological tradition ("mnemic waves") of antiquity is largely determined by the historical traditions and conditions ("foundations") of his ethnic identity. In the case of Burckhardt and Nietzsche, he traced their different perceptions of their profession as cultural historians to the respective Latin-Germanic and romantic traditions in which they lived and in which they believed. In his meditations at Bellevue, Warburg had already used the same idioms to describe himself: "But now, in March 1923, in Kreuzlingen, in a sealed institution, where I find myself a seismograph made of pieces of wood stemming from a growth transplanted from the Orient into the nourishing north-German plain while carrying a branch inoculated in Italy, I allow the signals that I have received to be released from me, because in this epoch of chaotic defeat even the weakest one is beholden to strengthen the will to cosmic order."[28] The central images in this self-description allude to the three major cultural traditions in Warburg's life: the Jewish tradition ("a growth transplanted from the Orient"), the Hamburgian tradition ("into the north-German plain"), and the Florentine tradition ("while carrying a branch inoculated in Italy"). In what follows I probe how all of Warburg's three traditions contributed to the making of his identity and how they all "signaled" to him his peculiar mythistorical perception of human reality.

II

"Ebreo di Sangue, Amburghese di Cuore, d'Anima Fiorentino."[29] As befitting an expert on "the art of portraiture," this self-depiction aptly exposes the inner, invisible features of Warburg's physiognomy but also reveals the larger background behind it, allowing us to decipher in that integration of personal identity in natural and cultural reality the deeper structures of meaning in Warburg's life, the historical traditions that form, in Charles Taylor's influential formulation, his "sources of the self."[30]

The question of Warburg's problematic "Jewish identity" has received much attention from scholars.[31] In her reconstruction of Warburg's early life from his letters to his family, Anne Marie Meyer showed how this offspring of the most prominent Jewish family in Hamburg rebelled against its most sacred rules and ways of life.[32] He regarded himself as a "political opponent" of the clerical institutions of Judaism, openly defied its "cultic" rites, and refused to be considered a member of the Jewish community, claiming, "I am dissident."[33] In the first years of World War I, Warburg accentuated his German identity. In his essay on Luther, he praised him as a great liberator of mankind from dogma and superstition and added in a letter that Luther had helped to free him from a Jewish orthodoxy that had tried to enslave him.[34] Toward the end of the war, as anti-Semitic propagandists intensified their attacks on German Jewry and singled out his brother Max as the main enemy of the nation, Aby was consumed by guilt and shame. In October 1918, upon his final collapse into madness, he drew his pupil Carl Georg Heise into a corner in order to make a terrible confession. He said that he had once told a university professor during a conversation, "At the bottom of my soul I am Christian!"—an admission that he now took to be a sin against his family, his people, and God, the reason for all his current punishments.[35] This frightful reaction is not so much atonement as a statement on how Warburg conceived of Judaism—as a magical religion, possessed by vengeful demons and omens. As Felix Gilbert has observed, "[t]he alienation from the Jewish world of his family, and the identification with the social world of the Empire refined his feelings for the survival of residues from earlier times. It increased his perceptivity for the continuation of beliefs of an older culture in a later one." [36]

Against this background Meyer raises the crucial issue: "Exactly what was the relation between Warburg's research on paganism in the Renaissance and his meditations and fears about Judaism (and Jews) remains of course the problem." [37] Apparently that was not the problem for Gombrich, who abhors this kind of "psychoanalytical" examination. However, as Hans Liebeschütz has argued against Gombrich's all-too-"intellectual" biography of Warburg, the personal and the professional are inseparable in this case. [38] He asserts that Warburg's desertion of the Jewish religion for the quintessential German profession of "art history" initiated a "dialectics of assimilation" that was crucial to his development as an "Interpreter of Civilization." For by continuing to see himself as both a "primitive" Jew and a "progressive" German and refusing to choose between the two, Warburg was able to recognize and analyze people who were likewise permanently torn between religious and sacrilegious tendencies. In his works on Renaissance artists and humanists, he singled out those individuals who, like himself, rejected facile reconciliation between the opposite forms of pagan and Christian life and sought rather to maintain both alongside each other, *Nebeneinander,* in what Cusanus hailed as *concordia oppositorum.* In one of his last letters, Warburg confided to the Romanist Karl Vossler that he would not lie down until he had resolved that crucial manifestation in early modern intellectual history, the riddle of the most enigmatic personality that had fascinated him for forty years: Giordano Bruno. [39] Warburg, in his own terms, sought compatibility (*Kompatibilität*) of magic and logic everywhere, in his life as well as in his cultural history, and admired those who achieved it in mythic sublimation. "When conflicting worldviews kindle partisan emotions, setting the members of a society at each other's throats, the social fabric inexorably crumbles; but when those views hold a balance within a single individual—when, instead of destroying each other, they fertilize each other and expand the whole range of the personality—then they are powers that lead to the noblest achievement of civilization. Such was the soil in which the Florentine early Renaissance blossomed." [40] His main tacit argument against his fellow German Jews was that they failed to achieve that sublimation. Living as Jews have always done, in their closed community of belief according to the strict rules of their ancient tribe, impelled by their "partisan emotions," they could not "expand the whole range of the personality" as Aby Warburg, the "dissident," had done. In his study of Warburg's Kreuzlingen lecture, Michael Steinberg has gone so far as to argue that Warburg's observations on the Indians actually refer to the Jews, whom he regarded as equally "primitive," an ancient and "magical" tribe in modern "logical" civilization.[41]

Warburg's *Wahlverwandschaft* to the pagan, Christian, and German traditions clearly affected his conception of Judaism as primarily "magical." Although he never converted, he seems to have adopted, however inadvertently, the common misconception that Christian historians such as Ernest Renan had applied to Judaism—that it was either too magical (in its ritualistic forms) or too logical (in its legalistic norms), but never properly mythical. This misconception is evident also in Warburg's work as a cultural historian of the mythological tradition in Western civilization. Note his remarks on the harsh treatment of the serpent in the Old Testament: whereas the Greek and medieval Christian traditions managed to transform the serpent into a mythical symbol of salvation, the biblical Hebrew tradition remained magical and insisted on its physical destruction. Warburg's library contained many books on Kabbalah and other works of Jewish mythology, but he does not refer to any of them. He was probably unaware of the contemporary theological-historical controversies over the "the essence of Judaism"—whether it was *mythosfrei*, as Leo Baeck and Hermann Cohen claimed, or whether it was as mythical as any other religion or nation. The latter version acquired much credibility during Warburg's lifetime, as a new generation of Jewish scholars, led by Martin Buber, Franz Rosenzweig, and Gershom Scholem rediscovered myth in and for Judaism.

Warburg devoted his life to the study of renaissance. He explored in depth the renaissance of pagan classical antiquity in European civilization after a thousand years of medieval Christian domination. He traveled all the way to New Mexico in order to record the renaissance of Indian pagan antiquity after four centuries of Christian indoctrination and American modernization. Yet he remained utterly impervious to the phenomenal renewal of Judaism in his own lifetime and country, to what Martin Buber in fact described as "Jewish Renaissance," a term that has now become widely used by modern scholars of German Jewry.[42] In his life and works, Warburg was not interested in Judaism but in anti-Semitism.[43] And it was ultimately this seismographic attention to the anti-Semitic waves in Germany that enabled him to emerge as one of the discoverers of what his colleague Ernst Cassirer called "modern political mythology." As George

Mosse points out, the anti-Semitic and other *völkisch* movements in Germany forced Warburg and fellow "German Jews beyond Judaism," such as Freud and Cassirer, to perceive myth in political categories: "Myth was no longer confined to the thought of primitive man but was treated as a present concern, an enemy to be defeated and exorcised."[44] More generally, because Warburg assumed the position of an "outsider [*Außenseiter*]" in German society, he was able to become what Peter Gay called its "insider," namely a critical observer who could perceive in the apparent civility of the Second Reich the brutality of the Third Reich.[45]

Warburg defined his relation to his hometown, Hamburg, in the same metonymic terminology that he used to define his relation to Judaism: the "blood" and the "heart" signify a physiological connection, a belonging based on hereditary rather than voluntary affiliation with either community. Consequently, he turned into a "dissident" burgher in his own city-state, as he was in the Jewish community. In his letters to his mother during his student years in Bonn, he described his life as a "Zwei-Fronten-Krieg," a battle of liberation from both his religious and his bourgeois affinities.[46] Yet, like Warburg's "dialectical engagement" with his Judaism, his *Auseinandersetzung* with Hamburg proved to be very beneficial for his mythistorical project. In an autobiographical note that Warburg wrote in 1927, he mentioned that among the formative influences on his life was his "opposition towards wealth and Frenchifying elegance—Alsterufer," this location being the elegant quarter in Hamburg where he grew up.[47] Warburg expressed his animosity toward the cultural manners and conventions of his hometown already in the little play, *Hamburger Kunstgespräche,* that he wrote for the family's New Year's Eve party of 1896–97. In that play he contrasted the modern art of impressionism with the so-called Hamburg taste in art in order to expose the latter as mere sentimental *Kitsch.* Whereas the older generation in that play rejoices in the banal realism of paintings like *Maternal Bliss,* Warburg's protagonist in the play is a young artist who fights for radical impressionism and admires above all the works of the Swiss painter Böcklin. In his commentary on this play, Gombrich writes: "Clearly in these circles the 'costume picture' . . . was still much in vogue, while the sensuality of Böcklin's nymphs and satyrs who disported themselves in the nude was suspect. For Warburg and his friends Böcklin stood for liberation from philistinism."[48] When Böcklin died in Florence in 1901, Warburg composed a draft report on the funeral, in which he expressed his admiration for Böcklin's artistic achievement: "In our age of traffic, of distance-destroying chaos, he should still be found to stand against the current and forcefully assert the pirate's right of romantic idealism: to evoke through the mythopoeic power of image." [49]

When Warburg wrote these words, he was already contemplating how to exercise his own "pirate's right of romantic idealism." In the summer of 1900, he discussed with his brother and main benefactor, Max, "the idea of a Warburg Library for the Science of Culture," which he hoped to found around his already sizable collection of books on Renaissance mythology and related topics in cultural history.[50] At that point he could not yet make up his mind whether to build it in Florence or in Hamburg. In 1904 he came to the conclusion that if there was to be a Warburg Library, it ought to serve as "an observation post for cultural history in Hamburg." During Warburg's lifetime his native town became a major city: between 1870 and 1914 its population grew from 200,000 to 1,200,000. As a free Hanseatic City, Hamburg had a strong economic foundation and a great civic tradition that had long been safeguarded by a patrician senatorial oligarchy, to which Warburg was closely associated by marriage (his wife, Mary Hertz, was the daughter of a city senator). But it still lacked those qualities of life that were most important to Warburg, artistic and academic institutions. Eventually he resolved to create both in his own fashion, by his own means, through the foundation of the Warburg Library, which he intended to be part of a future Hamburg University. From the moment he resettled in Hamburg, Warburg was one of the main advocates of the university, and after its foundation in 1921, he continued to serve it as a curator, a benefactor, and a *Honorarprofessor*.[51] His letters and early plans for the library indicate that he intended it to be a public institution, a "transcendental home" for *Kulturwissenschaft* in the widest meaning of this term, where scholars from all humanistic disciplines could gather and work on sources that had once inspired the artists of the Italian Renaissance to revolt against medieval stagnation and could still inspire a modern artist like Böcklin "to evoke through the mythopoeic power of image" a radical transformation of the ethical-aesthetical norms of the "Hamburg taste."

The subsequent development of the library according to these original guidelines attests to the immensity of Warburg's initial conviction. As Fritz Saxl, who served as Warburg's assistant in the library and later succeeded him as director, recalls, "[i]t took some time to realize that his aim was not bibliographical. This was his method of defining the limits and contents of his scholarly world and the experience gained here became decisive in selecting books for the Library." Twenty years later, when the library

contained about fifty thousand volumes, Saxl could still observe: "Warburg's lifelong and often chaotic and desperate struggle to understand the
expressions of the mind, their nature, history, and interrelation, ended
with the creation of a library system which appeared as natural as if it had
been not the result but the starting-point of Warburg's activities."[52] The
acquisition and classification of the books reflect Warburg's plan for a new
science of the "historical psychology of human expression." Starting on
the first floor, with books dealing with primal images (*Bild*), such as those
of the earliest cosmological and astrological fantasies, the collection moves
on to show how the ancient pictorial figurations reappear in the history of
art. It then moves up to the second floor, which contains sources of oral
and literal representation (*Wort*)—languages, literatures, and other scrip-
tural traditions that have made up the classical legacies and libraries of our
civilization. On the third floor of the library, the collection pursues the
transition of these fundamental forms of representation into theoretical
modes of "orientation [*Orientierung*]," such as religion, philosophy, and
the sciences. On the top floor, the fourth, is seen their transformation into
practical modes of "action [*Handlung*]" that recur in social and political
affairs.[53] The guiding principle of the whole arrangement seems to be
mythological in the strict sense of the term: it follows the logic of myth—
and thereby exposes the myth of logic—from its initial creation to its
eventual recognition as such. The placement of books on philosophy next
to astrology, magic, and folklore may be traced back to Aristotle's fundamental assumption on the mythopoeic origination of philosophical
speculation.[54]

During the Weimar years, the library attracted many scholars, who,
inspired by Warburg's personality and work, drew from the mythological
sources he had accumulated new ideas for their own works.[55] Among
them were the art historians Gustav Pauli, Adolph Goldschmidt, Erwin
Panofsky and Edgar Wind; classical philologists like Karl Reinhardt and
Bruno Snell and the medievalists Richard Salomon, Hans Liebeschütz, and
Percy Ernst Schramm; the literary scholars André Jolles, Clemens Lugow-
ski, and Ernst Robert Curtius; Walter Benjamin sought in vain to get into
this *Kreis*.[56] By all accounts, the most prominent fellow of the library in
those years was the philosopher Ernst Cassirer. Fritz Saxl reports that when
Cassirer first came to visit the library in 1920, he was already at work on
his *Philosophy of Symbolic Forms:* "It came as a shock to him, therefore, to
see that a man whom he hardly knew had covered the same ground, not
in writings, but in a complicated library system, which an attentive and

speculative visitor could spontaneously grasp . . . Cassirer became our most assiduous reader. And the first book ever published by the Institute was from Cassirer's pen."[57] Significantly, that book was on myth—*Die Begriffsform im mythischen Denken*.[58] Two years later Cassirer completed in the library the second part of his *Philosophy of Symbolic Forms*, the volume titled *Mythical Thought*, which, on his testimony, had been much enriched by the library's "abundant and almost incomparable material in the field of mythology and general history of religion, and in its arrangement and selection."[59] In June 1926 he published his study *The Individual and the Cosmos in Renaissance Philosophy*, which he dedicated to Warburg on his sixtieth birthday with these gracious words: "The work I am presenting to you on your sixtieth birthday was to have been a purely personal expression of my deep friendship and devotion. But I could not have completed the work, had I not been able to enjoy the constant stimulation and encouragement of that group of scholars whose intellectual center is your library."[60]

Cassirer's book, along with other studies on the mythological and mystical traditions in the Italian Renaissance that were published by the Warburg Library in those years, attests to the intellectual stimulation that Warburg provided to his fellow scholars. The young theologian Paul Tillich visited the Warburg Library in 1922 and summed up his impressions in a short essay, in which he pointed out that the main aim of this institution was to revise the superficial conception of the Renaissance as an age of modernity, marked by realism and secularism that apparently triggered the religious reaction of the Reformation and the Counter Reformation, and it did so by repossessing its deeper spiritual and intellectual obsessions with antiquity.[61] Warburg's revision began in his doctoral dissertation on the formation of Botticelli's *Birth of Venus* and *Primavera* in the mythological ambience of his fellow humanists in the court of Lorenzo the Magnificent, and it culminated in the great essays on Ghirlandaio's frescoes, wherein he exposed the innermost tribulations of their donors, Florentine merchant bankers like Tornabuoni and Sassetti, who wished to reconcile their pagan and Christian identities. These studies impressed on his fellows a new vision of the Renaissance as an age in which this confrontation between pagan antiquity and Christianity forged a very tenuous modernity, a new cultural identity that was not so much an ascendance or dominance of the logical over the magical but rather a concordance of the two in the mythical. More concretely, Warburg's deep engagement with the humanists in the court of de' Medici instilled in him their belief in *concordia oppositorum*, the pluralistic or "syncretic" ideology of cultural compatibility that inspired Pico's *Oration on the Dignity of Man* and our modern notion of the "humanities,"[62] and it was ultimately this conviction that led him to model the Warburg Library in Hamburg on the Platonic Academy in Florence. Assuming the role of its benefactor and director was the last stage in the self-transformation of a man who was born *Ebreo di Sangue* and *Amburghese di Cuore* into what he really wanted to be in his *Anima*—a *Fiorentino*.

Warburg's decision to build his library in Hamburg was motivated by his conviction that this "free town" of private merchant bankers could achieve, under the patronage of families like the Warburgs, a kind of cultural Renaissance like that of Florence under the Medici. His letters to his brothers show that he envisaged for his family the same glory possessed by the Florentine families of Bardi and Strozzi, Tornabuoni and de' Medici, Rucellai and (Warburg's main example) Francesco Sassetti. Gertrud Bing remarked: "One can almost say that in his works on Florence, Warburg wrote his own *Buddenbrooks*." And like Mann in his novel, Warburg could explore the bourgeois mentality of these families so emphatically and yet so critically because he was a dissident member of their class, of his own family. In his insightful comments on this *Wahlverwandschaft*, Horst Günther calls attention to an uncanny similarity between the picture of the young Warburg brothers in a photograph taken in 1890 and the young de' Medici brothers in Domenico Ghirlandaio's painting of 1485, *The Confirmation of the Order of St. Francis*, on which Warburg wrote one of his seminal and most personal essays, "The Art of Portraiture and the Florentine Bourgeoisie." The portraits in both pictures impart the same basic patrician expressions and visions of life.[63] A closer look at this essay may reveal what Warburg meant by his self-identification as "*d'Anima Fiorentino*."

Warburg's main task in that essay was to elaborate the social meanings and functions of the Florentine "Art of Portraiture." Whereas Burckhardt regarded this art as a prime example of the individualistic and aesthetic tendencies in the Renaissance, Warburg considered it an art that revealed also the most "typical" in an age. "In a living art of portraiture, the motive forces of evolution do not reside solely in the artist; for there is an intimate contact between the portrayer and the portrayed," the latter habitually seeking to conform the personal to the communal.[64] Accordingly, in his study of Ghirlandaio's work in the memorial chapel of Francesco Sassetti in Santa Trinità in Florence, Warburg sought to show how this work evoked the vibrant communal life of all the Florentine characters who partook in its creation—not only the "client" Sassetti and the "executant"

Ghirlandaio, but also those whom both resolved to portray, namely Lorenzo de' Medici and his entourage. Warburg's elation after arduous years of archival research is obvious:

> Florence, the birthplace of modern, confident, urban, mercantile civilization, has not only preserved the images of its dead in unique abundance and with striking vitality: in the hundreds of archival documents that have been read—and in the thousands that have not—the voices of the dead live on. The tone and timbre of those unheard voices can be recreated by the historian who does not shrink from the pious task of restoring the natural connection between word and image. (187)

Turning to Ghirlandaio's painting, Warburg notes that it depicts two narrative scenes: the first and most visible is the nominal one, the historical moment of the confirmation of Saint Francis and his fellow friars by the pope; the second occurs in the foreground, where the Sassetti family and Lorenzo de' Medici are standing. They are ostensibly present at the historical scene but are totally impervious to it: their gazes and attention are directed at a stairway beneath their feet, on which three children and three men are climbing up toward Lorenzo. Warburg duly identifies them, one by one, as Lorenzo's three sons and their teachers, led by Angelo Poliziano. He then devotes his entire essay to analyzing this sudden "intrusion" of the Medici deputation into the solemn ceremony.

The general historical meanings of this painting are clear. Warburg in fact spells them out in a brief preliminary comparison of Ghirlandaio and Giotto, who around 1317 painted the same scene in his decoration for the Bardi chapel in Santa Croce: "whereas Giotto, in his rapt and lapidary simplicity, concentrates on the unsought elevation of a group of unworldly monks to the status of sworn vassals of the Church Militant—Ghirlandaio, armed with all the self-regarding culture of civilized Renaissance man, transforms the legend of the 'eternally poor' into a backdrop for Florence's opulent mercantile aristocracy" (189). Yet these ultimate meanings, significant as they are, are less important to Warburg than the immediate means by which they were attained. "Der liebe Gott steckt im Detail." Warburg often repeated (and may even have invented) this aphorism, and in this study he exemplifies it by his close attention to the features and gestures of his "portraits."

> So eloquent is the mute interaction between Lorenzo and this group that on close consideration one comes to see the "deputation on the stairs" as the artistic and spiritual center of gravity of the entire composition, and

to wish that these lively presences could speak for themselves. Let us try, therefore, to find what these individuals—whose entrance means so much to Francesco Sassetti that he has so remarkably given over the foreground of his picture to them—may have to say. They are quite willing to talk. Only resort to a variety of subsidiary evidence—documents, medals, paintings, and sculptures—and they will begin to tell us all manner of intimate, beguiling, and curious things about the family life of Lorenzo il Magnifico. (193)

Warburg's admiration for Lorenzo is evident in every description of this man "who could pay pious homage to the past, relish the fleeting moment, and look the future shrewdly in the eye, all with equal vigor," "a thoughtful and prescient statesman" as well as a philosopher and poet who "achieved a degree of spiritual self-liberation through artistic creativity" (200). Warburg chides Machiavelli for having failed "to appreciate the lively and unconventional side of Lorenzo's character": "Perhaps the keen eye of that intelligent historian—usually so startlingly unprejudiced—was clouded by the sense of stylistic dignity that he derived from Livy, and above all by the utterly different, ideal political type whose advent he longed to see" (200). Like father, like sons, courtiers, partners, and painter: all of them emerge almost as "magnificent."

It is all the more surprising, then, that in the last paragraphs of his essay, Warburg strikes a different tone, more critical and almost inimical to the "three little princes and their professor—learned in all matters pagan, privy dancing master to the nymphs of Tuscany—together with a witty domestic chaplain and a court balladeer, all ready to launch intermezzo. As soon as they reach the top step, even the cramp space still occupied by Saint Francis, the pope, and the consistory will be taken over as a playground for secular diversions" (203). The fact that even on this occasion of commemorating the "eternally poor," they all appear clad in their most ornate costumes "is no mindless arrogance: these are churchgoers who love life, and whom the Church must accept on their own terms" (189). In one of his most original discoveries, Warburg detected in this exhibition traces of an ancient pagan Etruscan tradition that had become fashionable among Florentine magnates: they commissioned life-size wax effigies of themselves, dressed in their own clothes, to be set up in churches. Even Lorenzo il Magnifico himself, whom Warburg otherwise hails as "a prudent custodian" of the classical tradition, was still bogged down by such ritualistic and materialistic fashions of Florentine society. In the very last lines of the essay, Warburg remarks that the "concentrated assurance of these figures, so filled with individual life—portraits detaching themselves from their ecclesiastical background—carries a distinct reminder of the figures in Northern European territories" (204). In Warburg's vocabulary the "Northern European" type usually signified a degenerate hedonist, a materialist who craved luxurious life and goods *alla franzese* rather than the virtuous life *all' antica*.

Warburg accentuated these tendencies in his studies "Flemish and Florentine Art in Lorenzo de' Medici's Circle around 1480" (1901) and "Flemish Art and the Florentine Early Renaissance" (1902), in which he showed that the great Florentine patrons of art, above all the Medici themselves, were in fact extraordinarily fond of Flemish and other Northern "Gothic" lifestyles. Upon examination of archival records of collections and inventory lists of the Medici, he found out that they preferred to surround themselves with the rich costumes and tapestries of northern manufacturers rather than with the artistic creations of Florentine artists: "in living-rooms and bedrooms, halls and chapels, that is in the rooms where the Medici spent the private hours of their bright and their dark days, and where, next to the fragments of classical statues, one should only expect to see the choicest flowers of native art, one finds instead the artistic products which had come from contemporary Burgundy."[65] In a letter to his brother Paul, he exposed the darker features of these magnificent Medici, their indulgence in "pleasure-loving swells, till Piero was overtaken by gout at an early age and Giovanni died of over-eating." Warburg adds: "Naturally our high-flown art history never takes this impact of manners and conventions into account, though the preference given to an artist of the kind of Benozzo Gozzoli should provide food for thought, if we recall that at the time Castagno and Donatello were at the peak of their powers. Things, in other words, were then as they are now: the amiable compromise was preferred to the sublimely impressive."[66] What, then, was the real *anima Fiorentina* that Warburg craved for himself, and who represented it for him? Clearly, Warburg could not identify with the Medici sons and courtiers, whose secular revolution led to the profanation and degeneration of the Florentine Renaissance. And for all his boundless admiration for Lorenzo il Magnifico, Warburg could not see in that much-too-perfect and all-too-modern man a typical Florentine either: his "largeness of spirit soared beyond the common measure in the range, and above all in the force, of its evolutions."[67] Lorenzo fits (and may well have served as model for) Burckhardt's famous definition of Renaissance Man as the one who "became a spiritual *individual,* and recognized himself as such" after he had discarded the medieval communal categories of personal identity and learned to see the world as it is, beyond the "veil woven of faith, illusion, and childish prepossession, through which the world and history were seen clad in strange hues."[68] Warburg seems to have had this definition in mind when he offered his own definition and actual identification of Renaissance Man:

> The citizen of Medicean Florence united the wholly dissimilar characters of the idealist—whether medievally Christian, or romantically chivalrous, or classically Neoplatonic—and the worldly, practical, pagan Etruscan merchant. Elemental or harmonious in his vitality, this enigmatic creature joyfully accepted every psychic impulse as an extension of his mental range, to be developed and exploited at leisure. He rejected the pedantic straightjacket of "either-or" in every field, not because he failed to appreciate contrasts in all their starkness, but because he considered them to be reconcilable . . . Francesco Sassetti is just such a type of the honest and thoughtful bourgeois living in an age of transition who accepts the new without heroics and without abandoning the old. The portraits on the wall of his chapel reflect his own, indomitable will to live.[69]

In 1902 Warburg still hesitated to accord Sassetti the full attention and distinction that his personality deserved. He acknowledged his role in the production of Domenico Ghirlandaio's work but qualified it: "With his clear and sure sense of the task in hand, Sassetti surely eased Domenico's departure from convention; but the real magical inspiration stemmed not from him but from Lorenzo de' Medici. It is toward Lorenzo that the members of the little deputation ascend, like chthonic spirits rising into their master's presence."[70] But Warburg's intuitive identification with Sassetti compelled him to find out what made this rather unremarkable merchant banker such a great patron of artists and scholars. He thus set out to discover the deeper motivations of Sassetti's "indomitable will to live," those that made him, rather than Lorenzo il Magnifico, the quintessential Renaissance Man, the perfect personification of the *anima Fiorentina*. After several years of arduous work in the Florentine archives, Warburg finally completed the study in Hamburg and published it in 1907 under the title "Francesco Sassetti's Last Injunctions to His Sons."[71]

Warburg's point of departure is a record of Sassetti's life, drawn by his great-grandson in 1600, which revives a controversy that Sassetti had with the Dominican friars of Santa Maria Novella over his wish to decorate the family chapel with paintings in honor of his own namesake and patron saint, Saint Francis. The Dominicans objected to this plan because, as longtime adversaries of the Franciscans, they could not see the patron saint of the rival mendicant order being glorified in their church. Sassetti promptly transferred his patronage to Santa Trinità, where, on his commission,

Ghirlandaio painted the fresco *The Confirmation of the Order of St. Francis*, discussed above, and *Miracle of the Revivification of Saint Francis*. Yet in his last will, Sassetti beseeched his descendants to reassert the family rights and honor in the Santa Maria Novella, a fact that, together with his deep devotion to his patron saint, signaled to Warburg that this man was much more devout than Warburg himself had assumed in his earlier study of his personality. There, we recall, Sassetti's posture alongside Lorenzo de' Medici seemed to be all too secular and utterly disrespectful to the Franciscan ceremony in the background. Warburg now came to reassess that "intrusion" of the Sassetti and their friends into the paintings as a sign of respectful and, above all, fearful devotion: "They are there to commend themselves to the saint's protection" (232). A letter from Marsilio Ficino, commending Sassetti on his devout attention and generous donations to religious institutions, confirms this conclusion. At the same time, in the same religious productions he had commissioned, Sassetti presents himself in the guise of a chivalrous philanthropist-humanist, and in other representations—as in his bust in the Bargello—he even appears as a pagan Roman emperor. Assuming that Sassetti was both a man about the world and a devout Christian, Warburg then seeks to explain why and how he attained this duality in his personality. He finds a crucial clue in Sassetti's letter to his sons, written on 4 April 1488, before Sassetti, by then a sixty-eight-year-old man, embarked on a dangerous business journey to Lyons on the Rhone. Reflecting on the dangers ahead, Sassetti writes to his sons: "Where Fortune intends us to make landfall, I know not, in view of the upheavals and the changes amid which we now find ourselves (may God grant us a safe haven)," and then goes on to tell them that even "if I were to leave you more debts than assets, I want you to live and die in the same state of Fortune" (240).

The evocation of the pagan deity Fortune, who originally was the goddess of windstorm, who rules the fate of maritime merchants and could thus assume the dual meaning that Sassetti induces in his letter of both "chance" and "wealth," indicates for Warburg how Sassetti conceived of the power that ruled his life. The employment of Fortune is "a symbolic illustration of the inner life of the individual" that reveals the immanent duality of Renaissance Man in that age of transition from medieval Christian religiosity to modern Machiavellian virtuosity. "It was characteristic of the early Renaissance to use words and images of a revived antiquity to express, in terms of pagan heroism, the stance of the individual at war with the world": for only a myth like that of Fortune, with its immanent duality of meaning, could enable men like Sassetti or Rucellai, who still trusted in both providence and free will, to resolve, at least in their imagination, the ambivalent predicament in which they lived and believed, to reconcile the "two still compatible forms of the cult of memory, Christian-ascetic and antique-heroic" (240). Warburg thus concludes: "We now feel why the wind goddess, Fortune, came into Francesco Sassetti's mind in the crisis of 1488 as a measure of his own tense energy: for Rucellai and for Sassetti alike, she functions as an iconic formula of reconciliation between the 'medieval' trust in God and the Renaissance trust in self" (242).

Warburg substantiates this interpretation with two other examples from Sassetti's personal expressions of self. The first concerns Sasseti's choice of the family coat of arms, or *impresa,* depicting another ancient elemental deity—a centaur hurling a stone. Warburg shows how in this *impresa* Sassetti evokes the same impression of reconciliation between the pagan-individual and Christian-providential conceptions of life, for the pagan symbol of natural energy is here welded to David's sling (244). Warburg discovers a more explicit expression of this *Weltanschauung* in the two mottoes that Sassetti used in his letters and inscriptions on bookplates: "*A mon pouvoir* [In my power]" and "*Mitia fata mihi* [Fate merciful to me]" (244– 45). Moving then to the Sassetti Chapel in the Santa Trinità and to its decorations, Warburg turns his attention from Ghirlandaio's frescoes, which he dealt with in his earlier essay, to the pagan reliefs underlying them and shows that their death scenes were copied from the Meleager sarcophagus. Warburg thus states and asks: "It is just not possible to suppose that so strong a personality would have admitted this wild, pagan horde to his own Christian tomb out of some purely aesthetic delight in their formal qualities . . . How did Francesco Sassetti attempt to reconcile the pagan histrionics of the sarcophagus with a traditional, medieval view of the world?" (246–47). His answer to this question is the climactic conclusion to the entire essay, to the very notion of Sassetti's—and his own—identity: he reasons that Sassetti consciously used the marble pagan sarcophagus as a "crib for the Christ child and as a manger for the ox and the ass" shown above in Ghirlandaio's *Adoration of the Shepherds* in the alter of the chapel.

> In all good faith, Francesco Sassetti could thus display his Christian piety amid the signs and portents of the Roman world; not because he was at all capable of kneeling in guileless prayer, like one of the shepherds, oblivious of the alien stonework all around, but because he believed that he had laid the unquiet spirits of antiquity to rest by building them into the solid conceptual architecture of medieval Christianity . . . The apparently bizarre incompatibilities between the shepherds' Flemish garb and the panoply of the Roman general, between God and Fortune, between David with his sling

and the centaur, between "*mitia fata mihi*" and "*à mon pouvoir*," between the death of the Saint and the death of Meleager, may therefore be viewed as a whole. This was the organic polarity that existed within the capacious mind of cultivated early Renaissance man: a man who, in an age of transformed self-awareness, strove for a positive balance of his own. (249)

These last words are as much about Warburg himself as they are about Sassetti. His analytic description of Sassetti as a modern man possessed by atavistic obsessions and superstitions is quite clearly self-reflective. Yet this description is much more comprehensive. The attempt to understand the modern Sassetti through the ancient myths that motivated him is a truly modernistic interpretation of Renaissance Man as truly "modern." Whereas Burckhardt and his followers conceived of Renaissance Man as "modern" because he seemed to be so sovereign in his temporal and immoral manners, so imperiously free from all burden of the past, Warburg's description of this man as essentially primitive is redolent of how artists like Conrad, Picasso, and Stravinsky, or human scientists like Freud, Bergson, and Sorel rendered Modern Man in their works.[72] In the next section I show how Warburg developed his new, distinctly "modern," conception of the Renaissance through "dialectical engagement" with Burckhardt and Nietzsche.

III

Ever since the publication of Burckhardt's *Civilization of the Renaissance in Italy* in 1860, his very notion and characterization of the "Italian Renaissance" as the beginning of the modern age have stimulated generations of cultural and art historians to test the validity of this image against new discoveries and theories. This was especially so during Warburg's formative years as a student and young scholar around the turn of the century, when the image of the Renaissance generated a whole new fashion of life in aristocratic and upper-middle-class circles. For the masses of European and American visitors who flocked into the Italian towns turned the "Italian Renaissance" into a general cultural code for a life of beauty, liberty, and modernity. E. M. Forster's novel *A Room with a View*, published in 1908, neatly evoked the spiritual pretensions of these secular pilgrims. Among them were also fashionable scholars, most notably Bernard Berenson, whom Warburg met and disliked, dismissing him along with other "connoisseurs" and "professional admirers" as "hero-worshippers" who sought self-realization through idealization and emulation of "Renaissance Man."[73] In his essay "The Problem of the Renaissance" of 1920, the Dutch historian Johan Huizinga showed how this "heroic" image evolved from Burckhardt's original conception and description of Renaissance Men as "absolute villains":

> Burckhardt had summoned the man of the Renaissance before the face of time like one of those magnificent sinners from the *Inferno*, demonic in his unbending pride, self-satisfied and audacious, the *uomo singolare*, the "unique man." This was the only figure from his book which captured the fancy of the dilettantes. The concept of "Renaissance Man" became associated with notions of impetuous acceptance and domination of life . . . None of this was Burckhardt's fault. The melody he had sung a later generation had orchestrated à la Nietzsche, who, as is known, was a disciple of Burckhardt.[74]

Although Warburg spared Burckhardt from his wayward followers and was particularly allergic to the *Heroenverehrer* who vulgarized his legacy, he hinted that Burckhardt's celebration of Renaissance artists as "morally heroic," even if "reconstructed on historical foundations," was bound to produce a "parody [*Affe*]" like Gobineau.[75] Warburg used to mock this typical visitor to Italy—himself included—as "the Northern superman on his Easter holiday [who wishes] to experience the divinely pagan freedom of the Renaissance individual."[76]

Warburg learned to distrust this heroic image of Renaissance Man early on from one of his teachers at the University of Bonn, the theological scholar Henry Thode. In 1885 Thode published *Francis of Assisi and the Beginnings of Renaissance Art in Italy*, in which he sought to invert the common Burckhardtian equation of the Renaissance with modern secularity by relating it to medieval religiosity.[77] Thode's main argument was that the inspiration for the realism and artistic innovation of painters like Giotto in the early fourteenth century stemmed not from the rediscovery of pagan antiquity, as Burckhardt had taught, but rather from the influential theories and activities of Saint Francis, who redirected the attention of his contemporaries to human and natural affairs in this world. In the European fin de siècle, this antimodernistic conception of the Renaissance became more acceptable, even fashionable. It appealed to the "spirit of the age," with all its notions and prognostications of "degeneration" into modernity. Its most effective promoters were John Ruskin, Walter Pater, and other aesthetes who managed to forge, against their own "material" bourgeois society, "spiritual" Gothic and Renaissance realities. Their decadent fellow travelers and art-lovers, the Pre-Raphaelites, were particularly enchanted by those poetic-pietistic artists—Giotto, Fra Angelico, and Botticelli—who preceded the age of prosaic realists such as the Borgia and Medici popes, Machiavelli, and their kindred modernist Michelangelo and were thus still able to indulge in all kinds of ethereal visions and pleasures, as their modern admirers did. Warburg often scorned the "modern languid art-lover who has gone to Italy to refresh himself" in spiritual exercises of that kind: "Ruskin's word of command sends him to the cloisters, to a mediocre Giottesque fresco, where he must discover his own primitive mentality in the charming, unspoiled and uncomplicated Trecento work."[78] Warburg rejected all the neoromantic attempts to create a new, very idyllic conception of the Middle Ages and to impose it on the Renaissance. Although he ultimately came to acknowledge that the Renaissance was much more medieval than Burckhardt had assumed, he perceived the Middle Ages in the old pejorative terms as a "dark" era of repression and superstition. In the controversy between Burckhardt and the revisionists, he remained loyal to Burckhardt's original conception of the Renaissance as emancipation from the Middle Ages. Yet since Warburg enhanced the inner difficulties and complexities of this movement, the "daemonic" compulsions in the regeneration of pagan antiquity, his conception of the Renaissance turned out to be more critical, dialectical, and radical than Burckhardt's own rather mild conception.

Warburg's main contention against Burckhardt's followers and adversaries, and ultimately against the master himself, was that they all failed to account for what the Renaissance had really meant to those who performed it. Few, if any, of the many commentators on Burckhardt's book bothered to elaborate the questions concerning this phenomenal confrontation of the modern Christians with pagan antiquity: What did antiquity mean to them? What did they actually discover in it? How were they affected by what they discovered? And above all, why were they, as we still are, so entranced by the images and tales of classical mythology? Burckhardt himself did not help to clarify this problem. Although he virtually created the modern notion of renaissance, Burckhardt was never entirely satisfied with its fashionable meanings and came to regret the undue attention that readers had given to this particular notion in his book, where, he reminded them, it was introduced only in the third section, following the discussion of topics that he considered more significant for the cultural development of modern civilization then and there—such as the political conditions in the Italian city-states and the new moral and cultural concessions for abrasive individualism. Burckhardt stated in the introduction to that section of *The Civilization of the Renaissance in Italy:* "We must insist, as one of the chief propositions of this book, that it was not the survival of antiquity alone, but its union with the genius of the Italian people, which achieved the conquest of the western world."[79] For Burckhardt, then, the notion of renaissance of classical antiquity was important only as one mode among others by which the Italians became modern. He was not interested in the ancient images and tales as such, but only as sources that the Italians had consciously employed in order to express their modern desires, interests, and views. He disregarded both the old romantic and the new scientific mythology. In one of his letters, he passed this judgment on the mythological studies of Johann Jakob Bachofen: "Have you seen Bachofen's book? I have seen it but have not yet read it, because as soon as I began 'my mind drained away.' I am not at all fit to be an explorer of myths or anything like it and have no right to opinion in this matter."[80] Consequently, he did not explore the deeper psychological and historical reasons for the phenomenal reanimation of pagan mythology in Renaissance life and art. This was to be Warburg's task.

Aby Warburg hardly mentioned Burckhardt's name in his writings. Yet it is significant that his two closest companions and collaborators, Fritz Saxl and Gertrud Bing, saw fit to emphasize the seminal importance of Burckhardt's *Civilization of the Renaissance in Italy* for Warburg's life and works. According to Saxl, since his student days Warburg had loved, admired, and read this book more than any other book.[81] In a letter that Aby Warburg sent to his brother Max in 1900, asking, as usual, to increase the family's subsidy for his work ("we should demonstrate by our example that capitalism is also capable of intellectual achievements"), he clinched his arguments with these words: "If one day my book is mentioned in connection with and as a complement to Jacob Burckhardt's *Civilization of the Renaissance in Italy,* this will be the compensation for what I and you have done."[82] Two years later, in the opening lines of the prefatory note to his essay "The Art of Portraiture and the Florentine Bourgeoisie," he stated: "With all the authority of genius, that model pioneer, Jacob Burckhardt, dominated the field that he himself had opened up for scholarship: that of Italian Renaissance civilization. But it was not in his nature to be an autocratic exploiter of the land he had discovered . . . If he could only sow the seeds undisturbed, then anyone might garner the harvest." Warburg did so in his own essay, which he dubbed "a supplement" to Burckhardt's essay "The Portrait." Throughout his life he held onto this conviction: "Our perception of the greatness of Jacob Burckhardt must not deter us from following in his footsteps."[83]

Nonetheless, as Bing remarks in her admirable assessment of this case,

Warburg was not a servile follower of Burckhardt. "He did not follow him in his presentation of the state as a Work of Art and in the course of time he was to modify profoundly Burckhardt's view of the Development of the Individual. But certain themes to which Burckhardt had drawn attention became Warburg's fields of exploration: Italian festivals, Florentine relations with Burgundy, and, of course, the rediscovery of Classical Antiquity."[84] Above all, Bing continues, Warburg adhered to Burckhardt's historical methodology of gathering facts from all types of sources for his vivid depiction of the Italian Renaissance. In so doing he adopted "one of Burckhardt's leading terms: Life. As a descriptive term for an object it is ill defined and neither of the two men explains what he understood by it. Its value to them was that it circumscribed the historian's task. It was a reminder that in dealing with the past the historian is faced with a reality as burning and as bewildering to those who lived through it as our own is to us."[85] This is an important observation, but it obscures the fact that on a more fundamental level, Warburg did not adhere to Burckhardt's conception of "Life": whereas Burckhardt aspired in his life and in his historical studies to attain the "aesthetic" life, Warburg sought the "ecstatic" life, "das bewegte Leben," life in motion, life moved by deep emotion.

Warburg's critical engagement with Burckhardt's idealistic conception of the Renaissance had begun in his doctoral dissertation, which he completed in 1892 and published a year later under the title "Sandro Botticelli's *Birth of Venus* and *Spring:* An Examination of Concepts of Antiquity in the Italian Early Renaissance.[86] In the prefatory note to his study, Warburg announces his aim "to adduce . . . the analogous ideas that appear in contemporary art theory and poetic literature, and thus to exemplify what it was about antiquity that 'interested' the artists of the Quattrocento." His main discovery was that "the artists and their advisers recognized 'the antique' as a model that demanded an intensification of outward movement."[87] Concentrating on Botticelli's mythologies, he argued that what the Florentine painter looked for, found, and copied from antiquity were not forms of "noble simplicity and quiet grandeur," the qualities that Winckelmann had ordained as essential for the "classical," but rather models of dynamic and dramatic movements.[88] Further investigations into other cultural activities in late-fifteenth-century Florence revealed that Botticelli's vibrant representation of ancient mythology was common among his contemporaries and moreover that they were indeed able, as Burckhardt had suggested, to revive it in their festive ceremonies.

The detection of some remarkable similarities between Botticelli's two paintings and Poliziano's poem *Giostra* enabled Warburg to identify the

real occasion for both artistic creations: the tournament that Giuliano de'
Medici organized in 1475 in honor of the fair Simonetta Cattaneo, the
young wife of Marco Vespucci, who was widely admired as *La Bella* of
Florence. The glorification of Simonetta as the Princess of Beauty in that
celebration turned into deification after her sudden death in the spring of
1476. Her ritual commemoration may have inspired Botticelli to depict
her as the Goddess of Spring in floral attire, who holds Venus's cloak in
Birth of Venus and who receives Venus and her court upon their ceremonial return to the City of Flowers in *Primavera*. Warburg surmises that she
also inspired Botticelli's ideal profile of the *innamorata*. The identification
of Botticelli's mythical goddess with the historical Simonetta has been criticized by Gombrich and other scholars as a "romantic myth."[89] But, as
Charles Dempsey has argued, in this case, as in the analogous cases of
Dante's Beatrice and Petrarch's Laura, Simonetta "or someone very much
like her" must have been a "true poetic myth," for the aesthetic and erotic
conventions of the time required that the ideal images of Beauty and Love
should appear through real personages.[90] In any case, Warburg harked back
to the figure of "La Bella Simonetta" because to her contemporaries (as
well as to Warburg himself) she appeared to have been a "fair Nymph," a
real manifestation of that singular image from classical antiquity—a young
maiden with flowing hair and garments—that epitomized the "pagan
spirit" of the age.

Warburg's attention to the concrete cultural-historical traditions and
conditions in which Botticelli's mythologies germinated is as much ideological as it is methodological: he consciously used this kind of "historicism" in order to rebut the "aestheticism" of Botticelli's "sentimental" admirers. This was the first of many attacks on the "prevailing aestheticism"
in art history.[91] According to Warburg, Botticelli indeed tended to indulge
in "tranquil moods that gave his human figures the dreamy, passive beauty
that is still admired as the especial mark of his creations," and this tendency
was visible in the elegant position and facial expression of Venus in both
paintings.[92] Yet, once Warburg turned his attention from features to gestures, to motions like dancing or running around, and above all to what he
called "accessories in motion [*bewegte Beiwerke*]," namely, to swirling winds
and to motions that were "unmotivated by any bodily movement"—
whether flowing locks of hair or wind-blown draperies—a whole new
impression emerged (95–104). For these accessories were "affective signs"
of psychological (rather than physiological) ag\itation. Assuming that Botticelli "turned to antique sources whenever accessory forms—those of
garments and hair—were to be represented in motion" (89), Warburg duly

noted that already Botticelli's contemporary, the art theorist Leon Battista Alberti, had described and recommended these "accessories" in his treatise *On Painting* (1435) as classical artistic conventions for the evocation of intense emotions and passions. Angelo Poliziano, who served as the humanistic adviser in the Medici court, where Botticelli worked, was likewise fond of Roman images of storms, of intensified movement, and of unbridled experiences, which he used in his own poetic and dramatic works. According to Warburg, Poliziano's *Orfeo* was "the first attempt to confront an Italian audience with flesh-and-blood characters from classical antiquity," and his depiction of the vengeful furies, the Maenads, is visible in many pictorial representations of the nymphs (121–25). Warburg concludes that it must have been Poliziano who forced Botticelli—who, like so many other Renaissance artists, was a "weak person" and "all too pliable"—to recognize these darker aspects of the human psyche and "to show human figures in a state of excitement, or even of inner emotion" (141).

Late in his life, Warburg sought to reassess Burckhardt's contribution to the study of the Renaissance from slightly different perspectives, to ask, as it were, not what life meant for his history but rather what history meant for his life. This formulation recalls, of course, the terms by which Burckhardt's colleague from Basel, Friedrich Nietzsche, sought to revise the historical lessons of his "great teacher": "Does anybody at last understand, will anybody understand what the renaissance was? The transvaluation of Christian values, the attempt undertaken with all means, all instincts and all genius to make the opposite values, the noble values triumph." [93] Nietzsche believed that this was one of those "truths" that Burckhardt had discovered yet sought "to conceal," like any other subject that "fringes on the problematical." [94] Warburg knew and often referred to these words, most conspicuously so in his address to the participants in his seminar on Jacob Burckhardt. In these final reflections on Burckhardt's life and achievements, Warburg judged him against Nietzsche, and, moreover, he did so by Nietzsche's terms and standards. He thus came to see that Burckhardt's reluctance to immerse himself in pagan mythology betrayed his acute perception of what it might reveal about man, life, and art in the civilization of the Renaissance: "The art of pageantry was discovered by him [Burckhardt] and it compelled him to respond to a slice of untamed life that had not existed before and that he was really afraid to present." [95]

"Warburg was no more a Nietzschean than he was a Freudian." Gombrich's assertion stands even if, as usual, it attests as much to Gombrich's own Popperian aversion to all "irrational" doctrines. As Gombrich notes,

Warburg opposed the Nietzschean vision of the Renaissance, which de-
generated scholarship into worship and produced that most ignominious
"type of tourist"—"the superman on Easter holiday with *Zarathustra* in the
pocket of his tweed cape, seeking fresh courage from its mad cascadings
for his struggle for life, even for political authority."[96] Yet even Gombrich
acknowledges that, quite apart from Warburg's disparaging comments on
the historical methodology in Nietzsche's *Birth of Tragedy,* "few students of
art at the turn of the century could remain uninfluenced by that seminal
book."[97] Warburg became acquainted with the main psychological and
anthropological assumptions of Nietzsche's existential conception of myth
through the teaching of the great scholar of antiquity Hermann Usener.
He attended Usener's course on mythology at the University of Bonn in
the winter term of 1886-87 and was enchanted by his assertion that the ancient deities were primarily imaginative projections (*Vorstellungen*) of natural anxieties onto supernatural entities. On these assumptions Usener
instructed how to deduce the original intentions and functions of these
myths from their names. He indicated that these intentions and functions
still permeated "our own religion": "All study of myth, unless it is no more
than a game, will ultimately bring us back, in spite of ourselves, to what
most intimately concerns us—our own religion—and will further our understanding of it."[98] As noted above, in those formative years, Warburg was
much impressed by the psychological theories of Nietzsche's colleagues in
Basel, Friedrich Vischer and his son Robert. Later on Warburg read Erwin
Rohde, another "professor in Basel," whose influential *Psyche: The Cult of
Souls and Belief in Immortality among the Greeks* (first published in 1894) syn-
thesized the theories of both Nietzsche and Usener to portray the "Olympian" Greeks as ecstatic and cultic primitives. Hence, even if, as in the case
of Burckhardt, there is hardly a reference to Nietzsche in Warburg's publications, there is much evidence in his diaries, letters, and lectures that
shows that his preoccupation with Nietzsche's "Dionysian" conception of
antiquity was pervasive and endured till the very last phase of his work on
Mnemosyne-Atlas.[99]

Warburg was profoundly impressed—though not convinced—by
Nietzsche's theory concerning the mythical-musical origin of Greek tragedy and its potential modern revivification in Wagner's mythical-musical
drama. His critical engagement with that theory is evident in his early essay "The Theatrical Costumes for the Intermedi of 1589," which he published in 1895 and then continued to revise upon further readings of
Nietzsche's book in 1905.[100] His description of the aesthetic (and rather
pathetic) attempts of Florentines in the age of the baroque to revive the

classical myth in their own fashion is redolent of Nietzsche's critical attack on liberal "bourgeois" attempts in his time (like those of David Friedrich Strauss's *Das Leben Jesu*) to reconcile the ancient primitive mythology with modern theology or philology. And as in Nietzsche's book, where the rebirth of tragedy in modern civilization required a resurrection of pagan mythology, as in Wagner's music-dramas, Warburg realized that the rebirth of humanism in the civilization of the Renaissance in Italy required a break into—and of—that ancient source of expression.

Already in his doctoral dissertation, Warburg discerned that crucial breakage in the "bourgeois" mentality of Florentine society in a singular pictorial representation: the "fair Nymph." Why were so many prominent Florentine artists—Botticelli, Ghirlandaio, Filippo Lippi, Leonardo, and Michelangelo—attracted to this character of a young maiden with flowing hair and garments? What did she mean to the patrons who commissioned her depiction in their palaces and chapels? Around 1900 Warburg began to investigate a particular representation of that *nympha* in Ghirlandaio's frescoes *Birth of St. John the Baptist* and *The Sacrifice of Zacharias* in the Tornabuoni Chapel in Santa Maria Novella. Each painting depicts a feminine figure—a servant girl and an angel, respectively—wearing light sandals and a billowing veil rushing into a solemn religious ceremony. Warburg expressed his thoughts in the form of a fictitious correspondence with his friend, the Dutch scholar André Jolles. In his masterful reconstruction of this correspondence, Gombrich calls attention to the meaning of this erotic figure in the social imagination of an age that had seen in women like Isadora Duncan the embodiment of passion. The erotic sensuality of Ghirlandaio's nymph certainly enticed Jolles to imagine himself as her "lover." But Warburg was more concerned with the cultural meanings and implications of that figure for Giovanni Tornabuoni and his family: why did these people, who were all "patrician churchgoers, with innately impeccable manners," permit this tempestuous maiden to break into their virtuous company? Warburg's answer to this question is that the sudden appearance of this nymph in this setting represents the eruption of primitive pagan emotion into the decorum of Christian convention. He writes to Jolles: "The fact that your pagan stormy petrel is permitted to rush into this slow-moving respectability of subdued Christianity reveals to me the enigmatic and illogical aspects of the Tornabuoni in their primitive humanity." [101] Mindful that "a conscious profanation was surely far from the mind of Giovanni Tornabuoni and Domenico Ghirlandaio," Warburg assumes that their decision to introduce the nymph into their chapel signifies the emergence of the new civil convention of compatibility in Florentine society, a realization that an admission of pagan passion into Christian life is both respectful and useful, because it restores the classical ideal of virtuous life, *das bewegte Leben* of passion and action that energetic men like Tornabuoni found congenial to their own *vita nuova* and very *activa*. The symbol of the nymph enabled them to reconcile pagan intensity with Christian piety. "Exuberant vitality, the awareness of a germinating, creative will-to-life, and an unspoken, maybe an unconscious opposition to the strict discipline of the Church . . . demand an outlet for their accumulated pent-up energy in the form of expressive movement."[102] The nymph is a pictorial representation of that conviction, a mythic resolution of the tension between magic and logic in the life and times of a Florentine burgher and his modern observer. "Who, then, is the 'Nympha'? As a real being of flesh and blood she may have been a freed slave from Tartary . . . but in her true essence she is an elemental sprite, a pagan goddess in exile."[103]

Several years later Warburg invoked this pagan goddess again in his essay on Francesco Sassetti, where she reappears as Fortuna. In late-fifteenth-century Florence, this goddess was primarily a "symbol of energy in the antique vein [*antikisierendes Energiesymbol*]" that could, and did, invoke different reactions and interpretations—wisdom in Ficino, self-assertion in Rucellai, and submission in Sassetti. They all reverted to this ancient pagan image precisely because it was a "symbolic illustration of the inner life of the individual," a mythic rather than a rationalistic resolution to the insoluble mystery of human life, which Rucellai expressed in his "momentous question: 'Have human reason and practical intelligence any power against the accidents of fate, against Fortune?'"[104] Unable to find an adequate answer in the great philosophers of antiquity, Aristotle, Boethius, or Seneca, or in those of modernity (Ficino), Rucellai harked back to the symbolic-heraldic meanings of the goddess Fortuna, which are signified by the three connotations of the Latin word *Fortuna*—"chance," "wealth," and "storm wind." "To him, as a merchant venturer, these three distinct meanings were the attributes of a single being: Storm-Fortune, whose uncanny ability to switch from daemon of destruction to bountiful goddess fostered the atavistic image of her single, anthropomorphic, mythical identity."[105]

Clearly, then, whatever Warburg may have thought of Nietzsche's scholarship, he was aware that it had radically changed the common perceptions of classical antiquity. In 1908 he thus opined: "Every age can see only those Olympic symbols which it can recognize and bear through the development of its own inner visual organs. We, for instance, were taught by Nietzsche a vision of Dionysius." [106] Following Nietzsche, he realized that ancient mythology could no longer be perceived as an *Existenzbild* with the idealistic and rather romantic meanings that Burckhardt ascribed to it when he mused about that "wonderful vision" that "illuminated the whole of the present for the Greeks . . . and essentially presented a sublime reflection of the perceptions and the life of the nation itself." Rather, as Nietzsche saw, it was a projection of deeper nihilistic emotions into aesthetic perceptions of reality that enabled the Greeks "not to die of the truth" (of the mortality and futility of all human endeavors) and might still enable us (as Wittgenstein would put it) to experience these "dark and sinister" impressions "in our own inner selves." As elemental existential expressions of psychic energy, the ancient pagan myths were essentially neutral, "beyond good and evil," like the tradition that carried them on, and their appropriation depended on the interpretation that later generations and individual persons gave them.

This new perception into the atavistic and agonistic psychic energies that empower the "mythological tradition" in modern civilization enabled Warburg to invert Burckhardt's basic notion and interpretation of the renaissance as a reappropriation of the ancient by the modern. He perceived it rather as a reappropriation of the modern by the ancient, because he considered the revivification of primitive emotions through ancient images and tales to have been so powerful that it rendered this entire process of renaissance much more sensational, impersonal, and irrational than Burckhardt had portrayed it. Whereas Burckhardt appraised the great humanists and artists of the Renaissance as creators of our modern cultural tradition, Warburg came to see them rather as mediators of a very ancient tradition. Against the immensity of this tradition, the individual "makers" of the Italian Renaissance appeared not so important, or at least not so potent, as Burckhardt had made them to be. Curiously, for a historian of art, Warburg did not even regard the great artists as the real harbingers of the Renaissance. All too often, he noted, the artists were "weak personalities" and conformists who just worked out what their humanist advisers instructed them to do in accordance with the standard *Pathosformeln* of their professional guidebooks. Warburg was particularly fascinated by the psychological process of "dynamic inversion" of the orgiastic ecstasies of ancient pagan mythology into the pietistic amenities of Christian theology. He could thus trace how the famous legend of Trajan's clemency to a widow who asked and received justice from the emperor on his way to war grew out of Christian attempts to accommodate a relief in the Arch of Constantine in Rome, which depicts the gruesome scene of Trajan and his soldiers massacring their barbarian enemies. The "dynamic inversion," not suppression, of the original energy of pagan agitation in this Christian rehabilitation ensured that its pictorial expressions could still empower later artists like Ghirlandaio and Raphael to re-create the scene in new guises, thereby renewing, however inadvertently, the myths of pagan antiquity in modernity.[107] Ghirlandaio introduced the triumphal Arch of Constantine into the background of his *Adoration of the Shepherds* in the Sassetti Chapel at Santa Trinità and several years later copied its combative motifs into *Massacre of the Holy Innocents* in the Tornabuoni Chapel, assuming, as did his patron Sassetti, that he thereby managed to reconcile Roman and Christian virtues. "In all good faith, Francesco Sassetti . . . believed that he had laid the unquiet spirits of antiquity to rest by building them into the solid conceptual architecture of medieval Christianity. He was not to guess— before the advent of Savonarola—just how critical a test this optimistic attempt to absorb and enlist antiquity would prove to be."[108] As much as he admired Sassetti, in this case Warburg was inclined to admit that Savonarola knew better: the revivification of ancient pagan mythology was dangerous, and ultimately disastrous, to Christianity. On this matter Warburg sided with Nietzsche, against Burckhardt.

The crucial difference between Warburg and Burckhardt lies, then, in their antithetical conceptions of "tradition": Burckhardt, always loyal (as he prided himself) to his "conservative convictions," appraised "tradition" in the common "classical" categories of *Bildung* as one "great spiritual continuity [*grosses geistiges Kontinuum*]" on which events and people are borne along, "guarded by time-honored myths"—and here we may recall the idle impression of the Platonic Academy in Florence that Burckhardt evokes in the very last lines of *The Civilization of the Renaissance in Italy* as a medium wherein "echoes of mediaeval mysticism here flow into one current with Platonic doctrines, and with a characteristically modern spirit"; Warburg, in contrast, held to a Nietzschean, agonistic conception of "tradition." His early confrontation with the ritual commandments of his own Jewish tradition—keeping kosher meals, reciting Kaddish at his father's burial, the prohibition against marriage with gentiles, all of which he had violated—alerted him to the racial and other primitive superstitions that always lurk in that and any other tradition that pretends to convey a continuous and homogeneous message from antiquity to modernity. His later historical investigations into the origins and transformations of European civilization showed that its Christian tradition was equally prone to irrational fixations, even though, in his view, it was ultimately more successful than Judaism in the sublimation of such atavistic tendencies as blood sacrifice into the sacramental rite of the Eucharist. This acute attention to the essential tension between magic and logic in his own Jewish–Christian tradition enabled Warburg to discern the signs of disruption that the fusion of antagonistic psychic orientations and religions— Dionysian and Apollonian, pagan and Christian—brought into the "classical tradition." These signs—flowing hair and draperies in Botticelli's mythological paintings, the sudden appearance of a maiden in windblown diaphanous garb among respectable Florentine citizens in Ghirlandaio's frescoes in the Tornabuoni Chapel in Santa Maria Novella, the evocation of the Roman goddess Fortuna in the letters and family emblems of Sassetti and Rucellai—were all expressions of cultural contradictions, proofs that the ancient pagan compulsions were still vibrant after many centuries of clerical or "classical" attempts to repress them.

Evidently, around 1908 Warburg became thoroughly disenchanted with all the "heroic" conceptions of the Renaissance. Since his studies of the Flemish infiltration into Florentine life and art in the early 1900s, he had had reservations about the Burckhardtian contradistinction between the Renaissance south and the Gothic north. In a lecture in Berlin in 1901, "Flemish and Florentine Art in Lorenzo de' Medici's Circle around 1480," he criticized this—then still his own—tendency: "For we are reluctant to acknowledge how mediaeval the man of the renaissance really was, the man whom we salute as superman, the liberator of the individual from the dark prisons of the Church."[109] By 1908, in his lecture "The Gods of Antiquity and the Early Renaissance in Southern and Northern Europe," he was much more categorical:

We are used to regarding the new forms of the High Renaissance as the unsought by-product of the spontaneous revolution, which began when the artistic genius woke up to the awareness of his own personality. It is believed that such geniuses proudly ignored the mediaeval past which was to them a dark, Gothic age when the ancient gods were no more than a crowd of demons dwelling in forbidden obscurity. And yet the Middle Ages had followed late antique traditions and had perfectly preserved the memory of the ancient gods in its literary and artistic forms . . . I am confident that reflective and trained historians will not feel that I have spoiled their pleasure and deprived them of their faith in the achievements of the early Renaissance if I try to prove to them that that age first had to liberate the serene Olympians from scholastic and non-visual erudition and heraldically rigid astrological manuals in a deliberate and difficult struggle with a fossilized late ancient tradition (which we wrongly call medieval).[110]

Reflecting on this programmatic declaration and its later ramifications, Gombrich concludes: "The year 1908 proved in fact a turning-point in Warburg's life."[111] From that year on and to the end of his life, Warburg sought to describe this fateful struggle of liberation of "the serene Olympians" from the ancient-medieval magical and astrological traditions that made them so frightful. Even as he recognized the powerful role of astrology in the transmission of classical mythology into Renaissance art, he deplored the "baneful" exploitation of its Olympian deities in this oldest "form of onomastic fetishism." He duly saw that the transformation of these classic symbols of humanity and beauty into forces of fatality has always served magicians and other politicians to stupefy the ignorant masses.

The "curious rebirth" of this ancient primitive superstition in the early modern age of enlightenment alerted Warburg to the modern political meanings of ancient classical mythology, to its demonological potentialities in religious controversies and in nationalistic and anti-Semitic ideologies. In 1913 he carried on a fervent campaign against some astrological swindlers in Hamburg.[112] His diaries, letters, and public lectures, such as the one that he gave at the Tenth International Congress of Art History in Rome in October 1912 ("Italian Art and International Astrology in the Palazzo Schifanoia"), reveal his acute awareness of the magical and astrological superstitions that were rising in those last years of European civilization and were soon to engulf it once the war broke out.[113] After centuries of "classical" European civilization, the ancient demons that seemed to have been defeated by the forces of enlightenment suddenly reappeared to drag modern nations into the sacrificial rites of World War I.

Warburg himself eventually succumbed to these demons. Locked in his room in Bellevue, he formed a cult around the night flies that were buzzing around; trusting them to be his only "soul mates" in that world, he would spend whole nights talking to them. In his delusions he believed that the cries in the clinic's hallway were his wife's cries under torture and that the meat served at supper was his children's flesh. As William Heckscher has observed, Warburg's "study of mythological types in the service of Astrology affected his entire personality and did so, finally, to the detriment of his psychological balance . . . Victimized by his madness, he seems to have identified himself with Kronos."[114] The philosopher Ernst Cassirer, who visited Warburg at Bellevue in January 1924, later reported that Warburg had confessed to him that "the demons, whose sway in the history of mankind he had tried to explore, had taken their revenge by seizing him, and were finally about to overcome and destroy him."[115]

Ernst Gombrich seems to have had this melodramatic version in mind when he inveighed that "the inferno into which [Warburg] descended should not be romanticized."[116] Gombrich notes that Warburg's diaries during his illness "hardly sustain the legend which has grown up that the patient's main preoccupations at the time were connected with his past researches into demonology and superstition."[117] As Gombrich would have it, Warburg was and remained even during his illness an agent of enlightenment, a scholar who did not really believe, and therefore could not actually live, in a world of demons. And yet, as Edgar Wind has argued, the circumstances in this case are more complicated because "the 'legend' did not 'grow up' at random but was apparently started by Warburg himself"[118]—a fact that implies that even if Warburg did not actually think in those mythical terms while he was ill, he eventually employed them when he was able to reflect on what he had been through. And if, as both Cassirer and Gombrich agree, Warburg was thoroughly aware of his psychotic condition and, moreover, managed to overcome it precisely because he saw so deeply into his own obsessions, then the "legend" he had created ought to be seen rather as a myth in the sense that Vico gave the term: it was Warburg's "true narration" of his life as he had come to realize it. Warburg, like all mythmakers, could master his animalistic reactions only after he had transformed them into artistic creations. His immersion in "demonology" enabled him to discover a new methodology in art theory and history, which has subsequently been refined and defined, primarily by Erwin Panofsky, as "iconology."[119]

IV

In his classic essay "The Genesis of Iconology," William Heckscher has proposed to examine Warburg's new methodology in conjunction with other major "modernistic achievements" in the sciences and humanities that likewise occurred around 1912—Einstein's theory, Freud's method of psychoanalysis, motion pictures, and art movements such as German expressionism, cubism, Orphism, futurism, and suprematism. According to Heckscher, all these new theories and practices emerged as attempts to expose the deeper affinities between various manifestations of chaotic reality by the "synthetic" means of association and collation. This perception is coeval with my definition of modernism as the recognition of myth. It was certainly Warburg's mode of operation in his lecture-essay on the

astrological paintings in the Palazzo Schifanoia in Ferrara, which Heckscher credits with the invention of iconology.[120]

Warburg's aim in that essay was to examine the historical origins and
transformations of the iconic astral deities in the calendrical fresco of Schifanoia, whose "complicated and fantastic symbolism has hitherto resisted
all attempts at interpretation." By "extending the purview of investigation
to the east," Warburg revealed these deities to be "survivals of astral images
of the Greek pantheon . . . symbols for the fixed stars—although over the
centuries, in their wanderings through Asia Minor, Egypt, Mesopotamia,
Arabia, and Spain, they have lost their Grecian clarity of outline."[121] The
fact that Renaissance artists usually received the mythological tradition
in the hideous modifications of astrology required them to rediscover its
"human forms" directly from the classical sources. Most of the painters of
the Schifanoia ceiling, like the anonymous painter of the July fresco, failed
to do so because they could not stand up to their patrons and advisers, who
were totally ensnared by astrological beliefs and images (584). Even an individualistic and realist painter like Francesco Cossa was unable to shake
off the dogmatic indoctrination of his supervisors. The numerous varia-
tions and transmutations of these mythological representations of late classical antiquity inevitably diminished their original meanings as "serene
Olympians." Yet they retained their elemental meanings as "icons" in
graphical and astrological guides, and a goddess like Venus could still inspire Renaissance artists like Botticelli "to restore her to her Olympian
freedom" that had once made her so vital and immortal (585). The real liberation of the Renaissance from "medieval bondage" occurred a decade or
two later, in the High Renaissance between 1490 and 1520, as both humanists like Pico della Mirandola and artists like Raphael, who despised astrology, combined to produce "a more elevated, idealized, quasi-antique
style in the depiction of the great figures of ancient myth and history"
(584). On his visit to Rome in 1908, Warburg was profoundly impressed
by Raphael's ceiling mosaic in the Chigi Chapel, with its representation of
the seven planets in all their original humanity and beauty. Yet, as much
as Warburg admired Raphael's Olympians on the ceiling of the Villa Farnesina, he reminded us that "only a step away, in an adjoining room of the
Farnesina, Agostino Chigi simultaneously commissioned Peruzzi to fill the
ceiling with pagan astral deities . . . For Chigi chose to spend his hours of
rural leisure beneath the protection of his own auspicious horoscope,
which—deceptively—promised him long life."[122]

Such observations led Warburg to the conclusion that the reception of

the classical tradition in the European civilization was not a harmonic process of transition and easy translation to modernity, as Burckhardt had
made it out to appear, but rather a process of confrontation, "part of an international process of dialectical engagement with the surviving imagery
of Eastern Mediterranean pagan culture." [123] The "classical tradition," with
its serene conception of antiquity, was the synthetic resolution of this "dialectical engagement," fashioned by humanist scholars and artists in the Renaissance and ever after who sought to emancipate the pagan deities, and
themselves, from the allegorical, magical, astrological, and other clerical
disciplines. "It was with this desire to restore the ancient world that 'the
good European' began his battle for enlightenment in that age of interna-
tionally migrating images that we—a shade too mystically—call the Age
of Renaissance." [124] Again we see that, for Warburg, the mythical prevailed
over and against both the magical and the logical. Warburg used this example of deep mythic continuity and unity of meaning to argue for a new
kind of art history, which he termed *iconological,* a method "that can range
freely, with no fear of border guards, and can treat the ancient, medieval,
and modern world as a coherent historical unity." [125] Heckscher rightly
points out that the intellectual origins of this methodology may be traced
to Vico, whose work Warburg knew, although he never cited him in his
writings. [126]

Warburg continued to elaborate these notions in his study of the astrological prophecies in the age of Luther, on which he worked during the
war years (the essay was eventually published in 1920). Of all his studies in
art history, this is the most historical, political, and ideological. The actual
circumstances of war seem to have made Warburg impatient with his lifelong artistic preoccupations.

> Only when we bring ourselves to consider the figures of the pagan gods—
> as resurrected in early Renaissance Europe, North and South—not merely
> as artistic phenomena but as religious entities, do we begin to sense the
> power of the determinism of the Hellenistic cosmology, even in Germany,
> even in the age of the Reformation . . . Those astral symbols that had sur-
> vived in the literature of divination—the seven personified planets, above
> all—gained a new lease on life from the social and political upheavals of the
> day and became, as it were, the presiding deities of contemporary politics. [127]

Warburg is clearly fed up with the very notion of "classical" art and history: "A classically rarefied version of the ancient gods has been so suc-
cessfully imposed on us, ever since Winckelmann, as the central symbol
of antiquity, that we are apt to forget that it was entirely the creation of

humanist scholars: this 'Olympian' aspect of antiquity had first to be wrested from its entrenched, traditional, 'daemonic,' aspect" (598). The war all but destroyed this "creation" of humanist scholarship. Warburg's essay, the last one he published, was an attempt to save its essential message from complete demolition through reconstructing the heroic efforts of Luther and Dürer to sustain a humanistic belief against demonological superstitions in the German Reformation.

Warburg's study revolves around a controversy concerning Luther's birth date. In the critical years of the Reformation, Luther's adversaries tried to demonize him by falsifying his actual birth date of 10 November 1483 to 22 October 1484, the date their chief astrologer, the Italian papist Lucas Gauricus, had fixed as suitable for this maleficent man. Warburg traced these astrological prognostications to prophecies that had circulated in Germany since 1465 and connected the conjunction of Jupiter and Saturn in that year to the birth of a prophet nineteen years later, whose evil deeds would cause great cataclysmic events in 1524. Luther's enemies relied on an oracle book by Johannes Lichtenberger, who claimed that this prophet would be a monk. They identified Luther in a woodcut illustration in that book showing a monk with a devil on his neck. Warburg is primarily concerned with the different reactions of Martin Luther and his comrade Philipp Melanchton to this war of defamation, principally to the very notion of astrological and teratological divination. Luther emerges as a champion of reason and enlightenment: he dismissed astrology as sheer nonsense, arguing, for example, that the twins Jacob and Esau were completely contrary in character, a proof that only God, and not the stars, determines human fate (611). He also ridiculed the attempt to identify him with the monk in Lichtenberger's illustration, saying that, if anything, it proves his righteousness—for he carried Christ in his heart while the devil on the monk's neck was the pope, who persecuted him (630).

Unlike Luther, Melanchton was still thoroughly absorbed by superstitious fears. Warburg starts his essay by citing a long letter that Melanchton sent to his friend the astrologer Johann Carion, in which he inquired about the meanings of the comet that had appeared in 1531 and frightened all Germany and also asked for a personal favor—a special horoscope for his newborn daughter. This personal opposition between the two leaders of the German Reformation signified, for Warburg, the fundamental "polarity" of the age, indeed the polarity of all ages and stages of history, which are always strained, and sustained, by the contradictory forces of the magical and the logical. "That age when logic and magic blossomed, like trope and metaphor, in Jean Paul's words, 'grafted to a single stem,' is inherently timeless: by showing such a polarity in action, the historian of civilization furnishes new grounds for a more profoundly positive critique of a historiography that rests on a purely chronological theory of development" (599). Following his studies of the Renaissance, where he had demonstrated how this polarity of magic and logic evolves dialectically so as to produce a mythic resolution—be it Botticelli in the Early Renaissance or Raphael in the High Renaissance—Warburg sought a similar resolution in the German Reformation. He found it in Albrecht Dürer's works.

An early print illustration of a man suffering from syphilis who is surrounded by ominous astrological signs reveals that the young Dürer was "deeply rooted" in the "archetypal, pagan cosmological belief" that was so rife in the age of his great patron Emperor Maximilian I (636). The engraving of an eight-footed pig from the same year (1496) suggests that Dürer had already begun to emancipate himself from this belief. For while his fellow humanist Sebastian Brant still associated this monstrosity with ancient Assyrian augury and with Vergil's description of Aeneas's sow, Dürer's realistic representation proves that he "had already put this Babylonian mentality behind him. His engraving bears no inscription . . . The impulse that guided Dürer's burin was his scientific interest in a phenomenon of nature" (640–41). This tension between the magical and logical conceptions of reality found its resolution in Dürer's famous print *Melancolia I* of 1514. This dark image of a winged genius, apparently in deep depression, sitting pensively amid enigmatic objects and creatures, had already been identified by Karl Giehlow as pertaining to the astrological deities Saturn and Jupiter, whose conjunction was liable to cause "saturnine melancholy." Dürer's depiction of a "magic square of Jupiter" hanging over the genius's head betrays his affinity with the astrological theories of Maximilian, who considered himself a "child of Saturn," and of contemporary humanists such as Ficino and Agrippa, who commonly prescribed this "jovial" remedy against "saturnine melancholy." Warburg's counterargument was that Dürer's composition indeed retained yet subverted these elemental astrological explanations and representations by the creative transformation of the deities into allegories of human qualities:

> The truly creative act—that which gives Dürer's *Melancolia I* its consoling humanistic message of liberation from the fear of Saturn—can be understood only if we recognize that the artist has taken a magical and mythical logic and made it spiritual and intellectual. The malignant, child-devouring planetary god, whose cosmic contest with another planetary ruler seals the subject's fate, is humanized and metamorphosed by Dürer into the image of the thinking, working human being . . . Here, the cosmic

conflict is echoed in a process that takes place within man himself. The daemonic grotesques have disappeared; and saturnine gloom has been spiritualized into human, humanistic contemplation. Deep in thought, the winged figure of Melancholy props her head on her left hand and holds a pair of compasses in her right; she is surrounded by technical and mathematical instruments and symbols, and before her lies a sphere. (644–45)

Warburg is careful, however, to add that "Dürer's Melancholy has yet to break quite free of the superstitious terrors of antiquity. Her head is garlanded not with bay but with *teukrion,* the classic herbal remedy for melancholy; and she follows Ficino's instructions by protecting herself against Saturn's malefic influence with her numerological magic square" (647). The "liberation of modern humanity" from these ancient fears and superstitions would come only in the scientific revolution of the next century. The German Reformation marks a transitional age in that process of enlightenment from magic to logic, the quintessential mythic age of modernity, which Warburg defines, suggestively, as "the age of Faust, in which the modern scientist—caught between magic practice and cosmic mathematics—was trying to insert the conceptual space of rationality between himself and the object" (650).

Dürer's apparent transition from a magical to a logical conception of reality was not final, and not only because it could not yet be so but also because as an artist, not a scientist, his achievement in the creation of *Melancolia I* was due to his ability to retain a "symbolic connection" to the mythological tradition. Warburg's last and much-debated assertion in the statement on the "age of Faust" quoted above—"Athens has constantly to be won back again from Alexandria [*Athen will eben immer wieder neu aus Alexandria zurückerobert werden*]"—was not a declaration of war, let alone of the victory of logic (Athens) over magic (Alexandria), but rather a final admission that logic could not ever overcome magic completely, nor indeed should it do so, for it was precisely their "polarity in action" that marked the cultural achievements of transitional ages like the German Reformation. As Felix Gilbert writes, "[h]e certainly did not believe that the removal of repressions or superstitions would smooth the way to cultural achievement."[128] In a similar vein, Michael Steinberg has shown that Gombrich's slight mistranslation of Warburg's assertion ("Athens must always be conquered afresh from Alexandria") has imposed on it rationalistic and much too deterministic meanings, whereas a closer attention to what Warburg actually wrote—*Athen will*—reveals that he was more ambivalent about the process of civilization, closer, as Steinberg rightly notes, to Nietzsche as well as (I would add) to more modern proponents of the

Dialektik der Aufklärung such as Adorno and Horkheimer.[129] The "liberation of modern humanity" is not *from* myth, as Gombrich would have it, but rather *through* myth. Only in these terms can we understand the motto of Warburg's essay on Luther, which comes from Goethe's *Faust*, part 2: "There's an old book for browsing in / From Harz to Hellas all are akin [*Es ist ein altes Buch zu blättern / Vom Harz bis Hellas immer Vettern*]." In Goethe's poetic play, as in Warburg's essay, modern Germany is akin to ancient Greece in that they both consist in the same primitive mythological tradition. Warburg evokes the same association in the motto he affixed to his lecture at Bellevue on the Indians of Oraibi: "There's an old book for browsing in / Athens and Oraibi all are akin [*Es ist ein altes Buch zu blättern / Athen-Oraibi, alles Vettern*]." The appropriation of this motto attests to the inner connection between the two essays, indeed to the mythistorical conviction that permeates all of Warburg's works and is well captured in the title of his posthumous volume of collected papers: that the crucial moment in art history, from the Renaissance to modern times, has always been the renewal of pagan antiquity—*die Erneuerung der heidnischen Antike*.

As Salvatore Settis has recently argued, this was also the main aim of his journey to the Pueblo Indians in 1896: to examine artistic creation *in statu nascendi*.[130] Having just discovered in his doctoral dissertation the historical origins of Botticelli's *Festwesen* in the Maenadic dances and Bacchantic frenzy of the ancient Greek tribal communities, Warburg now believed that an ethnological exploration of the primitive rites and artifacts of the Hopi tribal community might enable him to discover in their images the psychological origins of all artistic creation—the *Pathosformeln* that still retain the primeval motivations of "expression" and "orientation." During his preparations for the lecture in Bellevue, as he reflected on the original aims of his journey, Warburg wrote: "I had acquired an honest disgust of aestheticizing art history. The formal approach to the image—devoid of understanding of its biological necessity as a product between religion and art— . . . appeared to me to lead merely to barren word-mongering."[131]

Toward the end of his life, Warburg formulated this conviction in his theory of "social memory [*soziales Gedächtnis*]." In that theory he also reiterated the conservative conclusion he had reached in his lecture at Bellevue, namely that modern advancement in logical sciences and technologies is liable to destroy the magical and mythical traditions of antiquity, and with them the essential "symbolic connection" to reality. Whereas other theorists of "collective memory" at the time, most notably Maurice Halbwachs, employed the critical terms of modern sociology to accentuate the intentional and institutional means by which the past is being used for some present "topocentric" policy, Warburg was still bound by the evolutionary and hereditary terms of biological psychology. Thus he forged a theory that enhanced the emotional and irrational origins of memory, its organic function in the conservation of primeval energetic reactions and psychic impressions in symbols, or "dynamograms," that encode the most crucial lessons for the preservation of civilization.[132] Warburg was aware that social memory was essentially regressive and as such could revive racial sentiments and myths; he in fact employed this notion in order to account for the eruption of ancient anti-Semitic and Fascist prejudices in modern European civilization. But he nevertheless continued to appraise this kind of atavistic memory as a useful creation of society, a form of resistance to what he called the "disconnected dynamograms" of the baroque.[133] Noting that "one aspect of the development towards the Baroque was that expressive values [Ausdruckswerte] were cut loose from the mint of real life in movement," he stated: "Here the task of social memory as a 'mnemic function' emerges quite clearly: through renewed contact with the monuments of the past, the sap should be enabled to rise directly from the subsoil and imbue the classicizing form in such a way that a creation charged with energy should not become a calligraphic dynamogram."[134] He derided the reanimation of demonic antiquity, but he also knew that its symbols were inevitable and indispensable in any cultural renaissance. Although Warburg did not elaborate his theory of soziales Gedächtnis, he worked it out in the major project of his last years—the Mnemosyne-Atlas—which is utterly modernistic in its conception and execution.[135] As Matthew Rampley has seen, Warburg's "critique of allegorical signification feeds into the modernist cultural-philosophical theories of figures such as the young Lukács, Sigfried Kracauer, and Adorno," who likewise came to perceive modernity as "a rootless alienation from and loss of immediacy to Being."[136]

In his lecture "Italian Antiquity in the Age of Rembrandt," which he delivered in his library in May 1926, Warburg reiterated his old conviction—which he had expressed already in his early study "The Theatrical Costumes for the Intermedi of 1589," of 1895—that the "baroque" was an age of cultural degeneration because its predilection for allegorical sophistication and decoration of myth led to a loss of authentic "symbolic connection" to this crucial source of our civilization. According to Warburg, the Dutch painter regained this vital connection to life. Rembrandt's etching of Medea proves that, much like Raphael and Dürer before him, he had rediscovered the true content of myth in its deep and full humanity. For while his contemporaries used to portray Medea as a frantic avenger stirred by phobic desires, Rembrandt chose to consign her to the shadow of the stage on which Jason and Creusa are celebrating their marriage, a lonely woman who, like Hamlet, has become too self-reflective and thus inactive, lost in her "agonies of conscience."[137] Rembrandt's interpretation of the Medea myth is a model of a sovereign, and quintessentially modern, confrontation with the ancient mythological tradition. Warburg sums up its lesson most poignantly: "We must not demand of antiquity that it should answer the question at pistol point whether it is classically serene or demoniacally frenzied, as if there were only these alternatives. It really depends on the subjective make-up of the late-born rather than on the objective character of the classical heritage whether we feel that it arouses us to passionate action or induces the calm of serene wisdom. Every age has the renaissance of antiquity it deserves."[138]

What was the "renaissance of antiquity" that Warburg deemed appropriate for his own age? The two alternative options he mentions—"classically serene" and "demoniacally frenzied"—correspond, respectively, to the two scholars whom he esteemed as "prophetic" for the age: Jacob Burckhardt and Friedrich Nietzsche. Yet Warburg also beckons us not to judge "as if there were only these alternatives," a pointer, it seems, to a third alternative (his own), which mediates between the two: in his view the "renaissance of antiquity" was both "classically serene" *and* "demoniacally frenzied," and whether and how to reconcile them really depended on the moderns, be they humanists and artists in the Renaissance or "late-born" scholars like Burckhardt, Nietzsche, or Warburg. This is the final message of Warburg's lifelong reflections on Burckhardt and Nietzsche, which he delivered in the last session (*Schlussübung*) of his seminar on Jacob Burckhardt at Hamburg University on 27 July 1927.

V

Warburg originally planned to conduct a methodological-historical seminar on the various types of Renaissance scholarship. He eventually decided to concentrate only on Jacob Burckhardt, a tacit recognition that Burckhardt was the first and foremost scholar of the Renaissance, incomparable to all others. Bernd Roeck has recently reconstructed in minute detail Warburg's plan and long preparations for this seminar.[139] On the folder containing his massive collection of documents and notes for the seminar, Warburg stuck two stamps—of Kant and Goethe, who symbolized for him the two alternative modes of Enlightenment. Warburg disliked Kant, whom he usually associated with Winckelmann and his idle "classicism," a doctrine that Kant exemplified in his life of detachment and philosophy of enlightenment that advocated a total emancipation from myth. In a note that Warburg wrote in 1929 while he assembled his *Mnemosyne-Atlas*, he toyed with the idea that out of this project might come a book to counter Kant's *Kritik der reinen Vernunft*, under the title *Bilder Atlas zur Kritik der reinen Unvernunft*. In Goethe's life and works, above all in *Faust*, Warburg found and praised a more moderate enlightenment, a dialectical movement, *eine Auseinandersetzung*, between magic and logic that kept a "symbolic connection" to the mythic. According to Warburg, Burckhardt was a follower of Goethe. Moreover, he even intimates that Goethe prefigured Burckhardt in the figure of the watchman Lynkeus in *Faust*, part 2. Sitting high up in his watchtower, Lynkeus appears as a seer who observes the world from afar and rejoices that he sees only the beauty of nature and not the cruelty of man.

> For my keen vision noted
> Set to watch day and night
> To my tower devoted
> The world's my delight
>
> . . . .
>
> Thus a charm never-failing
> I see all around
> And I am glad, hailing
> The joy I have found.[140]

Such was also, according to Warburg, the ascetic–aesthetic position that Burckhardt secured for himself in Basel. Warburg describes him as Lynkeus, who "sits in his tower and speaks." Warburg does not think, however, that Burckhardt's notorious withdrawal to a life of *Anschauung* and *Genuß* was just a hedonistic reaction of a pessimist who could not bear to counter the harsh reality (*die plumpe Wirklichkeit*) of human life, as some of Burckhardt's critics, most notably Nietzsche, had alleged. Rather, it was a sign of *Sophrosyne*, of his ability to draw prudential lessons from history, above all from the study of ancient Greek civilization and its resuscitation in the Italian Renaissance, where Burckhardt learned how men could cope with the chaotic affairs of their dreadful human reality by the creation of meaningful myths. The crucial problem facing Burckhardt was how to cope with these myths and the dreadful truths they disclosed.

We must learn to see Burckhardt and Nietzsche as the receivers of mnemic waves and realize that the consciousness of the world affects the two in a very different way . . . Both of them are very sensitive seismographs whose foundations tremble when they must receive and transmit the waves. But there is one important difference: Burckhardt received the waves from regions of the past, he sensed the dangerous tremors and he saw to it that the foundations of his seismograph were strengthened. Though he experienced the extremes of oscillation he never surrendered to them completely and unreservedly. He felt how dangerous his profession was, and that he really should simply break down, but he did not succumb to romanticism. For a time he accepted this compulsion to resonate with such intensity that he looked back upon it—without any resentment—as on a period of psychological crisis he had overcome. He would not have reacted in this way if this experience had not concerned an essential aspect of his mnemic role: he must resonate for new areas to surface from the hidden layers of forgotten facts. The art of pageantry was discovered by him and it compelled him to respond to a slice of untamed life that had not existed before and that he was really afraid to present. It will not do to approach these matters with an ethical standard. Burckhardt was a necromancer, with his eyes open. Thus he conjured up specters which quite seriously threatened him. He evaded them by erecting his observation tower. He is a seer such as Lynkeus; he sits in his tower and speaks.[141]

Zum Sehen geboren / Zum Schauen bestellt. Warburg copied these words of Goethe's Lynkeus into his notes and recited them to his listeners, as if to remind them that this ability to transform natural vision into contemplation, the essential mythic capability, is a human quality common to all human beings who are always compelled, as he was during his mental illness, to transform the beautiful and awful visions they inevitably inherit or create into meaningful contemplation. For the same myths that help humanity to escape dreadful reality—the stories of salvation from mortality, brutality, and futility—may also draw them back into it if they do not recognize them as such. Having once succumbed to these myths, Warburg knew that modern mythology required sublimation, not revitalization, of their images. This was the lesson of the great humanists, from Botticelli, Raphael, and Dürer to Burckhardt, a lesson that Nietzsche consciously rejected.

Warburg's thoughts then turn to Nietzsche's life. "What role did Burckhardt play in Nietzsche's life?" he asks, and then he recounts—or perhaps indeed relives—Nietzsche's last moments of sanity in Turin in the first days of January 1889, as he withdrew from the lighted street to his dark hotel room, where, engulfed by religious frenzies, he sent out his final letter to Jacob Burckhardt. "The man whose sole concern was the unconditional dedication to the belief in the greatness of the future became, in this attempt, the victim of his own ideas . . . He who so frequently had written about man's *Passion* and had demanded the privilege of standing above it now lay prostrate—a worm wriggling in fear."[142] Warburg is eager to fend off from Burckhardt any accusations that he had not done enough to help Nietzsche before and during this last fatal attack. He mentions Burckhardt's old age and weakness and commends him for having alerted Franz Overbeck to Nietzsche's condition. "The collapse of this superman is something that Burckhardt had constantly feared for his esteemed colleague. There is nothing more foolish than to believe that he may have dismissed him with cool irony."[143] Rather, as Warburg would have it, Burckhardt distanced himself from Nietzsche because he discerned in him a certain insolence (*Vermessenheit*) toward the common norms and forms of civilization that was superhuman, all too superhuman for a "simple teacher" like himself. "In Nietzsche the orgiastic states of the ancient world produced a dream world, which he could not live up to, though as a poet he produced invocations arising from a musical sphere that Burckhardt never attained."[144] Thence, whereas "Nietzsche wooed Burckhardt very much," Burckhardt recoiled and "turned away from him like someone who sees a dervish run through the streets of Jerusalem"— because he was all too aware of "how dangerous his profession was": he realized that, unlike himself, Nietzsche did not seek to sublimate the ancient myths but rather to reanimate them.

Warburg noted in the opening words of his lecture: "We must learn to see Burckhardt and Nietzsche as the receivers of mnemic waves and realize that the consciousness of the world affects the two in a very different way." This, for Warburg, is the crucial difference between the two, the crucial problem for all modern cultural historians: How does one deal with ancient mythology, this quintessential pagan expression of beauty and liberty? How did Burckhardt and Nietzsche respond to its radical message of deconstruction that exposes, and celebrates, all ultimate truths as our own mythopoeic creations? Or, in Warburg's words, "What part does antiquity play in the development of prophetic personalities?"[145] The religious affinities are crucial, as both Burckhardt and Nietzsche are "sons of clergymen who react so differently to the feeling of God's presence in the world. One of them feels the uncanny breath of the demon of destruction and withdraws to his tower, the other wants to make common cause with him." Warburg, who had just survived his own struggle with the "demon of destruction," naturally identified with Burckhardt. He praised Burckhardt as a scholar who looked for a loftier form of cultural tradition, which he eventually found in Rubens, whose art and way of life exemplified "the discipline of form and the standards to go with it";

Nietzsche, however, longed for the "mystic drama" of the Greeks, which he thought he had found in Wagner. Once Nietzsche realized his delusion, he was lost. "Nietzsche perished because in his loneliness he had exposed himself to the most violent shocks, believing as he did in a superior logic of fate. He had reacted against the complacent pathos formula [*Pathosformel*] he found in Wagner. Thus we suddenly see the influence of antiquity in both its currents, the so-called Apollonian and Dionysian." [146] According to Warburg, then, Nietzsche failed to transmit the "mnemic waves" that he had received from prehistoric traditions, the myths of antiquity, into adequate cultural history because unlike—and against—Burckhardt, he wished to be a prophet rather than a teacher.

In 1929, shortly before his death, Warburg presented himself to the governing body of the Warburg Library using the same metaphorical terms he applied to Burckhardt: as "an old Jewish watch-man in a lighthouse on the North Sea." [147] His identification with Burckhardt was thus complete. Warburg's last words on Burckhardt may serve as our last words on Warburg himself: "We have reached the limits of his ability. But he possessed what lifts him above us and what remains our example: the ability to feel by virtue of his *Sophrosyne* the limits of his mission, perhaps even too poignantly, but at any rate not to transcend them since his mental poise restrains him." [148] Till the end of his life, Warburg managed to keep this "mental poise" and did not succumb anymore to the "mnemic waves" of ancient mythology. He remained, however, acutely sensitive and responsive to the demonic waves of that mythology in modern Germany. Unlike his fellow scholars in the Warburg Library, he did not abide by the rules of *Gelehrtenpolitik*, which forbade mixing scientific, value-free knowledge with contemporary events. In 1925 Ernst Cassirer could still write with academic detachment that the swastika was the "earliest form of the four-pronged cross" that symbolized "primeval religious-cosmic motifs," which are to be found in various religions, and this was at a time when the swastika had already acquired some distinct Nazi meanings.[149] Warburg, however, was alert to the new political meanings that the ancient mythology had acquired in modern Germany. In the last months of his life, he added three screen-plates to his cultural-histocral *Bilderatlas,* which are unique because they contain material images from contemporary newspapers alongside reproductions of works of art. Warburg obviously saw visual associations and deeper spiritual and intellectual affinities and continuities between the mythical and the political realities they display.

As Charlotte Schoell-Glass has recently shown, Warburg was particularly impressed by one contemporary event: the signing of the Lateran

Treaties on 11 February 1929 by Mussolini and Pope Pius XI.[150] According to Warburg, by this Concordat the Church resigned all real-political power and claims to the Italian state, while the Italian state in turn affirmed the Catholic faith as a state religion. Warburg, who happened to be in Rome on that day and witnessed the popular celebrations in the streets, described them as "the repaganization of Rome." On the screen-plate he juxtaposed the photograph of the Eucharistic Procession in Rome in 1929 with a reproduction of Raphael's fresco *Mass of Bolsena* in the Vatican, which depicts a famous mythical—not historical—moment in the history of the Church, when Pope Urban IV determined to institute the Feast of Corpus Christi. The fact that the newspaper that published the photograph of the Eucharistic Procession intruded upon it by placing next to it a photograph of a swimmer boastful of his beautiful body signified for Warburg the entire process of secularization, in which "the cheerful *hoc meum corpus est* can be set beside the tragic *hoc est corpus meum* without this discrepancy leading to an outcry against such barbarous breach of decorum."[151] The juxtaposition of the images thus calls attention to the political appropriation of theological myth, to the intrusion of racial brutality into Christianity, to the sacralizing of political treaties and parties, and ultimately to the creation of what Ernst Cassirer called the Myth of the State.[152] Warburg, however, believed that the persistence of myth *in* the state, of the classical and theological imagery in modern political history, retained the crucial "symbolic connection" to sources of spiritual vitality that might guarantee sublimation and the eventual salvation of Western civilization from both logical profanity and magical brutality. He thus placed underneath the reproduction of Raphael's fresco Giotto's figure of *Speranza* (hope), an early Renaissance depiction of the *nympha* (who also appears in Raphael's fresco), and next to it Botticelli's *St. Jerome's Last Communion*, as if to signify the long mythological tradition of human passion stemming from pagan antiquity and moving through Christianity to modernity.

Warburg died in October 1929. Within a year a book appeared— Alfred Rosenberg's *Der Mythus des zwanzigsten Jahrhunderts*—that destroyed this mythological tradition of *Speranza*.[153] For Rosenberg's new *Mythus* was a "myth of the blood," an impulsion of primeval biological and mystical passions that had long been lurking in the German *Rasse* and were now ready to break through the ancient mythology of the Judeo-Christian tradition and impose on its history a new mythology—the swastika over against the cross. "The new Mythus and the power to create a type cannot in any way be refuted," wrote Rosenberg. "They will establish themselves and they will create facts."[154] Indeed they did: already in late 1933 the Warburg Library was moved from Hamburg to London, depriving Germany of that cultural-historical institution which guarded its vital "symbolic connection" to the classical-theological tradition of Western civilization.

For many intellectual historians, then as now, this transition from Warburg's conception of history as ancient mythology to Rosenberg's conception of history as new mythology was inevitable and betrays the dangerous and ultimately disastrous consequences of the recognition of myth in historiography. This was the final judgment of Ernst Cassirer on what he and his fellow members in the Warburg Library had done. But there were also other historical scholars, who had contributed even more significantly to the revision of history into new mythology and who subsequently came to reassess this transition differently. The most notable among those myth-istorians was Ernst Kantorowicz.

Ernst Kantorowicz: History as New Mythology

I

In April 1945, shortly before his death in exile in New York, Ernst Cassirer completed his last book, *The Myth of the State,* which he introduced with these words:

> In the last thirty years, in the period between the first and the second World Wars, we have not only passed through a severe crisis of our political and social life but have also been confronted with quite new theoretical problems . . . Perhaps the most alarming feature in this development of modern political thought is the appearance of a new power: the power of mythical thought. The preponderance of mythical thought over rational thought in some of our modern political systems is obvious. After a short and violent struggle mythical thought seemed to win a clear and definite victory. How was this victory possible? How can we account for the new phenomenon that so suddenly appeared on our political horizon and in a sense seemed to reverse all our former ideas of the character of our intellectual and our social life?[1]

Why has myth become so crucial in the modern state? And why, of all modern states, was it so acutely expressed, and explained, during the fateful years of the Weimar Republic? Cassirer's urgent queries still resound in the debate over the mythological origins and manifestations of the state, even though his actual theories, let alone his auguries, about the fatalistic consequences of political mythology have lost much of their original cogency. Henry Tudor opines that this is true because Cassirer's observations and interpretations of modern political mythology, and principally his apparent puzzlement that this mythology is still so viable in this age of reason, expose the "primitivistic" assumptions in his conception of myth.[2] This conception, which was implicit already in Cassirer's studies of myth in the 1920s, ultimately led him to conceive of any "modern" form of mythmaking as some kind of "sudden aberration" of irrationality or "reversion" to primitive mentality, which would therefore—as Tudor put it—"complicate and mystify matters which prove, on inspection, to be perfectly straightforward . . . Myth-making is characteristic of culture as such and is no more a reversion to 'the first rudimentary stages of human culture' than are dancing, painting and architecture."[3]

Cassirer accounts for the "victory" of modern political myths by pointing out that they "acted in the same way as a serpent that tries to paralyze its victims before attacking them. Men fell victims to them without any serious resistance. They were vanquished and subdued before they realized what actually happened."[4] His pejorative terms imply that, whereas in his works of the 1920s, he treated myth rather objectively, even positively, and at any rate acknowledged that "it is inconceivable that a nation should exist without a mythology,"[5] by 1945 he had come to identify all myths with the Nazi *Mythus*. This association is evident in his essay "Judaism and the Modern Political Myths" (1944), where he employs the Nazi self-perceptions to describe the war of the Germans against the Jews as a sudden eruption of the eternal war between the mythical forces and the ethical forces in human life and history.[6] Cassirer employed this jargon as a rhetorical weapon in the war, but his description of myth nevertheless reveals that he had come to adopt, however inadvertently, Alfred Rosenberg's contentious definition of myth as an aboriginal and irrational form of life.[7] In that way, much like the Nazis—even if in order to combat them—Cassirer came to confine myth solely to manifestations of primeval compulsions in social-political reality, and thereby he ignored other, "higher" forms of mythopoeic manifestations even in his own *Volk*. For, as contemporary scholars of Judaism such as Martin Buber and, above all, Gershom Scholem have explained, mythological images and practices have permeated all the spheres of Jewish life and history:[8] They recur in apocalyptic visions in the Bible, in mystic figurations in the Kabbalah, in magic rites in Hasidism, and in some recent messianic ideologies in Zionism. These latter examples, that is, the political myths of Judaism,[9] are particularly important to our discussion, and not only because they so clearly defy Cassirer's main claims in his essay, but also because they prove, yet again, that Jewish history, like that of any other nationality, is fundamentally and inevitably mythological. Cassirer rightly emphasized the strong antimythical impulsion in the ethical and legal principles of Judaism; and yet, as Scholem maintains, it is exactly this permanent dialectical tension between the mythical and the ethical-legal that has always regenerated Judaism.[10]

On more concrete historical grounds, Cassirer's "primitivistic" conception of myth betrays a basic intellectual disposition—typical to the German *Aufklärung*—that may have made Cassirer and many other liberal intellectuals, or *Vernunftsrepublikaner,* in Weimar Germany immune, for better and worse, to the power of political myth.[11] His late realization in *The Myth of the State* that "it is beyond the power of philosophy to destroy the power of political myths," that they are "invulnerable" to rational arguments and historical refutations,[12] may be taken as a certain admission on his part that his own philosophical work on myth was inadequate. He himself eventually came to acknowledge: "When we first heard of the political myths [in the mid-1920s] we found them so absurd and incongruous, so fantastic and ludicrous that we could hardly be prevailed upon to take them seriously. By now [in the mid-1940s] it has become clear to us that this was a great mistake. We should not commit the same error a second time. We should carefully study the origin, the structure, the methods, and the technique of the political myths."[13] In *The Myth of the State,* Cassirer certainly did much to rectify his earlier mistakes. As Tudor writes in his study *Political Myth,* "[t]he theorist who, more than any other, has drawn attention to the use of myths in contemporary politics is Ernst Cassirer. Indeed, as a study of political myths, his *The Myth of the State* has yet to be superseded."[14] And yet, as some prominent reviewers of the book pointed out, Cassirer ultimately failed to account satisfactorily for the "victory" of political myths, because he had not really come "to take them seriously." This is the main contention of Hans Kohn in his review of *The Myth of the State:* Cassirer should have taken the German national myths as seriously as those who believed in them did. According to Kohn, these political myths were (or could be interpreted as) intellectual reactions to the crises of European societies in the age of revolution; that is, they were authentic (even when horrific) attempts to re-create political integration and legitimation.[15] In another review of the book, Leo Strauss raised similar objections, arguing that the main question was not how the Nazis had used myth but rather why so many people had become so susceptible to it.[16] As long as Cassirer continued to regard myth as incongruous and ludicrous in itself, he could not quite understand why and how the nationalistic and anti-Semitic Nazi mythology proved to be so effective, even among German *Aufklärer* like himself.

This hermeneutic fallacy is evident in the actual explanation that Cassirer offers for the phenomenal "victory" of political myth in Nazi Germany and in other modern nations. His assertion that Nazi myths were "made according to plan . . . fabricated by very skillful and cunning artisans" and his more general observation that in this age of modern technology in mass communication, "myths can be manufactured in the same sense and according to the same methods of any other modern weapon" are ingenious, even though they run counter to what he himself wrote, correctly in my view, two decades earlier in his *Mythical Thought*. There he stated, "No one who understands what a mythology means to a people, what inner power it possesses over that people and what reality it manifests therein, will say that mythology, any more than language, was invented by individuals."[17] As in the case of so many other theories of "manipulation" put forth by Marxian, Frankfurterian, or similar experts on the "masses," Cassirer's theory does not quite explain how these new myths, if they were mere fabrications and inventions by the "rulers," came to be believed by so many very rational people. Peter Gay's contention that Cassirer did not conduct any "*social* history of ideas,"[18] that he did not care to explain the specific conditions in which ideas—or myths—arise at certain times and places, is correct; it might best be exemplified in the final chapter of *The Myth of the State,* where Cassirer grounds the Nazi myth of the state in the philosophical theory of Spengler or Heidegger, not in the political history of Germany during and after the World War I, when, according to his account, there appeared "a new power: the power of mythical thought."

The thinker who explained those conditions was Max Weber. On 7 November 1917 he delivered a lecture to the Union of Free Students at the University of Munich in which he discussed, under the now famous title "Science as a Vocation," the spiritual and intellectual conditions for the resurrection of myth in German society. In his lecture Weber characterized the predicament of modern society in words that have become canonical in all subsequent discussions of modernity:

> The fate of our times is characterized by rationalization and intellectualization and, above all, by the "disenchantment of the world." Precisely the ultimate and most sublime values have retreated from public life either into the transcendental realm of mystic life or into the brotherliness of direct and personal human life . . . It is not accidental that today only within the smallest and intimate circles, in personal human situations, in *pianissimo,* that something is pulsating that corresponds to the prophetic pneuma, which in former times swept through the great communities like a firebrand, welding them together.[19]

Weber's aim in this lecture was not only to refute the positivistic doctrines that had reduced life and history to such dull regularities but also to rebut the various idealistic movements that flourished in Germany in the first decades of the century. He was particularly concerned to warn his listeners of such wayward followers of Nietzsche as Stefan George, whose *Kreis* exemplified, for Weber, those "smallest and intimate circles" where "prophetic" visions could still arouse majestic emotions and actions. Yet, although Weber opposed George and other proponents of "modern intellectual romanticism of the irrational," he realized that George's poetry and policy, conducted on the reactivation of myth, were not just efficient but also pertinent to an age that had become again so susceptible to myth—through such modern developments as nationalism, commercialism, and aestheticism.[20] Weber observed:

> We live as did the ancients when their world was not as yet disenchanted of its gods and demons, only we live in a different sense. As Hellenic man at times sacrificed to Aphrodite and at other times to Apollo, and, above all, as everybody sacrificed to the gods of his city, so do we still nowadays, only the bearing of man has been disenchanted and denuded of its mystical but inwardly genuine plasticity. Fate, and certainly not "science," holds sway over these gods and their struggles . . . Many old gods ascend from their graves; they are disenchanted and hence take the form of impersonal forces. They strive to gain power over our lives and again they resume their eternal struggle with one another.[21]

Weber's words proved to be prophetic for Weimar Germany. During that period myth became a category of absolute conceptual and historical primacy in the major cultural and political ideologies, as well as in critical theoretical works on them across the humanities and social sciences. The emergence of new human sciences like psychology, sociology, and anthropology, along with the modernist movements in the arts, inspired also German historians and philosophers of history to ask whether, and to what extent, history is determined by mythology. Oswald Spengler's epochal *Untergang des Abendlandes* (1918) and Theodor Lessing's polemical *Geschichte als Sinngebung des Sinnlosen* (1919) affirmed this assumption in the most resounding theoretical terms, as did many historical scholars in more practical terms.[22]

Among them was the young Ernst Hartwig Kantorowicz, whose famous historical biography *Frederick the Second* of 1927 was inspired by Weber's epochal oration of 1917 and the controversies it aroused in the George Circle. In the winter of 1919, before he moved to Heidelberg and became a follower of George, Kantorowicz studied history at the University of Munich. Although he came to Munich more than a year after Weber had delivered his lecture there, it is safe to assume, with Karl Löwith, that like most of his fellow students in Munich, the young Ernst Kantorowicz must have been affected by the phenomenal soundings of Weber's oration in the local academic community and in ever wider circles in Weimar Germany.[23] Moreover, when Weber returned to the university in the winter of 1919, Kantorowicz attended his seminar and may have heard Weber's second lecture to the Union of Free Students, "Politics as a Vocation," which was a sequel to the first.[24] Mindful of the Marxist revolutionaries who were then active in the streets of Munich, as well as in the lecture hall, Weber demanded that his listeners and all political activists adopt a scientist's objective detachment and calm rationality in dealing with such radical actions and other revolutions that had rendered modern political reality so unbearable. They were also to be acutely aware of the ancient revelation that lurks in the modern revolution: "Whoever wants to engage in politics at all, and especially in politics as a vocation, has to realize [that] . . . he lets himself in for the diabolic forces lurking in all violence. The great *virtuosi* of cosmic love of humanity and goodness, whether stemming from Nazareth or Assisi or from Indian royal castles, have not operated with the political means of violence. Their kingdom was 'not of this world' and yet they worked and still work in this world."[25] Having thus realized the precarious function of the myth of salvation in the permanent reformation of societies, Weber evokes again the notion of political virtuosity, this time in its Machiavellian interpretation, and recalls the "beautiful passage" in *History of Florence* where the author "has one of his heroes praise those citizens who deemed the greatness of their native city higher than the salvation of their souls," so as to iterate his message that the political vocation in modern society requires the ability to attain ethical responsibility in and for various orders of life.[26]

Throughout his life Kantorowicz was a devout follower of George, and thus, in Weber's terms, committed to the ethic of absolute conviction (*Gesinnungsethik*) of the religious or romantic believers in myths rather than to the ethic of responsibility (*Verantwortungsethik*) of scientists and other objectivists who profess detachment and calm rationality. Moreover, during his studies in Heidelberg, Kantorowicz adopted and advocated the theory of his fellow Georgeaner Erich von Kahler, who in 1921 published a polemical essay, *Der Beruf der Wissenschaft*, which, as implied by its title, aimed to counter Weber's very notion of the objective scientific vocation in the humanities and social sciences by the Nietzschean notion of the subjective artistic vocation.[27] But at two critical moments in his life, first in Nazi Germany in 1933, and then in the United States during the anti-Communist craze of 1949, Kantorowicz proved that the two political options were not necessarily incompatible and that it was possible, indeed indispensable, to take the right ethical action out of mythical conviction.

Ernst Hartwig Kantorowicz was born in 1895 into a wealthy Jewish merchant family in Posen, then the capital of a Prussian province in Poland.[28] In World War I he served as an officer in the German army. In 1918, following the German capitulation and the abdication of the monarchy, he joined the *Freikorps*, the paramilitary troops of the German nationalists, and participated in their attacks on the Polish "separatists" in his hometown Posen and against the "Spartakists" and their *Räterepublik* in Munich.[29] He began his studies at the University of Munich in 1919 and then moved to Heidelberg, where he met and became a close disciple of the poet and seer Stefan George. His intimate association with the *Meister* and his young "men of destiny" determined his life as a young man and a scholar in Germany: he dedicated himself completely to its spiritual mission—the creation of "Das neue Reich" through reviving its foundational myths. This turned out to be Kantorowicz's vocation as a historian of medieval Germany. In 1927 he published the historical biography *Kaiser Friedrich der Zweite*.[30] The book was not only one of the biggest best-sellers of German historiography between the wars—by 1939 it had sold five editions, more than fifteen thousand copies!—but also the source of the most famous *Historikerstreit* of the Weimar Republic: the so-called *Mythenschau* controversy over the book. It culminated in 1929–30 with a hostile review of the book in the official journal of the historical profession in Germany, the *Historische Zeitschrift*, written by its coeditor Albert Brackmann, under the title "Kaiser Friedrich der Zweite in 'mythischer Schau.'" Kantorowicz responded in the same journal with an essay called "'Mythenschau': Eine Erwiderung."[31] The controversy thus hinged on the question of whether it was the author who rendered history mythological according to poetical and political guidelines, or whether it was history itself that was essentially mythological. In later years the *Mythenschau* controversy became primarily political rather than merely historiographical, and it persists to this day. For many reviewers of the book, not least Kantorowicz himself, came to see that this book created the model Führer for the new Germany before it actually got one. Thirty years later, in his second major book, *The King's Two Bodies*, Kantorowicz reexamined the particular case of Frederick II and the whole problem of political mythology, and he did so by critical engagement with Ernst Cassirer's book *The Myth of the State*.[32] Much like Cassirer, but ultimately arriving at different conclusions, Kantorowicz was forced to rethink his early work *on* myth by the actual work *of* myth in modern German history.[33]

II

From the moment of its appearance in 1927, *Frederick the Second* was recognized as more than just a new historical biography of the medieval emperor. In his memoirs, *A European Past,* Felix Gilbert recalls the vivid impressions that Kantorowicz made on the younger generation of historians in the renowned *Historisches Seminar* in Berlin: his book "demonstrated that a different kind of medieval history, one that revealed the ideas and values that motivated the rulers of the Middle Ages, was possible . . . one admired his book for overcoming the rigidification that had set in in medieval history because of an overemphasis on historical techniques."[34] This, of course, was precisely the reason why older guardians of the profession attacked Kantorowicz so vehemently. The huge popular success of his book unnerved them because it was so evidently a work of the highest historical scholarship.[35] This was acknowledged even by a radical critic like Eckart Kehr, who otherwise dismissed works of this kind as "historische Belletristik."[36] For favorable reviewers of the book, such as Karl Hampe and Friedrich Baethgen, Kantorowicz's teachers in Heidelberg, the main problem with his work was not that he treated old myths as history but rather that he treated his own history as just another new myth.

And indeed, right from its very first lines, his book is thoroughly mythical: it begins with a recitation of Vergil's Fourth Eclogue, the famous celebration of the future ruler of the world. The medieval evocations of this prophecy in the visions of the Sibyllines, Joachim of Fiore, and Peter of Eboli provide the background to the life and times of "the last and greatest Christian Emperor of the German Roman Imperium."[37] Throughout the book, this was Kantorowicz's pattern: to describe Frederick through the legends, panegyrics, hymns, and similar poetic visions by which his contemporaries, and primarily he himself, perceived the Kaiser as *Stupor Mundi*—the Amazement of the World. Here is how Kantorowicz recounts Frederick's birth: "Not in Palermo, but in Jesi, a small town dating from Roman times, in the March near Ancona, Constance brought her son to birth. After he was Emperor, Frederick . . . called Jesi his Bethlehem, and the Divine Mother who bore him he placed on the same plane as the Mother of our Lord."[38] The book ends, as befits a myth, not with the death of Frederick but with his *Fortleben* and eventual resurrection:

"The greatest Frederick is not yet redeemed, him his people knew not and sufficed not. 'Lives and lives not,' the Sybill's word is not for the Emperor, but for the German people."[39] Kantorowicz, of course, was wrong. The German people were ready for an emperor, and they got one.[40]

Modern readers of the book have commonly attacked Kantorowicz on this score. Thus, Peter Gay writes that Kantorowicz "put much reliable history into his biography," but this only "made his myth all the more persuasive to the educated, all the more dangerous to the Republic." By creating "a superman who had defied all authority," he rendered "history as political poetry."[41] Moreover, Kantorowicz himself seems to have come to share these opinions. Although he berated as "stupidity [*Dummheit*]" any insinuations that he had written this work under the impact of the rising tide of National Socialism, he hardly ever referred to the book in his later works and generally dismissed it as a "Jugendwerk."[42] For many years he forbade the republication of his book in Germany. In 1962 he finally gave in, yet he immediately came to regret his decision when the first letter he received was from General Hans Speidel, a NATO commander and a former high officer in Rommel's army, who congratulated him on this "outstanding work about the great Staufen, which again and always moves us so deeply."[43] Kantorowicz then wrote to his publisher that "a book that once lay on Himmler's night table and that Göring sent as a gift, with his inscription, to Mussolini"—and, one could add, that Hitler claimed to have read twice—"really ought to be abandoned to oblivion."[44]

Alas, books have their own fate, and Kantorowicz's book has not had the fate his author wished for. It is still the standard work on the topic for modern medieval scholars and biographers of Frederick.[45] Moreover, it is one of those rare historical works that are not only studied by professional scholars but also actually read by common readers. Yet, over the years, even those who have otherwise been impressed by Kantorowicz's historical research on Frederick have deplored his mythological presentation of the emperor. His reputation in the wider academic circles nowadays stems chiefly from his last major work, *The King's Two Bodies*. Nevertheless, as Robert Lerner has argued, "had Kantorowicz not begun to draw on prophecies and legends while seeking to create a superhuman Frederick, in the service of Stefan George, he might never have become the author of *The King's Two Bodies,* his landmark study of 'Medieval Political Theology.'"[46] The question remains, however, whether *Frederick the Second* itself and, more generally, the mythistorical genre that Kantorowicz developed present viable options for modern historiography.

The most common objection to Kantorowicz's mythological method is that by depicting historical reality in essentially personal and epiphenomenal idioms, he created a reified reality, in which images become more real than the facts of life and experiential impressions of the events more actual than the events themselves. Kantorowicz did seem to be so concerned with collective experiences and deep impressions of historical events, rather than with the events themselves, that he often failed to answer the main historical question of what actually happened in those events. The critical remarks of the great medievalist Richard W. Southern on Kantorowicz's *King's Two Bodies* ring all the more true in the case of his *Frederick the Second*. According to Southern, Kantorowicz "puts the symbol before the reality, and seems to assume that without the symbol men will be incapable of grasping the reality they wish to express. But men are never so absorbed in the shadow-world of symbols that they cannot express without them whatever is necessary for their practical ambitions."[47] As Karl Hampe, the eminent medieval historian and Kantorowicz's teacher at Heidelberg, pointed out in his review of *Kaiser Friedrich der Zweite:* "A confusion between history and myth may easily arise when legends, prophecies, fables and anecdotes which date from later periods are taken as historical sources."[48] Hampe notes that this fallacy might be easier to deal with in the case of a Caesar or a Charlemagne than in the case of an emperor who was so deeply immersed in religious disputations and whose life had thus been marked and marred—primarily by himself—by so much "mythic" information, which is liable to distort any historical reconstruction.[49] Although Hampe agrees with Kantorowicz that the historian must use this information, he chides him for having all too often succumbed to it, as, for example, in the uncritical recitation of the pristine myths of the emperor's miraculous birth and growing up as *"Puer Apuliae."*[50] This apparent fallacy might best be illustrated by one episode, which received much critical attention from Brackmann: Frederick's crusade to the Holy Land in 1228.

According to Kantorowicz, Frederick set out on his crusade in order to fulfill an imperial mission that was more mystical than political: his aim was to establish himself as heir to King David and thereby assert his divine right to world rule, in place of the pope. The famous coronation mass in the Church of the Holy Sepulchre on 18 March 1229, in which Frederick lifted the crown and placed it on his own head, convinced Kantorowicz that "not through the Church, but alongside and without the Church, Frederick the Second had consummated his triumph as if it were a *unio mystica* ... As the Sibylline saying had foretold—though in far other wise than the world had understood—the rulers of East and West were united in

Jerusalem in the one person of Frederick, and the Holy City was free."[51] Brackmann attacked this entire conception and description of the crusade. He pointed out that Jerusalem at that time was not the seat of an empire but only a small town that bore the name of the great kingdom. He also argued that Frederick did not seek to overcome the pope but to curry favor with him after the pope had excommunicated him; and he resolutely denied any metaphysical significance to the act of self-coronation. The whole scene, for Brackmann, was just a minor political event, inflated to metahistorical dimensions by Frederick's propagandists and by his modern biographer.[52]

Kantorowicz was acutely aware that the images and legends he had used were largely the creation of Frederick's *Kanzler* Petrus de Vinea and his team of clerks and artists in the imperial court: "Behind the adulation of the courtiers, often grossly overdone, we can see the truth: the impression the Emperor wished to make, especially on his own followers."[53] Nonetheless, in contrast to Brackmann, who simply dismissed these myths as rhetorical means to disguise real political ends, Kantorowicz maintained that they expressed the innermost convictions of Frederick himself and were therefore crucial for what was ultimately his greatest achievement as a political ruler: the construction of a permanent image or myth of the emperor. By assuming the figures of both "David and Caesar, the Biblical and the Roman prototypes," Frederick and his courtiers constructed an image of an ideal ruler that was meant to be, and duly became, stronger than the real ruler: "The picture for which Frederick II posed and which the imperial Chancery painted was quickly apprehended near and far."[54] The biography thus concentrates on Frederick's awareness of his role, which grows with each experience of war and conquest in Sicily, Italy, Germany, and above all in the Holy Land, and with his attempt to codify these notions in laws and social organization.

Kantorowicz deems the crusade so crucial to the *Bildung* of the emperor in modern European civilization because Frederick's confrontation with oriental norms and forms of life opened up not only his political horizons but also the general European cultural horizons to new artistic and scientific sources. Kantorowicz's infatuation with the Roman-oriental legacy of European civilization and his attempt to reconcile it with its dominant Catholic-occidental tradition, which began during his wartime service in Turkey and became permanent intellectual preoccupations throughout his life, are evident on almost every page of *Fredrick the Second*. As a result, it appears that not only Frederick but also his biographer became totally immersed in oriental folklore. Thus, Kantorowicz relates many fabulous stories about Frederick, some of them utterly fictitious, even lunatic. For example, there is the story that associated him with the Assassins, or *Hashishin*, a cult of hashish smokers and killers from the slopes of Lebanon, and which was really no more than one of their hallucinations. Kantorowicz concedes that "these tales, of course, lack all historic truth, but it is interesting to note how tales of horror and wonder tend to focus round one great name, partly in order to gain greater credence from its authority and partly out of a strange desire to see two incongruous elements brought together in one person's story—the real and the fantastic; Muhammad and Christ; Kaiser and Khalif" (193–94). Kantorowicz thus concludes that this "oriental atmosphere was a necessary factor in the evolution of the autocratic mind": the myth of the immortal emperor was not "invented" by Frederick and his courtiers but rather grew out of the mythological images and tales that surrounded him during the crusade and pervaded his own perceptions of himself: "The *Puer Apuliae* has developed and revealed himself: he is no longer the fate and destiny of individuals; but as the Emperor, imitating the Old Man of the Mountain and playing God to his little prisoners in the cellar, he becomes himself the fate or destiny of communities and peoples" (194–95). After the coronation in Jerusalem, he literally assumes mythological dimensions, as in "a metamorphosis, when a mythic hero becomes suddenly aware of his divine origin and the god in him springs visibly to life . . . From the moment that the divine sonship is proclaimed the career of the monarch takes a new direction: from the phase of mere personal activity and self-assertion he grows in stature, obeying the eternal law of his being by creative activity in empire and in state" (215).

Whereas Brackmann regarded Frederick as just a typical medieval emperor, who generally tried (but mostly failed) to observe all the rules of the Catholic creed and establishment, Kantorowicz used the mythopoeic idioms by which Frederick conceived of himself to show that in Frederick there emerged a new type of emperor, who might well be seen as the prototypical modern ruler, and precisely because he knew how to gain his absolute authority by the manipulation of classical and biblical mythology, or, as Kantorowicz ultimately called it, by the creation of a new "political theology." Although Kantorowicz duly noted that Frederick's greatest achievements as a statesman, such as the Constitutions of Melfi of 1231, were the creation of the jurists who compiled the commentaries and glossaries on Roman law at the University of Bologna, he insists that it was Frederick himself who instructed them to substantiate their legislation by way of a new imperial theology that would counter the papal theology. On

that basis Frederick could show that the emperor is not an agent of punishment to sinful mankind but rather an agent of its salvation. This is the
main message of his *Liber Augustalis,* which depicts the emperor as an "in-
carnation" of the messianic prophecies of antiquity, a *Divus Augustus* who
merges the universal Roman ruler (*Imperator*) with the universal Christian
Redeemer (*Soter*) into a new and most powerful political-theological authority (241–44). According to Kantorowicz, this new theological justifi-
cation of political domination proved conducive to the new "Machiavellian" morality of the modern secular polity. For Frederick's notion of
Necessitas Monarchiae, that the state was a natural and therefore a moral necessity for the preservation of humanity, eventually evolved into the modern notion of Reason of State, allowing the tyrants of the Renaissance and
the absolute monarchs of the Enlightenment to justify their egomaniacal
policies as moral just because they were natural (245–54).

Such propositions might make it appear that Kantorowicz endorsed
Burckhardt's judgment that Frederick was "the first ruler of the modern
type," a despot whose "Gewaltstaat" in Sicily was the model for all later
tyrannies of the Renaissance princes. For Kantorowicz, however, Frederick was not so much the first modern ruler as the last and greatest Christian emperor. For all his apparent modernity, Frederick II did not espouse
secularity: he still adhered to what Kantorowicz came to call "Medieval
World Unity,"[55] namely to the eschatological conception of reality that
imparted metaphysical meaning to all beings, assuming that the world in
which he acted was part of a greater *sacrum imperium* where the vision of
perfect society—The Myth of the State—"stands out and becomes almost
reality."[56] His imperial policy and real-political operations were still largely
determined by ideal-theological considerations. Kantorowicz admits that
Frederick created in the kingdom of Sicily "a visible mirror of princes for
the days to come."[57] But he insists that because Frederick still acted according to certain metaphysical and eschatological guidelines, which his
followers discarded, his tyranny was not as bad as that of the latter. As his
friend Maurice Bowra recalls, even during the hard times of Nazi persecution, Kantorowicz insisted that "brutality based on metaphysics was
better than brutality for its own sake."[58] This is how he judged the case
of Frederick: what was still "true for Frederick"—the Aristotelian and
Christian ideals of Natural Law—was "no longer true for the Renaissance
princes," just as Frederick's conception and execution of the Roman *virtus*
were no longer congruent with "what Machiavelli called *virtu,* this combination of strength and talent, not incompatible with evil," after which

"each of the Renaissance tyrants had to show *virtu* or genius if he was to maintain his illegitimate rule over his State."[59] Ultimately, the Frederick who emerges from Kantorowicz's biography is a tragic hero, a ruler whose good intentions led him to Dante's *Inferno*.[60] He was a model ruler whose legacy to posterity was no more than a model, "the structure of the State" and not the actual content, ideal, or "myth" that permeated it—hence the conclusion that he "dominated the Renaissance anonymously and illegitimately."[61] In his biography Kantorowicz thus set out to redeem Frederick's true legacy, to retrieve the original "myth of the state" that had inspired all his actions and creations. He properly identified this myth in Frederick's slogan of *Renovatio Imperii Romanorum*.[62]

Kantorowicz readily found in the vision of *Renovatio Imperii Romanorum* the historical myth of his own life and nation. For George and his followers, as well as for the many German royalists and imperialists who opposed the Weimar Republic, this myth signified the real German Reich, that which the Second Reich had so miserably failed to create. Among those who adhered to this myth were reactionaries as well as more moderate "conservative revolutionaries" such as Oswald Spengler, Max Scheler, Hugo von Hofmannstahl, and, in his own way, Thomas Mann, that is, *unpolitische* intellectuals who abhorred the political and technological "modernization" of German society and sought to rebut this process by the reassertion of medieval German features of hierarchy, rusticity, and spirituality. Kantorowicz's attempt to reassert the Roman virtues of medieval Germany aligns him with another conservative intellectual movement that emerged in the mid-1920s, whose members pursued what they called a "Third Humanism." According to the founder and leader of this movement, the eminent classical scholar Werner Jaeger, the rapid process of modernization in Germany led to the vulgarization and radicalization of its venerable tradition of *Bildung* and consequently to the degeneration of the basic virtues of "humanism." The new political ideologies, from both left and right, that promised to overcome this degeneration by means of "revolution" merely served to perpetuate it. The only remedy, according to Jaeger and his followers, was the "classical" solution, namely the revivification of the ancient Graeco-Roman humanistic education through the study of classical languages and spiritual traditions. After the two renaissances of humanistic education in ancient Greece and medieval Italy, it now fell upon Germany to generate a new renaissance, a "Third Humanism."[63]

These neohumanistic aspirations echo in Kantorowicz's book, especially in his celebration of Frederick's imperial mission as a great moral and cultural achievement, the decisive moment in the movement of the European Renaissance. Again, as in his evocation of Frederick's spiritual mission in the crusade, Kantorowicz drew on the symbolic gestures and pictures "for which Frederick posed and which the imperial Chancery painted," assuming that as "poets, chroniclers and writers began to compare Frederick with Caesar and with Augustus and to seek resemblances in individual episodes," they revealed in their imaginary and literary fabrications the real reasons, or historical myths, that motivated Frederick throughout all his military operations.[64] This is how Kantorowicz divines Frederick's vision after his victory in the battle of Cortenuova in November 1237:

> ROMA CAPUT MUNDI! This age-old phrase graced like a challenge, a seal of Frederick II's. If this rune was as tangibly and literally fulfilled as the ancient claim of the Emperors to be the successors of David; if Frederick II was Maximus Imperator of Italy and with the Pontifex, a Caesar again in Rome . . . then the Empire of the Caesars, so oft invoked in manifesto, had become tangible once more and the Empire had been perfected as befitted the time. An Emperor celebrating a triumph in Rome itself would, in some mystic way, become possessed of all the kingdoms of the West.[65]

Kantorowicz knew that Frederick never realized this dream, but he nevertheless reiterates it in his biography, so as to prove yet again the efficacy of such historical myths. This was also the main argument of his fellow medieval historian Percy Ernst Schramm. In 1929 Schramm published with the Warburg Library his magisterial study *Kaiser, Rom und Renovatio,* in which he analyzed the millenarian epoch of the Saxon ruler Otto III (983–1002) and his teacher Gerbert of Aurillac (later Pope Sylvester II).[66] The ideological and methodological affinities between his book and Kantorowicz's biography of Frederick are evident and date from the time they were both students of medieval history at Heidelberg in the early 1920s. As they later pursued the study of medieval imperial sources in the Monumenta Germaniae Historica in Berlin, they extended the German art of *Quellenforschung* beyond its rigid antiquarian boundaries: whereas Kantorowicz, following George, concentrated on literary sources such as poetry and hagiography, Schramm, who studied and worked with Aby Warburg, was much more attentive to iconographical and ethnographical sources of medieval civilization. Concentrating thus on liturgical sources such as the illustrated edition of the Gospels in the imperial court of Otto III, Schramm sought to discover therein the "dream" of the young emperor and his adviser so as to argue that the main aim of their imperial policy was the *renovatio* of ancient and Christian Rome rather than the building of a German empire, as nationalist political historians have argued then and now. Although Emperor Otto III and Pope Sylvester II failed to accomplish their dream of *Renovatio Imperii* around the turn of the millennium, Schramm regards their aspiration as the first and most significant attempt at renaissance in the Middle Ages. Kantorowicz traced this imperial legacy into Frederick's life and times, showing how his hero inherited the message and bequeathed it in the form of our modern conception of Renaissance: "As he sought to re-quicken not only Roman forms (like his predecessors) but Roman life, the ancient state-life of the Romans, his *renovatio* ended by heralding the Renaissance."[67]

Kantorowicz devotes many pages to proving this point.[68] By describing Frederick as a "statesman and philosopher, politician and soldier, general and jurist, poet and diplomat, architect, zoologist, mathematician, the master of six or it might be nine languages, who collected ancient works of art, directed a school of sculpture, made independent researches in natural sciences," and so on, he makes Frederick appear not only to have prefigured but really to have exemplified the "Genius of the Renaissance."[69] Kantorowicz's positive description of Frederick's all-around achievements in the arts and sciences, above all in those of statecraft, are clearly meant to revise Burckhardt's negative description of the emperor in the opening paragraphs of *The Civilization of the Renaissance in Italy,* where Frederick is portrayed as the prototypical Renaissance tyrant, the mastermind of "the transformation of the people into a multitude destitute of will and of the means of resistance."[70]

Kantorowicz's presentation of the medieval emperor as a Renaissance Man seems to align him with the so-called Revolt of the Medievalists of the 1920s, that is, with the contention that there was no real break or distinct age of renaissance between the Middle Ages and modern times or, if there was a renaissance at all, it must have occurred in the Middle Ages.[71] This was the argument of Charles H. Haskins in *The Renaissance of the Twelfth-Century,* which appeared in the same year as Kantorowicz's book and betrays the same revisionist tendencies.[72] However, unlike the American revisionists, Kantorowicz did not set out to refute Burckhardt's basic assumption on the Italian origins and manifestations of the movement; instead, he wished to revise it by new temporal and cultural definitions: he relocated the Italian Renaissance in an era that was both earlier and holier than the age of Burckhardt's *Gewaltmenschen.* Its harbingers were not only the new type of "The Emperor" but also the new type of "The Saint." In his biography, Frederick's contemporary Francis of Assisi emerges as the second major protagonist of the new movement. According to Kantorowicz, Frederick's actions against the pope were motivated by emotions and notions similar to those that inspired Francis's attempt at a *renovatio* of the Church through radical renunciation of all papal possessions and devotion to clerical poverty.[73] He argues that Frederick would have accepted "a penniless Peter as pope, side by side with him as emperor, an emperor of boundless possessions, both immediately appointed by God. To such a Pope who by his holiness made kings and princes to serve him, Frederick was prepared to render, as Dante demanded, 'that reverence which a first born son must show his father'" (616). But the deep division and opposition between the two empires in the thirteenth century prevented the realization of this ideal vision of a new society, or "earthly paradise," based on the original and seminal notions of justice, which both Frederick and Francis—as well as Kantorowicz—appear to have craved. "Frederick, it is true, realised his dream only in part, but the vision never faded—Dante took it up and gave it a soul" (456). "The Poet" thus emerges as the real messenger of the Renaissance, precisely because he was able to transform in the *Commedia,* the greatest historical mythology of the postclassical era, the ideal vision of both his predecessors, "The Emperor" and "The Saint," into a real provision.

Kantorowicz's discussion of Dante concentrates on the presentation of Frederick in the *Commedia.* His main contention is that Dante construed his entire philosophy of man upon Frederick's political-theological affirmation of the emperor as a secular savior of mankind. Dante indeed consigned Frederick to the infernal "sepulchres of those who despise immortality, the 'Epicureans,'" but Kantorowicz insists that he "had the most profound respect and admiration for the Hohenstaufen," especially because Frederick personified the new and ideal emperor that the Ghibelline Dante had portrayed in the *Monarchia:* a sovereign ruler who in his secular actions restores to man his original ability to be what Adam had been in paradise—a just emperor over creation. This is the message that Kantorowicz gleans from Frederick's pronouncement in the preamble to his law code: "Taking Man from a clod of earth He [God] breathed life into him and Spirit and crowned him with the diadem of honor and fame" (258). As Kantorowicz would have it, the same message is then repeated, and much amplified, in the dramatic moment in the *Commedia* when Vergil bids farewell to Dante: "No longer expect a word or sign from me. Free, upright and whole is your will, and it would be wrong not to act according to its pleasure; wherefore I crown and miter you over yourself."[74]

Kantorowicz refers this humanistic message back to Frederick's perception of himself: "The Emperor's earthly goal: to attain once more the divine image by the fulfilment of the Law on earth and in the State, was the exact premise of Dante's formula of faith, that in every man the contemplative element needs salvation through the Church, the active element needs a no less sacred fulfilment on earth in the Law and in the State."[75]

By insisting on the essential unity of the poetical and the political in Dante's life and works, Kantorowicz intimates that principle which was to guide him in all subsequent struggles: that the real leaders of the state are not its rulers but its mythmakers. Indeed it was Dante, not Frederick, who was the real hero of Kantorowicz's work—just as it was a modern poet, and not any modern ruler, who was the real hero of his life.[76] And this, ultimately, was also the main reason that Kantorowicz composed his own work along poetical lines, rather than strict historical ones.

As already noted, during the 1920s there were many works concerning historical myths—even some on the myths about Frederick II.[77] Had Kantorowicz confined himself to that kind of investigation, his work would not have been so outrageous, even to positivists like Brackmann. Kantorowicz, however, sought to do more than this: he wanted to create a new kind of historiography, which would be more useful to life, as Nietzsche had demanded, and according to Nietzsche's terms and goals. It had to be an artistic rather than a scientific historiography, openly subjective rather than seemingly objective, "monumental" and not just "critical," and above all "suprahistorical," this being the term used by Nietzsche in his historiographical theory for what he elsewhere defined as mythical.[78] It was indeed Nietzsche's radical transvaluation of myth and history that initiated the notion and tradition of *Mythenschau* in German historiography. It was largely due to Nietzsche's perpetual legacy in Germany during the early decades of the twentieth century that the historiographical controversy over Kantorowicz's work assumed greater cultural and political significance.

III

In his first major work, *The Birth of Tragedy,* Nietzsche praised the Greek myths as "timeless allegories" of the human condition. Assuming, with the Greeks, that the truth about the crude reality (*plumpe Wirklichkeit*) of the world—that in itself this world was utterly chaotic and meaningless— would have made the world impossible to believe and live in, Nietzsche came to admire the great achievement of "the profound Hellene" who, "having looked boldly right into the terrible destruction of so-called world history as well as the cruelty of nature," resolved to overcome the "terror and horror of existence" by creation of "the Olympian middle world of art," in which reality was not exposed, nor disguised, but merely "veiled and withdrawn from sight."[79] As Nietzsche put it, "we have art in order not to die of the truth."[80] He concluded, therefore:

> Without myth every culture loses the healthy power of its creativity: only a horizon defined by myths completes and unifies a whole cultural movement . . . The images of the myth have to be the unnoticed omnipresent demonic guardians, under whose care the young soul grows to maturity and whose signs help the man to interpret his life and struggles. Even the state knows no more powerful unwritten laws than the mythical foundation that guarantees its connection with religion and its growth from mythical notions. (135)

Nietzsche conceded that "it is the fate of every myth to creep by degrees into the narrow limits of some alleged historical reality, and to be treated by some later generation as a unique fact with historical claims" (75). But he argued that this gradual emancipation from mythological beliefs and truths—as carried out, for example, by liberal theologians like David Friedrich Strauss—was not really a process of enlightenment but a process of vulgar trivialization and profaning of the world, which has left modern man not more enlightened but only more disenchanted about it: "The tremendous historical need of our unsatisfied modern culture, the accumulation of countless other cultures, the consuming desire for knowledge—what does all this point to, if not to the loss of myth, the loss of the mythical home, the mythical maternal womb?" (136).

This early recognition of the constructive function of myth in classical civilization led Nietzsche in his later works, primarily in his essay *On the Utility and Liability of History for Life*, to a critical examination of history in modern civilization and set the standard by which history was to be judged: its utility and liability for life. He sought to replace "that rule of chance and accident that has hitherto been called 'History'" by a new conception of history, an artistic rather than a scientific one, which does not reduce the total chaos of crude reality to the perfect form of its human representation but rather sustains both in a precarious and fully conscious balance—as in classical mythology, where reality in general, and human life along with it, were conceived as freely *made* by human beings rather than as necessarily *given* by divine or natural laws. However, unlike the Greeks, who realized, and therefore fully exploited, the essentially artistic structure and potentialities of the human condition, modern man has been deprived of his artistic capabilities by excessive claims for methodical rationalism and realism in all spheres of life. Modern historiography, with its scientific pretensions to a realistic representation of human affairs, was a prime example of that deprivation. Nietzsche's radical solution to this predicament was to redeem myth in and for history. Accordingly, the task of the historian is to enhance and to elevate even the most common theme "to a comprehensive symbol," to disclose in it "a whole world of profundity, power and beauty." This "requires above all a great artistic power, a creative floating above things, a loving immersion in the empirical data, a poetic elaboration of given types" in later historical configurations, such as had been achieved by the Greek tragedians in their mythological interpretations and representations of their historical reality.[81] "The genuine historian [echter Historiker] must have the power to recast what is age-old into something never heard before, to proclaim a general truth with such simplicity and profundity that we overlook the simplicity due to the profundity, and the profundity due to the simplicity."[82] Nietzsche thus urges all modern historians to "seek our models in the primordial world of ancient Greece with all its greatness, naturalness, and humanity. But here we will also find the reality of an essentially ahistorical cultivation and of a form of cultivation that despite—or precisely because of—this fact is indescribably rich and vital."[83]

These famous pronouncements on the mythological origins and potentialities of modern historiography had an enormous impact on a whole generation of Kulturkritiker in Germany, most notably—and for Kantorowicz most crucially—on his Meister, the poet and leader Stefan George.[84] According to Steven Aschheim, George and his followers were rather ambivalent in their attempt to appropriate Nietzsche's legacy;[85] but they were wholly devoted to fulfilling Nietzsche's pronouncement in Human All Too Human:

> The poetic power available to men of today which is not used up in the depiction of life ought to be dedicated, not so much to the representation of the contemporary world or to the reanimation and imaginative reconstruction of the past, but to signposting the future:—not, though, as if the poet could, like a fabulous economist, figuratively anticipate the kind of conditions nations and societies would prosper better under and how they could then be brought about. What he will do, rather, is emulate the artists of earlier times who imaginatively developed the existing images of the gods and imaginatively develop a fair image of man.[86]

Nietzsche's attempt to replace the pretentious Verwissenschaftlichung of historiography by new modes of Ästhetisierung acquired new political meanings after World War I. As Ernst Troeltsch has shown in his classic studies on the crisis of German historicism, Nietzsche's message became particularly attractive and effective as the German *Ersatzreligion* of "Scientific History" collapsed with all other secular foundations and institutions of the German Reich.[87] Nietzsche's call for the mythopoeic construction of history clearly reverberates in Friedrich Gundolf's explication of George's theory of historiography:

> The true task of the poet, from a new view of the world to acquire a new power of utterance, was in the nineteenth century more nearly accomplished by the three great historiographers Ranke, Mommsen, and Burckhardt . . . Ranke's pictures of the Reformation, Mommsen's Roman history and Burckhardt's Renaissance will (regardless of whether they have since been "superseded" scientifically) be seen to have most readily retained their power of mythical illumination, while the plays, novels and poems of even the most talented writers have long since been the concern only of the psychologists or the literary historians.[88]

George himself recited such Nietzschean notions in many of his poems and sermons on great historical figures, whom he deemed worthy of mythologizing.[89] This is the main message of his poem "The Graves of Speyer," which he wrote around the turn of the century, against the official decision to celebrate this occasion by reopening the imperial graves in the Dome of Speyer. This sacrilegious act betrayed all the profanity and vanity of modernity, of a German nation that had become so obsessed with the material possessions of its history that it could not perceive anymore its spiritual lessons. George described in the poem how

> summoned by his Staufen ancestress
> From regions of the South, a splendid guest
> A people's god: the greatest of the Fredericks
> Approaches . . .
> His gaze unites the plans of Ottos, Carls
> With his own boundless dreams of the Levant
> Wisdom of Cabbalists and Rome's decorum.[90]

His poem carried a message of redemption for those who could decipher its mythological expression. Kantorowicz sought to achieve that redemption in his historical biography of Frederick, the Hohenstaufen emperor whom members of the George *Kreis* used to call "Friedrich der Grössere," so as to distinguish him from his namesake, the Prussian king Frederick II. Following George's orders and the examples set by other members of his

Kreis, he composed it along the Nietzschean lines of "monumental" historiography, namely as a history that was or could become a *Mythologie.* Ernst Bertram's book on Nietzsche himself, published in 1918 and aptly subtitled *Versuch einer Mythologie,* was precisely that, a conscious attempt to apply Nietzsche's mythological axioms to his own life and works.[91] Friedrich Gundolf's historical biographies of Caesar and Goethe were predicated on the same principles. In his work on Caesar's reputation in history, Gundolf, in fact, preceded Kantorowicz in claiming that Frederick II was the first modern ruler who really understood Caesar as a "personal role model" and accordingly sought to emulate him in all his actions.[92] All these attempts at a new historiography are restated in theoretical terms in Erich von Kahler's polemical essay *Der Beruf der Wissenschaft* of 1921. Kahler's main aim in this tract was to mold the neoromantic, antipositivistic theories of his fellow Georgeaner into a respectable historiography, claiming that as an artistic composition it was scientific in the new and more radical sense of the term given to it by Nietzsche, precisely because it pertained to truths beyond factual limitations. Kantorowicz, a lifelong friend of Kahler, used Kahler's distinction between research (*Forschung*) and representation (*Darstellung*) in his book (and subsequent controversies) about Frederick II.[93] He may also have borrowed the notion of "Mythenschau" itself from Kahler's argument against the rigidity of Weber's conception of science and his claim that the aim of science was to transform *das Leben* through *Schau.*[94] Like Nietzsche and George, Kantorowicz maintained that the task of the historian was not only to gather and test facts about the past but also to transform them into truths about the present. Above all, however, he believed that since historiography was essentially an art, not a science, it belonged to and had to be practiced as "national literature."

In view of what happened in Germany at that time and after, Kantorowicz's notions on the vocation of historiography may seem outrageous and dangerous. His pedagogical conception of history as "nationale Literatur" is redolent of the demagogic conception of history as "Belehrung für die Nation."[95] As critical commentators have pointed out, Kantorowicz's attack on objective "truth" in historiography served those who sought to reduce all the old universal "truths" to new German "myths." According to Otto Gerhard Oexle, such "historicistic" attacks on scientific historiography proved fatal to German historical scholarship. Oexle singles out Kantorowicz's *Frederick the Second* as a prime example of the fabrication of a "new Middle Ages" that suited the conservative revolution in Germany. He notes that even though Kantorowicz himself did not espouse the Nazi doctrines of racial and imperial superiority, he propagated similar notions in his book, as well as in his public appearances, where he openly called for the "nationalization of historiography."[96] However, as other German scholars have argued, Kantorowicz's notions of "German," "Nation," and the "German Nation" were not at all the same as those of the Nazis.[97] The crucial difference between Kantorowicz's "nationalistic" notions and the Nazi conceptions was that Kantorowicz did not ground any of his notions in racial theories and all but ignored the very notion of *Volk*. Most scholars of German historiography would argue that this ought to be the distinction between the various forms of nationalistic historiography in Germany before and during the Nazi rule.[98] The fact that Nazi ideologists used Kantorowicz's book does not make him or his book organs of National Socialism. Helmut Scheuer, a harsh but fair critic of Kantorowicz's book, gets it right when he commends Kantorowicz for his courageous opposition to the Nazis but points out that "the heroism and messianism which he espoused flowed into the syncretic ideology of National Socialism."[99] More fundamentally, the connection between historical methodology and political ideology in this (and probably in any other) case is not so simple, as can be gauged from the fact that Kantorowicz's main antagonist in the controversy on the equity of historiography was the notorious Albert Brackmann: in 1930 Brackmann championed all the right (i.e., objective, nonrelative, corroborative) principles of the historical profession, but he himself did not live up to them: during the Nazi period he became the most powerful official historian of the regime.[100]

This counterexample may at least indicate that in 1930 the historical controversies in Germany were still more methodological than ideological. In any case, the one and only ideology that Kantorowicz believed in and served during those years—and ever since—was George's, and this, as we saw above, was then concerned with the spiritual and intellectual traditions of German cultural history. In his book and his polemical essays, Kantorowicz sought to make his readers and fellow historians fully aware of these traditions and, moreover, of their predicament in them, as essentially and inevitably "Germans." As Johannes Fried writes, "[t]he biographer of Frederick II was far from taking visions as reality; but he had realized the implications of the methodological dilemma which lands historians into trouble, namely, that no historian, not even the strongest positivist, could conceive of or analyse a fact and tell a story without an idea and a metaphysical concept of the subject, without an image of the past, with which he is concerned."[101]

This was the main message of Kantorowicz's public lecture at the

Seventeenth Congress of German Historians, held at Halle on the Saale in April 1930, which seems to have been his most explicit pronouncement ever regarding his historiographical aims and methods.[102] After reiterating his "Mythenschau" claim that the "the positivistic *Geschichtsforschung*" should not attempt to impose "its own rules of research" on "the artistic *Geschichtsdarstellung*," Kantorowicz stated, in opposition to Brackmann and the entire establishment of historical scholarship in Germany, that human affairs were not determined by "causes [*Kausalitäten*]" but by "tensions [*Spannungen*]," which often arose out of irrational perceptions (*Wahrnehmungen*) of reality and thus rendered it unsuitable to positivistic explanations. The main task of historiography is artistic, not scientific: it must set up "pictures [*Bilder*]" of the past, yet such as describe not only "how something really *was*" but also, and primarily, "how it was perceived" (116–17). Hence myths are indispensable to historiography: "For inasmuch as legends and myths are recognized as such, their interweaving in the historical narration does not pose any danger to truth but is rather part of that historical truth itself" (119). He further states that since the new historiography seeks to evoke the "totality" of human life, with all its emotional and even irrational experiences, it is more akin to the ancient epic or dramatic arts than to any of the modern sciences. Accordingly, this historiography demands from its practitioner the "commitment of the whole man," by which he means to say that, like the creative artist who brings his whole being into the work, the historian ought to bring his "life" into his work. Yet the "life" of the historian is not merely his own; it is also the life of his nation. For Kantorowicz believed that national identity determined the lineage and language of the historian to such an extent that any attempt at an objective treatment of facts was a fallacious pretension. "The severe positivism faces the danger of becoming romantic when it claims . . . to find the blue Flower of truth without any preconceptions [*Voraussetzungen*]" (120). On these premises he rejects the "cosmopolitan" ideology and methodology of the old German historiography that saw, with Ranke, all nations "equally close to God" as impractical and hypocritical; he insists instead on the indispensability of "nationalistic historiography."

Having thus committed himself to "nationalistic historiography," Kantorowicz readily assumes the role of a very German historian. He refers proudly to *Frederick the Second* as a work in which he sought to inspire his readers with descriptions of the "German" qualities of Frederick. In his description, Frederick's features exemplified the "God-and-Father type of earlier German emperors as Barbarossa embodied it, and as the Renaissance Emperors revived it," and his "total impression" was "a German trait to which neither a Caesar nor a Napoleon could lay claim."[103] And all this was concerning a Norman-Sicilian ruler who, despite his German ancestry, never learned German and hardly considered himself to be German! Clearly, Kantorowicz was less concerned with the way Frederick really was than with the ways in which he had been ideally interpreted and the way he had lived on. Or, as modern theorists would put it, the real *Geschichte* of any historical figure was truly and fully revealed only in its *Wirkungsgeschichte*. Recall again the coronation scene in Jerusalem. Kantorowicz concludes his discussion of this historical event with its metahistorical meanings for Frederick and his contemporaries: "The question was whether he could awaken an echo in some nation, whether some people could comprehend him, as the divine power within him seemed to portend."[104] In the final lines of the work, these enigmatic suggestions become explicit commands for the German people to awake to—and to awaken like—"the radiant, the ever-young, the stern and mighty judge . . . who slumbers not nor sleeps but ponders how he can renew the 'Empire.'" Having realized that "Germany's dream was changed, and change of myth reflects the changing life and longings of the people," he sought to represent Frederick as a still living figure, not only in his age but also in all ages of German history, a myth-dream that had been forgotten by, though not lost to, modern Germany.[105] More precisely, Frederick epitomized the ideal ruler for those Germans who adhered to a certain ideal of their nation—that of "The Secret Germany."

Das geheime Deutschland: this notion has been much discussed by cultural historians of the period, who traced its transformations from the patriotic sentiments of Hölderlin, Schiller, Hebbel, and Heine through the nationalistic aspirations of de Lagarde and Langbehn and finally to the mystic and elitist meanings it acquired in the George *Kreis*. Common to all the interpreters was the belief that the spiritual identity and destiny of Germany were hidden in—but also from—its people; they differed over the political means to perpetuate the secret mission: whether through "a hidden emperor . . . whether he be artist, sage or thinker";[106] a *völkisch* movement; or, for George, a group of virtuous artists and intellectuals, such as his own *Kreis,* whose task was to forge the ideal *Volk* out of and eventually against the real people. In order to regain this "Secret Germany," it was necessary to reveal the heroic mythology inherent in its mundane history. This is precisely what Kantorowicz performed in his work. He made it clear in the prefatory note to the book, in which he recalled his visit to Frederick's tomb in the Cathedral of Palermo in 1924. There, he writes, "a wreath might have been seen on the emperor's sarcophagus with this inscription: Seinen Kaisern und Helden / Das Geheime Deutschland." It was a symbolic action, he added, that proved that "not alone in learned circles enthusiasm is astir for the great Germans of the past: in a day when Kaisers are no more." [107]

The rhetorical accentuation of such political considerations in historical composition was too abrasive even for an extreme nationalist like Brackmann, who concluded his review with the warning that one cannot write history "either as a George disciple, or as a Catholic, Protestant, or Marxist, but only as a truth-seeking human being." [108] Kantorowicz responded that on these terms neither could one write history as a German, or indeed even as a human being who had any opinions or passions. [109] More to the point, he noted that Brackmann objected to his methodology because by downplaying the "mere political facts" in favor of the "total way of life" of the emperor and by relying, as he openly did, on subjective and colorful chronicles of his contemporaries rather than on official diplomatic sources, he appeared to compound history with myth, and therein, so argued Brackmann, lay the great danger for knowledge of the truth. Kantorowicz agreed that this was the crucial issue: whether his method posed "the great danger for knowledge of the truth." [110] The controversy, in other words, was not really or solely about "historical method" but about "historical truth," more concretely about historical truth's relation to myth: were they opposed, as Brackmann thought, or was myth, as Kantorowicz thought, the appropriate form in which certain truths could be told. He concluded that Brackmann's attack on him was not really a *Methodenstreit* but an *Anschauungsstreit*. [111]

And so indeed it was. The debate was not whether to use myths as historical sources—this, as we have seen, was fairly common in German historiography—but how to appraise these myths: were they false or true manifestations of historical reality? How, for example, should one account for the divine idioms by which Frederick and his courtiers conceived of the emperor as having merged with King David and Christ? Were they political manipulations of religious beliefs, as Brackmann thought, or were they expressions of these beliefs, as Kantorowicz argued? [112] Kantorowicz, in any case, did not think that these questions could be answered in a *Methodenstreit*, for they were not so much methodological as ideological. Moreover, even when he seemed to engage in a professorial *Methodenstreit* with fellow German historians and performed all the ritual gestures of *Quellenforschung*, he did not really respect its academic rules and results. In reply to Brackmann and like-minded critics who accused him of having written his book according to some arbitrary and subjective idée fixe rather than by the objective *Regeln* of the profession, he published in 1931 a supplementary volume (*Ergänzungsband*) of footnotes and annotations to every page of the text, as well as ten learned excursuses on particular problems. Brackmann was now satisfied, and in the final words of his *Nachwort* to Kantorowicz's *Mythenschau* essay, he expressed the hope that Kantorowicz, who was then working in the Monumenta Germaniae Historica in Berlin, would henceforth abide by its "positivistic" regulations.[113] Yet Kantorowicz himself did not think that his additional publication was significant to the book itself: "There may be as many quotations of sources as possible. They will, however, never prove the essential: the basic conception . . . and as its result: *das historische Bild*."[114] Clearly, what mattered to Kantorowicz, what mattered in history itself, were the "historical images" that emanated from the factual sources, the ideal fictions that survived and revived the real actions in the imagination of later generations. In order to deal with these images adequately, the historian had to forge a new historical *Methode* out of this new historical *Anschauung*.

From these larger perspectives, the *Anschauungsstreit* over *Frederick the Second* was not confined to Brackmann and Kantorowicz. The preponderance of *Anschauung* over *Methode* already indicates that in this case both represented traditions in German historiography, which had long been divided over the problem of historical myths. The two traditions were then associated with the respective universities, Berlin and Heidelberg, of the two medieval historians. Brackmann represented the positivistic tradition of Ranke's *Historisches Seminar* in Berlin, whose most prominent spokesman in his generation was Theodor Mommsen, the great classical scholar who, in the name of real-political historiography, demolished many ancient political myths, such as those of Romulus and Coriolanus. Kantorowicz studied and worked in Heidelberg, where Max Weber's teachings inspired a whole generation of historical scholars to counter the positivistic methodology of the Berlin school with new humanistic and hermeneutic perceptions. The two teachers who initially directed Kantorowicz's historical studies represented this countertradition: the historian of antiquity Alfred von Domaszevski, in whose seminar on Alexander the Great the young student presented a paper, "The Divine Exaltations of Alexander," which was his first attempt in what he would later define as political theology; and the economic historian and Kantorowicz's *Doktorvater*, Eberhart Gothein, who had studied in Basel with Jacob Burckhardt and Wilhelm Dilthey and did much to propagate their message of *Kulturgeschichte* in Heidelberg.[115] As the *Nachfolger* to Max Weber's *Lehrstuhl* for political economy, Gothein was able to combine the cultural-Burckhardtian and the social–Weberian conceptions of history in a way that clearly inspired his student Kantorowicz to create his own very "modern" historiography. Gothein, in fact, anticipated Kantorowicz's *Streit* with Brackmann and the Prussian school in historiography already in 1889 when he argued against the political historian Dietrich Schäfer for the primacy of "cultural history" in the comprehension of human affairs as well as in moral instruction regarding them.[116] The origins of the *Mythenschau* controversy must therefore be traced back to Basel in the age of Burckhardt and his fellow champions of *Kulturgeschichte*. As Lionel Gossman has shown, the Basel school of historical scholarship differed most radically from that of Berlin's in its atavistic conception of history. For scholars like Burckhardt, Bachofen, Nietzsche, Overbeck, and Rohde all assumed that the psychological origins of human life and history were mythical and therefore sought to regain them for modern historical scholarship.[117] Kantorowicz tried to do the same as he set out to expose the archaic beliefs and traditions that have made up and sustain all our modern political institutions, above all that of the nation-state.

This was the task that he took up in his last major work, *The King's Two Bodies*, which he published in 1957. I conclude my discussion with some comments on that work, which contains, as it were, Kantorowicz's final reflections on history as *Mythenschau*. It will serve me also to elaborate on the ideology of Kantorowicz's methodology. For even if one believes, as I do, that his biography of Frederick is defensible on methodological grounds, it is still disconcerting to recall what it meant to Hitler, Göring, and other Nazis. Karl Löwith's judgment on the members of the George Circle applies to Kantorowicz's book as well: "They prepared paths for National Socialism which they then themselves did not take."[118] Although Kantorowicz consistently refused to discuss this problem of contamination by association and generally assumed professorial immunity to such charges, he must have been acutely aware of his predicament, and at one point in 1946 he obliquely referred to it. At the end of his book *Laudes Regiae*, recalling some *Laudes*-like hymn used by the Italian Fascists to acclaim Mussolini, he remarks that cases like this may give the historian full scope for "meditations on the dangers implicit in his profession of excavator of the past."[119] His correspondence with the German publisher of *Frederick the Second* in the last years of his life reveals that he was all too aware of how his book and ideas had been abused in such ways.[120] Yet Kantorowicz never revoked his admiration for Frederick, or his notion of "universal monarchy," or his devotion to "Secret Germany." In *The King's Two Bod-*

ies, he clarified and justified his position by other means—analytical rather than mythical, or, more precisely, by analytical examination of the mythical.[121] His task in that book, he wrote, bore on "the problem of what has been called 'The Myth of the State' (Ernst Cassirer)," but his very notion and evaluation of that myth were radically different from those of Cassirer.[122] Whereas Cassirer was committed to the liberal philosophy of the Enlightenment and therefore sought to edify an ever more rational conception and organization of the state, Kantorowicz was rooted in the metaphysical theology of the Middle Ages: he sought to reveal the mythopoeic beliefs and traditions that have constituted and sustain the state. For him, as for Burckhardt, the state was, or at least ought to have been, "A Work of Art," a mythopoeic creation. This humanistic conviction motivated Kantorowicz throughout his life and may ultimately explain his apparent political conversion from German nationalism in the twenties to American liberalism in the fifties: in both cases he was primarily loyal to the myth of the state rather than to the state itself.

IV

As in his biography of Frederick, Kantorowicz calls our attention in his last book to the political circumstances and the precise moment of personal experience in which he came to realize what his task was. "One day I found in my mail an offprint from a liturgical periodical published by a Benedictine Abbey in the United States, which bore the publisher's imprint: *The Order of St. Benedict, Inc.*" To a European medieval scholar, he says, "nothing could have been more baffling than to find the abbreviation *Inc.,* customary with business and other corporations, attached to the venerable community of St. Benedict."[123] Having thus realized that in the United States even the monastic congregations were incorporated, along with other institutions that were supposed to be autonomous, such as the universities, Kantorowicz began to query how this had come about: how did the modern state become so powerful, so totalitarian? Kantorowicz was particularly alert to such signs, because as a scholar he had twice fought against state domination over universities—first during the Nazi occupation of the University of Frankfurt in 1933 and then, between 1949 and 1951, during Senator McCarthy's persecutions, when he opposed the regents of the University of California who demanded that all professors in that university take a loyalty oath to the state.[124]

In *The King's Two Bodies,* Kantorowicz thus set out to trace the history of the notion of the state as a corporation from its inception in medieval political theology. He found its origins in the legal formulations of the political theories of the later Middle Ages, principally in the idea that the king has two bodies: one that is physical and dies with him and one that is mystical and never dies. His main contention was that the political notion of the state as a mystical body of the king grew out of the theological notion of the Church as the "corpus mysticum" of Christ. He asserted that the political notion of the king's body proved to be equally effective in securing the unity and continuity of the secular organization through social divisions and historical ruptures. According to Kantorowicz, this "mystic fiction" served not only the legal theorists of the medieval monarchies but also subsequent theorists of the state, and it survived in many modern political theories that deified the state, most notoriously so in the Nazi ideology. Kantorowicz mentions "the horrifying experience of our own time in which whole nations, the largest and the smallest, fell prey to the weirdest dogmas and in which political theologisms became genuine obsessions defying in many cases the rudiments of human and political reason." [125] He adds that his study might be seen as a contribution to the problem that Ernst Cassirer has called "the Myth of the State." Yet Kantorowicz immediately follows this reference with some harsh words against Cassirer's and others' "all-too-sweeping and ambitious histories of ideas"—a sign that their differences were not just methodological but primarily ideological.[126] The issue, again, was not whether to work on "the myth of the state" but how to appraise it. For Cassirer this—and any other—political myth was pernicious to the very process of Western civilization, an "enemy" of reason and morality that must be exposed and destroyed.[127] Kantorowicz, in contrast, thought that the original myth of the modern state, as revealed in the king's two bodies, was crucial for the establishment of secular organization on norms and forms of communion that were truly universal and therefore human, much more human than the parochial norms and forms of the modern nation-state. The difference between Kantorowicz's conception of the myth of the state and Cassirer's is obvious: not only is Kantorowicz's theological (as any real myth must be) rather than philosophical, but it is also actual and historical: the notion of the king's two bodies really animated and affected political reality, whereas Heidegger's notion of *Geworfenheit,* on which Cassirer dwells, was known, if at all, to very few intellectuals, many of whom may have been Nazis; nevertheless, even they surely had other sources for their political mythology. In order to explain the fascination of the myth of the state in modernity, it was necessary to probe deeper layers of consciousness and cultures—primarily the

Christian ideas of the polity that are hardly mentioned in Cassirer's account. This was Kantorowicz's task.

He began it in one of his most famous essays on the medieval conception of *Pro Patria Mori,* which he published in 1951 and later inserted into *The King's Two Bodies.* The main polemical aim of this essay was to expose the modern notion of patriotism as a perversion and distortion of the prior and, in his view, superior Christian myth of the state.[128] The essay is a magisterial historical reconstruction of the phases by which the ancient theological notion of *corpus mysticum* acquired new political connotations in the wake of the holy wars of the crusaders, when the notion of *patria* assumed both new physical and new metaphysical dimensions, and thereafter transferred them into an ever more secular notion of the new "state." This process culminated in the Renaissance, when Enea Silvio Piccolomini (later Pope Pius II) dedicated to the Habsburg emperor Frederick III a sermon in which he replaced the "mystical body of church the head of which is Christ" with the "mystical body of the state the head of which is the prince." In that way, "at a certain moment in history the 'state' in the abstract or the state as a corporation appeared as a *corpus mysticum* and death for this new mystical body appeared equal in value to the death of a crusader for the cause of God."[129] Kantorowicz then invites the reader "to figure out all the distortions which the central idea of the *corpus mysticum* has suffered by its transference to national, party, and racial doctrines in more distant and in most recent times." In the final discussion, he exemplifies but also clarifies what he means by these "distortions":

> The so-called "Tombs of Martyrs" of the National-Socialist movement in Munich, or the gigantic streamer *Chi muore pe Italia non muore* covering, on Christmas, 1937, the façade of the Milan cathedral for the commemoration service for the dead soldiers of the Fascist Italian divisions in Franco's Spain, illustrate some of the recent nationalistic ravings which so terribly distort an originally venerable and lofty idea. On the other hand, the disenchantment of the world has progressed rapidly, and the ancient ethical values, miserably abused and exploited in every quarter, are about to dissolve in smoke. Cold efficiency during and after the Second World War, together with the individual's fear of being trapped by so-called "illusions" instead of professing "realistic views," has done away with the traditional "superstructures," religious as well as ideologic, to the effect that human lives no longer are sacrificed but "liquidated." We are about to demand a soldier's death without reconciling emotional equivalent for the lost life. If the soldier's death in action—not to mention the citizen's death in bomb-struck

cities—is deprived of any idea encompassing *humanitas*, be it God or king or *patria*, it will be deprived also of the ennobling idea of self-sacrifice. It becomes a cold-blooded slaughter or, what is worse, assumes the value and significance of political traffic accident on a bank holiday.[130]

It is, above all, this singular attempt at a clarification or rehabilitation of the myth of the state that distinguishes Kantorowicz, for better and worse, from so many other modern political historians and theoreticians, who have more often merely opposed these "distortions" rather than really exposing them for what they are. For Kantorowicz knew that the myth of the state as a *corpus mysticum* could quite easily be distorted, as indeed it had been, by Fascists and other reactionaries. But he nevertheless upheld it, because without this metaphysical myth, there was no meaning to physical life and death in—or for—the state.

This metaphysical conception of the state may clarify Kantorowicz's apparent "nationalistic" political conception of modern Germany during the Weimar years of his life. His Georgean notion of "The Secret Germany" was akin to what theorists from Schiller to Marcuse called "the aesthetic state."[131] He believed in Germany not as a *Staatsnation* but as a *Kulturnation*, a nation that transcends territorial and ethnical definitions so as to include among its members a Norman Sicilian emperor like Frederick and a poet like Dante. For him poets, rather than legal and political theorists, were the true guardians of the state, because they created and upheld its myth. Hence, whereas Cassirer builds his entire progressive theory and history of the myth of the state on the example of Plato, who first realized what it was and therefore expelled the poets, the mythmakers, from his Republic, Kantorowicz, at all times the follower of George, inverts this entire process by reaffirming the role of "the poet as leader" in cultural and political history. In 1954, while Kantorowicz was working on *The King's Two Bodies*, he confessed to his fellow George follower Robert Boehringer that even though he did not say much about George in public, "there is not a day in which I do not become aware that everything I have ever managed to achieve derives from that *singular* source and that this source continues to flow even after 20 years. Against that indomitable force, which has come out from over there, all the direct relations remain ephemeral."[132]

Believing that poetry is paramount, above history and all other theories, Kantorowicz opens *The King's Two Bodies* with Shakespeare, who exposed that myth of the state as merely a myth, yet one that still held— at least for Shakespeare, if no longer for secular jurists in his time— enormous metaphysical meanings. Moreover, Kantorowicz adds, "if that curious image, which from modern constitutional thought has vanished all but completely, still has a very real and human meaning today, this is largely due to Shakespeare."[133] Kantorowicz then reconstructs the history of the image as a "fiction" that acquired ever more realistic connotations (*fictio figura veritatis*) in the theological-political treatises of legal scholars in the thirteenth century.[134] Yet it was above all Dante who knew how to imbue the fiction of the continuity and unity of the state with its quintessential human meanings. In his *Monarchy* Dante foresaw in the eventual mastery of the emperor over the pope a new vision of the state as essentially "man-centered," namely as a creation of—and for—human sovereignty; he transformed the ancient theological myth of the state as preordained by *deitas* into a new political myth of the state as freely ruled by *humanitas*. Dante, like later Renaissance scholars from Pico to Vico, identified this notion of *humanitas* with the political ability to exercise "supreme jurisdiction over man *qua* mortal man"; he thus came to regard the ruler, and by extension all men, as *homo instrumentum humanitatis:* as agents who serve the absolute ideas and ideals—or what I have defined as the myths—of humanity. Thus, while the jurists and political theorists elaborated the tension between the king's natural body and his political body, "it remained to the poet to visualize the very tension of the 'Two Bodies' in man himself, to make *humanitas* . . . the sovereign of *homo*."[135] And just as the ideas and ideals of *humanitas* were necessarily universal, the state, which they all served, had to be universal; in Dante's vision it "embraced not only Christians or members of the Roman Church, but was conceived of as the world community of all men, Christians and non-Christians alike"—much like *das geheime Deutschland*.[136]

Dante's notion of universal monarchy was, then, the quintessential myth of the state—a myth that Kantorowicz held to be " 'always' and 'all at the same time' actuality."[137] He held on to it even when this myth seemed not only impossible but also reprehensible. Thus, in the darkest days of 1942, Kantorowicz sought to resuscitate the myth in a remarkable paper, "The Problem of Medieval World Unity," that he wrote for the *Annual Report of the American Historical Association for 1942*.[138] This romantic "slogan" was widespread in German historiography, as in Ranke's notion of "Romano-Germanic Nation," but, Kantorowicz admits, "[t]oday, the historian finds it difficult to defend the case of Medieval World Unity on similar lines and in similarly sanguine way" (76). In fact, he adds, "the much-hailed unity of language, letters and learning, of customs, education and crusading spirit, or even ecclesiastical matters" never materialized in historical reality: it was and remains "a mirage" (76–77). How, then, should the historian deal with the medieval conception of world unity? The fact that this conception is untenable on current historical—let alone geopolitical—grounds does not mean that it is not veritable for the historian: he must recognize it for what it is and always was, "a myth" of metaphysical reality that elevated and united the whole medieval world above all its theological and political dissensions.

> Therefore, if it be our desire to defend the myth of Medieval World Unity, we should remember that indeed this unity was myth, nay, that it was this very "Myth of Unity" which East and West alike professed. In other words, the "Myth" is the seemingly nebulous though yet quite solid substance of Medieval World Unity . . . The absence of unity was considered a momentary defection which could be overlooked because sooner or later the unity would have to be restored. A united world was indispensable for achieving that state of perfection which, it was generally recognized, would be established just before time ends and doomsday dawns. Thus, the medieval Myth of World Unity has a predominantly messianic or eschatological character. Against this background the myth stands out and becomes almost reality. (77–78)

On these premises Kantorowicz shows how the metaphysical myth "manifested itself daily in the Eastern and Western Churches alike, despite the profound differences between their rituals," notably above all in their similar exaltations of the universal Church, and how "the materialization of these hopes and expectations was the task not only of the Church but also of the secular power," who managed to exercise "a permanent spell upon the minds of people" (78–80). Hence, because the "vision of the unity to come proved stronger than the perception of the disparity that was," it was not just "a mirage," even if that is what it actually was. "It is obvious that the conception of World Unity has nothing whatever to do with what today would be called reality," but, just like the conceptions of "Christian Empire" or "Christian Army," which were similarly immaterial entities, such visions were real enough: "Mythically, however, or eschatologically, these were nevertheless realities" (80).

Although Kantorowicz refrains from comparative allusions to actual affairs, his message is clear. Once we realize what the medieval myth of world unity was and how it helped unite rival nations and religions into a universal community of believers, we must not give up our myth of universal humanity, even if, and precisely because, it is a myth. The vision of unity in 1942 could equally prove stronger than the perception of the disparity that was. In our modern civilization even more than in medieval civilization, metaphysical and eschatological myths of unity were indispensable. "This consideration should prevent us from confounding medieval ideas of World Unity with modern ideas of International Unity" (78). This reassertion of affirmative and redemptive theological myths over against deliberative political treaties betrays the deep conservative convictions of Kantorowicz. But it does not turn him into a political reactionary, as many rash commentators have described him. Rather, his lifelong attempt to save the myths of the state or of universal monarchy from "distortion" by reactionaries is akin to those of other modern conservative humanists in Germany at the time, whose aim was, in Thomas Mann's words, to have "myth taken out of Fascist hands and humanized down to the last recess of its language."[139]

These words are particularly pertinent to George's followers in Nazi Germany, as they were exemplified in the case of Claus Schenk Graf von Stauffenberg, a fellow member of Kantorowicz's in the George *Kreis*. His fateful story is well known: he was the leader of the German resistance to Hitler, and he became its tragic hero when the time bomb he carried to Hitler's headquarters Wolfschanze at Rastenburg in East Prussia on 20 July 1944 failed to kill the Führer.[140] The story of his life and death is profoundly associated with Kantorowicz's life and works through their deep and total devotion to the George *Kreis* and to the myth of *das geheime Deutschland*.[141] During Kantorowicz's student years in Heidelberg, Claus von Stauffenberg moved in the George Circle and was deeply influenced by its cultural ideas, ideals, and idols—above all, by the figure of Frederick II, the Staufer. Already in 1923 he alluded to himself and to his brothers as heirs of the Staufens. Among members of the group, he was in fact compared to Frederick: Max Kommerell hailed him in 1925 as "chief of the myth" and described him as a "miraculous lad" and the heir of the Staufen emperor "in the Staufen mountain."[142] Claus's twin brothers Berthold and Alexander were closely associated with Kantorowicz during his Heidelberg years while he was working on *Frederick the Second:* in 1924 they participated in the rite of laying the wreath at Frederick's tomb in the Cathedral of Palermo.[143] Berthold was entrusted by George with preparing Kantorowicz's book on the emperor for publication. The book itself was dedicated to Stauffenberg's cousin, Woldemar Graf von Uxküll-Gyllenband. During the 1930s and early 1940s, Claus von Stauffenberg continued to cherish the memory and message of Stefan George, principally the notion of *das geheime Deutschland*.

Das geheime Deutschland was the last poem that George himself had recited in public in 1928, and this was also the code name that Claus von

Stauffenberg and the other conspirators—many of whom were followers of George—used for their group.[144] In the last weeks before the decisive day in July 1944, when many of their comrades still doubted whether an assassination of the Führer was just, the Stauffenberg brothers sought to encourage them by reciting George's poem "The Anti-Christ." On 4 and 5 July 1944 they discussed at length Alexander von Stauffenberg's poem "Der Tod des Meisters" on George, which expressed their innermost spiritual and political convictions about their Germany.[145] And in the last horrible moment of his life, as he was lined up against the wall facing the firing squad of the Gestapo, Claus von Stauffenberg is reported to have called: "Long live the Secret Germany!"[146]

The actions of the Stauffenberg brothers and the works of Ernst Kantorowicz might thus be explained by the one myth that inspired them— that of *das geheime Deutschland*. As Peter Hoffman has observed, the Stauffenberg brothers never joined the Nazi party: "Their 'party' was the Secret Germany, their 'Führer' was Stefan George, their future was the 'vision' to which their small band was summoned." Claus Stauffenberg "remained committed to the living Secret Germany to which the Stauffenbergs had become heirs through Stefan George's last will and testament. This neo-classicist and neo-romantic side-road of German intellectual history drove them to action with greater force than the intellectual milieu to which the other conspirators belonged."[147]

The same might be said of Kantorowicz: the myth of *das geheime Deutschland* motivated him to his most significant intellectual and political actions. After the Nazi seizure of power in the early months of 1933, as militant students and officials at the University of Frankfurt boycotted and disrupted his classes, Kantorowicz was forced to stay away for several months. Yet even under the new extreme conditions, he held on to the Georgean notion of *das geheime Deutschland,* a mythical nation that existed, as it were, beyond and above the real-political one and included all—and only—the true patriots. This conviction inspired his actions in those fateful months. On 20 April 1933 he wrote a letter to the minister of education, in which he informed him of his resignation in protest against the anti-Semitic regulations of the University of Frankfurt:

> Although I, because of my published writings on the Staufen Emperor Frederick II, need no credentials from yesterday or today to vouch for my sentiments towards a nationally re-orientated Germany; although my fundamentally positive attitude towards a nationally geared Reich goes far beyond current trends or events and has not wavered even in the light of the most recent occurrences . . . nevertheless I, as a Jew, am forced to draw

certain conclusions from what has happened and to set aside my professional duties in the coming summer semester. For as long as any German
Jew—as in this present period of upheaval—can be considered almost a
traitor just because of his origin; as long as every Jew is deemed racially in-
ferior; as long as having any Jewish blood in one's veins implies a defect in
national convictions . . . so long will every German and truly patriotic Jew
who wishes to escape such suspicion have to hide his patriotism shame-
facedly instead of proclaiming it proudly.[148]

Then in November 1933 Kantorowicz resolved to fight back and resume
his teaching duties. To mark the occasion, he decided to deliver a special
public lecture in the auditorium of the University of Frankfurt carrying
the title "Das Geheime Deutschland."[149] In a letter to George, he stated
that the moment had come for their vision of *das geheime Deutschland* to reveal and assert itself.[150] His decision was precipitated by the realization that
the Nazi seizure of power had enticed some members of the George *Kreis,*
among them Ernst Bertram and Woldemar von Uxküll-Gyllenband (to
whom Kantorowicz dedicated *Friedrich der Zweite*), to declare that this
was the "break [*Umbruch*]" into new reality that George had called for, the
"Drittes Reich" being the realization of George's vision of the "Neues
Reich" and hence of all the ideas and ideals of *das geheime Deutschland.* Under the circumstances, Kantorowicz performed the most courageous and
virtuous act of resistance by setting out to defend *das geheime Deutschland*
against its detractors, those who used the "weapons" of vulgarism and rac-
ism to "drag its image to the streets, make it fashionable for the market
and then celebrate it as their own flesh and blood!"[151] He insists that *das
geheime Deutschland* "is a *Reich* which is at the same time in this world
and not in this world . . . a *Reich* which is at the same time here and not
here . . . a *Reich* which is at the same time of the dead and of the living,
that changes and yet remains eternal and immortal."[152] Recalling the *Di-
vina Commedia,* Kantorowicz reminded his listeners that a spiritual *Reich*
like that of *das geheime Deutschland* might open up only for those who are
willing to live in the shadows of humility, whereas "those who merely wish
to boast about it, or worse to abuse it for some impure purposes—should
not even be allowed to look at this secret *Reich* . . . By sheer force [*Gewalt*]
they will never be able to conquer this heaven."[153] Kantorowicz thus reiterated the Georgean notion of *das geheime Deutschland* as a mythical, not
political, entity, a nation that existed beyond any territorial or any other
material limitations: it signified rather the biblical-classical notion of an
"elected" or elitist nation, which Max Kommerell (paraphrasing Hölderlin) defined as "a nation among whom the gods dwell and sire their heroes,

a nation whose life resembles the life of the gods down to the most trivial activity."[154]

As in the case of the Stauffenbergs, Kantorowicz conceived of this lecture as his "last testament" to a "better Germany"—the old mythical Germany over against the new real-political one. The German *Reich* that emerged in his lecture was not defined by the modern notions of *Blut und Boden* but by the medieval virtues of beauty and nobility. Kantorowicz presented this Germany as a myth, indeed, but one that had once been real—for the heroes of classical Greece; for the saints of the Christian *civitas dei;* for the Ottonian, Salien, and Staufen emperors; for the Renaissance adherents to Dante's *humana civilitas;* for modern Germans like Holbein, Frederick the Great, Herder, Goethe, Hölderlin, Nietzsche, and George; and for all others who could bring into being "all primeval human forms and forces." By quoting both Goethe ("es müße der vollkommene Deutsche stets mehr sein als Deutsch") and Nietzsche ("um Deutscher zu werden müße man sich entdeutschen") to support his claim that Germany was a *Kulturnation* rather than a *Nationalstaat,*[155] Kantorowicz grounded his historiographical argument against Brackmann in historical reality: just as the real Germany was supranational, its true historiography was suprahistorical.

Several months after his last public lecture, Kantorowicz found another occasion to reiterate this message, in an essay, "German Papacy," which he wrote in 1933 and then managed to have broadcast, under a pseudonym, in the Reichssender Berlin late in the night of 22 February 1935.[156] It dealt with the attempts of the German emperors in the eleventh century to unite the German and Roman crowns and to initiate thereby a *renovatio imperii.* Starting with the Roman expedition of the young emperor Otto III, who deposed the Crescentine pope, John XVI, and then made both his cousin and his teacher popes, as Gregory V and Sylvester II, Kantorowicz then describes the attempts of Otto's successors Heinrich II and Heinrich III (who managed to appoint three German popes) to reform the papacy according to the new provisions of Cluny; these reform attempts, he notes, failed. The Nazi officials who allowed the transmission of Kantorowicz's text probably found it congenial to the new concordance between Hitler and the political and papal authorities in Rome. Yet Kantorowicz perceived in this episode a deeper and very different truth about the political destination of Germany, that it was to renew its Roman rather than its Aryan orientation and therewith to reach beyond the narrow political boundaries of German nationality to universality.[157] Kantorowicz notes that even though this policy failed, its myth of "German Papacy" survived in the poetic visions and prophecies of Hildegard von Bingen and may still be seen in the Dome of Bamberg, which contains the tombs of the emperor Heinrich II as well as of pope Clemens II and where, he adds, "two statues, one of *Ecclesia* that does not boast in its triumph and the other of *Synagoge* that restrains its sorrow, are equally noble," as if to signify that a Roman Germany promises also a reconciliation of Christians and Jews.[158] Apart from his letter of resignation of April 1933, Kantorowicz did not write about the fate of German Jewry; but his evocation of *das geheime Deutschland* in the eleventh century as a model state of toleration and reconciliation clearly indicates how and where he perceived the eventual redemption of German Jewry.

Stauffenberg believed that a new and better Germany could arise, like the mythological Phoenix, only from the ashes of destruction. Kantorowicz too was fascinated by this "fabulous bird of classical and Christian myths" and devoted to its history and meanings many pages in *The King's Two Bodies,* where it appears to symbolize the most sublime notion of human perseverance in medieval political theology: *Dignitas quae non moritur.*[159]

V

The historical case of the Stauffenberg brothers, much like the historiographical work of Ernst Kantorowicz, seems to defy the conventional norms by which we commonly judge political and historical issues. Kantorowicz was well aware of this. In his reflections on Dante's legacy to modernity, Kantorowicz remarks that "if in a superficial manner he has often been labelled reactionary, it is simply the prevalence of the imperial idea in Dante's works . . . which obscured the overwhelmingly unconventional features of his moral-political outlook. Dante, of course, cannot easily be labelled at all."[160] The same might be said—and is, I think, being said in this passage—about Kantorowicz himself: his conservative political ideology obscured the radical features of his historical methodology. For, just like Dante, who regained myth in and for literature and thereby modernized it, Kantorowicz attempted to regain myth in and for historiography, and in so doing he contributed to its new, distinctly modern, formation.

In his final reflections on the persistence of the myth of the "King's Two Bodies," Ernst Kantorowicz acknowledged that this "kind of manmade irreality—indeed, that strange construction of a human mind which finally becomes slave to its own fictions—we are normally more ready to find in the religious sphere than in the allegedly sober and realistic realms of law, politics, and constitution."[161] The term "allegedly" betrays Kantorowicz's true opinion. In fact, his entire historical work clearly defies this common assumption. As in his previous work on Frederick II, where he presented the legal and political works of the ruler as epitomes of that quintessential dignity of man, namely, the ability to believe and live in fictions that man himself has made; or in the *Laudes Regiae,* where he traced the perpetuation of royal hymns from medieval theology to Mussolini's Fascist ideology; so too in this last work, *The King's Two Bodies,* Kantorowicz demonstrates that our modern social and political reality is made up by historical myths and must be interpreted—and possibly even written— in their terms. The lesson of his life and works was clear to him: history *is* a *Mythenschau.*

Kantorowicz's notions on the theological origins and functions of modern political theories and institutions have in recent years won the attention of social theorists and historians. His work on the charismatic authority of kings has been hailed by Clifford Geertz as "magisterial" and "seminal" for the evolution of modern political anthropology.[162] English scholars have likewise come to rediscover the aptness of Kantorowicz's theories and histories of "royalty" for their project on the invention and— more significantly—the continuation of that tradition.[163] His more general observations on the political significance of "bodies" and other symbols of power have been recognized by Michel Foucault and other French genealogists of the "human sciences" as conducive to their counterhistory of modernity, in which "power" has been detached from visible bodies and thus has become much more pervasive and authoritative.[164]

As I show in this chapter, Kantorowicz's notions on the mythopoeic origins and potentialities of modern historiography warrant attention, especially from mythistorians, because in his two great books he exemplified how the "recognition of myth," which all mythistorians must attain, might be used either positively for the realization of historical myths, as in *Frederick the Second,* or more objectively for critical reflection on historical myths, as in *The King's Two Bodies.* Kantorowicz failed to combine the two strategies because he believed, with Nietzsche, that history is, or must become, a new mythology, a suprahistorical affirmation of the myths by which we live. He therefore failed to transform mythistory into "modern historiography" in the way that Joyce, Eliot, or Thomas Mann created the "modern novel" out of—but also against—the old mythology. He did not use their "mythical method." In order to accomplish this task, it would have been necessary to attain a new critical recognition of myth, such as would counter, mediate between, and overcome both Cassirer's philosophical derision of myth and Kantorowicz's theological-political submission to it. Walter Benjamin attained this kind of recognition in his "redemptive criticism [*rettende Kritik*]" of myth.

Walter Benjamin: History as Modern Mythology

I

In his "Recollections of Walter Benjamin," Ernst Bloch recounts a typical meeting with Benjamin, sometime in the spring of 1927: "We saw him strolling pensively, so to speak, with his head bowed, on the Kurfürstendamm—and my fiancée Karola, who was seeing him for the first time after having heard so much about him from me, asked him what he had been thinking about. He answered: 'Dear lady, have you ever noticed the sickly appearance of the marzipan figures?' " [1] In her memoirs Karola Bloch recalls this incident and adds that after Benjamin had made his remark, "he pulled out of his bag a half-shell made of walnut and in it Mary and infant Jesus in a crib all finely carved in marzipan," a *Kunstwerk* that they then all studied with admiration! [2]

This anecdote epitomizes the manner in which Benjamin conducted his life and intellectual inquiries. The *Marzipanfiguren* were legitimate, indeed consummate, objects for philosophical and historical reflections, manifesting, as it were, the entire spiritual and material compulsions that made up modern civilization. As Theodor Adorno noted, Benjamin's philosophy consists in "a kind of concretion," whereby scant and seemingly insignificant objects—be they material (toys, stamps, postcards) or literal (proverbs, legends, quotations)—yield, under his "Medusan glance," secret meanings. [3] Benjamin's predilection for the tiniest and most concrete aspects of grand theories and institutions might best be exemplified by another anecdote, recounted by Gershom Scholem: "In August 1927 he dragged me to the Musée Cluny in Paris, where, in a collection of Jewish ritual objects, he showed me with true rapture two grains of wheat on which a kindred soul had inscribed the complete Shema Israel." [4] From this story, as from so many others concerning Benjamin's "micrology," we may infer a possible reason for his meditation on the *Marzipanfiguren:* just as it was possible to write the essential Torah on two grains of wheat, it is feasible to comprehend the entire modern world by meditating on just one of its typical goods. Benjamin himself defined his historical methodology as consisting in "the attempt to retain the image of history even in the most inconspicuous corners of existence—the detritus of history, as it were."[5]

Why, then, *Marzipanfiguren?* What did Benjamin learn from them about modern society and history? Since, to the best of my knowledge, neither Ernst or Karola Bloch nor Benjamin himself ever elaborated on their discussion of this particular incident, I would like to explain—in a *Gedankengang* that, in itself, pays homage to Benjamin—his entire worldview out of this episode, which, as Benjamin would have it, is so original precisely because it is so marginal. A possible starting point for this inquiry might be the motto that Benjamin affixed to his autobiographical work *A Berlin Childhood around Nineteen Hundred:* "O Victory Column, baked to perfection, ornamented with the sugar of winter out of the days of childhood."[6] Whatever Benjamin may have meant by these words (which, as Scholem notes, were probably written during one of Benjamin's hashish experiments),[7] his decision to use this luscious image as the key to his social memories and experiences is significant and may also explain his reaction to the *Marzipanfiguren.* For the sugar or the snowflakes that cover up the harsh socio-political reality of the "Victory Column"—the Berlin monument that disguises the awful reality of death and destruction reminiscent of "Dante's *Inferno*"[8]—are like the sweet but "sickly" *Marzipanfiguren.* The fact that modern society still produces and consumes these "wishful images [*Wunschbilder*]" implies that these fabrications, like so many other mythic figurations that still abound in all other "cultural expressions," pertain to some real needs and desires in our social life and history. My main contention in this chapter is that Benjamin conceived of the *Marzipanfiguren* as yet another manifestation of the general "reactivation of the mythic forces" in modern civilization and that this realization, which he termed *modern mythology,* permeated his entire philosophy.

Benjamin's "puzzlement" at the sight of the *Marzipanfiguren* displays that singular kind of mythological thought which, according to Aristotle, is "metaphysical" in the original sense of the term:

> It is owing to their amazement that men both now begin and first began to philosophize; they wondered originally at the obvious difficulties, then

advanced little by little and stated difficulties about the greater matters, e.g. about the phenomena of the moon and those of the sun and of the stars, and about the genesis of the world. And a man who is puzzled and wonders thinks himself ignorant; whence even the lover of myth [*philomythes*] is in a sense a lover of wisdom [*philosophus*] for the myth is composed of wonders.[9]

These words aptly characterize Benjamin's style of philosophical reasoning. As Scholem has observed, although Benjamin often assumed materialist guises, he was primarily "a metaphysician" in the classical, Aristotelian sense of the term: "Philosophical experience of the world and its reality— that is how we can sum up the meaning of the term *metaphysics,* and that is certainly the sense in which it was used by Benjamin."[10] Having thus defined Benjamin as "a metaphysician pure and simple," Scholem makes this important observation, which deserves to be quoted in full:

But it was borne in on him that in his generation the genius of a pure metaphysician could express itself more readily in other spheres, any other sphere rather than in those traditionally assigned to metaphysics, and this was precisely one of the experiences that helped to mold his distinctive individuality and originality. He was attracted more and more by subjects that would seem to have little or no bearing on metaphysics. It is a special mark of his genius that under his gaze every one of these subjects discloses a dignity, a philosophic aura of its own which he sets out to describe.[11]

In his memorial biography of Benjamin, *The Story of a Friendship,* Scholem shows that Benjamin was well aware of the essentially "mythological" origins and potentialities of his metaphysical inquiries. He also draws attention to Benjamin's deep immersion in Aristotle's *Metaphysics* during the formative years of their philosophical education.[12] Although Benjamin's interest in myth in those years was primarily philosophical, he was well informed about the major trends in the new science of mythology. During his studies at the University of Munich between 1915 and 1917, he attended, along with other inspired participants, including the poet Rilke, a private seminar given by Walter Lehmann, the eminent scholar of pre-Columbian ethnology and comparative mythology, in which Benjamin came to understand the wider philosophical meanings and historical implications of ancient mythology.[13] This understanding was intensified by other members in that circle, such as Max Pulver, who introduced Benjamin to the romantic philosopher of myth Franz von Baader, whom Benjamin found "more impressive than Schelling."[14] The circle also included

Felix Noeggerath, with whom Benjamin discussed the avenues that the new discipline of "comparative mythology" might open up for his own personal "tasks and goals."[15] These notions affected Benjamin's reading of mythological literature during 1918–19 and informed his general theories of myth as well as his critical interpretations of other works on the topic during the early 1920s. Scholem recalls one memorable conversation with the young Benjamin in Seeshaupt near Munich in June 1918: "During a discussion of whether Hegel had wished to deduce the world we turned to mathematics, philosophy, and myth. Benjamin accepted myth alone as 'the world.' He said he was still not sure what the purpose of philosophy was, as there was no need to discover 'the meaning of the world': it was already present in myth. Myth was everything; all else, including mathematics and philosophy, was only an obscuration [*Verdunkelung*], a glimmer [*Schein*] that had arisen within it."[16]

These observations impressed Scholem profoundly. In his diary he wrote: "Benjamin's mind revolves, and will long continue to revolve, around the phenomenon of myth, which he approaches from the most diverse angles: from history, with Romanticism as his point of departure; from literature, with Hölderlin as the point of departure; from religion, with Judaism as that point; and from law."[17] Reflecting on these words, Scholem notes that "Benjamin's decided turn to the philosophic penetration of myth, which occupied him for so many years, beginning with his study of Hölderlin and probably for the rest of his life, was manifested here for the first time and left its mark on many of our conversations."[18] These conversations proved decisive for Scholem's own intellectual development as the first and foremost scholar of Jewish mythology. Scholem himself states: "I frequently presented to him my ideas about Judaism and its fight against myth, something I had reflected on a great deal . . . I suppose it was in these days that we especially influenced each other."[19]

As to Benjamin's own intellectual development, Scholem's observation that the deep sources, or "origins," of Benjamin's life and works are to be found in "the world of myth," implies that in order to understand Benjamin adequately, one ought to observe that practically every image, idea, or theory that Benjamin had ever had of "the world" grew out of some concrete mythological perception of this reality, even if ultimately it turned against its origin. Moreover, Benjamin's reflections on his life and works in his autobiographical study *A Berlin Childhood around Nineteen Hundred* demonstrate that he had come to think of his own intellectual development as having been always immersed in mythological configurations, from his earliest infantile visions of the labyrinth and the monumental figures in the Tiergarten Park of Berlin to his last mature recognition of these impressions as indicative of real forces in the commercial quarters of Paris. In his monumental work *The Arcades Project*, he sought to discover the deep reasons for this compulsion in the collective unconsciousness of modern society. He assumed that the exposition of the "latent mythology" in the social and cultural forms of life in Paris of the nineteenth century would reveal the basic obsessions that still haunted the early decades of the twentieth century.[20] Benjamin himself affirmed: "Only a thoughtless observer would deny that correspondences come into play between the world of modern technology and the archaic symbol-world of mythology."[21]

Alas, in the vast literature on Benjamin, there are only scant attempts to deal with his lifelong immersion in myth. John McCole has recently observed that "[t]he importance of Benjamin's preoccupation with myth has often been noted; both Adorno and Scholem stressed it. All the more surprising, then, is the lack of any sustained and rigorous treatment of the issue."[22] And indeed, though many scholars have duly noted Benjamin's predilection for mythological images, only a few have understood, as Scholem did, that for Benjamin myth was a category of absolute conceptual and historical primacy, the key to all further inquiries into human affairs. Moreover, because so many scholars still tend to perceive Benjamin as a Marxist or a "Critical Theorist" in the fashion of the Frankfurt School, they all too readily take Benjamin's critical observations on myth to be inimical to mythology in the same pejorative manner in which Marx and other modern radical theorists, such as Adorno and Horkheimer, Marcuse, or Eagleton have commonly portrayed it, that is, as being a "false consciousness" of reality, an "ideology" of society, a "linguistic manipulation" of mentality, and the like.[23] However, as Jürgen Habermas has argued, Benjamin's very notion of *Kritik* and therewith his conception and investigation of mythology were very different from those of his fellow critical theorists: he practiced what Habermas terms a "redemptive [*rettende*]" rather than a "corrective [*bewußtmachende*]" critical inquiry. According to Habermas, Benjamin believed that "the semantic potential from which human beings draw and with which they invest the world with meaning, permitting it to be experienced . . . is deposited in myth to begin with and must be released from it—but it cannot be expanded, just continually transformed."[24] Hence Benjamin attempted to regain this meaning through linguistic and mystic inquiries into the origins of modern cultural traditions: he feared that if "the streams of semantic energies" preserved in myth were to be lost to humanity, "the poetic faculty to interpret the world in terms of human needs would falter."[25]

In his work on mythology, Benjamin praised those artists and scholars who understood this new "critical" task and treated myth accordingly. Such were the Greek tragedians in classical antiquity and the German creators of the *Trauerspiel* in the seventeenth century, Goethe and the early romantic poets in the late eighteenth and early nineteenth centuries, and modern authors like Baudelaire and Balzac, Kafka and Gide: however critical they may have been of the ancient myths, they knew that they still contained some important messages for their respective modern societies. "But precisely the modern, *la modernité,* is always citing primal history [*Urgeschichte*],"[26] Benjamin observed, and he explained why: because the gradual emancipation from mythological beliefs and truths that Kant and his followers equated with "enlightenment" deprived the moderns of some archaic "forms of experience," such as the mimetic or magic faculties that once were, and still are, crucial for full human orientation and integration in the world. Benjamin generally defined these perceptions or "illuminations" of reality as "auratic."

These "auratic" perceptions consist in the apprehension of deeper temporal and spatial dimensions in the object, "the unique appearance of a distance, however close it may be," as in a work of art that generates these mythic associations through its mystic images and cultic uses.[27] The auratic life thus depends on the mental disposition of distance and reverence that prevailed in religious communities yet might still be evoked in modern society by artificial means of "intoxication [*Rausch*]"—whether they were artistic (as with the surrealists) or militaristic (as with the Fascists). Benjamin would strongly reject such attempts at auratic illumination, but he could also see that they signified authentic aspirations for liberation and transformation of the dull experience of secular modernity. This is what Benjamin describes in the last scene, entitled "To the Planetarium," of his book of aphoristic episodes, *One-Way Street.* In this miniature Benjamin counters the modern rational-technological attitude toward the natural world with the archaic, distinctly mythic one: "Nothing distinguishes the ancient from modern man so much as the former's absorption in a cosmic experience scarcely known to later periods . . . It is in this experience alone that we gain certain knowledge of what is nearest to us and what is remotest to us, and never of one without the other."[28] The fact that such aesthetic and mythic sensations still arise in us when we look at a work of art or at natural objects like "a mountain range on the horizon" indicates that a reenchantment of the world could still be viable through the reactivation of myth.

Benjamin was acutely aware of the potential dangers in such "reactivation." As McCole has rightly emphasized, "auratic perception has something literally atavistic about it": it implies "that atavistic, mythic compulsions continue, unrecognized, to dominate the forms of perception and experience throughout modern society."[29] The Great War proved just how forceful and fateful these compulsions have become.

> It is the dangerous error of modern men to regard this experience as unimportant and avoidable, and to consign it to the individual as the poetic rupture of starry nights. It is not; its hour strikes again and again, and then neither nations nor generations can escape it, as was made terribly clear by the last war, which was an attempt at new and unprecedented commingling with the cosmic powers. Human multitudes, gases, electrical forces were hurled into the open country, high-frequency currents coursed through the landscape, new constellations rose in the sky, aerial space and ocean depths thundered with propellers, and everywhere sacrificial shafts were dug in Mother Earth.[30]

The phenomenal allurement of mythological movements in Weimar Germany showed just how much the modern age had become again susceptible to these auratic experiences, especially when propagated by new ideologies and technologies of mass communication. In some of his later "materialistic" works of the mid-1930s, most notably in the essay "The Work of Art in the Age of Mechanical Reproduction," which Benjamin composed according to Brecht's strict antimetaphysical guidelines, he rejected the notion of the "auratic" as conducive to mere hypnotic trances like those of the surrealists or, worse, to the ritualistic *Blut und Boden* of the Fascists. Yet even in his most critical attacks on these new modes of auratic reenchantment—as, for example, in a review of Ernst Jünger's war novels, which glorified the horrific experiences of the war as heroic *Fronterlebnis*—Benjamin pointed out that both the surrealistic revolutionaries and the fascistic reactionaries were successful because they appealed to certain fundamental "forms of experience" that their opponents on the left had failed to recognize and to utilize for their purposes.[31]

Eventually, in his last works Benjamin sought to reconcile the auratic with the peculiar realization of modernists like Baudelaire, that some kind of an experience that "includes ritual elements" from prehistoric times was crucial for "modern man," who "has been cheated out of his experience."[32] Such, for example, is the experience of "festive days": what makes them "great and significant," Benjamin writes, "is the encounter with an earlier life."[33] Benjamin points out that Baudelaire's poetry, for all its "images of caves and vegetation, of clouds and waves," was not a romantic attempt at reenchantment of the world but a distinctly modern one: it grew out of, expressed, and sought to transcend the modern experience of *spleen,* that is, of seeing "the earth revert to a mere state of nature. No breath of prehistory surrounds it: there is no aura."[34] In poems like *Correspondances* or *La vie antérieure,* Baudelaire rekindled the auratic experience by the metaphorical description of the modern city as an ancient forest, a dramatic refiguration that exemplified, for Benjamin, the quintessential modern comprehension of human reality as a permanent "prehistory," ruled by the same mythical compulsions. Benjamin notes: "The important thing is that the *correspondances* record a concept of experience which includes ritual elements. Only by appropriating these elements was Baudelaire able to fathom the full meaning of the breakdown which he, a modern man, was witnessing."[35]

Assuming thus that myth was once "the meaning of the world" and in many ways still is, since "all else"—all modern images, ideas, and theories of the world—came into being as "only an obscuration, a glimmer that had arisen within it," Benjamin redefined the critical task of the modern mythologist as primarily hermeneutic rather than scientific: its aim was to show how any new meaning of the world was in fact a new meaning of myth. He explained in his essay on Gide's modernistic version of *Oedipus:* "What is important rather is how the modern meaning gains a distance from the old, and how that distance from the old interpretation is just a new closeness to the myth itself, from which the modern meaning inexhaustibly offers itself up for renewed discovery."[36] As we recall Scholem's conversation with Benjamin in 1918, it appears that Scholem was absolutely right to predict that "Benjamin's mind revolves, and will long continue to revolve, around the phenomenon of myth, which he approaches from the most diverse angles." Yet what exactly was Benjamin's conception of myth? And what did Scholem mean by saying that throughout all his works on myth, Benjamin was mainly preoccupied with one major problem, "the philosophic penetration of myth, which occupied him for so many years, beginning with his study of Hölderlin and probably for the rest of his life"?

II

Although Benjamin was fairly interested in modern psychological, sociological, and anthropological theories of myth, his notion of what myth is all about was largely confined to its "classical" connotations. Scanning his references to actual myths reveals that he was particularly concerned with the artistic transformations of Greek mythology in the works of later generations. Among modern scholars of myth, he paid more attention to those who dealt with classical mythology—Hegel, Bachofen, Nietzsche—than to romantic theorists such as Schlegel, Schelling, and Creuzer, who were primarily concerned with Indian and oriental mythologies. And although he admired his teacher Walter Lehmann, with whom he studied pre-Columbian ethnology and comparative mythology, Benjamin all but ignored him in his studies. Even more striking is his rather evasive attitude toward the work of his closest friend and intellectual confidant, Scholem: as much as he learned from Scholem on Jewish theology, Benjamin hardly refers to, let alone makes use of, Scholem's radical rediscoveries and theories of Jewish mythology. On those few occasions when Benjamin explicitly dealt with Jewish perceptions of life and history—as, for example, in the essay "Critique of Violence" of 1921—he deliberately pitted Jewish *theology* over against all forms of *mythology*. Nonetheless, unlike German Jewish *Aufklärer* such as Cohen or Cassirer, he did not rule out the very notion and manifestations of "Jewish mythology." The evocation of the messianic image of the Angel from Paradise in his final reflections on history might even suggest that he ultimately came to recognize and utilize this mythology, even if, as he would insist, he did so only in order to overcome its domination over our imagination.

On the whole, though, Benjamin consistently stuck to the classical definition of mythology and its philosophical interpretation by thinkers like Hegel, Nietzsche, and Weber, all of whom identified myth with the notion of "fate." This is the main contention in Benjamin's references to the meaning of myth in his first major essay, "Two Poems by Friedrich Hölderlin" (1914-15); through his essays of the early 1920s "Fate and Character," "Critique of Violence," and "Goethe's Elective Affinities"; to his last reflections on the topic in his essay on Baudelaire and in *The Arcades Project*. Myth, for Benjamin, was any state of affairs in which human beings perceived reality as governed by forces that were too immense and opaque for their comprehension, whether they were real *Machthaber* like the gods in Greek mythology or the fathers and judges in Kafka's stories or, more generally, any law or institution that has made up and sustains the authority of tradition by mystification of its human, all too human, origin.

Assuming the role of a "literary strategist" in the ideological struggles over the meanings of tradition and its keywords, Benjamin sought to discern the origins of the fatalistic mentality in the classical mythical sources of Western civilization. In his essay "Oedipus, or Rational Myth" (1932), he thus reiterates André Gide's assertion: "With this repellent word [fate], we concede much to chance—more than is merited. The dreadful workings of fate are in evidence wherever we dispense with explanations. I now maintain, however, that the deeper we drive fate back into the myths, the more instructive they are."[37] In his works on classical myths, Benjamin tried to show how the archaic notion of "fate"—the perception of human life as being ruled by superhuman gods and supernatural forces—has reproduced throughout the ages the same kind of "mythical fatality" in its various forms. Thus, the heroes in Greek tragedy are still "mythic," even though they dare to counter the divine laws and orders, because ultimately they always come to the "cathartic" realization that fate is omnipotent and therewith reaffirm it. "In tragedy pagan man realizes that he is better than his gods, but this realization strikes him dumb and it remains unarticulated."[38] Benjamin seems to concur with Hegel's observation that this recognition—of myth as "myth"—makes the tragic hero "mute," as well as with Nietzsche's subsequent conclusion that in Greek tragedy human motions and action are more significant than words. However, since Benjamin was mainly concerned with the "philosophic penetration of myth," namely with the first signs of critical confrontation with mythic fatality, he also points out how this first attempt at self-assertion of human rights against divine laws is the beginning of liberation from myth.[39] For even though the tragic hero is doomed to acquiesce in mythic fatality, the message of his action regains notability in the Chorus's more reflective, objective, and collective incantations on his particular case. This dialectical process of liberation through myth occurs also in Greek philosophy: "The Socratic dialogue needs to be studied in relation to myth. What did Plato intend with it? Socrates: with this figure, Plato annihilates the old myth while adopting it. Socrates: this is the offering of philosophy to the gods of myth who demand human sacrifice. In the midst of the terrible struggle, the young philosophy attempts to assert itself in Plato."[40]

Similarly, in his essay on Goethe's novel *Elective Affinities* (written between 1919 and 1922, published in 1924), Benjamin argues that the fateful consequences that befall the "unfaithful" lovers Eduard and Ottilie are "mythic" not because the two violate the sacred bonds of marriage but because they still cling to this legal institution, even though it has become so irrelevant to them. Their guilt feelings prove that their punishment is determined not by some external authorities but by their own internal tribulations, which they do not understand and seek to expiate by all kinds of atavistic-fetishistic beliefs in portents and other bleak "pagan tendencies."[41] Yet, as in the analogous case of the Greek tragedians, Benjamin finds in Goethe's novel signs of the liberation from myth—and also, as we shall see, for the liberation *of* myth—in Goethe's serene composition of the entire novel. He shows how Goethe consciously chose to intensify, and thereby petrify, the mythic fatality that permeates his heroes' mentality by depicting their entire world of appearances as ruled by uncanny forces. Nevertheless, Goethe's critical attempt to turn "the mythic" into the essential problem of his novel has been entirely perverted by modern readers such as Friedrich Gundolf. According to Benjamin, Gundolf rightly perceived the prevalence of mythic compulsions in Goethe's life and works, but he failed to see that in *Elective Affinities* Goethe began his struggle to release himself from these forces. Gundolf took all the apparent mythopoeic presentations in this work to be yet another expression of (his own) neoromantic conception of reality as thoroughly mythical, rather than as a subversion of that conception. "Yet no mode of thinking is more disastrous than that which bewilderingly bends back into the myth the very thing that has begun to grow out of it."[42] The "mythic elements" in Goethe's life and works "testify not only, and not at the deepest level, to the mythic world in Goethe's existence. For there is in him a struggle to free himself from its clutches, and this struggle, no less than the essence of that world, is attested to in Goethe's novel."[43] Gundolf's attempt "to present Goethe's life as a mythical one" thus approved, however inadvertently, what Goethe had sought to disapprove—submission to "mythical fatality."

This new realistic conception of mythology was further intensified by Benjamin's growing disenchantment with the idealistic philosophies of mythology of Schelling, Creuzer, von Baader, and Hegel, which he had hitherto so esteemed. He also became impatient with Nietzsche's "purely aesthetic conception of myth," which led to his "renunciation of its understanding . . . in historical-philosophical terms."[44] Moreover, in the mid-1920s Benjamin turned against these and other late or neoromantic theorists, because he realized how their old notions had become prevalent in many new philosophies of mythology in Germany. Thus, in December 1925, upon reading Ernst Cassirer's book *Die Begriffsform im mythischem Denken,* Benjamin wrote to Hugo von Hofmannsthal that he "remained unconvinced that it is feasible not only to attempt to present mythical thought in concepts—i.e. critically—but also to illuminate it adequately in contrast with what is conceptual."[45] In order to "illuminate it adequately," it was necessary to treat myth more realistically than Cassirer had done. Hence, whereas Cassirer still employed strict epistemic, ethic, and aesthetic categories in order to explain what myth is, Benjamin would rather ask what myth does; and where Cassirer was primarily concerned with the problem of (how myth distorts) "truth," Benjamin would simply dismiss the whole notion of "truth" from mythology. Benjamin perceived myth itself in neutral terms, as a primeval form of perception that was as yet neither true nor false, beyond good and evil, essentially "ambiguous" about natural and human affairs.[46] In his essay on Goethe's *Elective Affinities*, Benjamin thus opined that "the relation between myth and truth" is one of "mutual exclusion."[47] The one and only philosophical question about myth pertained to the "philosophic penetration of myth."

For Benjamin, Goethe's novel marked the truly modern perception of reality, whereby man has become fully aware of the mythical compulsions in his life and works. Benjamin found in this novel, and in his own work on it, the critical methodology by which to confront modern mythology. For just as Goethe was able to begin his liberation from the ensnarement (*Verschlingung*) in myth only after he had immersed himself in it, Benjamin sought through various works and experiments to cultivate that critical method of "losing himself" in the "forest" of symbols of mythology while being aware of what he was doing. Eventually Benjamin defined this new critical methodology as "dialectical enchantment." Its main aim was to counter both the "disenchantment" of mythology in modern scientific ideologies (e.g., futurism or Marxism) and the "re-enchantment" of mythology in neoromantic ideologies (e.g., surrealism or Fascism) by a new critical attempt to re-fuse mythology.[48]

What Benjamin meant thereby might be illustrated by his critical reaction to the new German translation of the Bible by Franz Rosenzweig and Martin Buber, which appeared in 1926. Although Benjamin accepted their basic contention that Judaism was not as *mythosfrei* as many German Jewish *Aufklärer* had maintained, and although he must have been familiar with Scholem's methodical restoration of Jewish mythology, he opposed the attempt to render Judaism entirely mythical, as, in his view, Buber and Rosenzweig had done in their *völkisch* translation of the Bible. Upon publication of the first volume of this translation, Benjamin wrote to Scholem that its appearance was most inopportune.[49] He rightly saw that Buber and Rosenzweig sought to inspire their modern, all too rational, German Jewish readers by using all kinds of archaic and magic terms, whereas he thought that precisely because the Bible itself was so mythical, it required a most literal and historical translation, to enable the modern reader to recognize this very fact from critical perspectives. What was needed in this case, as in similar translations of ancient and modern mythopoeic works, was not an "enchantment" but a "dialectical enchantment" of the myth, which would reveal the extension of countermythical tendencies within that text. Benjamin's meditation on Kafka's parable "The Silence of the Sirens," a "myth" about myth, neatly demonstrates how this "dialectical enchantment" could be used in the creation and interpretation of modern mythology.[50]

In Kafka's version of the myth, the Sirens have "an even more terrible weapon than their song . . . their silence"—a sign, for Benjamin, that the myth might continue to allure even when it is no longer sound. Only a Ulysses who "was so full of guile, was such a fox that not even the goddess of fate could pierce his armor" was able to overcome the "myth" of the Sirens: "Reason and cunning have inserted tricks into myths; their forces cease to be invincible." As Benjamin would have it, this interpretation proves that Kafka did not succumb to the mythical "temptation of redemption" and shows how he succeeded in turning away from the immediacy and delicacy of mythical fantasies by means of self-negation, resignation, and alienation: "A latter-day Ulysses, he let the Sirens go by 'his gaze which was fixed on the distance, the Sirens disappeared as it were before his determination, and at the very moment when he was closest to them he was no longer aware of them.'"[51] Nonetheless, Kafka then adds: "If the Sirens had possessed consciousness [Bewußtsein] they would have been annihilated at that moment. But they remained as they had been; all that happened was that Ulysses had escaped them." This signified, if not for Benjamin (who does not cite this crucial passage) then certainly for Horkheimer and Adorno, that modern rational man has never really overcome myth, and that is precisely because myth lacks, or operates without, "consciousness."[52] Benjamin does cite the final lines of the parable: "Perhaps he [Ulysses] had really noticed, although here the human understanding is beyond its depths, that the Sirens were silent, and opposed the afore-mentioned pretense to them and the gods merely as a sort of shield."[53]

Kafka's Ulysses exemplifies the two basic critical methods by which the moderns have commonly dealt with myth—the rationalistic and the artistic, which are akin to Habermas's distinction between the "corrective" and the "redemptive" or to Benjamin's distinction between the "disenchantment" and the "dialectical enchantment" of myth. Whereas Ulysses' first strategy is to confront myth with ironic derision ("reason and cunning have inserted tricks into myths; their forces cease to be invincible"), the more sober realization that the myths "remained as they had been; all that happened was that Ulysses had escaped them" proposes a second strategy of "reconciliation." For the very last lines of Kafka's parable imply that Ulysses, who must have known that the "Song of the Sirens" was merely a fiction that had been devised to capture its listeners, nevertheless continued to "pretend" that the myth was very real, if only because his fellow travelers still believed in it, and as long as it still resounded in Kafka's own life. Likewise, modern mythologists must beware of the "latent efficacy of myth" even if, and precisely because, they themselves do not believe in it anymore.

This was the main message Benjamin had gleaned from Aragon's novel *Paris Peasant,* which he read in 1926, and on his own admission he was profoundly impressed by its notion and description of "modern mythology." [54] In his novel Aragon does not describe a "peasant" in Paris. Rather, his hero is an inhabitant of the city who has become so mesmerized by its modern manifestations of gaslights, arcades, shops, filling stations, and moving cars that he begins to imagine them as monsters and deities. In so doing he reacts like a peasant who habitually fills the landscape in which he dwells with such mythical figurations.

> New myths spring up beneath each step we take. Legend begins where man has lived, where he lives. All that I intend to think about from now on is these despised transformations. Each day the modern sense of existence becomes subtly altered. A mythology ravels and unravels . . . and thus our cities are peopled with unrecognized sphinxes which will never stop the passing dreamer and ask him mortal questions unless he first projects his meditation, his absence of mind, towards them. But if this wise man has the power to guess their secret, and interrogates them in his turn, all that these faceless monsters will grant is that he shall once again plumb his own depths. [55]

This is exactly what happens to Aragon's hero. As he abandons himself to the flow of new sensations, he notices how his mind forms certain "fixations" around static objects and how these then cohere and grow into images of gods, monsters, and other strange idols.

> It became apparent to me that man is as full of gods as a sponge plunged into the open sky. These gods live, attain the zenith of their power, then die, leaving their perfumed altars to other gods. They are the very principles of every transformation of everything. They are the necessity of movement. So I was walking tipsily among countless divine concretions. I set about forming the idea of mythology in motion. It was more accurate to call it the modern mythology. And it was under that name that I conceived it. [56]

According to Benjamin, the main problem with this novel, as with all other artworks of surrealism, was that it did not offer any critical, let alone theoretical, assessment of "modern mythology." In his essay on this movement, Benjamin is sympathetic to the basic impulsion of the surrealists: "But anyone who has perceived that the writings of this circle are not literature but something else—demonstrations, watchwords, documents, bluffs, forgeries if you will, but at any rate not literature—will also know, for the same reason, that the writings are concerned literally with experiences, not with theories and less with phantasms." [57] Throughout his life Benjamin revered such extreme states of mind as dreams, hypnotic trances, feverish attacks, and drug hallucinations as authentic attempts to break through the normal perceptions of reality. Since his first major philosophical essay, "On the Program of the Coming Philosophy" (1918), Benjamin always sought to elucidate a new theory of experience that would open up to such intuitive and imaginative perceptions of reality, which surpass the rigid Kantian categories of permissible *Vernunft*. [58] He approved the "surrealistic experiences" because they were analogous to mystical ecstasies and epiphanies and other "forms of experience" that have been likewise repressed, forgotten, or dismissed as unreasonable, and yet they were conducive to Revelation, or, as Benjamin would rather have it, to Revolution: "To win the energies of intoxication [*Rausch*] for the revolution—this is the project on which Surrealism focused in all its books and enterprises. This it may call its most particular task." [59]

However, although Benjamin praised the surrealists as "visionaries and augurs" of the revolution, he judged that they failed to accomplish their task and moreover did not even help "to overthrow the intellectual predominance of the bourgeoisie and to make contact with the proletarian masses," as they so avidly claimed. What rendered them so ineffective, in Benjamin's view, was that they had "an inadequate, undialectical conception of the nature of intoxication," by which he meant to suggest that they did not have any theoretical terms—anthropological, historical, or political—to account for all the various forms of "intoxication" they had so perceptibly noticed and practiced. In order "to win the energies of intoxication for the revolution," as the surrealists wished to do, they could not indulge in individualistic, and all too often narcissistic, feats of their own imagination; instead, they had to realize the collective origins and potentialities of their images, dreams, hallucinations, and other fantasies. For the meanings of images and dreams, like those of words and things, are objective, communicative, and reactive to common prehistoric experiences. In his essay Benjamin redefined this new kind of "auratic" perception of the deeper mythical-historical associations of prosaic empirical mundane reality as "a *profane illumination,* a materialistic, anthropological inspiration, to which the hashish, opium, or whatever else can give an introductory lesson."[60] Like religious illumination, profane illumination uses spiritual intoxication in order to produce a "revelation," a sudden vision that transcends the normal perception or experience of reality, yet it does so in a methodical and critical manner. Benjamin conducted his own experiments with hashish along the same critical lines: he probed drug hallucinations methodically, seeking to remain as self-reflective as possible even during intoxication, for his aim was to analyze those rare "forms of experience"— the epiphanies of mystical revelations or artistic inspirations—which he deemed crucial for an "absolute experience" of reality.[61]

Shortly after he finished his essay on the surrealists, Benjamin wrote a "complement" essay on Marcel Proust, whose masterpiece *À la recherche du temps perdu* he had long been engaged in translating and commenting upon.[62] The affinity that Benjamin found between Proust and the surrealists is evident in his evocation—or rather creative imitation—of Proust's *Lieux de mémoire:*

> In the last century there was an inn by the name of "Au Temps Perdu" at Grenoble; I do not know whether it still exists. In Proust, too, we are guests who enter through a door underneath a suspended sign that sways in the breeze, a door behind which eternity and rapture [*Rausch*] await us . . . It is the world in a state of resemblances, the domain of the *correspondences;* the Romanticists were the first to comprehend them and Baudelaire embraced them most fervently, but Proust was the only one who managed to reveal them in our lived life.[63]

Benjamin considered this capability to perceive things in the world in the mythic terms of their "similarity" rather than in the analytic terms of their strict "individuality" or "identity" to be crucial for the original and still most seminal illuminations of reality. As Scholem writes, "[t]he origin of the constellations as configurations on the sky surface was, so he [Benjamin] asserted, the beginning of reading and writing, and this coincided with the development of the mythic age. The constellations were for the mythic world what the revelation of the Holy Writ was to be later."[64] Benjamin elaborated this notion in his fragment "On the Mimetic Faculty" of 1933, where he explained how this imagistic capability that enabled the ancients to forge sensuous relations to natural reality, and in our times survives merely in such negligible occupations as astrology and graphology, exemplified the ability "to read what was never written." In other words, it may teach us how to open up and emancipate our cognition from the rationalistic and mechanistic conceptions it imposed on our human reality as well.[65] Benjamin commends Proust because, unlike the romanticists and, implicitly, in contrast to the surrealists, he managed to reveal these new dialogical relations "in our own lives" in a methodical and critical fashion, through the conscious activation of what he called "involuntary memory." As we shall see, Benjamin regarded this novelistic invention as a major contribution to modern historiography. He used it later in his own autobiographical and historical investigations of modern mythology.

Benjamin coined a new term for this memory—*Eingedenken*—which connotes both meditation (*denken*) and commemoration (*gedenken*) and is generally descriptive of the more critical way in which we regain past and lost experience in magical occasions, as, for example, in the celebration of "holidays [*Feiertage*]." No matter how secular they have become, and precisely because they are now secular, such occasions function as "days of remembrance [*Tage des Eingedenkens*]," as occasions for recognition of the initial "holy days."[66] The methodic, even ritualistic performance of *Eingedenken* is thus redolent of what Benjamin meant and sought to achieve by "profane illumination"—a voluntary production (by hashish or other means of intoxication) of involuntary visions of empirical reality that would offer a new secular "revelation" of its immanent—not transcendent—sources of meaning. Or, to use the concrete example that Benjamin must have had in mind when he thought up this term, *Eingedenken* is akin to the "involuntary memory" that Proust conjured up by dipping the *madelaine* in the cup of tea. Benjamin elaborates:

> In the reflection that introduces the term [involuntary memory] Proust tells us how poorly, for many years, there appeared in his memory [*Erinnerung*] the town of Combray in which, after all, he spent part of his life. One afternoon the taste of a kind of pastry called *madelaine* (which he later mentions often) transported him back to the past, whereas before then he had been limited to what memory [*Gedächtnis*], which is always attentive to the dictates of caution, had made available to him.[67]

What made Proust's task of recollection so difficult, then, was not only the "disintegration" of the memorial impressions in the "destructive" *Erinnerung*, but also their total integration and preservation in the "conservative" *Gedächtnis*, whose function, according to the psychologist Theodor Reik (whom Benjamin cites) is the "protection" of—or, more crucially, from—such impressions by adding and adapting them to the ready

forms of recognition and tradition (162). Under these conditions of repression, "*À la Recherche du temps perdu* may be regarded as an attempt to
produce experience synthetically . . . for there is less and less hope that it
will come into being naturally" (159). That is why "involuntary memory"
is indispensable: the sudden sensation of the *madelaine* enabled Proust to
break into the "voluntary memory" and release from its repository of past
and lost experiences the indefinite series of mythic or, in Benjamin's terms,
"auratic" associations "which, at home in the *mémoire involontaire,* tend to
cluster around the object of perception" (188).

Benjamin prized Proust's "involuntary memory"; he considered it useful for the novelist as well as for the historical materialist because, unlike
the "voluntary memory," which adjusts the past for the careful and purposeful subject, the "involuntary memory" stirs up the past "in some material object (or in the sensation which such an object arouses in us),"
thereby recharging or (in Benjamin's term) "rejuvenating" the "object of
perception"—be it Proust's *madelaine* or, we may add, Benjamin's *Marzipanfiguren*—with significance.[68] Yet, whereas for Proust, the novelist, the
significance of the object and the mythical associations it arouses in memory lies in the experiences of the *temps perdu,* for Benjamin, the historical
materialist, that "image" of the past becomes significant only in and for the
present, that is to say in the acute historical recognition of why and how,
say, the object and the mythical associations of the *Marzipafiguren* have become so "sickly." Proust was unable to actualize his image of happiness in
that way in his life, because he held onto an "elegiac idea of happiness,"
which compelled him to seek "the eternal repetition, the eternal restoration of the original, the first happiness" that he had "once upon a time"
had in Combray (206). Proust exercised the most "radical attempt at self-
absorption [*Selbstversenkung*]" in the past and was thus doomed to remain
therein. In his novel, as in his life, he subsequently came to "the intellectual renunciation" of all mundane affairs and finally of their memories as
well (214–16).

This is the lasting "Image of Proust" that Benjamin evokes in the essay
bearing that title. As much as Benjamin tried to correct the common "image" of Proust as "the insignificant snob, the playboy and socialite" by
presenting him, rather implausibly, as an insider whose real aim was to
"subvert" the social snobbery in which he indulged (207–12), he had to
concede that, for all his obsessive engagement with the petty affairs of the
Parisian high society, Proust really lived, or at least aspired to live, in and
for the nostalgic image of the blissful *temps perdu:* "To it he sacrificed in his
life friends and companionship, in his works plot, unity of characters, the

flow of the narration, the play of the imagination" (206). Benjamin describes how Proust sought to capture that "image which satisfied his curiosity—indeed, assuaged his homesickness. He lay on his bed racked with homesickness, homesick for the world distorted in the state of resemblance, a world in which the true surrealist face of existence breaks through. To this world belongs what happens in Proust, and the deliberate and fastidious way in which it appears. It is never isolated, rhetorical, or visionary; carefully heralded and securely supported, it bears a fragile, precious reality: the image" (207). This imagery of the past, then, was the "precious reality" that Proust created for himself, in "true surrealistic" fashion, a reality where virtual memories of the events prevailed over their actual histories: "For an experienced event is finite—at any rate, confined to one sphere of experience; a remembered event is infinite, because it is only a key to everything that happened before it and after it" (204). Nevertheless, as Benjamin (and other mythistorians) would have it, Proust failed to use that key adequately, because, much like the surrealists, he confined his novel to the subjective memories of the events and did not care to account for anything that had objectively happened in his life, let alone in history. Benjamin comments in his last critical reflections on Proust: "Where there is experience in the strict sense of the word, certain contents of the individual past combine with material of the collective past. The rituals with their ceremonies, their festivals (quite probably nowhere recalled in Proust's work) kept producing the amalgamation of these two elements of memory over and over again. They triggered recollection at certain times and remained handles of memory for a lifetime. In this way, voluntary and involuntary recollection lose their mutual exclusiveness." [69]

As already noted, Benjamin regarded Proust as the prototypical "modern novelist." His critical judgment on the apparent fallacies in À la recherche du temps perdu indicates that the novelist had the same problem that the surrealists and other modernists had: there was a fatal individualistic flaw in the very conception of the "modern novel." For the main distinction of the modern novel, as Benjamin came to identify it in the novels of Kafka, Aragon, and Proust, has been the realization of such "involuntary" motivations in all human actions and creations. Much like the first modern poet, Baudelaire, these novelists were modern precisely because they recognized the mythic correspondances and la vie antérieure in "our own life," perceiving the "prehistoric forces" that dominate our historic traditions and institutions in the "labyrinths" of the courtrooms or of the Parisian arcades and saloons. Benjamin admired their artistic ability to describe how these myths were still operative in their own memories, stories, and histories, but he ultimately criticized all three novelists for their apparent inability to explain in adequate critical and historical terms the myths they had so well exposed. Much like the surrealists, they all failed to recognize the objective and collective sources of the self, to utilize such "handles of memory" as ritual ceremonies in order to open the doors of perception to what Benjamin calls "experience [*Erfahrung*] in the strict sense of the word." In his essays "Experience and Poverty" (1933), "The Storyteller" (1936), and "On Some Motifs in Baudelaire" (1939), Benjamin attempted to discover the fundamental transformations in modern society that have thus hampered experience itself and the narrative capability to convey it.

Setting out from the assumption that experience consists in the human capability to render the contingencies of life recognizable and hence bearable, he argued that the revolutions that invigorated modern civilization and all but destroyed it in World War I have eroded this prudential capability: "With the [First] World War a process began to become apparent which has not halted since. Was it not noticeable at the end of the war that men returned from the battlefield grown silent—not richer, but poorer in communicable experience? . . . For never has experience been contradicted more thoroughly than strategic experience by tactical warfare, economic experience by inflation, bodily experience by mechanical warfare, moral experience by those in power." [70] In his finest essay, "The Storyteller," Benjamin relates this predicament of "modern man" who "has been cheated out of his experience" to the deterioration of certain communal conditions that have long sustained the most basic of all experiential capabilities: storytelling. For the ability to tell and listen to a story in community consists in "the ability to exchange experiences." [71] This art thrived in premodern societies, among villagers and voyagers, whose slow rhythmic life and habitual occupations—weaving and spinning, riding and sailing—allowed and required them to indulge in this archaic manner of passing time and information (84). For the storytellers and their listeners, "the intelligence that came from afar—whether the spatial kind from foreign countries or the temporal kind of tradition—possessed an authority which gave it validity, even when it was not subject to verification" (89). Thus Nikolai Leskov, the protagonist of Benjamin's essay, was an author who could still endow his stories with such "authority" because he "was at home in distant places as well as in distant times" (85–86). Benjamin insists that this kind of authority is crucial to the construction of experience, because, as the term *Erfahrung* implies, experience consists in lessons culled from traveling (*fahren*) in distant places and times, into other realities of

life, and even beyond it: "All great storytellers have in common the freedom with which they move up and down the rungs of their experience as
on a ladder. A ladder extending downward to the interior of the earth and
disappearing into the clouds is the image for a collective experience to
which even the deepest shock of every individual experience, death, constitutes no impediment or barrier" (102).

The ultimate function of the story in traditional society was to make
this most painful of all experiences *natürlich,* literally *heimlich*—visible, pal-
pable, predictable, acceptable, bearable—to its listeners, by its integration
into a coherent narrative representation of the cyclical-mythical order of
things: "The idea of eternity has ever had its strongest source in death . . .
Death is the sanction of everything that the storyteller can tell. He has borrowed his authority from death. In other words, it is natural history to
which his stories refer back." The storytellers were able to convey this experience because they lived in Christian communities, where dying was "a
public process in the life of the individual and a most exemplary one." But
"in the course of modern times dying has been pushed further and further
out of the perceptual world of the living. There used to be no house,
hardly a room, in which somebody had not once died . . . Today people
live in rooms that have never been touched by death, dry dwellers of eternity, and when their end approaches they are stowed away in sanatoria
or hospitals by their heirs." We may also recall Benjamin's description of
Proust's illness, in which he shows how Proust disguised his own dying in
melodramatic fashion (93–94). The modern novel, too, with its melodramatic descriptions of death, turns this most ordinary moment into an extraordinary and exemplary one, presenting "the character in a novel" as if
"the 'meaning' of his life is revealed only in his death." The reader of the
novel does not get any real instruction for his own life and death, only satisfaction, from this description. Benjamin remarks: "The novel is significant, therefore, not because it presents someone else's fate to us, perhaps
didactically, but because this stranger's fate by virtue of the flame which
consumes it yields us the warmth we never draw from our own fate. What
draws the reader to the novel is the hope of warming his shivering life with
a death he reads about" (101).

Benjamin culled his negative conception of the modern novel from
Lukács's study *The Theory of the Novel,* which, as Scholem and other commentators have noted, had long been one of his major sources of inspiration.[72] According to Lukács, the main task of the novelist is to recharge
modern life with some meaning; but, since he can no longer find the
objective and authentic "meaning of life" in his bourgeois society, he has

come to construct it synthetically and subjectively. In "The Storyteller" Benjamin cites this important observation by Lukács:

> Only in the novel are meaning and life, and thus the essential and the temporal separated; one can almost say that the whole inner action of a novel is nothing else but a struggle against the power of time . . . And from this . . . arise the genuinely epic experiences of time: hope and memory . . . only in the novel . . . does there occur a creative memory which transfixes the object and transforms it.[73]

Following on these assumptions, Benjamin comments: "The 'meaning of life' is really the center about which the novel moves." But this "meaning of life" is radically different—and indeed totally absent—from "the moral of the story," because its very notion is alien to life in traditional society where meaning was still immanent and transparent in life. This is the essential difference between the story and the novel:

> What differentiates the novel from all other forms of prose literature—the fairy tale, the legend, even the novella—is that it neither comes from oral tradition nor goes into it . . . The storyteller takes what he tells from experience—his own or that reported by others. And in turn makes it the experience of those who are listening to his tale. The novelist has isolated himself. The birthplace of the novel is the solitary individual, who is no longer able to express himself by giving examples of his most important concerns, is himself uncounseled, and cannot counsel others. To write a novel means to carry the incommensurable to extremes in the representation of human life. In the midst of life's fullness, and through the representation of this fullness, the novel gives evidence of the profound perplexity of the living. (87)

Unlike the solitary novelist, the storyteller "is a man who has counsel for his readers," and this counsel, when "woven into the fabric of life is wisdom": it acquaints the listeners or readers of the story with the "epic side of truth," namely with the many different meanings of the happening that the story has acquired in history, recalling, as in the Hasidic story, "the chain of tradition which passes a happening on from generation to generation," from its "archaic" past, which might still be "divined" in Homer, to the present, where it becomes significant (86–87, 98). In that way, Benjamin adds, the story constitutes "the oldest form" of historiography, whose "first storyteller"—not quite or yet a proper historian—was Herodotus (97). His story of the Egyptian king Psammenitus in the third book of the *History* manifests, for Benjamin, "what the nature of true story is":

"It does not expend itself. It preserves and concentrates its strength and is capable of releasing it even after a long time" (89–90), because "Herodotus offers no explanations" for the happening he describes: he merely tells how Psammenitus, after he was beaten and captured by the Persian king Cambyses, was forced to watch the Persian triumphal procession. He endured without visible emotion the sights of his daughter taken to slavery and of his son being led to execution, yet he broke down in tears when he recognized in that rank of prisoners one of his old servants. Where a modern historian would seek to explain Psammenitus's reactions by delving into his psychological motivations, the ancient historian just reports the story as he heard it, much like his predecessors in the epic tradition, who used to *mythologein,* "recount what they say," allowing it to pass into history. Herodotus still possessed those objective and collective certainties of Greek mythology that endowed his *History* with that definitive quality of "every real story": it "contains, openly or covertly, something useful," whether "a moral," "some practical advice," or "a proverb," which, in Benjamin's wonderful simile, "is a ruin which stands on the site of an old story [*alte Geschichte*] and in which a moral twines about a happening like ivy around a wall" (86, 108).

These pragmatic assumptions determined Benjamin's new realistic, and eventually materialistic, conception of mythology, as well as the methodical procedures of its study, which were more practical, anthropological, and historical. To use Benjamin's terms, the creation and interpretation of myth ought to be "allegorical" rather than "symbolical." Cassirer and other idealistic "symbolists," such as the neoromantic poet Stefan George, have commonly believed in the emanation of some original and eternal meanings of the myth that they merely had to evoke. Benjamin espoused instead the "allegorists," those realistic modernists, such as Baudelaire or Gide, who duly realized that the historical process of dissociation and alienation had rendered all meanings temporal and conjectural, "cultural" rather than "natural," and were thus able to imbue myth with new relevant meanings—actual as well as spiritual, political as much as theological, in short equally historical and mythological. Only those who achieved liberation *from* myth could achieve the liberation *of* myth in artistic creations and allegorical interpretations.

This was the great achievement of the creators of the German *Trauerspiel* in the seventeenth century. In the *Habilitation* book that came out in 1928, Benjamin showed how these Protestant clergymen, who witnessed the catastrophes of the Thirty Years War, came to perceive the world as a stage that had been deserted by God and destroyed by man. Their plays abound with brutal scenes in which all men appear barbarous and treacherous, as if to show that the physical reality of human life and history is in itself devoid of any metaphysical meaning. The radical inversion of common Christian myths of martyrs and saints implied that these idealized fictions could not be realized in this world. Alas, this critical presentation of Christian mythology was not heretical as much as allegorical: it juxtaposed the myth of salvation with historical reality in order to redeem the myth from that reality. The *Trauerspiel* playwrights achieved this aim by showing to their viewers-believers that the only true reality was not the actual but the spiritual, the mythical beyond the historical. In order to save the Christian myth of salvation, they had to expose this myth as such.[74]

For Benjamin, the greatest modern allegorist of myth was Charles Baudelaire. "It was owing to the genius of allegory that Baudelaire did not succumb to the abyss of myth that gaped beneath his feet at every step."[75] Whereas other mythologists in his time, most notably the late romantics, forged archaic visions or "myths" of bygone ages to counter the revolutions of modernity, Baudelaire was able to resist this temptation (except when he succumbed "to the rage for Wagner")[76] because he managed to discern these mythopoeic images and visions in fashionable Paris, to expose, as it were, the archaic in the anarchic, the eternal in the phenomenal, *La vie antérieure* in the vicissitudes of modern life itself. As Baudelaire himself put it in his famous essay "The Painter of Modern Life," the "heroic task" of the modernist must be "to extract from fashion whatever element it may contain of poetry within history, to distill the eternal from the transitory"[77]—a statement that resounds in Benjamin's notion of modernity as a "recognition" of the mythical in the historical. For Benjamin, Baudelaire's poetry amounted to a "phenomenology of modernity," because it was responsive to the dialectical historical transformation of myth from an aesthetic into an allegorical comprehension of reality: "In the poetry of Baudelaire, notwithstanding the original signature which allegory inscribes there, a medieval substrate makes itself felt beneath the Baroque element. This involves what Bezold calls 'the survival [*Fortleben*] of the ancient gods in medieval humanism.' Allegory is the vehicle for this survival."[78] The term *Fortleben*, which Benjamin employs here to define Baudelaire's poetry as a "continuation of the life" of myth by artificial (allegorical) means is significant, for it was the same term that Benjamin used elsewhere to define the task of literary criticism, his own vocation, as a "continuation of the life" of the work of art after it had lost its immediate (organic-auratic) meanings by similar dialectical means. For just as the eternal "truth content [*Wahrheitsgehalt*]" of artistic and poetic creations could be fully realized only after the phenomenal impressions that emanated from its "material content [*Sachgehalt*]" had waned, the real meanings of myth could be evident only after its forceful sensations and fateful compulsions had abated. The dissociation of myth from its primordial associations, or its "dialectical enchantment," also reveals its beauty: "The genuine period of beauty is fixed from the earliest decay of myth until its eruption [*Sprengung*],"[79] that is to say, after the mythic images have ceased to be menacing and can be used for further artistic elaborations, as in Greek sculpture, Gothic architecture, or baroque theater. "The presupposition for all beauty is the latent efficacy of myth. The beauty of a poem avers even if its mythic elements are evident." This is most notably so in Baudelaire's poetry, where the mythic elements that still permeate modernity are evident yet not dominant, recognized and thereby neutralized.[80]

Theodor Adorno realized as much when he argued that "the reconciliation [*Versöhnung*] of myth is the theme of Benjamin's philosophy."[81] By that he meant to suggest that Benjamin did not perceive myth as essentially opposed to reason and law but as utterly impervious to them, that his aim was not to set the rational over against the mythical but rather to mediate between them, to recognize the archaic in the modern, so as to expose the mythopoeic sources of our consciousness and civilization. By the reconciliation of myth, he sought to show, as it were, what Adorno and Horkheimer came to define as the inevitable dialectic of enlightenment, whereby not only does myth become rational, but reason also becomes mythical.[82]

In the remainder of this chapter I illustrate Benjamin's lifelong attempt at a "reconciliation of myth" in his works and life by reviewing some "micrological" investigations in which he revealed this intention, his amazement at the *Marzipanfiguren* being one (the very last) of them. I pay special attention to Benjamin's essay on the nineteenth-century Swiss scholar of mythology Johann Jakob Bachofen.[83] I first discuss the more general and circumstantial reasons that led Benjamin to write this essay and then turn to the more personal and deeper existential reasons that confined him to that task. I conclude by a brief discussion of Benjamin's last and greatest work on myth, *The Arcades Project*.

III

Benjamin's essay on Bachofen has not received much attention from scholars, and this fact is in itself significant. It was precisely the realization that Bachofen's discoveries and theories of myth were all but lost to the new critical theory of society that prompted Benjamin to write his essay.

Benjamin wrote this essay during the last months of 1934 for the *Nouvelle Revue Française,* which had commissioned him to present to the French public an important but unknown modern thinker. He submitted the work in January 1935, but it was rejected by the journal, apparently for being too obscure. This essay is only a minor work and was deemed to be such by Benjamin, who wrote in a letter to Max Horkheimer that the essay—the first that he ever wrote in French—was only "meant to introduce Bachofen, who is completely unknown in France. With this in mind, I tried to portray him rather than describe his theories."[84] However, the essay may now seem more important than its author thought. It was, after all, Benjamin himself who exercised to perfection the micrological method in cultural studies (and in life), showing how attention to marginal, seemingly unimportant details in major works might illuminate them anew. As Scholem noted, in his Bachofen essay Benjamin "conducted a kind of general inspection of some of his old motives, without however identifying them as such" and, moreover, without controlling them, so that they seem to have swept him in directions that were totally opposed to his intentions. According to Scholem, this fact may render this essay particularly revealing and yet may also explain why the editors of the *Nouvelle Revue Française* rejected it.[85]

Although Benjamin wrote his essay late in his life and claimed at the time that he had not previously read Bachofen's works,[86] he seems to have become acquainted with Bachofen's main discoveries and theories as early as 1914. Benjamin was by then in contact with Ludwig Klages and later met other members of the *Kosmische Runde* such as Karl Wolfskehl, Alfred Schuler, Jula Radt, and Franz Hessel, who propagated Bachofen's legacy in Germany. During his student years in Munich, between 1915 and 1917, Benjamin deepened his mythological studies and convictions, and, as Scholem indicates, he "must have been familiar around this time with the writings of Johann Jakob Bachofen."[87] Benjamin was particularly impressed by Klages's theories on the longevity of archaic mythology.[88] Klages's graphological and ethnohistorical—or, as they were then known, "characterological"—notions on the mythological origins of mankind, and specifically the assertion that the *Urbilder* of these mythologies persist as cultural memories in modernity, impressed the young Benjamin profoundly. He held onto them even when they were later abused, primarily by Klages himself, in the propagation of racial and anti-Semitic policies.[89] Nevertheless, in 1926 he came to the conclusion that a "confrontation with Bachofen and Klages" was "unavoidable."[90]

In that year the leading Nazi ideologist Alfred Baeumler published his edition of Bachofen's writings under the title *Der Mythus von Orient und Occident*, in which he presented Bachofen's work as the last and most accomplished achievement of the "Mythology of Romanticism."[91] According to Baeumler, in that "mythology" Bachofen demonstrated the efficacy of the irrational in—and ultimately in opposition to—the process of civilization: the forces of mystery, myth, cult, race, and *Blut und Boden*. At the same time, Bachofen's animosity to the very notion and various manifestations of modern *Zivilisation*—atheism, rationalism, materialism, imperialism, patriarchalism, in short what Bachofen's admirer Ludwig Klages called *der Geist*, which has overpowered *die Seele*—endeared him to many antiliberal thinkers on the left. As Lionel Gossman has pointed out,

> Bachofen's work was a point of reference for the entire German tradition of *Kulturkritik*, or criticism of liberal, bourgeois culture, in the first half of the twentieth century, whether the criticism came from the right or from the left. A complete account of Bachofen's legacy would have to explain how it came to be shared by Marxists and Nazis, how it could inspire Erich Fromm and Walter Benjamin, as well as Alfred Baeumler and Manfred Schröter, and how it could happen that Thomas Mann, who warned of the dangerous political significance of the Bachofen revival of the 1920's, was at the same time so profoundly moved by the Swiss scholar's approach to myth.[92]

"Der Kampf um Johann Jakob Bachofen," as one of Baeumler's followers called it, was thus a battle in a larger war over the meaning of the ancient mythology in and for modern civilization. It was above all this realization that spurred Thomas Mann's lifelong work on the "redemption of myth [*Erlösung des Mythus*]."[93] This was the main message of his essays on Schopenhauer, Wagner, Nietzsche, and Freud, whom he considered great modern mythologists, as well as of his "mythical novel" *Joseph and His Brothers*, on which he worked from 1926 till 1942 and which was thoroughly inspired by Bachofen's notions.[94] Upon completion of this work, Mann stated that "so often, in the last decades, had the myth been abused as a means of obscurantic counter-revolution that a mythical novel like [his own] *Joseph and His Brothers*" became almost infeasible; but he nevertheless worked it out because, like Bachofen, he wished to reveal why and how certain mythological creations, such as religious beliefs and rites, moral inhibitions, and social conventions, have evolved and become crucial for our civilization. Mann trusted that this ancient mythology was crucial for the unity and continuity of Western civilization especially in times of "historic convolutions, adventures and tribulations." Mann resolved, therefore, to save Bachofen's mythology from its "tendentious political abuses" by the Fascists.[95]

Benjamin's intervention in the *Kampf* over Bachofen was motivated by the same humanistic conviction. He defined his task as a "critical redemption [*kritische Rettung*]" of Bachofen's legacy, because, like Mann, he was alert to the close and dangerous affinity of Bachofen's mythopoeic theories to actual policies. But this affinity only enhanced his resolution to save Bachofen—and through him mythology—from the clutches of German National Socialism. This conviction motivated him till the end of his life. Thus, as late as May 1940, he could still write to Adorno and commend him on his essay on Stefan George, which Benjamin appraised as an effort "to rescue" Stefan George from the Fascists. Benjamin was impressed by Adorno's ability to reassert the message of "defiance" as "the poetic and political foundation" of George's poetry: "Your work has made imaginable what was previously unimaginable, and would constitute the beginning of George's afterlife."[96] The same could be said about Benjamin's essay on Bachofen.

Benjamin makes his intention clear in the opening paragraph of his essay, where he alludes to the new ideological distortions of Bachofen's legacy, noting that Bachofen's mythological discoveries of "archaic symbols, fertility rites, divination cults, and death magic" were "scientific prophecies." Yet, he said, since they informed the modern sciences of psychology and anthropology, they also inspired modern political ideologies: "This image of reality, in which the irrational forces were endowed with so much metaphysical and legal-political significance, inevitably drew rash and immense attention from the theoreticians of Fascism." Benjamin adds, however, that Bachofen's image of archaic community was equally effective among "Marxist thinkers," such as Engels, Lafargue, and Morgan, who found in it "the presentiment of a communist society."[97] As he seeks to account for this apparent anomaly, Benjamin argues that Bachofen's work defies all conventional categories because it deals with a certain human reality that is in fact much more archaic than the "classical antiquity" of the philologists and archaeologists as well as—for this very reason—much more modern than Bachofen himself could see. For as he explored early Roman or pre-Columbian societies, Bachofen came to idealize them as the golden age of humanity. In his peculiar terms, this was the age of the mothers, which preceded, both temporally and morally, the age of the fathers. Bachofen sought to prove that this mythical reality of Edenic sensuality and spirituality was once, and could still become again, a historical reality.

Benjamin's first task in his "kritische Rettung" of Bachofen's mythology was to save it from such romantic associations. He thought that Bachofen's own "scientific discoveries" of the archaic and anarchic forces that prevailed in these societies defied his theory. "To speak of any order or hierarchy is impossible here": thus observes Benjamin in his essay on Franz Kafka, which he wrote around the same time he was working on his Bachofen essay and in which he found the most powerful evocation of the dark *Urnwelt* that Bachofen had discovered yet failed to illuminate. For the psychic energies that Kafka sensed and exposed in that underworld were much more animalistic than spiritualistic, and its creatures were promiscuous rather than sensuous; its apparent equality was in fact utter laxity. Kafka's representation of ancient mythology (as in "The Silence of the Sirens") is allegorical rather than symbolical because, unlike Bachofen, he sensed that it was already a reflection on—rather than of—that primordial reality, an attempt at sublimation rather than reanimation of its energies: "Even the world of myth of which we think in this context is incomparably younger than Kafka's world, which has been promised redemption by the myth."[98] As Benjamin would have it, then, what Bachofen discovered in antiquity was a "scientific prophecy" of what Kafka was to discover in modernity: it was just a continuation or configuration of antiquity.

> Kafka did not consider the age in which he lived as an advance over the beginnings of time. His novels are set in a swamp world. In his works, created things appear at the stage which Bachofen has termed the hetaeric stage. The fact that it is now forgotten does not mean that it does not extend into the present. On the contrary: it is actual by virtue of this very oblivion. An experience deeper than that of an average person can make contact with it.[99]

To regain this kind of deeper experience—that which reaches and reveals the mythic compulsions in modern reality—was the main task of Benjamin's essay on Bachofen and, more generally, of all his works and life experiments in the last years of his life. As I explain in the final section of this chapter, around 1935 Benjamin came to believe, with Bachofen, in what he called the "primal history [*Urgeschichte*]" of our civilization, that is, in a history that is animated by certain primordial experiences that are "stored in the unconscious of the collective." There they recur as "primal images [*Urbilder*]" like that of "Paradise," the original myth of all messianic expectations and actions, which, as Benjamin described it in his "Theses on the Philosophy of History," has generated in the history of our civilization a "storm" that is liable to destroy it. A brief discussion of

Benjamin's autobiographical work *A Berlin Childhood around Nineteen Hundred* would reveal that Benjamin came to comprehend his own life in the mythological terms of Bachofen's anthropological history.

Benjamin fashioned his collection of reminiscences and reflections on his life after Proust's *À la recherche du temps perdu*.[100] In his essay on Proust, he noted that "in this work Proust did not describe a life as it actually was, but a life as it was remembered by the one who had lived it."[101] Having realized, via Proust, that "an experienced event is finite—at any rate, confined to one sphere of experience; a remembered event is infinite, because it is only a key to everything that happened before it and after it," Benjamin composed his own recollections accordingly: in the exploration of his own memorial impressions, he sought to reveal in them the same "auratic" associations that Proust had evoked in his recollections. In Proust, "the materials of memory no longer appear singly, as images, but tell us about a whole, amorphously and formlessly, indefinitely and weightily, in the same way that the weight of his net tells the fisherman about his catch"; the materials of Benjamin's memory were to be like that, too.[102] And as to the crucial question—"What was it that Proust sought so frenetically? What was at the bottom of these infinite efforts?"—Benjamin offers a simple answer: "happiness," the blissful pleasures that he once experienced in his childhood at Combray. Benjamin defines Proust's quest for happiness as "elegiac," and the terms by which he describes how Proust went through this "eternal repetition . . . eternal restoration of the original, the first happiness," which "transforms existence into a preserve [*Bannwald*, literally "magic forest"] of memory" indicate that, for Benjamin, Proust's entire work derives from, or at least involves him in, immersion in myth.[103] Having understood where Proust failed, Benjamin conducted his own immersion in myth by more critical standards and methods. In *Berlin Childhood around Nineteen Hundred*, he used the Proustian "involuntary memory" in order to trace some concrete images of his childhood that flashed in his memory thirty years later; yet he did so to explore them not merely in his own life but also in the life of the German Jewish community and well beyond it in the "primal history" of civilization.

Thus, in the first chapter of his work, Benjamin returns, as it were, to the Garden of Eden in the Tiergarten in Berlin. He recalls how as a child he experienced the paths, monuments, and people of the park as a "labyrinth" replete with all kinds of mythological figures. Entering the park like a second Theseus following his Ariadne along the thread of erotic sensations, he discovered therein the myth-realm of the ancient gods as transfigured in the bourgeois decorations of the Second Reich, most visibly so in the aristocratic monuments of Friedrich Wilhelm and Queen Louise: "They towered up from their round pedestals among the flower beds as if spellbound by magic curves that a watercourse had inscribed before them in the sand."[104] As he invoked these primal visions thirty years later, Benjamin realized that they "preformed" the historical experiences and "the features of what is to come"; in other words, he recognized in his early impressions the topical concerns that were to determine his life and works.[105] From then on, he now understood, he had found signs of "the return of the ancient gods" everywhere: "Under their sign the Old West of Berlin was transformed into the West of antiquity, whence the western winds come to the mariners, who navigate their boat with the Hesperidan apples slowly up the Landwehrkannal, in order to cast anchor near the Herkules Bridge. And yet again, as in my childhood, the Hydra and the Nemean lion found a place in the wild bushes around the big star."[106] As this description reveals, Benjamin believed that the circumstances and events of his life had always been determined by strong mythological compulsions. In Bachofen's work he found the psychological, anthropological, and historical affirmations for his atavistic impression of life. Benjamin himself reveals as much when he writes of his experience in the Tiergarten that his steps there, which had led him "downward, if not to the mothers of all being, then certainly to the mothers of this garden," predestined his life to be a quest to regain this lost paradise of maternal bliss.[107] The similarity between Bachofen's maternal conception of history and Benjamin's maternal conception of his own life is telling.[108] Therein we may find the ultimate reason for Benjamin's *Wahlverwandschaft* to Bachofen.

Already in the first chapters of his memories, Benjamin contrasts the maternal and paternal impressions that have made up his world. Whereas the "patriarchs"—his father, his teachers—are figures who ruled him (and the whole world) by command, force, and heroic efforts at work or in battlefield, the maternal figures—his mother, aunts, nurses, serving women, even the selling women in the *Markthalle*—are full of love, care, and wisdom. For Benjamin this was the wisdom that was "counsel woven into the fabric of real life."[109] The patriarchs rule by reason and laws, but the matriarchs rule by compassion and prejudices, which they derive from the most ancient sources of tradition—the proverb, the legend, the fairy tale, ultimately the myth. They too are "guardians of tradition," but, unlike the patriarchs, who perform this duty using dogmatic and autocratic measures, the matriarchs use empathetic and pragmatic ways, which are much more truthful and useful to that tradition. His maternal aunts appear to be such figures in the episode "At the Corner of Genthiner and Steglitzer Streets." Their tales, houses, and lifestyle evoke the entire memorial history of a typical bourgeois Jewish family in Germany. The serving women in the house also fulfill this role: they "were mostly . . . more massive and powerful than their mistresses" and represented a different sagacious tradition, simpler but more prudential, like the "old helper" who "whenever I came, took my coat from me as if it were a great burden and, whenever I left, pressed my cap onto my forehead as if she wanted to bless me."[110] In the same vein, the market women in the shopping center on Magdeburg Square appear as "corpulent matrons lying on their thrones, priestesses of the commercial Ceres, sellers of fruits of tree and field, of all edible birds, fishes and mammals"—revealing, as it were, the archaic mythology inherent in modern commercial society.[111] In their traditional tales and practices, these and other women intimate a different kind of reality, which pertains to the world "as it might have been" rather than to the world "as it is." This "other" reality is like a dream, in which all kinds of wishful options that have not been realized are preserved, waiting to be resolved and fulfilled. This is the message of the figure of the nurse in the episode "Winter Morning." She is the *Magd* with the oil lamp who appears as the archaic guardian of the fire, in whom Benjamin comprehends that "the fairy who guards a wish exists for everyone. It's just that only a few can remember the wish they made, and, accordingly, only a few recognize its fulfillment later in their own life."[112]

However, as Bachofen, Kafka, and Proust had shown, such wishes are never entirely forgotten. "What has been forgotten is never something purely individual. Everything forgotten mingles with what has been forgotten of the prehistoric world"; so writes Benjamin in his Bachofenian interpretation of Franz Kafka.[113] Along with other auratic "forms of experience," such as magic trances, mystic revelations, or utopian visions that have been repressed, forgotten, or dismissed as unreasonable by our modern, all-too-modern, civilization, these personal wishes pass into and survive in myths, which are collective "wish-images," waiting to be remembered by future generations. They attest to what "people we could have talked to, women who could have given themselves to us" once sought— amelioration and eventual redemption of the human predicament. And though their hopes and dreams have been falsified by the terrible events of history, they must still be pursued: "our image of happiness is indissolubly bound up with the image of redemption . . . Like every generation that preceded us, we have been endowed with a *weak* messianic power, a power to which the past has a claim."[114] We must regain this messianic message not only from the biblical tradition but also from the mythical tradition, being aware that it is only a "temptation of redemption."[115]

Ever since Plato perceived the potential ethical and political dangers posed by the mothers and nurses who were reciting Homeric tales to their children, there have been those who attempted to suppress this art and its agents. Benjamin sought instead to reaffirm their virtues, most notably through the figure of his mother in the episode "Fever," where she literally assumes mythological dimensions. He recalls how, while he was lying ill in his bed, his mother used to bring him medicine and food, which his body detested.

> Against these he craved tales. The strong current that empowered them gushed through him carrying along with it, like driftwood, the illness. Pain was a dam that blocked the tale only initially; later on, when the tale became more powerful, it undermined the pain, and swept it down to oblivion. Caressing carved the riverbed of this stream. I loved this because in my mother's hand trickled already stories that would soon flow out of her mouth. With them surfaced all that I ever got to know of my forefathers.[116]

The child overcomes his illness by continuing the maternal narration of myth: he conjures up shadows of real and mythological creatures (*der Fenriswolf*) on the walls of his bedroom, letting them free to roam and rule his world.[117] The awakening from this nocturnal world of maternal protection to the daylight of bare life is traumatic: "Servants began again and more frequently to replace my mother at my side. And one morning I gave myself up again, after a long pause and with weakened power, to the beating of the carpets, that came up into my room through the window."[118] With this rude transition from archaic pleasures to modern pressures, from the ideal to the real, reason overcomes myth. Yet from that moment on, and throughout his life, Benjamin sought in dreams, books, and dream-books the lost mythical-maternal sensations of blissful existence: "In the books everything was turbulent. Opening one of them would lead me into a womb, wherein a changing and ruffling text, pregnant with colors, was clouding."[119]

As these recollections indicate, Benjamin's *Berlin Childhood* is not concerned primarily with the private life of the author, nor is it confined to the social conditions and institutions that dominated his growing up in the Wilhelmine age around the turn of the century. Rather, it reaches deeper, to the traditions that have permeated the world from prehistoric

---

times. Benjamin owed this peculiar perception of himself to Kafka. According to Benjamin, among all modern mythologists, it was Kafka who sensed the mythic compulsions everywhere and was thus able, or rather forced, "to move cosmic ages in his writings," even, and especially, in the description of the most common experiences.[120] A simple gesture like that of his sister knocking on the gate of a great house was enough to open and call up epochal experiences from the depths of primeval times. Benjamin relates "such experiences" of Kafka's sister and other "female characters" to the prehistoric age of myth that Bachofen unearthed.[121] He then advances this "mythological interpretation" against the "theological interpretations" of Kafka's works that were fashionable at the time among scholars like Hans-Julius Schoeps, Bernhard Groethuysen, or Willy Haas (127–28): "Only from this vantage point [the mythological] can the technique of Kafka the storyteller be comprehended. Whenever figures in the novels have anything to say to K., no matter how important or surprising it may be, they do so casually and with the implication that he must really have known it all along. It is as though nothing new was being imparted, as though the hero was just being subtly invited to recall to mind something that he had forgotten" (131). Kafka's K. must recall what he had forgotten, his archaic mythology, because, as already noted in the passage quoted above, he still lives by it: "The fact that it is now forgotten does not mean that it does not extend into the present. On the contrary: it is actual by virtue of this very oblivion" (130). This oblivion is the reason why the "laws and definite norms [that] remain unwritten in the prehistoric world" continue to affect those who are unaware of these laws and therefore liable to transgress them. Thus Joseph K. in *The Trial* or K. in *The Castle* must live and die in permanent "ambiguity" because they have failed to understand the "fatal" forces—or myths—that operate through "the legal authorities" that are directed against them (114–15). This is how Benjamin eventually came to see Kafka:

> Kafka's work is an ellipse with foci that are far apart and are determined, on the one hand, by mystical experience (in particular, the experience of tradition) and, on the other, by experience of the modern city-dweller . . . What is actually and in a very literal sense wildly incredible in Kafka is that this most recent world of experience was conveyed to him precisely by this mystical tradition. This, of course, could not have happened without devastating processes . . . within this tradition. The long and short of it is that apparently an appeal had to be made to the forces of this tradition if an individual (by the name of Franz Kafka) was to be confronted with that

reality of ours . . . But Kafka's experience was based solely on the tradition, to which he surrendered; there was no far-sighted or "prophetic vision." Kafka listened to tradition, and he who listens hard does not see.[122]

Kafka thus failed to explain what he had so well expressed because he lacked adequate critical terms by which to account for the mythical traditions that made it up, the very same forces that compelled him "to move cosmic ages in his writings." Benjamin's attempt to clarify this predicament in Kafka's life and works, as well as in his own, and his ability to rectify it in his later works by the "adequate" categories of social theory and history reveal just how crucial Bachofen's mythological discoveries and theories were for him. As the passages from his autobiographical writings indicate, he eventually recognized the mythical compulsions in his own life as inevitable, and even valuable, sources of his German Jewish identity and was thus able to come to terms with the awful forces and truths that Kafka had perceived in human reality and yet failed to reconcile within his own life. Benjamin observes:

> It is easier to draw speculative conclusions from Kafka's posthumous collection of notes than to explore even one of the motifs that appear in his stories and novels. Yet only these give some clue to the prehistoric forces that dominated Kafka's creativeness, forces which, to be sure, may justifiably be regarded as belonging to our world as well. Who can say under what names they appeared to Kafka himself? Only this much is certain: he did not know them and failed to get his bearings among them.[123]

Every word in this observation might be said about Benjamin himself. It is certainly easier to draw speculative conclusions from Benjamin's posthumous collection of notes that makes up *The Arcades Project* than to explore even one of the motifs that appear in his last works. Yet only these give some clue to the prehistoric forces that dominated his creativeness, forces that, to be sure, may justifiably be regarded as belonging to our world as well. Unlike Kafka, Benjamin did come to know these prehistoric forces and was able in his last works to get his bearings among them.

IV

In mid-1927 Benjamin began to collect notes and reflections for an essay with the provisional title "Paris Arcades: A Dialectical Enchantment."[124] In 1929 he read it to Adorno and Horkheimer at Königstein and Frankfurt. This early version of the work is important because it contains the most seminal notions around which Benjamin subsequently construed *The*

Arcades Project and, moreover, reveals these notions in their purest form before Benjamin refitted them into the thirty-six Convolutes that now make up the book. He starts with a brief factual description of the arcades, cited from contemporary sources (primarily the *Illustrated Guide to Paris* from 1852) and then writes:

> All this is the arcade in our eyes. And it was nothing of all this. They [the arcades] radiated through the Paris of the Empire like grottoes. For someone entering the Passage des Panoramas in 1817, the sirens of gaslight would be singing to him on one side, while oil-lamp odalisques offered enticements from the other. With the kindling of electric lights, the irreproachable glow was extinguished in these galleries, which suddenly became more difficult to find—which wrought a black magic at entranceways, and peered from blind windows into their own interior. It was not decline but transformation. All at once, they were the hollow mold from which the image of "modernity" was cast. Here, the century mirrored with satisfaction its most recent past.[125]

"All this is the arcade in our eyes. And it was nothing of all this." In order to know what the arcades really were and always had been in history, Benjamin turned to probe their deeper metaphorical and mythical meanings in history.[126] He reasoned that a proper historical investigation and psychological interpretation of the modes of construction, the commercial production, and the ornamentation that materialized in the arcades could disclose the original spiritual motivations that have always generated such passageways:

> One knew of places in ancient Greece where the way led down into the underworld. Our waking existence likewise is a land which, at certain hidden points, leads down into the underworld—a land full of inconspicuous places from which dreams arise. All day long, suspecting nothing, we pass them by, but no sooner has sleep come than we are eagerly groping our way back to lose ourselves in the dark corridors. By day, the labyrinth of urban dwellings resembles consciousness; the arcades (which are galleries leading into the city's past) issue unremarked onto the streets. At night, however, under the tenebrous mass of the houses, their denser darkness protrudes like a threat, and the nocturnal pedestrian hurries past—unless, that is, we have emboldened him to turn into the narrow lane.[127]

In his specific observations and interpretations of this "mythological topography," Benjamin follows Bachofen's direction. His descriptions of the city abound with chtonic metaphors, in which the arcades are likened to "mineral springs," "aquariums," "cells," and "labyrinths" that lead further down and ever deeper into the prehistorical origins of civilization—the Metro, the sewage channels, and further down into the river basin and "the limestone quarries, the grottoes and catacombs which, since the early Middle Ages, have time and again been reentered and traversed" by those "who knew their way around it." Among them were enemies of law and order, such as smugglers, but also the victims of law and order—from the early Christian martyrs to current vagabonds, beggars, orphans, and other lost souls. "We know also that in times of public commotion mysterious rumors traveled very quickly via the catacombs, to say nothing of the prophetic spirits and fortunetellers duly qualified to pronounce upon them." [128] The arcades thus served as actual "passages of myth" that could still contact, as it were, the earliest and lowest levels of the city as well as its newest and grandest levels of the grand boulevards, *Magasins de Nouveautés,* and fashionable boutiques of the upper classes. Entering these arcades might still enable the modern historian to step down from these upper superficial levels of modernity to the deeper and truer levels of antiquity. Benjamin employed the same topographical and archaeological modes of observation while he toured other modern European cities.[129] Paris of the nineteenth century, however, was the prime site of "mythological topography." Benjamin pays homage to Balzac, who described the city in these terms:

> Balzac has secured the mythic constitution of his world through precise topographic contours. Paris is the breeding ground of his mythology— Paris with its two or three great bankers (Nucingen, du Tillet), Paris with its great physician Horace Bianchon . . . with its sundry advocates and soldiers. But above all—and we see this time and again—it is from the same streets and corners, the same little rooms and recesses, that the figures of this world step into the light. What else can this mean but that topography is the ground plan of this mythic space of tradition [*Traditionsraum*], as it is of every such space, and that it can become indeed its key—just as it was the key to Greece for Pausanias, and just as the history and situation of the Paris arcades are to become the key for the underworld of this century, into which Paris has sunk.[130]

As this passage shows, Benjamin's work on the "mythological topography" of Paris was closely modeled on Pausanias's *Guide to Greece:* he reasoned that like the ancient traveler who "wrote his topography of Greece in the second century A.D. as the places of worship and many of the other monuments began to fall into ruin," the modern historian should decipher and invoke in the "ruins" of modernity their ancient mythologies.[131] His fascination with the arcades, "being the galleries, which lead into its past existence," was intensified by the sensation that they functioned like the ancient labyrinths that Pausanias had entered: they transferred their visitors from the pomp-world of the street into its deeper reality of the "swamp-world." In Bachofen's life and works—not least in the *Griechische Reise,* which Benjamin reviewed in 1928—Benjamin found a modern Pausanias, a fellow traveler who actually revisited those "sites in ancient Greece from which one could go down into the underworld" and could still drive us "as in a dream, once again to live the life of our parents and grandparents."[132]

In his early sketches for this work, Benjamin set forth his intention to "penetrate" the configurations of modern mythology as revealed in the various fabrications of Paris in the nineteenth century so as to expose and eventually to redeem their "utopian" potentialities—the unfulfilled dreams of past, and largely lost, generations about decent life and just society. Such were, for Benjamin, the "utopian" visions of a new society that nineteenth-century thinkers like Saint-Simon and Fourier, or indeed Bachofen, had evoked from ancient society. Benjamin seemed to recognize these old mythological meanings and messages also in the new technologies that emerged in Paris of the nineteenth century, above all in the arcades. "Only a thoughtless observer would deny that correspondences come into play between the world of modern technology and the archaic symbol-world of mythology."[133] For such were the topical subjects he had observed in its fashions, advertisements, and exhibitions: birth and death, fertility and sterility, sexuality and purity, sin and salvation.[134] The fact that these mythological figurations were still pervasive in modern reality—in linguistic phrases, conceptual idioms, religious doctrines, moral rules, social laws, political ideologies, commercial advertisements, names of companies and streets, architectural designs and monuments—implied that they still entailed some potential messages to mankind even in its modern period. What were the true meanings of the Parisian arcades? What was their utopian message to modernity? These were the questions that Benjamin sought to answer in *The Arcades Project.*

The conceptual inspiration of that work is found in the very first impression of the narrator in Aragon's novel *Paris Peasant,* who, passing by churches that seem deserted and utterly meaningless, opines: "Man no longer worships the gods on their heights . . . The spirit of religions, coming down to dwell in the dust, has abandoned the sacred places. But there are other places which flourish among mankind, places where men go calmly about their mysterious lives and in which a profound religion is very gradually taking shape."[135] These new shrines were the arcades, which "deserve . . . to be regarded as the secret repositories of several modern myths."[136] By the time Benjamin began to compose his own work on the arcades, his initial excitement with Aragon's powerful evocation of the surrealistic sensation of reality had abated. In his essay on surrealism he was already very critical of Aragon's apparent failure to offer any real explanation, or "profane illumination," for what he had so perceptively observed. In that essay he merely chided Aragon and Breton for their apparent "spiritualism," but in *The Arcades Project* he became quite militant in his opposition to such delirious states of mind and affairs: "Whereas Aragon persists within the realm of dream, here the concern is to find the constellation of awakening. While in Aragon there remains an impressionistic element, namely the 'mythology' (and this impressionism must be held responsible for many vague philosophemes in his book), here it is the question of the dissolution of 'mythology' into the space of history [*Geschichtsraum*]."[137]

Benjamin's urgent attempt to "awaken" Aragon from his impressionistic immersion in "mythology" by critical, practical, and historical considerations betrays his growing apprehension of the new meanings that "mythology" has assumed in modern political ideologies. This acute realization may explain his occasional reversion to the progressive ideology of enlightenment: "To cultivate fields where, until now, only madness has reigned. Forge ahead with the whetted axe of reason, looking neither left nor right so as not to succumb to the horror that beckons from deep in the primeval forest. Every ground must at some point have been made arable by reason, must have been cleared of the undergrowth of delusion and myth. This is to be accomplished here for the terrain of the nineteenth century" (456). Nonetheless, these desperate terms only enhance the impression that Benjamin must have had when he wrote that myth had not really been banished by reason and progress, nor could it be vanquished by them, because its "ground" or "reason [*Grund*]" is too fertile and its psychic roots, the "horror that beckons from deep in the primeval forest," are too deep for such inadequate weapons as the "axe of reason." His resolution to forge ahead "looking neither left nor right" implies that he detected mythic compulsions and delusions not only in Fascism and National Socialism on the "right," but also in anarchism and Communism on the "left." Only this deep realization can explain the curious fact that Benjamin does not confront directly the new political mythologies. In the massive compilation of notes and citations that make up *The Arcades Project*, he does not mention even once Alfred Rosenberg's *Mythus des zwanzigsten*

Jahrhunderts. He turns his attention, instead, to "the terrain of the nineteenth century."

Benjamin does so because he came to the conclusion that in order to understand the "reactivation of mythic forces" in modern European society, it was necessary to probe the historical conditions that generated them in the early decades of the nineteenth century, conditions that still prevailed because the forces they had reactivated still persisted (391). Aragon's city-dweller rightly perceives that he lives in "modern mythology," whereby "the newest, the most modern" assumes a "dream form of events," yet he fails to understand that this quintessential "modernistic" predicament is essentially "materialistic" rather than "mystic." According to Benjamin, this mythic sensation of reality emerged with the industrial revolution of the early nineteenth century and continued to exist because the new "materialistic" conditions of modern capitalistic society had been so devised as to generate in the city-dweller the same old "mystic" experiences of primitive mentality. Following Aragon into the arcades, Benjamin thus seems to conceive of them in these rather conventional critical theoretical terms. In "Convolute A (Arcades, *Magasins de Nouveautés,* Sales Clercs)," he presents these "shopping palaces" with their artificial light and bountiful goods as capitalistic fabrications that were designed to mesmerize the masses into a state of permanent fascination. Devoid of traffic and other public uses, "the arcade is a street of lascivious commerce only; it is wholly adapted to arousing desires" (42). Benjamin aptly demonstrates this materialistic conception of what the arcades are all about through a massive documentation of architectural plans, drawings and pictures, advertisements, journalistic descriptions, and poetic evocations, which are further accentuated in Convolute B, which deals with "Fashion." However, in "Convolute C (Ancient Paris, Catacombs, Demolitions, Decline of Paris)," he reiterates his incantation: "All this, in our eyes, is what the arcades are. And they were nothing of all this." And then he amends it with this insightful observation that Aragon made but utterly failed to understand: "It is only today, when the pickaxe menaces them, that they have at last become the true sanctuaries of a cult of the ephemeral, the ghostly landscape of damnable pleasures and professions. Places that yesterday were incomprehensible, and that tomorrow will never be known."[138]

What Aragon failed to see was that this "reactivation of mythic forces" in the Parisian arcades in the early decades of the twentieth century was primarily an expression of certain "historical" rather than of any "mythical" conditions, which theorists like Klages and Jung presumed to have discovered in the depths of human consciousness. Benjamin's call for "the dissolution of 'mythology' into the space of history" was meant to invert the neoromantic and nondialectic terms by which both the surrealists and the Fascists have commonly perceived the entwinement of myth and history. Against their common notion of *mythological history*, Benjamin proposed a theory of *historical mythology*. He wanted to show that history was not really determined by certain mythical beliefs, images, and tales but rather that certain historical conditions of material and anthropological necessities produced these mythic forms and compulsions everywhere and at all times. As Benjamin remarks in his essay on Karl Kraus of 1931, "there is no idealistic but only a materialistic deliverance from myth." [139]

This is the gist of Benjamin's argument against Carl Gustav Jung's attempt to mythologize real figures like that of "the beggar": whereas Jung thought that the reappearance of the beggar in various historical conditions was a manifestation of an eternal archetype that inhered in the collective unconsciousness of all nations and civilizations, Benjamin inverted this causal assumption so as to show that myths did not beget beggars but rather that beggars begot myths: "As long as there is still one beggar, there still exists myth." [140] This, then, is the rule of myth: as long as the social predicament remains the same—with irresoluble problems like material poverty, inequality, and inequity—there will be myth. The dissolution of myth will occur only with the coming of the Revolution or of the Revelation, which, for Benjamin, were bound to be coeval.

In "Convolute N (On the Theory of Knowledge, Theory of Progress)," the most substantial theoretical discussion of *The Arcades Project*, Benjamin seeks to reassess Jung's notion of myth as "collective dream" in accord with his new materialistic conception of historical mythology. Setting out from a comment he found in Marx's letter to Ruge—"The reform of consciousness consists *solely* in . . . the awakening of the world from its dream about itself" (456)—Benjamin argues that even if the surrealists and the Jungians were right to consider myths as collective dreams, they ought to have realized that in order to use these "collective dreams" for extension or correction of our conventional conception of reality, they had to treat these states of mind in the same way and for the same purposes that the Freudians used dreams: not to realize their fantasies, but to analyze their meanings. And, as in the case of dreams, this can be done not by association with them, but only by dissociation, or "awakening," from them. Crucially, however, Benjamin warns that a drastic "awakening" from dreams by forgetting and erasing them from consciousness is a "false liberation, whose sign is violence" (884, 388–89). In Freud's theory of "the return of the repressed," dreams that have not been properly recalled and resolved under wakeful conditions as pertinent to real problems in actual life are bound to reappear in nightmares; the same might be true of "collective dreams" such as myths, when they are simply dismissed as "fantasies."

This new perception of the arcades as "collective dreams" that contained some pertinent meanings and messages required a more fertile conception of "mythology" than the vulgar Marxists had derived from their "doctrine of the ideological superstructure." Benjamin duly culled this new conception from Marx himself. He noted that Marx did not fully abide by the assumption that there ought to be a "causal relation" of strict determination between the material conditions (infrastructure) and cultural manifestations (superstructure), for "already the observation that ideologies of the superstructure reflect conditions falsely and invidiously goes beyond this." Yet if "such determination is not reducible to simple reflection, how is it then . . . to be characterized?" Benjamin answers:

As its expression. The superstructure is the expression of the infrastructure. The economic conditions under which society exists are expressed in the superstructure—precisely as, with the sleeper, an overfull stomach finds not its reflection but its expression in the contents of dreams, which, from a causal point of view, it may be said to "condition." The collective, from the first, expresses the conditions of its life. These find their expression in the dream and their interpretation in the awakening. (392)

On these new hermeneutic premises, Benjamin goes on to reinterpret Marx's notion of the "fetishism of commodity." Whereas a commodity, as Marx observed in *Das Kapital,* initially appears as "a very trivial thing [that] is easily understood," in capitalist society, where commodities have been dissociated from all material relations (to their producers) and functional considerations (for their users), the commodity has acquired "theological subtleties and metaphysical niceties." Marx and his followers did not pay much attention to these mythical—or, as Benjamin preferred to call them, "phantasmagorical"—guises. Benjamin, however, was particularly attentive to this "thread of expression," because its wish-images (*Wunschbilder*) revealed, as it were, the authentic human aspirations that had always inspired all material productions. "At issue . . . is the attempt to grasp an economic process as a perceptible *Ur*-phenomenon, from out of which proceed all manifestations of life in the arcades (and, accordingly, in the nineteenth century)" (460).

This, then, is what the Parisian Arcades really are: "cultural expressions" of the "material conditions" of the nineteenth century that have assumed the form of "collective dreams." As such they preserve but conceal the traumatic experiences of previous generations as well as the expectations of future generations. These "dreams" are important sources of experience and knowledge that ought to be realized by a careful process of investigation and interpretation, as in a gradual awakening that allows us to grasp both the sensual images and the intellectual messages of the dream.

> Awakening as a gradual process that goes on in the life of the individual as in the life of generations. Sleep its initial stage. A generation's experience of youth has much in common with the experience of dreams. Its historical configuration is a dream configuration. Every epoch has such a side turned toward dreams, the child's side. For the previous century, it appears very clearly in the arcades. But whereas the education of earlier generations explained these dreams for them in terms of tradition, of religious doctrine, present-day education simply amounts to the distraction of children . . . What follows here is an experiment in the technique of awakening. An attempt to become aware of the dialectical—the Copernican—turn of remembrance. (388)

Benjamin's attempt to regain the utopian potentialities of collective dream-experiences attests to his conviction that historical myths are not just delusions or distortions. Rather, as repositories of youthful wishes of earlier generations that have not been fulfilled, they remain actual and may be conducive to the "re-generation" of social tradition. The fact that the messages of these collective dreams have so far been either conformed to "tradition" or annulled by "distraction" required a "Copernican revolution" in historical consciousness, such as could literally re-member, "put together again," the mythical images of historical dreams in a meaningful constellation. According to Benjamin, this constellation whereby the mythic images are revealed and recognized as such occurs only rarely, in certain historical moments of rapid transition from "old" to "new" forms of life, for example, those that prevailed in Paris of the early nineteenth century, and are visible in such quintessential "modern" creations as Baudelaire's poetry, Fourier's utopian theory, Bellangé's architectural constructions, and other cultural manifestations such as the World Exhibitions and advertisements, above all in the Parisian Arcades. On these premises, the "reactivation of mythic forces" that began in the early nineteenth century and has intensified ever since was not a degeneration to "prehistory" but rather a regeneration of what Benjamin called "primal history [*Urgeschichte*]" (463). Baudelaire's *Fleurs du mal* exemplifies this modern acuity: his recognition of the "correspondences" between the "primeval forest" and the "modern city" disclosed the "primal history of the nineteenth century" in "images appropriate to that century."[141] In *The Arcades Project* Benjamin defined these constellations of deep recognition of the primal in the epiphenomenal history as "dialectical images":

> Only dialectical images are genuinely historical—that is, not archaic—images . . . In the dialectical image, what has been within a particular epoch is always, simultaneously, "what has been from time immemorial." As such, however, it is manifest, on each occasion, only to a quite specific epoch—namely, the one in which humanity, rubbing its eyes, recognizes just this particular dream image as such. It is at this moment that the historian takes up, with regard to that image—the task of dream interpretation.[142]

Aragon failed to do so. He did not recognize the dream images or myths of the arcades he had so perceptively evoked in Paris of the early twentieth century as historical manifestations of the past that had become "legible" and "actual" for him and the modern generation. As Winfried Menninghaus has argued, Benjamin's theory of dialectical images, for all its apparent radicalism, "bears witness to the field of tension in Benjamin's reflections on myth. The dialectical image, on the one hand, tends to break up the mythical power of images [*Bildkraft*] by means of the dialectic of knowledge, and on the other hand, it implies that the genuine form of knowledge itself is, at least in part, based on images and thereby on myth."[143]

The eruption of all the major ideological movements of modernity—romanticism, Communism, and nationalism—in the early nineteenth century was likewise a regeneration of historical consciousness through the "reactivation of mythic forces." Benjamin elaborated this "revisionist" conviction in his essay "Paris, the Capital of the Nineteenth Century," the first Exposé of *The Arcades Project,* which he completed in 1934 while he was working on his Bachofen essay. After citing Michelet's claim that "each epoch dreams the one to follow," Benjamin asserts: "In the dream in which each epoch entertains images of its successor, the latter appears wedded to elements of primal history [*Urgeschichte*]—that is, to elements of a classless society. And the experiences of such a society—as stored in the unconscious of the collective—engender, through interpenetration with what is new, the utopia that has left its trace in a thousand configurations of life, from enduring edifices to passing fashions."[144] In 1935 such notions were suspiciously close to the Fascist ideology of "primal origins."[145] Theodor Adorno, at least, thought so and warned Benjamin of this perilous association with right-wing thinkers such as Bachofen's apostles Klages and Baeumler. Benjamin was willing to take this risk, because he thought that those and other political reactionaries, such as Nietzsche and Sorel, were, in their way, philosophical "revolutionaries." As Scholem has pointed out, Benjamin "was able to perceive the subterranean rumbling of revolution even in the case of authors whose worldview bore reactionary traits; generally he was keenly aware of what he called 'the strange interplay between reactionary theory and revolutionary practice.'"[146]

Benjamin duly saw that Bachofen's "regressive" attempt to ascertain the mythological compulsions in modernity did not necessarily entail reactionary political ideology; rather, it was, or at least could be used as, a critical attempt to expose the inevitable and ultimately valuable mythological legacy in such "progressive" ideologies as Marxism, especially because Marx and his modern followers commonly tended to disregard the efficacy of myth for (and in) their ideology. Following Engels, Lafargue, and Morgan, who found in Bachofen "the presentiment of a communist society," and his colleague Erich Fromm, who published an essay on Bachofen in the *Zeitschrift für Sozialforschung* of 1934,[147] Benjamin too regarded Bachofen's discovery of matriarchy as a great contribution to modern social science. Hence, whereas radical theorists from Marx to Adorno had attacked such invocations of the golden age as naive and "regressive" fantasies that inspired romantic or fascistic reactions against modernity, Benjamin attended to their "progressive" visions of social equity and unity, which in his view had at last become fully recognizable and thereby realizable. Benjamin sums up its message: "This state of things attests to a specific ideal of equity. The indisputable fact, that certain matriarchal societies have attained a high degree of democratic order and ideas of political equality, caught Bachofen's attention. It is for this reason that he perceived Communism as inseparable from Gynecocracy."[148]

Contrary to what Bachofen claimed, however, Benjamin saw that this myth of primary and exemplary society was bound to remain forever beyond anthropological or historical verification; he nevertheless accepted it as real enough, if only because it had survived and passed into our political tradition as a model of decent and just society and thereby had acquired significant political as well as historiographical meanings. For, as Benjamin understood, Bachofen's vision of matriarchy, which implied that women were superior to men in the ethical and political guidance of society, was part of a larger and more radical political-historiographical strategy, the ultimate aim of which was, according to Benjamin, "the subversion of the concept of authority."[149] And this, indeed, is what Bachofen must have meant it to be, if we recall that *Das Mutterrecht* was written in opposition to the "patriarch" of German historiography, the eminent Theodor Mommsen. Bachofen's extreme animosity to the Prussian historian of imperial Rome was as much personal as professional.[150] He was particularly incensed by Mommsen's "usurpation" of Roman history by the same positivistic-imperialistic means by which his hero Bismarck had taken over German history. Bachofen charged that Mommsen had conducted his *Quellenkritik* like a *Realpolitik*, seeking to demolish the mythological traditions and associations of Roman society so as to eliminate, very literally, all sources of opposition to his own real-political conception of its history. In his late historical works, above all in *Die Sage von Tanaquil* (1870), Bachofen sought to counter Mommsen and his followers by conjuring alternative images of life from—and of—antiquity, drawing on its mythological rather than its real-political histories, for these, in his view, contained the lost maternal messages of early Roman society. In a polemical tract on Mommsen's "critical" demolition of the historical authenticity of the renowned Roman myth of Coriolanus, he argued that this *Kritik* betrayed all that was wrong in Mommsen's political ideology and historical methodology of antiquity—imperialism, militarism, materialism, and secularism, all of which formed, or rather derived from, "patriarchalism."[151] Bachofen sought to counter this political-historiographical domination by the reassertion of "matriarchalism," whose legacy came from Roman mythology. In the introduction to his *Mutterrecht*, he thus insists on the historicity of the mythological stories of the Lycian queen Laodamia and the Danaïds and the stories recorded by Eustathius that seemed to affirm his theory of ancient matriarchy. He charges that

> those who hold to the prevailing view would have attempted to discredit Eustathius' story on the ground that its authenticity could not be supported by any older, not to mention contemporaneous sources; they would have argued that its cryptic character indicated invention by some foolish mythographer. They would have said, not that the myth had formed around the fact like a shell, but on the contrary, that the fact had been abstracted from the myth. They would have set it down as worthless rubbish and relegated it to the discard pile whose steady growth marks the destructive progress of the so-called "critical" approach to mythology.[152]

As Benjamin noted, Bachofen's attack on the positivistic methodology of the new *historische Wissenschaft* carried on Goethe's battle against Newton: Benjamin saw "the same proud, indeed imperious attitude; the same contempt for the established boundaries between the sciences; the same hostile reactions from professional colleagues." It was a fight that repeated itself in the attack of Willamowitz-Moellendorf on Nietzsche's *Geburt der Tragödie*, where, we recall, Nietzsche exposed the liberal-imperial historiography in his time in terms similar to those that Bachofen, his colleague at the University of Basel, used against Mommsen—as a pathetic substitution for "the loss of myth, the loss of the mythical home, the mythical maternal womb."[153]

In his last reflections on history, above all in his meditation on the "angel of history" in his "Theses on the Philosophy of History," Benjamin used this "regressive" conception of history against the major progressive ideologies and methodologies of history in modern times. As I shall point out, Benjamin's image of the historian in that famous text bears a tacit homage to Bachofen. For much like Bachofen, who denounced progressive historiography for having treated the Edenic lore of antiquity "as worthless rubbish and relegated it to the discard pile whose steady growth marks the destructive progress of the so-called 'critical' approach to mythology," Benjamin denounced, in similar idiomatic terms, the progressive conceptions of history as a "storm blowing from paradise," apparently moving away from the Edenic myth even if, unknowingly, by its own force, while producing a "pile of debris" that "grows skyward."[154]

V

Benjamin's main message in his "Theses on the Philosophy of History" is evident in the opening allegorical figuration of the "little hunchback" who sits within the "puppet called 'Historical Materialism'" and ensures that it "is to win all the time . . . if it enlists the services of theology, which today, as we know, is wizened and has to keep out of sight." This attempt at a rehabilitation of redemptive theology is amplified throughout the "Theses" until it culminates in its very last sentence, where Benjamin evokes the Jewish image of the Messiah, who might come "every second of time."[155] In his biographical-historical reconstruction of this text, Rolf Tiedemann relates Benjamin's theological turn in his last years and work to the general political developments and his personal experiences of life among left-wing intellectuals in Paris, which made him very wary of the standard Marxist explanations and solutions to the current political affairs.[156] By 1936 he had lost all faith in the Communist experiment in the Soviet Union and was particularly incensed by its crass antireligious policy. Tiedemann shows that during the early months of 1937, Benjamin was much occupied with André Gide's book *Retour de l'U.R.S.S.*, where the author berates the antireligious struggle waged "against a teaching which, after all, had brought the world a new hope and the most extraordinary revolutionary stimuli conceivable in those times." Gide adds, "One ought not here to begrudge me a remnant of my upbringing, my early convictions. I would speak in the same way about Greek myths; in them, too, I recognize a deep and lasting formative power. It would seem absurd for me to *believe* in them. But it would be equally absurd for me to ignore the truth in them and to try to dismiss them with a smile and shrug." This recognition impressed Benjamin, who wrote to Horkheimer: "The passage on religion is outstanding. Perhaps the best in the book." [157] A careful reading of Benjamin's last works reveals that, along with Gide and other French revisionists whom he encountered in Paris, he revised his earlier distinctions between theology and mythology accordingly and eventually came to see that "the service of theology" to historical revolution lay in its mythology.

This turn is evident in Benjamin's last publication, the preface to Carl Gustav Jochmann's "Regression of Poetry," which was published in the *Zeitschrift für Sozialforschung* in 1939. [158] Jochmann was a bourgeois intellectual from Riga, a *Spätaufklärer* who moved in the German literary and revolutionary circles of the early nineteenth century yet had been removed from the cultural and political traditions of modernity because he held to a regressive, not progressive, conception of history. [159] Benjamin's depiction of Jochmann as a seer who "turns his back to the future of which he speaks in prophetic words, and his visionary lights up at the sight of the mountain tops of earlier heroic human races and their poetry, which are receding ever more deeply into the past," inspired his last and most memorable conception of the "Angel of History." [160] Benjamin was particularly impressed by Jochmann's notion that poetry, along with other human faculties and creations that he deemed so crucial for an "absolute experience" of reality, was regressing with the process of enlightenment. [161] Benjamin goes on to ask, however, whether, in Jochmann's view, poetry really vanishes, and he says that "on this question Jochmann shows a profound indecision." [162] On the one hand, Jochmann is a typical man of the Enlightenment, who would concur with Plato's ban on mythological poetry, as long as this was pursued in disregard of moral and social virtues; on the other hand, Jochmann believes with the romantics in the indispensability of the "poetic spirit" for mankind and hopes for its rebirth in decent and just society. What set Jochmann against the romantics were his acute social and historical sensibilities; for the romantics indulged in the sentimental mystification of medieval myths and were utterly impervious to the implications of these "false riches" in social reality, a fallacy that consequently made their own works on these myths prone to the "aesthetic imperialism" of neoromantics in modern Germany—for "nothing motivates the Fascists so much as the will to seize the myth for themselves."[163] Jochmann countered these tendencies by insisting on the historical actuality of myths, both in their times, being the authentic expressions of human, albeit primitive, confrontations with natural and social realities, and for our times, because we can recognize in them certain intimations of problems that still beset mankind. According to Benjamin, Jochmann must have found this notion of "poetry" in Vico's *New Science*.[164] Although Benjamin does not offer any evidence that Jochmann actually knew Vico, it is quite possible that he did: the German translation of *The New Science* appeared in 1821 and was widely discussed by radical intellectuals with whom Jochmann was associated.[165] Jochmann was in Paris in the late 1820s, when Michelet's French translation of Vico's *New Science* appeared, and he was certainly aware of this work, which, according to Edmund Wilson, initiated the entire revolutionary movement through Sorel and up to Lenin.[166]

Clearly, then, Benjamin found in Jochmann's attempt to save the myth from the romantic reactionaries a precedent for his own attempt to save the myth from the Fascist reactionaries, as well as from the Marxist revolutionaries. When Benjamin wrote his essay on Jochmann, he was in the same intellectual predicament: a German scholar taking refuge among left-wing champions of the Enlightenment in Paris, yet one whose views on the mythopoeic origins and potentialities of civilization aligned him with their opponents. In the last years of his life, Benjamin became close to a group of French intellectuals who were likewise disillusioned with official Communism, above all with its apparent inability to counter the forces of Fascism. The group that called itself Acéphale and has become known as the College of Sociology set out to probe the social conditions underlying this political predicament, and ultimately it concluded that Communism had failed to appreciate, let alone create, the "sacred" in modern social life. On these assumptions they came to reappraise the efficacy of myth in modern society. The intellectual leaders of this group were Georges Bataille, with whom Benjamin ultimately entrusted the manuscripts of *The Arcades Project,* and Roger Caillois, whose essay "Paris, mythe moderne," of 1937, was much admired (and cited) by Benjamin in his own work on the same topic.[167] In the initial programmatic statements on the ideological and methodological purposes of the college that Caillois and Bataille published in the *Nouvelle Revue Française* in July 1938, they stressed the centrality of myth in their new social theory and practice. According to Caillois,

> For half a century now, the human sciences have progressed with such rapidity that we are not yet sufficiently aware of the new possibilities they offer, and are further still from having had the opportunity and audacity to apply them to the many problems posed by the interplay of instincts and "myths" that compose or mobilize them in contemporary society . . . This preoccupation with rediscovering the primordial longings and conflicts of the individual condition transposed to the social dimension is at the origin of the College of Sociology.[168]

Caillois elaborated and exemplified this notion in his lectures at the college, most notably on the social meanings and functions of "Festival" and in his collection of essays *Le mythe et l'homme,* published in 1938 and much admired by Benjamin. Bataille was equally assertive in his recognition of myth as a major source for the constitution and investigation of modern society. His programmatic statement owes much more to Nietzsche than to Marx:

> The man whom art, science, or politics was incapable of satisfying still has *myth* at his disposal . . . For one shattered by every trial, only myth reflects the image of a plenitude extending to the community in which men gather. Only myth enters the bodies of those whom it binds together and requires them to have the same expectations . . . For myth is not merely the divine figure of fate and the world in which this figure moves: It cannot be separated from the community whose creature it is and that ritually takes possession of its authority. It would be a fiction if a *people* in festival excitement did not show in their *accord* that it was the vital human reality. Myth is perhaps fable, but this fable is made the opposite of fiction if one looks at the people who dance it, who act it, and whose living truth it is. A community that does not succeed in the ritual possession of its myths possesses only a truth that is on the wane: It is living to the extent that its will to be brings all the mythical chances that figure its innermost existence to life.[169]

Although Benjamin was not a regular member of the college, he attended some of its secret meetings, and moreover, he was scheduled to deliver a lecture on fashion (which was canceled when the war broke out). In any case, according to the testimony of Pierre Klossowski, "Benjamin followed all these goings-on with as much consternation as curiosity. Although Bataille and I were at variance with him then on every position, we listened to him with fascination."[170] The members of the group were particularly intrigued by Benjamin's "personal version of (Fourier's) 'phalansterie,'" which he believed could be revived by "a liberal industrial production," as a result of which work might become again a source of free expression and even erotic enjoyment.[171]

In his "Theses on the Philosophy of History," Benjamin evokes Fourier's vision of harmonic reconciliation between human beings and between them and their natural resources: "According to Fourier, as a result of efficient co-operative labor, four moons would illuminate the earthly night, the ice would recede from the poles, sea water would no longer taste salty, and beasts of prey would do man's bidding." As Benjamin would have it, "Fourier's fantasies, which have so often been ridiculed, prove to be surprisingly sound" when compared with the "vulgar-Marxist conception of the nature of labor," precisely because they still retained mythic notions that forbade them to exploit the natural resources. Benjamin inveighs against the vulgar Marxists that because their "positivistic conception" of labor "recognizes only the progress in the mastery of nature, not the retrogression of society," it "already displays the technocratic features later encountered in Fascism."[172] In "Theses on the Philosophy of History," Benjamin sought, much like Fourier, to regain Paradise for humanity. This is the tacit message in his famous meditation on the "angel of history" in that text:

> A Klee painting named "Angelus Novus" shows an angel looking as though he is about to move away from something he is fixedly contemplating. His eyes are staring, his mouth is open, his wings are spread. This is how one pictures the angel of history. His face is turned toward the past. Where *we* perceive a chain of events, *he* sees one single catastrophe which keeps piling wreckage upon wreckage and hurls it in front of his feet. The angel would like to stay, awaken the dead, and make whole what has been smashed. But a storm is blowing from Paradise; it has got caught in his wings with such violence that the angel can no longer close them. This storm irresistibly propels him into the future to which his back is turned, while the pile of debris before him grows skyward. This storm is what we call progress.[173]

Against the common interpretations of this text, which usually read it as an attack on myth in history, I argue that Benjamin's theme in this last testament of his life and works remains "the reconciliation of myth." The crucial question pertains to the myth of Paradise. As I read the text, the apparent critical renunciation of this myth as destructive to human history betrays a deeper, more dialectical, recognition of this myth as essential to it. For the acute realization that "a storm is blowing from Paradise," namely that the myth of Paradise has produced only historical calamities, does not necessarily mean that the angel, whose "face is turned toward the past," could or should turn away from this myth. On the contrary, he "would like to stay [*verweilen*]" and eventually to regress so as to "make whole what has been smashed," a clear indication that he still seeks to regain Paradise. The question remains, though, whether this attempt to regain Paradise signifies the angel's capitulation to myth or, alternatively, a recapitulation of its message.

The unbearable vision of horrific history renders the angel unable to change its catastrophic pattern or even to avert his gaze from it: "His eyes are staring, his mouth is open, his wings are spread." Yet, at the same time, he does look "as though he is about [*im Begriff*] to move away" from this fixation and thus to overcome his apparent passivity and fatality. What moves him into but also away from this predicament in history is the memory of Paradise, the messianic myth that still empowers the theological and political visions of redemption through Revelation or Revolution. "But a storm is blowing from Paradise." Although Benjamin describes the angel at the critical moment when that myth "has got caught in his wings with such violence that the angel can no longer close them" and therefore "irresistibly propels him into the future to which his back is turned," he intimates that the angel knows what is happening to him, that he already comprehends how myth operates in history. "Where *we* perceive a chain of events"—that is to say, conceive of history in the teleological categories of the old theological or the new mechanical systems, which make history "appear to us [*vor uns erscheint*]" as if moving by law and purposive-progressive procedure—"*he* sees [*da sieht er*] one single catastrophe which keeps piling wreckage upon wreckage and hurls it in front of his feet." In other words, the angel realizes that history is a repetitive and ultimately regressive reaction to a "single catastrophe"—the expulsion from Paradise—which continues to torment humanity and is getting worse, since all attempts to build Paradise on earth have collapsed into a "pile of debris." The fact that the angel "would like to stay, awaken the dead, and make whole what has been smashed" implies that he too "has got caught" in "this storm" that the myth of Paradise has generated in history. In the wake of "this storm," any attempt to regain Paradise would seem to be not just naive but self-destructive. But in the last sentence of the text, Benjamin states: "This storm is what we"—not the angel—"call progress," as if to point out that unlike us, who "perceive" history in logical rather than in mythical categories, the angel knows what "this storm" is all about because he "sees" it as it really is: a mythical compulsion. As Gershom Scholem writes: "Paradise is at once the origin and the primal past of man as well as the utopian image of the future of his redemption—a conception of the historical process that is really cyclical rather than dialectical." Accordingly, the "storm" signifies "a history and its dynamic determined by Utopia and not, say, the means of production."[174] This acute recognition of myth in history enables the angel to transcend it. He ultimately appears to ride the storm that carries him away from Paradise.

Benjamin wrote the "Theses" at the beginning of 1940, while imprisoned in a camp for Jewish refugees in occupied France. His meditation on the "angel of history" reveals that, just like the *Trauerspiel* allegorists in the Thirty Years War, who saw the world as a stage that had been deserted by God and destroyed by man yet nevertheless sought to save the Christian myth of salvation from historical destruction, Benjamin sought in his allegorical text to save the myth of Paradise from all its brutal manifestations and total destruction in history. He believed that any mythic image that could be recognized in that way by modern civilization had become or might still become "genuinely historical"—it might inspire human beings in their social and political struggles for amelioration and eventual redemption of the human condition.[175]

This is what Benjamin means by *das wahre Bild der Vergangenheit:* "The true picture of the past flits by. The past can be seized only as an image which flashes up at the instant when it can be recognized and is never seen again . . . For every image of the past that is not recognized by the present as one of its concerns threatens to disappear irretrievably."[176] To recognize the "true image of the past" in, by, and for the present means to recognize the present in the past. This is what the French revolutionists did when they recognized themselves in—and as—the ancient Roman republicans. Their infatuation with the mythological history of Rome was not at all "self-deception," as Marx had thought, but rather a realization that history was a "time filled by the presence of the now [*Jetztzeit*]. Thus, to Robespierre ancient Rome was a past charged with the time of the now which he blasted out of the continuum of history. The French revolution viewed itself as Rome reincarnate. It evoked ancient Rome by the way fashion evokes costumes of the past. Fashion has a flair for the topical, no matter where it stirs in the thickets of long ago."[177] Benjamin believed that this literal re-presentation of historical images as topical was crucial to any political revolution because they might still stir up the emotions of vengeance and sacrifice, which are necessary motivations for radical actions, and "both are nourished by the image of enslaved ancestors rather than that of liberated grandchildren."[178] Here, as elsewhere in his last reflections on history, Benjamin's conception of the revolution as primarily imagistic and mythic aligns with Sorel, rather than with Marx, and attests to his close intellectual affinity with the Acéphale revisionists, who combined the revolutionary theories of both thinkers to forge a new theory of social revolution that was mythic and yet antifascistic.

Assuming thus that historians must concentrate on a recognition and evocation of images, Benjamin recommended that they revise their methodology accordingly, using the new artistic modes of imagistic composition, precisely as he had been doing over many years in *The Arcades Project*, in order "to carry over the principle of montage to history."[179] His resolution to rely only and so totally on the "images of history" was motivated by the realization that contemporary "history decays into images, not into stories."[180] For in those darkest days of civilization, its most meaningful stories, the classical-biblical myths, had already been abused beyond recognition by *Der Mythus des zwanzigsten Jahrhunderts,* whose principal target, so proclaimed its author, was to replace the cross (*Kreutz*) by the *Hakenkreutz*. In order to redeem that "true image" of the past from such distortions, the historical materialist must "recognize" it as such, which means to recognize it for what it is and has always been—a myth. How then should he treat that myth which has made up and sustained the "tradition" of our Western civilization but is now liable to destroy it? Benjamin insists that even at that "moment of danger" to this tradition, when Fascist ideology "affects both the contents of tradition and its receivers," the critical task of the historian is not to fight against the mythical tradition but rather to fight over it:

> In every era the attempt must be made anew to wrest tradition away [*abzugewinnen*] from a conformism that is about to overpower it. The Messiah comes not only as the redeemer, he comes as the subduer of the Antichrist. Only that historian will have the gift of fanning the spark of hope in the past who is firmly convinced that *even the dead* will not be safe from the enemy if he wins. And this enemy has not ceased to be victorious.[181]

According to Benjamin, contemporary historians have failed to counter the Fascists because they did not recognize the mythical compulsions in history. He asserts that both the "historicists" and the "historical materialists" have ignored or misread the regressive tendencies in contemporary history. For since both parties perceived history in similar optimistic and deterministic categories of "progression through a homogeneous, empty time," a mechanistic "chain of events" that operates by some causal law toward some universal goal—whether the perfect capitalist or the communist society—they could not quite account for the Fascist regression to myth; they merely explained it away as a momentary "aberration" or, worse, as a necessary "acceleration" in the otherwise "normal" process of progression: "One reason why Fascism has a chance is that in the name of progress its opponents treat it as a historical norm. The current amazement that the things we are experiencing are 'still' possible in the twentieth century is *not* philosophical. This amazement is not the beginning of knowledge—unless it is the knowledge that the view of history which gives rise to it is untenable." [182]

This oration refers back to that classical source in Aristotle's *Metaphysics* with which I began this chapter. As we recall, in that passage Aristotle relates the "beginning of knowledge" to the "amazement" at physical objects such as the moon, the sun, and the stars and furthermore asserts that the mythical attempt to overcome this amazement was already philosophical and distinctly *metaphysical*—for it was really and very literally an attempt to discover the significance of the object beyond its physical appearance. On these assumptions, the "current amazement" of contemporary historians that the events they experienced in the twentieth century were "still" possible was "*not* philosophical" because they did not adequately recognize these events as mythological, lacking, as it were, the distinct metaphysical capacities that enabled Benjamin to perceive these mythic or auratic associations beyond the physical objects and events. As in his previous critical engagement with "Theories of German Fascism," Benjamin thought that this new ideology was so successful because it thrived on and revived an ancient German mythology, which, in itself, pertained to authentic perceptions of the nation or of the relation of the nation to the landscape but has now been usurped by and for the destructive technology of oppression and expansion. The task of the historian or, shall we say, the mythistorian in such awful conditions of distortion and manipulation of myth is to attain a critical recognition—in Benjamin's terms, a "dialectical enchantment"—of that myth so as to understand and explain in anthropological-historical terms why it is still so powerful even (and especially) in our age of disenchantment. An example he cites in *The Arcades Project* might clarify his contention: "The bombers remind us of what Leonardo Da Vinci expected of man in flight: that he was to ascend to the skies 'in order to seek snow on the mountaintops and bring it back to the city to spread on the sweltering streets in summer." [183]

By making this observation in 1938, while bomber planes were devastating Ethiopian and Spanish towns, Benjamin redeemed a classical myth (Icarus) that encoded, as it were, the true necessities and aspirations of humanity. The fact that the mythological image of the flight of man has been deprived of these meanings in modern historical reality attests to the truth of that reality, not to the truth of the myth. The same might be said about the *Marzipanfiguren* of Mary attending baby Jesus in the manger: they represent authentic messianic aspirations for material and spiritual redemption. The fact that they now appear "sickly" attests to the truth of modern capitalistic society, which has thus distorted one of the great social myths of Christianity, not to the truth of that myth, which still exudes its utopian claim, a *promesse de bonheur*. One would like to assume that this is what Benjamin was thinking when Ernst Bloch saw him "strolling pensively, so to speak, with his head bowed, on the Kurfürstendamm," meditating on the *Marzipanfiguren*.

Ideareal History: A Lesson from Joyce

In the first chapter of this study, I claim that mythistory might well become that modern historiography which, as Eliot would have it, is capable "of controlling, of ordering, of giving a shape and significance to the immense panorama of futility and anarchy which is contemporary history." Against the majority of commentators on Eliot's famous assertion, I argue that what he and Joyce and many other modernists were aiming at in the "employment of myth" was not a mechanical and quite ironic imposition of some mythic order from literary history on the story but rather an exposition of that order in history through the story. It is quite possible, as Eliot also implies, that Joyce created the "parallels" between Homer's *Odyssey* and his *Ulysses* as a structural principle of novelistic composition, and he may well have used the majestic mythical ideality of classical antiquity in order to counter and even mock the pathetic historical reality of modern society; but, as attentive readers such as Samuel Goldberg have shown, at a more substantial level, the mythic allusions "project into *Ulysses* a sense, which the characters themselves partly possess, of the continuities and permanent patterns of human experience."[1] For Joyce believed, with Vico, that history is cyclical and prototypical: the fundamental human virtues of the nuclear family that induced Odysseus and Telemachus to perform their heroic actions still inspire Leopold Bloom and Stephen Dedalus, even if they themselves are not entirely aware of them, and however pathetic and even comic their attempts to achieve these virtues may appear to be. The evocation of such fundamental virtues from the mythical stories of Homer, the Gospels, Dante, Shakespeare, and Irish and Jewish folktales in the meditations and actions of the novel's two main heroes manifests the domination of the great myths of our civilization over their apprehension of life and history.

In his great book *After Virtue: A Study in Moral Theory,* the philosopher Alasdair MacIntyre has elaborated this Vichian-Joycean perception of the essential connection between the classical virtues, myth, and history.[2] According to MacIntyre, the basic rule of life is that "man is in his actions and practices, as well as in his fictions, essentially a story-telling animal . . . a teller of stories that aspire to truth" (216). What he means by this is that we live out and understand our lives (and those of others) according to certain narratives that lay out for us basic precedents, rules, and prescriptions for moral action in social situations. A successful life depends on whether the person who lives it possesses and exercises "the virtues," which are those qualities that his or her society has predetermined as crucial for the sort of life that person lives or the "role" in life that the person seeks to fulfill. According to MacIntyre each society defines those "roles" for its members through the typical heroes of its traditional stories. In order to survive, modern society must reassert its tradition through "narrative history." In his terms, this "is not the work of poets, dramatists and novelists reflecting upon the events which had no narrative order before one was imposed by the singer or the writer" but rather a form of life in which "stories are lived before they are told," an "enacted dramatic narrative in which the characters are also the authors" (215). Hence, MacIntyre concludes,

> It is through hearing stories about wicked stepmothers, lost children, good but misguided kings, wolves that suckle twin boys . . . , that children learn or mis-learn both what a child and a parent is, what the cast of characters may be in the drama into which they have been born and what the ways of the world are. Deprive children of stories and you leave them unscripted, anxious stutterers in their actions as in their words. Hence there is no way to give us an understanding of any society, including our own, except through the stock of stories which constitute its initial dramatic resources. Mythology, in its original sense, is at the heart of things. Vico was right and so was Joyce. (216)

Indeed Vico was right—as was Joyce in his interpretation of Vico. For it was Vico who first initiated this "mythic turn" among modern human scientists and artists, most certainly so in the case of Joyce himself. From the moment Joyce discovered Vico's *New Science* in Trieste around 1904, and during the years when he worked on *Ulysses,* he was inspired by the mythological discoveries and theories of Vico's book.[3] Whereas most other commentators on Joyce's attraction to Vico have traced it to his fascination with Vico's cyclical theory of history, which is indeed very evident in *Finnegans Wake*, I suggest that in *Ulysses* Joyce seems to have drawn mainly on Vico's mythopoeic theory of history, on what he called (in both novels) the "Vico road."[4] In my discussion of this Joycean idiom in the first and second chapters of this study, I suggest that the "Vico road" signifies the dialectical pattern in the development of modern historiography from the mythical through the historical and around to the mythistorical perceptions of reality. This pattern, which I have traced both in the history of the profession from classical antiquity to modernity and in the life story of each of the four major modern mythistorians in the subsequent chapters, generates one of the main narrative motions in *Ulysses*, which leads its two main heroes—Stephen Dedalus and Leopold Bloom—in the chapter "Ithaca" to what, in my terms, is the ultimate goal of mythistory: a critical recognition of myth. This, I think, is what Goldberg means when he writes that "what we actually feel in *Ulysses* . . . is its force of affirmation, and affirmation not of any doctrine superhuman or supernatural, but of *the mythopoeic imagination itself.* It is as if we come to apprehend in and through Bloom and Stephen—which is to say, in and through the total action— the vital truth of the myths of Ulysses and Christ and the Wandering Jew and Sinbad and so on."[5]

This indeed is what we have in *Ulysses:* not a reanimation of myth, as in Jung and other modern mythologists who presumed to disclose in the great myths of our civilization the ultimate mysteries (and their own theories) of the human condition, but rather, and merely, a recognition of myth as a repository of the stories by which, as Vico saw, "men themselves" have made and continue to remake their histories. Joyce, in fact, expressed his predilection for Vico's historical interpretation of myth over Jung's psychological conception.[6] As we shall soon see, for Joyce, this recognition of the historical vitality and volatility of myth implied and opened up possibilities for its critical interpretation and re-creation in *Ulysses.* Yet even in his most radical interpretations and re-creations of the classical myth—as, most notably, in the transformation of Ulysses into Bloom—Joyce preserved the main structure of adventure of the Homeric *Odyssey,* for he came to perceive this *mythos* of wandering and homecoming as the most pervasive narrative *logos* of Western civilization. It is above all this myth that Joyce pursued in the novel up to its magnificent culmination in the "Ithaca" chapter. In 1920, upon its completion, he wrote to a friend that his intention in that novel had been "to transpose the myth *sub specie temporis nostri*": the mechanical and tactical connotations of the sentence imply that he used the Homeric myth critically, methodically, aiming, as it were, to examine, not to undermine, its classical virtues and truths by modern historical standards and methods.[7] Hence, whereas postmodernists still seek to dismiss the "mythical method" of the modernists as yet another expression of their lingering obsession with some pristine metaphysical truth that lies in the great classical and biblical myths of our civilization, "a myth of myth" as Fredric Jameson calls it, which merely serves to expose "the bankruptcy of the ideology of the mythic . . . [and] the bankruptcy of the ideology of modernism in general,"[8] I would like to show that this "mythical method," as Joyce in fact practiced it, might still be conducive to modern historiography. For if, as Eliot hoped, the "mythical method" of *Ulysses* should have "the importance of a scientific discovery" comparable to those of Einstein and Freud, at least in historiography, then it must attain that *critical recognition of myth* which, on my terms, distinguishes mythistory from both myth and history.

I deliberately choose to conclude this study in modern historiography with a discussion of a modern novel because, as already noted in chapter 1, one of the most remarkable developments in the humanities and social sciences in our times has been the reassessment of the novel as a serious "method" of studying human agency in modern society. Unlike earlier generations of scholars, who read novels for "inspiration" or "examples" for further, more procedural and general inquiries into "truths" about human beings, the new scholars have come to read novels for the particular truths that their characters display in their emotions, reflections, and actions. Having realized, as Martha Nussbaum puts it, that "certain truths about human life can only be fittingly and accurately stated in the language and forms characteristic of the narrative artist," Nussbaum and other moral philosophers such as Stanley Cavell and Richard Rorty have come to read the novels of Jane Austen, Gustav Flaubert, Henry James, Marcel Proust, Vladimir Nabokov, and George Orwell as both dramatic and thematic illuminations of the moral deliberations that are characteristic of modern society—primarily those that pit individual agents against the historical traditions and institutions of their society.[9]

On these assumptions, I propose to read *Ulysses* as a novel that explores the moral deliberations of the mythistorian. For this is how one might characterize its young hero, Stephen Dedalus, a teacher of history who, in the course of one lesson of history, and thereafter through a day of wandering and wondering about Dublin, comes to a critical recognition of the myths that dominate his life and history. "To define, or even summarily to describe, the mythic vision of *Ulysses* is to define the whole book":[10] mindful of Goldberg's warning, I do not attempt to describe the evolvement of this recognition throughout the novel, nor even dare to offer an interpretation of its culmination in the penultimate chapter, "Ithaca." I limit the discussion to the second chapter of *Ulysses,* the "Nestor" episode, in which Stephen literally draws this lesson of history while teaching a history lesson in the private school for boys in Dalkey, a village just outside Dublin.[11] At a critical moment in that lesson, Stephen recalls that there is a "Vico road" nearby.

Significantly, this association flashes into Stephen's mind while he is reflecting on William Blake's depiction of history as "[f]abled by the daughters of memory." Blake wrote these words in "A Vision of the Last Judgment," where he argues that just as the Last Judgment is a "Vision" of history, graspable only by mystical revelation rather than by empirical and critical observation, so must we perceive all the major events in historical reality: as myths that require spiritual veneration and interpretation rather than factual explanation. The young artist Stephen is well disposed toward this notion, for he too has come to discover (in *Stephen Hero* and in *A Portrait of the Artist as a Young Man*) the metaphysical dimensions, or "epiphanies," in mundane reality.[12] But Stephen nevertheless objects to Blake's renunciation of any factual reality to history: "And yet it was in some way if not as memory fabled it. A phrase, then, of impatience, thud of Blake's wings of excess." Nevertheless, as the following association reveals, Stephen also perceives a certain historical reality in Blake's mythical-apocalyptical vision of history: "I hear the ruin of all space, shattered glass and toppling masonry, and time one livid final flame."[13] Stephen does not so much reject Blake's mythical conception of history, then, but rather seeks to curb its "impatient" and "excessive" ramifications, aiming, as it were, to retain Blake's intuition that the actual events of history have indeed been "fabled" by the mythopoeic faculties, or "daughters," of memory, within a new recognition that this history might still enable us to perceive not only that something actually happened "in some way" but also why and how it was rendered as myth. It is precisely this realization of the mythopoeic formation of history that alerts Stephen to the possibility of its transformation by critical interpretation and re-creation of its constitutive myths. In that way, Stephen's initial objection to Blake, which prompts him to discover the truth of history beyond its myths, would eventually lead him to recognize this truth through and in these myths. This revision sets in during the historical lesson he is actually teaching—the famous

"Pyrrhic Victory" in the battle in Asculum in 279 B.C.—and culminates in his later confrontation with the headmaster of the school, Mr. Deasy.

The classroom scene opens with Stephen going, rather absentmindedly, through a routine round of questions about and corrections of the facts and the main historical lesson of Pyrrhus in the battle in Asculum, which his pupils duly recite: "Another Victory like that and we are done for." Stephen ponders whether these trivialities ought to be the only lesson of history: "That phrase the world had remembered. A dull ease of the mind. From a hill above a corpsestrewn plain a general speaking to his officers, leaned upon his spear. Any general to any officers. They lend ear."[14] His students do not lend ear to this or any other lesson of history: "For them too history was a tale like any other too often heard."[15] Clearly, history, at least that kind of dull factual and much-too-actual history, had lost its meaning.[16] Stephen begins to look for an alternative, more imaginative, history. Still bearing in mind Blake's words on the mythopoeic modes by which history is recalled, he conceives of a new kind of history, a poetic history, such as would overcome the old Aristotelian dichotomy between poetry and history.

Aristotle's pronouncement that the task of the poet "is not to report what has happened but what is likely to happen; that is, what is capable of happening according to the rule of probability or necessity" resounds in Stephen's critical meditations on the vocation of history: "Had Pyrrhus not fallen by a beldam's hand in Argos or Julius Caesar not been knifed to death? They are not to be thought away. Time has branded them and fettered they are lodged in the room of the infinite possibilities they have ousted. But can those have been possible seeing that they never were? Or was that only possible which came to pass?"[17] Stephen thus doubts whether such queries about human affairs could be answered by Aristotelian natural teleology, namely, that all that has happened in history was "the fulfillment of what exists potentially, insofar as it exists potentially." For history is full of "infinite possibilities" that have not come to be, of potential reformations and revolutions that were forced out of history by the actual forces of authority, which also dictate the official records of historiography. Against this official history, which delimits and destroys all human potentialities, Stephen turns to that form of memory which retains such dreams, hopes, and visions—the myths that make up poetic history. He begins to conduct a new lesson of history. When his students appeal to him: "Tell us a story, sir," and again, "Oh, do, sir, a ghoststory," he responds willingly by "opening another book"—Milton's mythological poem *Lycidas*. And when he is asked by his students, "And the history, sir?" he answers: "After," as if to affirm, along with Vico, that poetry precedes history, both temporally and morally.[18] Stephen directs his students to this passage in *Lycidas:*

> Weep no more, woful shepherd, weep no more
> For Lycidas, your sorrow, is not dead,
> Sunk though he be beneath the watery floor.

Whereas in real history Lycidas died, in the ideal history of the poet, he "is not dead," an assertion that is certainly true in that his myth, and the myth of Christ the Savior, are still alive. This discovery of the human potentialities in myth enables Stephen to overcome Aristotle's deterministic conception of history. Following the recitation of Milton's poem, he comes to the conclusion that history "must be a movement then, an actuality of the possible as possible"; yet he now realizes that it must not be confined anymore to what actually happened: "Aristotle's phrase formed itself within the gabbled verses and floated out into the studious silence of the library of Saint Genevieve" in Paris, where he had first read it, and may now safely lie at rest with all other theological and teleological conceptions of history.[19]

Having thus dismissed the historical facts and lesson of the battle of Pyrrhus as no more than a "dull ease of the mind," Stephen discovers a deep historical truth in the myth of "him that walked the waves. Here also over these craven hearts his shadow lies and on the scoffer's heart and lips and on mine." Unlike the plain words of Pyrrhus that Stephen and his students memorize, the words of Jesus, like his actions, evoke the sensation of permanent mythical rather than transient historical relevance: "To Caesar what is Caesar's, to God what is God's. A long look from dark eyes, a riddling sentence to be woven on the church's looms."[20] In that way, while Pyrrhus's words remain a text, Jesus' words have acquired practical "textile" qualities. Nevertheless, Stephen also realizes that the myth of Jesus casts a "shadow" over history, affecting the life of those who believe in him and of those who do not—particularly, among the latter, the Jews. Their fate in (and because of) this mythical history will become significant in Stephen's subsequent deliberations on myth in history.

Once the lesson of history and poetry is over, Stephen confronts the headmaster of the school, Mr. Deasy. He is a silly old man who duly, even if inadvertently, supplies an apt characterization of himself as "an old fogey and an old tory." Like the old warrior Nestor in Homer's *Odyssey*, Mr. Deasy is liable to tell the young man lies rather than history.[21] As

Stephen is waiting in the headmaster's office, inhaling its "stale smoky air" and the "smell of drab abraded leather of its chairs," he recalls some words from the *Gloria Patri,* "As it was in the beginning, is now," an association that reflects his fresh comprehension of the mythical structure of history yet also reveals his nascent apprehension about that history, which has structured his own life according to all sorts of political and ecclesiastical historical mythologies. Looking around him, Stephen becomes acutely aware of the usurpation and manipulation of his own Catholic-Irish historical mythology by the Protestant and pro-English Deasy: "On the sideboard the tray of Stuart coins, base treasure of a bog: and ever shall be. And snug in their spooncase of purple flash, faded, the twelve apostles having preached to all the gentiles: world without end." [22] This discontentment intensifies as his conversation with his employer gets under way.

Deasy's historical lessons are outrageous, [23] especially because they are based on the same venerable Christian mythology that Stephen has just come to appreciate. Such images recur in Deasy's ruminations about the Protestant destination of Irish history ("Glorious, pious, and immortal memory. The lodge of Diamond in Armagh the splendid behung with corpses of papishes. Hoarse, masked and armed, the planters' covenant. The black north and true blue Bible. Croppies lie down"), as well as in his allegations against the Jews ("England is in the hands of the jews. In all the highest places: her finance, her press. And they are the signs of a nation's decay . . . They sinned against the light . . . And you can see the darkness in their eyes. And that is why they are wanderers on the earth to this day"), or against women ("A woman brought sin into the world. For a woman who was no better than she should be, Helen, the runaway wife of Menelaus, ten years the Greeks made war on troy. A faithless wife first brought the strangers to our shore here . . . A woman too brought Parnell low"). [24] Stephen is appalled. All he can see in Deasy's "glorious, pious, and immortal" history are futile "Jousts. Time shocked rebounds, shock by shock. Jousts, slush and uproar of battles, the frozen deathspew of the slain, a shout of spear spikes baited with men's bloodied guts" (32). Stephen's reaction to Deasy's garrulous lessons—"Is this old wisdom?"—implies that he is well aware of their origin in ancient Christian mythology and yet that he rejects their egregious interpretation. He understands that what determines the meaning of history is a subjective and creative interpretation of its constitutive myths. Hence, whereas for Deasy the "dark eyes" of the Jews attest to the mythical vision of their eventual oblivion, Stephen discovers in them, through Jesus' eyes, the historical mission of the Jews as the eternal wanderers: to carry on the Jewish prophecy of universal redemption that was so brutally abused not only by such fanatic Christians as Deasy, but also, and more disastrously, by the Twelve Apostles, who preached to all the gentiles, over against the Jews, "world without end." This myth has condemned the Jews to a life of isolation and alienation as permanent exiles in history. Stephen himself once witnessed the myth's effect:

> On the steps of the Paris Stock Exchange the goldskinned men quoting prices on their gemmed fingers. Gabbles of geese. They swarmed loud, uncouth about the temple, their heads thickplotting under maladroit silk hats. Not theirs: these clothes, this speech, the gestures eager and unoffending, but knew the rancours massed about them and knew their zeal was vain. Vain patience to heap and hoard. Time surely would scatter all. Their eyes knew the years of wandering and, patient, knew the dishonours of their flesh. (34)

Reflecting on this Jewish predicament, Stephen realizes that this is the real human condition in which he too, and all men, have always lived, even though, unlike the Jews, they have never recognized it as such, and some, like Mr. Deasy, never would: "—Who has not? Stephen said. —What do you mean? Mr Deasy asked." Stephen's prompt answer to Mr. Deasy's query, "History . . . is the nightmare from which I am trying to awake," thus signifies not so much a resignation from history as a recognition of what this history really is: a myth, indeed, yet not the one that Deasy believes it to be—a providential revelation that "moves towards one great goal, the manifestation of God"; rather it is a distortion of that mythical revelation (33–34). Yet this very critical recognition of the myth of "history" itself is, for Stephen, a moment of liberation from—but also for— that myth: from now on he will be able to fight over it.

Stephen's decision, which he conveys to Deasy—not to be a "teacher" of history but "a learner rather"—is the final conclusion of his lesson of history. From that moment and till the end of the day, he will seek to amend history by his story. This becomes clear in the next chapter of the book, in which Stephen turns away from the "big words" of "Nestor" to the "sounds" of "Proteus" and eventually reveals in them the new and yet older "protean" forms of history—the popular images and tales that Vico called "vulgar traditions" and rightly assumed that they "must have had public grounds of truth, by virtue of which they came into being and were preserved by entire peoples over long periods of time."[25] The realization of poetic history in this chapter enables Stephen to overcome the rigid naturalistic and fatalistic formulations by which history has been defined from Aristotle to Mr. Deasy and to redefine it in the "new scientific," humanistic, and mythopoeic terms of Vico.

In his last work, *Finnegans Wake*, Joyce invokes Vico again and characterizes him as "the producer" of images and tales that ultimately amount to an "Ideareal History," namely a history in which the ideal becomes real because what the people believe is what they actually live.[26] In that work Joyce also returns to the "Vico road" that "goes round and round to meet where terms begin": from history back to myth in order to begin again as mythistory.[27] This is also the final lesson of my study.

Notes

CHAPTER ONE

1. Herodotus, *History of Herodotus,* trans. G. Rawlinson (London: John Murray, 1880), 1.1.

2. Ibid., 7.152.

3. Ibid., 2.123, 4.195.

4. Arnaldo Momigliano, *The Classical Foundations of Modern Historiography* (Berkeley: University of California Press, 1990), 37. See also the important comments of Moses Finley, "Myth, Memory, and History," in his *Use and Abuse of History* (London: Hogarth Press, 1986), 11–33.

5. Thucydides, *History of the Peloponnesian War,* trans. B. Jowett (Oxford: Oxford University Press, 1881), 1.22.

6. On these connotations of the "mythic," see A. Wardman, "Myth in Greek Historiography," *Historia* 9 (1960): 403–13. See also John Marincola, *Authority and Tradition in Ancient Historiography* (Cambridge: Cambridge University Press, 1997), 117–27.

7. Thucydides, *History of the Peloponnesian War,* 1.22.

8. See Marcel Detienne, *The Creation of Mythology,* trans. M. Cook (Chicago: University of Chicago Press, 1986), 42–62.

9. Paul Veyne, *Did the Greek Believe in Their Myths?* trans. P. Wissing (Chicago: University of Chicago Press, 1988), 45.

10. Polybius, *The Histories,* trans. F. Hultsch (Bloomington: Indiana University Press, 1962), 9.1, 12.27, citing Homer, *Odyssey,* 1.1–4, 8.183.

11. Arnaldo Momigliano, "The Place of Herodotus in the History of Historiography," in his *Studies in Historiography* (London: Weidenfeld and Nicolson, 1966), 127–42.

12. John Gould, *Herodotus* (London: Weidenfeld and Nicolson, 1989), 111.

13. Wendy Doniger O'Flaherty, *Other Peoples' Myths: The Cave of Echoes* (New York: Macmillan, 1988), 27.

14. Mircea Eliade, *Myth and Reality,* trans. W. R. Trask (New York: Harper and Row, 1963), 19.

15. Irad Malkin, *The Returns of Odysseus: Colonization and Ethnicity* (Berkeley: University of California Press, 1998), 3.

16. G. S. Kirk, "On Defining Myths," in *Sacred Narrative: Readings in the Theory of Myth,* ed. A. Dundes (Berkeley: University of California Press, 1984), 58.

17. Percy Cohen, "Theories of Myth," *Man,* n.s., 4 (1969): 350. Though my study is not concerned with or committed to any particular theory of myth, it is much indebted to Cohen's ideas. In the vast literature on myth, Cohen's short essay is truly outstanding: not only does he offer the best analytic summaries of the major theories of myth, but he also manages to combine them into a most ingenious synthetic theory. Upon realizing that each of the major theories accounts for at least some aspects or functions of myth, Cohen concludes that a myth is that story—and only that story—which is capable of linking several functions and significances simultaneously.

18. Claude Lévi-Strauss, *The Raw and the Cooked,* trans. J. Weightman and D. Weightman (New York: Harper and Row, 1970), 18.

19. Claude Lévi-Strauss, *The Jealous Potter,* trans. B. Chorier (Chicago: University of Chicago Press, 1988), 189.

20. Clifford Geertz, "The Growth of Culture and the Growth of Mind," in his *Interpretation of Cultures* (New York: Basic Books, 1973), 82.

21. Victor Turner, "Social Dramas and Stories about Them," in *On Narrative,* ed. W. J. T. Mitchell (Chicago: University of Chicago Press, 1981), 164. Turner's major statement of this theory is *Dramas, Fields, and Metaphors: Symbolic Action in Human Society* (Ithaca, N.Y.: Cornell University Press, 1974).

22. Bronislaw Malinowski, "Myth in Primitive Psychology," in his *Magic, Science and Religion and Other Essays* (Boston: Beacon Press, 1948).

23. J. R. Gillis, ed., *Commemorations: The Politics of National Identity* (Princeton, N.J.: Princeton University Press, 1994).

24. Ernest Renan, "What Is a Nation?" (1882), in *Modern Political Doctrines,* ed. M. Zimmern (Oxford: Oxford University Press, 1939), 190–203.

25. Renan's ideas inspire many of the historical case studies in *Nation and Narration,* ed. Homi K. Bhabha (London: Routledge, 1990). See also John Armstrong, *Nations before Nationalism* (Chapel Hill: University of North Carolina Press, 1982); and Anthony D. Smith, "National Identity and Myths of Ethnic Descent," *Research in Social Movements, Conflict, and Change* 7 (1984): 95–130.

26. Anthony D. Smith, "The Myth of the 'Modern Nation' and the Myths of Nations," *Ethnic and Racial Studies* 11 (1988): 12. For a philosophical elaboration of this view, see David Miller, *On Nationality* (Oxford: Oxford University Press, 1993), 35–42.

27. Anthony D. Smith, "Nationalism and the Historian," in *Ethnicity and Nationalism,* ed. A. D. Smith (Leiden: E. J. Brill, 1992), 58–80, esp. 70–72.

28. Pierre Nora, introduction to *Realms of Memory: Rethinking the French Past,* trans. A. Goldhammer (New York: Columbia University Press, 1996), xv–xxiv.

29. Eric Hobsbawm, "Inventing Traditions," in *The Invention of Tradition,* ed. E. Hobsbawm and T. Ranger (Cambridge: Cambridge University Press, 1983), 7.

30. On the renaissance of the Arminian myth, see Frank L. Borchardt, *German Antiquity in Renaissance Myth* (Baltimore: Johns Hopkins University Press, 1971). On the subsequent modifications of this myth down to Anselm Kiefer, see Simon Schama, *Landscape and Memory* (New York: Vintage Books, 1996), 75–134.

31. Benedict Anderson, *Imagined Communities: Reflections on the Origin and Spread of Nationalism* (London: Verso, 1983).

32. Ibid., 19.

33. Donald R. Kelley, "Mythistory in the Age of Ranke," in *Leopold von Ranke and the Shape of the Historical Discipline*, ed. G. G. Iggers and J. M. Powell (Syracuse, N.Y.: Syracuse University Press, 1990), 3–20.

34. Donald R. Kelley, *Versions of History from Antiquity to the Enlightenment* (New Haven, Conn.: Yale University Press, 1991), 3. See also the chapter titled "Mythistory" in Kelley's history of historiography, *Faces of History: Historical Inquiry from Herodotus to Herder* (New Haven, Conn.: Yale University Press, 1998), 1–18.

35. George Eliot, *Middlemarch* (New York: Modern Library, 1977), 14, 331.

36. Richard Terdiman, *Present Past: Modernity and Memory Crisis* (Ithaca, N.Y.: Cornell University Press, 1993), 3–4.

37. T. S. Eliot, "Tarr," *Egoist* 5 (1918), quoted by James Longenbach, *Modernist Poetics of History: Pound, Eliot, and the Sense of the Past* (Princeton, N.J.: Princeton University Press, 1987), 230.

38. T. S. Eliot, "Tradition and the Individual Talent," in *Selected Prose of T. S. Eliot*, ed. F. Kermode (London: Faber and Faber, 1975), 38.

39. For a standard interpretation along these conventions, see Astradur Eysteinssohn, *The Concept of Modernism* (Ithaca, N.Y.: Cornell University Press, 1990), 8.

40. Paul de Man, "Literary History and Literary Modernity," in his *Blindness and Insight* (Minneapolis: University of Minnesota Press, 1983), 142–65, quotations on 148, 150.

41. T. S. Eliot, "Ulysses, Order, and Myth" (1923), in *Selected Prose of T. S. Eliot*, 177–78.

42. Peter Nicholls, *Modernisms* (Berkeley: University of California Press, 1995), 251–78.

43. This is the main argument of Cleanth Brooks's classic New Critical interpretation of Eliot's poem: "*The Waste Land:* Critique of the Myth" (1937), reprinted in his *Modern Poetry and the Tradition* (New York: Oxford University Press, 1965), 136–72.

44. Thomas Mann, *Joseph and His Brothers*, trans. H. T. Lowe-Porter (New York: Knopf, 1978), 1:33.

45. T. S. Eliot, *The Use of Poetry and the Use of Criticism* (London: Faber and Faber, 1934), 148.

46. T. S. Eliot, "Ulysses, Order, and Myth," 178. The best discussion of Eliot's "mythical method" is Michael H. Levenson, *The Genealogy of Modernism* (Cambridge: Cambridge University Press, 1984), 193–212. The academic literature on this topic is vast. For general assessments, see John J. White, *Myth in the Modern Novel* (Princeton, N.J.: Princeton University Press, 1972); Eric Gould, *Mythical Intentions in Modern Literature* (Princeton, N.J.: Princeton University Press, 1981); Ricardo J. Quiñones, *Mapping Literary Modernity* (Princeton, N.J.: Princeton University Press, 1985); and Michael Bell, *Literature, Modernism, and Myth* (Cambridge: Cambridge University Press, 1997).

47. Hayden White, "The Burden of History," in his *Tropics of Discourse: Essays in Cultural Criticism* (Baltimore: Johns Hopkins University Press, 1978), 41.

48. Burckhardt to Karl Fresenius, 9 June 1842, in *The Letters of Jacob Burckhardt*, ed. and trans. A. Dru (London: Routledge and Kegan Paul, 1955), 74.

49. Jacob Burckhardt, *Reflections on History*, trans. M. D. Hottinger (Indianapolis: Liberty Fund, 1979), 34.

50. Kelley, "Mythistory in the Age of Ranke," 20.

51. Friedrich Nietzsche, *The Birth of Tragedy*, trans. W. Kaufmann (New York: Vintage Books, 1967), 135.

52. M. Bradbury and J. McFarland, eds., *Modernism: A Guide to European Literature, 1890–1930* (London: Penguin Books, 1976), 82–83.

53. Ferdinand Tönnies, *Gemeinschaft und Gesellschaft: Grundbegriffe der reinen Soziologie* (Leipzig: Fues, 1887).

54. James Frazer, *The Golden Bough*, 1st ed., 2 vols. (London: Macmillan, 1890). The authoritative work on Frazer is Robert Ackerman, *J. G. Frazer: His Life and Work* (Cambridge: Cambridge University Press, 1987). On his influence on modernism, see John B. Vickery, *The Literary Impact of the Golden Bough* (Princeton, N.J.: Princeton University Press, 1973).

55. Frazer, *The Golden Bough*, 1:347–48.

56. Lionel Trilling, "On the Teaching of Modern Literature," in his *Beyond Culture* (New York: Penguin Books, 1965), 30.

57. Ibid., 32.

58. Joseph Conrad, *Heart of Darkness* (Harmondsworth: Penguin Books, 1973), 43.

59. George Steiner, *Tolstoy or Dostoevsky* (New York: Knopf, 1959), 40.

60. Conrad, *Heart of Darkness*, 70.

61. W. Rubin, ed., *'Primitivism' in Twentieth-Century Art: Affinity of the Tribal and the Modern* (New York: Museum of Modern Art, 1984).

62. H. Stuart Hughes, *Consciousness and Society: The Reorientation of European Social Thought, 1890–1930* (New York: Vintage Books, 1958); Fritz Stern, *The Politics of Cultural Despair: A Study in the Rise of Germanic Ideology* (Berkeley: University of California Press, 1961); Zeev Sternhell, *Neither Right nor Left: Fascist Ideology in France*, trans. D. Maisel (Berkeley: University of California Press, 1986).

63. Carl E. Schorske, *Fin-de-Siècle Vienna: Politics and Culture* (New York: Vintage Books, 1981).

64. Ibid., 145. See also William J. McGrath, *Dionysian Art and Populist Politics* (New Haven, Conn.: Yale University Press, 1974), 17–39.

65. Quoted by Schorske, *Fin-de-Siècle Vienna*, 134.

66. Sigmund Freud, "Group Psychology and the Analysis of the Ego," in *The Standard Edition of the Complete Psychological Works of Sigmund Freud*, ed. and trans. J. Strachey (London: Hogarth Press, 1964), 18:135. As Philip Rieff points out, Freud may have borrowed this notion of myth from Frazer. *Freud: The Mind of the Moralist* (New York: Viking, 1961), 224. See also the acute interpretation of this notion by Herbert Marcuse, *Eros and Civilization: A Philosophical Inquiry into Freud* (London: Sphere, 1987), 60.

67. Sigmund Freud, "Why War?" in *Complete Psychological Works*, 22:211.

68. Gillian Beer, "Wave Theory and the Rise of Literary Modernism," in *Realism and Representation: Essays on the Problem of Realism in Relation to Science, Literature, and Culture*, ed. G. Levine (Madison: University of Wisconsin Press, 1993), 193–213.

69. Owen Barfield, *Saving the Appearances: A Study in Idolatry* (London: Faber and Faber, 1965).

70. Bell, *Literature, Modernism, and Myth*, 12.

71. Lévi-Strauss, *The Raw and the Cooked*, 14.

72. Francis M. Cornford, *Thucydides Mythistoricus* (London: E. Arnold, 1907).

73. Ibid., 72−76.

74. Ibid., 136−52.

75. Marc Bloch, *The Royal Touch: Sacred Monarchy and Scrofula in England and France*, trans. J. E. Anderson (London: Routledge and Kegan Paul, 1973). On Bloch's life and work, see the comprehensive studies of Caroline Fink, *Marc Bloch: A Life in History* (Cambridge: Cambridge University Press, 1989); and Ulrich Raulff, *Ein Historiker im 20. Jahrhundert: Marc Bloch* (Frankfurt am Main: Fischer, 1995). See also the cogent assessment of R. R. Davies, "Marc Bloch," *History* 52 (1967): 265−82. For a thorough reevaluation of Bloch's book and its contribution to modern historiography, see Jacques Le Goff's preface to a new edition of *Les rois thaumaturges* (Paris: Gallimard, 1983).

76. Bloch, *The Royal Touch*, 28.

77. Ibid., 29.

78. For a positive appreciation of this book's contribution to the historical study of *mentalités*, see Peter Burke, *The French Historical Revolution: The Annales School, 1929−89* (Palo Alto, Calif.: Stanford University Press, 1990), 17−19.

79. On Febvre's initial reaction, see Le Goff, preface, xxix.

80. Bloch, *The Royal Touch*, 243.

81. Le Goff, preface, xxix−xxxii.

82. The same reductive methodology is evident also in Bloch's famous essay on the dissemination of fantasies among soldiers in World War I, "Réflexions d'un historien sur les fausses nouvelles de la guerre" (1921), reprinted in his *Mélanges historiques* (Paris: S.E.V.P.E.N., 1963), 1:41−57. Bloch examines the psychological and sociological conditions that generated these fantasies and made them "real" for the soldiers, and therefore also for the historians. But he does not examine their deeper spiritual origins and meanings in Christian mythology. For excellent reexaminations of these aspects, see Eric J. Leed, *No Man's Land: Combat & Identity in World War I* (Cambridge: Cambridge University Press, 1979), 115−62; and Jay Winter, *Sites of Memory, Sites of Mourning: The Great War in European Cultural History* (Cambridge: Cambridge University Press, 1995).

83. Ludwig Wittgenstein, *Remarks on Frazer's Golden Bough*, ed. R. Rhees, trans. A. C. Miles (Retford: Brynmill Press, 1979), 7.

84. Ludwig Wittgenstein, *On Certainty*, ed. G. E. M. Anscombe and G. H. von Wright, trans. D. Paul and G. E. M. Anscombe (Oxford: Blackwell, 1969), pars. 166, 336. See also *Lectures and Conversations on Aesthetics, Psychology, and Religious Belief*, ed. C. Barrett (Berkeley: University of California Press, 1966), 53−72.

85. Ludwig Wittgenstein, *Culture and Value*, ed. G. H. von Wright, trans. P. Winch (Oxford: Blackwell, 1980), pars. 83, 32.

86. For an excellent introduction, see Paul Rabinow and William M. Sullivan, "The Interpretive Turn," in *Interpretive Social Science*, ed. P. Rabinow and W. M. Sullivan (Berkeley: University of California Press, 1979), 1−30. See also the classic essay by Charles Taylor, "Interpretation and the Sciences of Man," reprinted in his *Philosophy and the Human Sciences* (Cambridge: Cambridge University Press, 1985), 15−57. On the implications of this turn in the respective theories mentioned above, see Stanley G. Clarke and Evan Simpson, eds., *Anti-Theory in Ethics and Moral Conservatism* (Albany: State University of New York Press,

1989); Stephen Mulhall and Adam Swift, *Liberals and Communitarians* (Oxford: Blackwell, 1992); Paul Feyerabend, "Realism and the Historicity of Science," *Journal of Philosophy* 87 (1989): 393–406.

87. Jerome Brunner, "The Narrative Construction of Reality," *Critical Inquiry* 18 (1991): 5. For a general discussion, see Wallace Martin, *Recent Theories of Narrative* (Ithaca, N.Y.: Cornell University Press, 1987). The best discussion of the "narrative turn" in historiography is Hayden White, "The Question of Narrative in Contemporary Historical Theory," in his *Content of the Form: Narrative Discourse and Historical Representation* (Baltimore: Johns Hopkins University Press, 1987), 26–57.

88. David Carr, *Time, Narrative, and History* (Bloomington: Indiana University Press, 1986), 177.

89. Jean-François Lyotard, *The Postmodern Condition: A Report on Knowledge*, trans. G. Bennington and B. Massumi (Minneapolis: University of Minnesota Press, 1984), 18–41.

90. William McNeill, "Mythistory, or Truth, Myth, History, and Historians," reprinted in his *Mythistory and Other Essays* (Chicago: University of Chicago Press, 1986), 1–10.

91. Lawrence Stone, "The Revival of Narrative: Reflections on a New Old History," *Past and Present* 85 (1979): 19. For excellent summaries and critical interpretations of this trend, see the essays in *The New Cultural History*, ed. L. Hunt (Berkeley: University of California Press, 1989); and in *New Perspectives on Historical Writing*, ed. P. Burke (Cambridge: Polity Press, 1991).

92. Among the classic works of the "New Cultural History" that exemplify these characteristics are Emmanuel Le Roy Ladurie, *Montaillou: Cathars and Catholics in a French Village, 1294–1324*, trans. B. Bray (Harmondsworth: Penguin Books, 1980); Robert Darnton, *The Great Cat Massacre and Other Episodes in French Cultural History* (New York: Vintage Books, 1984); Carlo Ginzburg, *The Cheese and the Worms: The Cosmos of a Sixteenth-Century Miller*, trans. A. Tedeschi and J. Tedeschi (Baltimore: Johns Hopkins University Press, 1981); Natalie Zemon Davis, *The Return of Martin Guerre* (Cambridge, Mass.: Harvard University Press, 1983); Jonathan Spence, *The Question of Hu* (New York: Knopf, 1988).

93. Natalie Zemon Davis, *Fiction in the Archives: Pardon Tales and Their Tellers in Sixteenth-Century France* (Palo Alto, Calif.: Stanford University Press, 1987), 4.

94. Carlo Ginzburg, *Ecstasies: Deciphering the Witches' Sabbath*, trans. R. Rosenthal (New York: Pantheon Books, 1991).

95. Ibid., 23.

96. Ibid., 24–25.

97. Hans Blumenberg, *Work on Myth*, trans. R. M. Wallace (Cambridge, Mass.: MIT Press, 1985), 118.

98. McNeill, "Mythistory," 8.

99. Jules Michelet, *History of the French Revolution*, trans. C. Cocks (Chicago: University of Chicago Press, 1967). On Michelet's mythological interpretation of history, see Lionel Gossman, "Michelet and the French Revolution," in *The French Revolution and the Creation of Modern Political Culture*, ed. Keith Michael Baker (Oxford: Pergamon Press, 1990), 3:639–63.

100. Michelet, *History of the French Revolution*, 164.

101. Albert Soboul, *The French Revolution, 1789–1799*, trans. A. Forrest and C. Jones (New York: Random House, 1975).

102. Ibid., 13, 139.

103. Simon Schama, *Citizens: A Chronicle of the French Revolution* (New York: Knopf, 1989).

104. Saul Friedländer, *Prelude to Downfall: Hitler and the United States, 1939–1941*, trans. A. Werth (London: Chatto and Windus, 1967); Saul Friedländer, *Pius XII and the Third Reich: A Documentation*, trans. C. Fullham (London: Chatto and Windus, 1966).

105. Saul Friedländer, *L'antisemitisme Nazi: Histoire d'une psychose collective* (Paris: Seuil, 1971); Saul Friedländer, *History and Psychoanalysis: An Inquiry into the Possibilities and Limits of Psychohistory*, trans. S. Suleiman (New York: Holmes and Meier, 1978).

106. Saul Friedländer, *When Memory Comes*, trans. H. R. Lane (New York: Farrar, Straus, Giroux, 1979), 143; Saul Friedländer, *Reflections of Nazism: An Essay on Kitsch and Death*, trans. T. Weyer (New York: Harper and Row, 1984), xiv–xvii, 81–85.

107. Saul Friedländer, *Nazi Germany and the Jews*, vol. 1, *The Years of Persecution, 1933–1939* (New York: HarperCollins, 1997), 73–112.

108. Giambattista Vico, *The New Science*, trans. T. Bergin and M. H. Fisch (Ithaca, N.Y.: Cornell University Press, 1968), par. 51.

109. Ibid., par. 376.

110. James Joyce, *Finnegans Wake* (London: Viking Press, 1939), 452.

111. Johan Huizinga, *The Autumn of the Middle Ages*, trans. R. J. Payton and U. Mammitzsch (Chicago: University of Chicago Press, 1996). The best discussion of Huizinga's historical vocation is Karl J. Weintraub, *Visions of Culture* (Chicago: University of Chicago Press, 1966), 208–46.

112. Ernst Cassirer, *The Philosophy of Symbolic Forms*, vol. 2, *Mythical Thought*, trans. R. Manheim (New Haven, Conn.: Yale University Press 1955), 5.

113. On the symbiotic immersion of Jewish intellectuals in German mythology, see Sidney M. Bolkosky, *The Distorted Image: German Jewish Perceptions of Germans and Germany, 1918–1935* (New York: Elsevier, 1975).

114. Peter Gay, "Encounter with Modernism: German Jews in Wilhelminian Culture," in his *Freud, Jews, and Other Germans* (Oxford: Oxford University Press, 1978), 95, 101.

115. Ernest Kahn, "Jews in the Stefan George Circle," *Leo Baeck Year Book* 8 (1963): 171–83.

116. Theodore Ziolkowski has measured this peculiar German "hunger for myth" by these figures: between 1907 to 1920 there appeared about 10 books with the term *myth* in their titles; in the 1920s, about 20; and in the 1930s, over 60! See his essay "Der Hunger nach dem Mythos: Zur seelischen Gastronomie der Deutschen in den Zwanziger Jahren," in *Die sogenannten Zwanziger Jahre*, ed. R. Grimm and J. Hermand (Bad Homburg: H. Gehlen, 1970), 169–201.

117. George Mosse, *German Jews beyond Judaism* (Bloomington: Indiana University Press, 1985), 47.

118. Steven A. Aschheim, "German Jews beyond Bildung and Liberalism: The Radical Jewish Revival in the Weimar Republic," in *The German-Jewish Dialogue Reconsidered*, ed. K. L. Berghahn (New York: Peter Lang, 1996), 125–40. See also Michael Löwy, *Redemption and Utopia: Jewish Libertarian Thought in Central Europe: A Study in Elective Affinity*, trans. H. Hope (London: Athlone, 1992).

119. Walter Benjamin, "Paris, the Capital of the Nineteenth Century," in *The Arcades*

Project, by Walter Benjamin, trans. H. Eiland and K. McLaughlin (Cambridge, Mass.: Harvard University Press, 1999), 10.

CHAPTER TWO

1. Livy, *History of Rome,* trans. B. O. Foster (Cambridge, Mass.: Harvard University Press, 1919), 1, pref., 6–9.

2. See, e.g., Peter Bietenholz, *Historia and Fabula: Myths and Legends in Historical Thought from Antiquity to the Modern Age* (Leiden: Brill, 1994). On Roman mythology in modern historiography, see Fritz Graf, "Der Mythos bei den Römern: Forschungs- und Problems-geschichte," in *Mythos in mythenloser Gesellschaft: Das Paradigma Roms,* ed. F. Graf (Stuttgart: B. G. Teubner, 1993), 25–43.

3. Livy, *History of Rome,* 25.16.4. On Livy's neostoic philosophy, see P. G. Walsh, *Livy: His Historical Aims and Methods* (Cambridge: Cambridge University Press, 1961).

4. Livy, *History of Rome,* 1.16.1–4.

5. R. M. Ogilvie, *A Commentary on Livy: Books 1–5* (Oxford: Oxford University Press, 1965), 85.

6. Livy, *History of Rome,* 1.16.7–8.

7. Gary Forsythe, *Livy and Early Rome: A Study in Historical Method and Judgment* (Stuttgart: F. Steiner, 1999), 133.

8. P. G. Walsh, "Livy's Preface and the Distortion of History," *American Journal of Philology* 76 (1955): 369–83.

9. Livy, *History of Rome,* 43.13.1. For a comprehensive discussion of Livy's religiosity, see D. S. Levine, *Religion in Livy* (Leiden: Brill, 1993).

10. On Livy and Cicero, see P. G. Walsh, *Livy: His Historical Aims and Methods,* 60.

11. Livy, *History of Rome,* 1.4.2.

12. Ibid., 1.4.7.

13. R. G. Collingwood, *The Idea of History* (Oxford: Oxford University Press, 1946), 38.

14. T. J. Luce, *Livy: The Composition of His History* (Princeton, N.J.: Princeton University Press, 1977), 231.

15. Gary B. Miles, *Livy: Constructing Early Rome* (Ithaca, N.Y.: Cornell University Press, 1995), 18, 138–39.

16. For general discussion, see Lidia Mazzolani, *Empire without End,* trans. J. McConnell and M. Pei (New York: Harcourt Brace Jovanovich, 1972).

17. Andrew Feldherr, *Spectacle and Society in Livy's History* (Berkeley: University of California Press, 1998), 76. On the Roman "invention" of authority through the consecration of foundation and tradition, see the brilliant observations of Hannah Arendt, "What Is Authority?" in her *Between Past and Future* (New York: Viking Press, 1961), 120–21.

18. Miles, *Livy: Constructing Early Rome,* 74.

19. Paul Zanker, *The Power of Images in the Age of Augustus,* trans. A. Shapiro (Ann Arbor: University of Michigan Press, 1990).

20. Feldherr, *Spectacle and Society in Livy's History,* 194–204.

21. Livy, *History of Rome,* 5.21.9.

22. Roberto Ridolfi, *The Life of Niccolò Machiavelli,* trans. C. Grayson (Chicago: University of Chicago Press, 1963), 83.

23. Niccolò Machiavelli, *The Letters of Machiavelli*, ed. and trans. A. Gilbert (New York: Capricorn Books, 1961), 142. For a close reading of this letter, see John M. Najemy, *Between Friends: Discourses of Power and Desire in the Machiavelli-Vettori Letters of 1513–15* (Princeton, N.J.: Princeton University Press, 1993), 215–40.

24. Niccolò Machiavelli, *Discourses on the First Ten Books of Titus Livius*, trans. L. J. Walker (London: Routledge and Kegan Paul, 1950). The assumption that Machiavelli wrote the *Discourses* only after he had written *The Prince* is affirmed by Hans Baron, "Machiavelli the Republican Citizen and Author of *The Prince*," in *In Search of Florentine Civic Humanism: Essays on the Transition from Medieval to Modern Thought,* by Hans Baron (Princeton, N.J.: Princeton University Press, 1988), 2:101–51.

25. Felix Gilbert, "Bernardo Rucellai and the Orti Oricellari: A Study on the Origins of Modern Political Thought," in his *History: Choice and Commitment* (Cambridge, Mass.: Harvard University Press, 1977), 215–46.

26. Machiavelli, *Discourses,* 1, pref., 2–3.

27. Ibid., 2.19.1. On Machiavelli's revision of "exemplary history," see the excellent discussion in Timothy Hampton, *Writing from History: The Rhetoric of Exemplarity in Renaissance Literature* (Ithaca, N.Y.: Cornell University Press, 1990), 62–79.

28. Machiavelli, *Discourses,* 1, pref., 4.

29. Machiavelli, *The Prince,* trans. R. Price (Cambridge: Cambridge University Press, 1988), 54.

30. Felix Gilbert, *Machiavelli and Guicciardini* (Princeton, N.J.: Princeton University Press, 1965), 180.

31. As John H. Geerken has shown, Machiavelli derived his notion and examples of political *virtù* from classical mythology. "Homer's Image of the Hero in Machiavelli: A Comparison of *Areté* and *Virtù*," *Italian Quarterly* 14 (1970): 45–90.

32. Machiavelli, *Discourses,* 1, pref., 1, my emphasis.

33. Ibid., 1.25.1.

34. Machiavelli, *The Prince,* 62.

35. Hanna Fenichel Pitkin, *Fortune Is a Woman: Gender and Politics in the Thought of Niccolò Machiavelli* (Berkeley: University of California Press, 1984), 34–42.

36. Niccolò Machiavelli, *History of Florence,* in *Machiavelli: The Chief Works and Others,* ed. and trans. A. Gilbert (Durham, N.C.: Duke University Press, 1965), 3:1123.

37. Leo Strauss, *Thoughts on Machiavelli* (Glencoe, Ill.: Free Press, 1958), 121–58.

38. This is also the judgment of Ronald Syme, "Livy and Augustus," in his *Roman Papers* (Oxford: Oxford University Press, 1979), 1:400–454.

39. Ridolfi, *The Life of Niccolò Machiavelli,* 4, 147–48.

40. Machiavelli, *Discourses,* 1, pref., 4.

41. On Livy's description of mass scenes, see P. G. Walsh, *Livy: His Historical Aims and Methods,* 173–90.

42. Machiavelli, *Discourses,* 3.1.3.

43. Ibid., 2, pref., 7.

44. Lisa Jardine and Anthony Grafton, "Studied for Action: How Gabriel Harvey Read His Livy," *Past and Present* 129 (1990): 31–78.

45. Machiavelli, *Discourses,* 1.4.2.

46. Ibid., 1.1–6; 2, pref., 1–4; 3.1.

47. Baron, "Machiavelli the Republican Citizen," 148.

48. Machiavelli, *Discourses*, 1.11.2.

49. Ibid., 3.33.2, citing Livy, *History of Rome*, 6.41.8.

50. Machiavelli, *Discourses*, 2.29.1

51. Ibid., 1.12.3

52. Ibid., 1.57.1

53. Livy, *History of Rome*, 6.14-20.

54. Machiavelli, *Discourses*, 1.24.4, 1.58.1, 3.8.2.

55. Ibid., 3.8.2.

56. Maurizio Viroli, *Machiavelli* (Oxford: Oxford University Press, 1998), 161.

57. Machiavelli, *Discourses*, 1.58.6-7.

58. Machiavelli, *The Prince*, 18-19.

59. Machiavelli, *Discourses*, 1.10.4.

60. Ibid., 2, pref., 2.

61. Ibid., 1.16.1.

62. Machiavelli, *The Prince*, 53.

63. Russell Price, "The Theme of *Gloria* in Machiavelli," *Renaissance Quarterly* 30 (1977): 588-631.

64. Isaiah Berlin, "The Originality of Machiavelli," in his *Against the Current* (Oxford: Oxford University Press, 1978), 62.

65. Mark Hulliung, *Citizen Machiavelli* (Princeton, N.J.: Princeton University Press, 1983), 256-57.

66. For critical judgments on Machiavelli as historian, see Federico Chabod, *Machiavelli and the Renaissance*, trans. D. Moore (New York: Harper, 1965), 85-120; and Eric W. Cochrane, *History and Historiography in the Italian Renaissance* (Chicago: University of Chicago Press, 1981), 265-70.

67. Machiavelli, *Discourses*, 1.9.1.

68. For a stimulating discussion of this notion, see Bruce James Smith, *Politics & Remembrance, Republican Themes in Machiavelli, Burke, and Tocqueville* (Princeton, N.J.: Princeton University Press, 1985), 84-93.

69. Mark Hulliung argues that for Machiavelli, whereas the assassination of Remus by Romulus was "constitutive" of Roman history, the assassination of Romulus by the senators had a destructive effect on it. *Citizen Machiavelli*, 188.

70. Strauss, *Thoughts on Machiavelli*, 90.

71. Machiavelli, *Discourses*, 3.1.1.

72. J. G. A. Pocock, *The Machiavellian Moment: Florentine Political Thought and the Atlantic Republican Tradition* (Princeton, N.J.: Princeton University Press, 1975).

73. Berlin, "The Originality of Machiavelli," 73.

74. Hulliung, *Citizen Machiavelli*, 266.

75. Livy, *History of Rome*, 25.16.4; see the discussion by Walsh, *Livy: His Historical Aims and Methods*, 53.

76. Niccolò Machiavelli, "On Fortune," quoted in Anthony Parel, *The Machiavellian Cosmos* (New Haven, Conn.: Yale University Press, 1992), 71. For general discussion, see also Pitkin, *Fortune Is a Woman*, 138-69.

77. Machiavelli, *Discourses*, 1, pref., 3.

78. Ibid., 1.39.1.

79. Giambattista Vico, *The Autobiography of Giambattista Vico*, trans. T. G. Bergin and M. H. Fisch (Ithaca, N.Y.: Cornell University Press, 1963), 119.

80. Ibid., 132.

81. Ibid., 134.

82. In 1692 Vico published a long philosophical poem, "Affetti di un disperato," in which he imagined himself as a wanderer lost in Lucretian moods and woods. As Elio Gianturco has noted, Vico's "formative years stand in a polemical relationship to the thinker whom, with a pride based on a consciousness of intellectual independence, he calls 'Renato.'" Translator's introduction to Vico, *On the Study Methods of Our Time*, trans. E. Gianturco (Ithaca, N.Y.: Cornell University Press, 1990), xxv.

83. See, for example, Peter Burke, *Vico* (Oxford: Oxford University Press, 1985), 8-9.

84. For a full reconstruction of Vico's intellectual setting in Naples, see Nicola Badaloni, *Introduzione a G. B. Vico* (Milan: Feltrinelli, 1961).

85. Max Harold Fisch, introduction to *The Autobiography*, by Vico, 35-36.

86. Benedetto Croce, *The Philosophy of Giambattista Vico*, trans. R. G. Collingwood (New York: Russell and Russell, 1964), 266. For a full interpretation of Vico's *Autobiography* along these lines, see Donald Phillip Verene, *The New Art of Autobiography: An Essay on the Life of Giambattista Vico Written by Himself* (Oxford: Oxford University Press, 1991).

87. Vico, *On the Study Methods of Our Time*, 33. For a perceptive examination, see John D. Schaeffer, "Vico's Rhetorical Model of the Mind: *Sensus Communis* in the *De nostri temporis studiorum ratione*," *Philosophy and Rhetoric* 14 (1981): 152-67.

88. René Descartes, *Discourse on Method*, in *Descartes' Philosophical Writings*, trans. N. Kemp Smith (New York: Modern Library, 1958), 97.

89. Giambattista Vico, *The New Science*, trans. T. G. Bergin and M. H. Fisch (Ithaca, N.Y.: Cornell University Press, 1968), par. 34.

90. Vico, *The Autobiography*, 166-67.

91. Vico, *The New Science*, par. 314.

92. Max H. Fisch, introduction to Vico, *The New Science*, xix-xx. On the various titles of *The New Science*, see Benvenuto Donati, *Nuovi studi sulla filosofia civile di G. B. Vico* (Florence: Le Monnier, 1936), 412-21.

93. Isaac Newton, *Opticks*, reprint of the 4th ed. (London: G. Bell, 1931), 401-2.

94. On Newton's reputation in the Enlightenment, see Peter Gay, *The Enlightenment: An Interpretation*, vol. 2, *The Science of Freedom* (London: Weidenfeld and Nicolson, 1970), 126-66.

95. Vincenso Ferrone, *Scienza, natura, religione: Mondo newtoniano e cultura italiana nel primo Settecento* (Naples: Jovene, 1982).

96. Cited and discussed by Donald R. Kelley in his essay "Vico's Road: From Philology to Jurisprudence and Back," in *Giambattista Vico's Science of Humanity*, ed. G. Tagliacozzo and D. P. Verne (Baltimore: Johns Hopkins University Press, 1976), 15.

97. Vico, *The New Science*, pars. 147, 344.

98. On this and other intellectual traditions that inspired Vico's *New Science*, see Joseph Mali, *The Rehabilitation of Myth: Vico's New Science* (Cambridge: Cambridge University Press, 1992), 16-41. I use some paragraphs from that book.

99. For comprehensive reviews of earlier formulations of this notion, see Croce, *The*

Philosophy of Giambattista Vico, 279–301; Rodolfo Mondolfo, *Il "verum-factum" prima di Vico* (Naples: Guida, 1969); Karl Löwith, *Vicos Grundsatz: Verum et factum convertuntur: Seine theologische Prämisse und deren säkulare Konsequenzen* (Heidelberg: C. Winter, 1968). For a provocative but perceptive discussion of current interpretations, see James Morrison, "Vico's Principle of *Verum* Is *Factum* and the Problem of Historicism," *Journal of the History of Ideas* 39 (1978): 579–94.

100. Giambattista Vico, *On the Most Ancient Wisdom of the Ancients*, trans. L. Palmer (Ithaca, N.Y.: Cornell University Press, 1988), 45–47.

101. Vico, *The New Science*, par. 331.

102. See the following anthologies: G. Tagliacozzo and H. White, eds., *Giambattista Vico: An International Symposium* (Baltimore: Johns Hopkins University Press, 1969); G. Tagliacozzo and D. P. Verne, eds., *Giambattista Vico's Science of Humanity* (Baltimore: Johns Hopkins University Press, 1976); G. Tagliacozzo, M. Mooney, and D. P. Verene, eds., *Vico and Contemporary Thought* (Atlantic Highlands, N.J.: Humanities Press, 1980); G. Tagliacozzo, M. Mooney, and D. P. Verene, eds., *Vico: Past and Present* (Atlantic Highlands, N.J.: Humanities Press, 1981); and numerous essays in the annual *New Vico Studies*. The excessive "comparativism" and "presentism" in modern Vico scholarship is duly criticized by Andrea Battistini, "Contemporary Trends in Vichian Studies," in Tagliacozzo, Mooney, and Verene, *Vico: Past and Present*, 1–47, esp. 16–22.

103. Vico, *The New Science*, pars. 202–3.

104. Ibid., par. 338.

105. Isaiah Berlin, *Vico and Herder: Two Essays in the History of Ideas* (London: Hogarth Press, 1976), 52–53.

106. Vico, *The New Science*, par. 412.

107. Vico, *The Autobiography*, 148.

108. Ernst Cassirer, *The Problem of Knowledge*, trans. W. H. Woglom and C. W. Hendel (New Haven, Conn.: Yale University Press, 1950), 296.

109. Gianfranco Cantelli, "Myth and Language in Vico," in Tagliacozzo and Verne, *Vico's Science of Humanity*, 48. Cantelli elaborates this view in his *Mente, corpo, linguaggio: Saggio sull'interpretazione vichiana del mito* (Florence: Sansoni, 1987).

110. Vico, *The New Science*, par. 352.

111. Ibid., par. 779.

112. Ibid., par. 51.

113. Ibid., par. 338. On Vico's innovative "anthropological history" of mythology, see Frank Manuel, *The Eighteenth Century Confronts the Gods* (Cambridge, Mass.: Harvard University Press, 1959), 149–67.

114. Vico, *The New Science*, pars. 94–95, 396. On Vico's theological-historical distinction and contemporary controversies, see Paolo Rossi, *The Dark Abyss of Time: The History of Earth and the History of Nations from Hooke to Vico*, trans. L. Cochrane (Chicago: University of Chicago Press, 1983), 251–61.

115. For an impressive interpretation of Vico's *New Science* on these assumptions, see Ferdinand Fellman, *Das Vico-Axiom: Der Mann macht die Geschichte* (Freiburg: K. Alber, 1976).

116. Vico, *The New Science*, par. 342.

117. Ibid., pars. 379, 473.

118. Ibid., par. 366.

119. Ibid., par. 503. On Vico's theory of religion, see Samuel Preus, *Explaining Religion: Criticism and Theory from Bodin to Freud* (New Haven, Conn.: Yale University Press, 1987), 59−83.

120. Vico, *The New Science*, par. 374.

121. Ibid., par. 470. See, e.g., Vico's interpretation of the myth of the foundation of Thebes by Deucalion and Pyrrha (pars. 79, 523).

122. Vico refers to his "four authors"—Plato, Tacitus, Bacon, and Grotius—in his *Autobiography*, 154.

123. For a full elaboration of this matter, see Mali, *The Rehabilitation of Myth*, 136−73.

124. Plato, *The Republic*, 378a.

125. For a modern interpretation of Plato's mythological theory along these lines, see Julius A. Elias, *Plato's Defence of Poetry* (London: Macmillan, 1984).

126. Vico, *The New Science*, par. 296.

127. Ibid., par. 375.

128. On Vico's debt to Bacon, see Enrico De Mas, "Bacone e Vico," *Filosofia* 10 (1959): 505−59.

129. Francis Bacon, *On the Wisdom of the Ancients*, in *The Philosophical Works of Francis Bacon*, ed. J. Spedding, R. L. Ellis, and D. D. Heath (London: Longman, 1858−74), 6:696.

130. Vico, *The New Science*, par. 127.

131. Ibid., par. 81. See, e.g., Vico's commentary on the myth of Apollo and Daphne (pars. 533−35).

132. In 1732 Vico delivered a special oration to the Royal Academy of Naples under the title "On the Heroic Mind." See the English translation by E. Sewell and A. C. Sirignano in Tagliacozzo, Mooney, and Verene, *Vico and Contemporary Thought*, 2:228−45.

133. Vico, *The New Science*, par. 158.

134. Ibid., par. 437.

135. Ibid., par. 34.

136. Erich Auerbach, "Vico and Aesthetic Historicism," *Journal of Aesthetics and Art Criticism* 8 (1949): 110−18.

137. The classic study is Andrea Sorrentino, *La retorica e la poetica di G. B. Vico* (Turin: Bocca, 1927). See also Andrea Battistini, *La degnità della retorica: Studi su G. B. Vico* (Pisa: Pacini, 1975); and Michael Mooney, *Vico in the Tradition of Rhetoric* (Princeton, N.J.: Princeton University Press, 1985).

138. On Vico's "poetic characters," see Donald P. Verene, *Vico's Science of Imagination* (Ithaca, N.Y.: Cornell University Press, 1981). For a more general assessment, see the important (but neglected) study of Karl-Otto Apel, *Die Idee der Sprache in der Tradition des Humanismus von Dante bis Vico* (Bonn: Bouvier, 1963).

139. Vico, *The New Science*, par. 138.

140. Ibid., par. 139. See also Tullio de Mauro, "Giambattista Vico: From Rhetoric to Linguistic Historicism," in Tagliacozzo and White, *Vico: International Symposium*, 279−95.

141. Vico, *The New Science*, pars. 390−92. For an insightful interpretation, see Kelley, "Vico's Road," 17.

142. For a brilliant elaboration of this notion, see Hayden V. White, "The Tropics of History: The Deep Structure of *The New Science*," in Tagliacozzo and Verne, *Vico's Science of Humanity*, 65–85.

143. Vico, *The New Science*, pars. 236–37.

144. Ludwig Wittgenstein, *Remarks on Frazer's Golden Bough*, ed. R. Rhees, trans. A. C. Miles (Retford: Brynmill Press, 1979), 10.

145. Vico, *The New Science*, par. 482.

146. Giambattista Vico, *The First New Science*, par. 391, in *Selected Writings*, by G. B. Vico, ed. and trans. L. Pompa (Cambridge: Cambridge University Press, 1982), 154–55.

147. Vico, *The New Science*, par. 814.

148. Ibid., par. 205.

149. Vico explains his predilection for Tacitus in *The Autobiography*, 138–39. See also the fine discussion of Santino Caramella, "Vico, Tacitus, and Reason of State," in Tagliacozzo and White, *Vico: International Symposium*, 29–37.

150. On the political background of Vico's antirepublican ideology, see Giuseppe Giarrizzo, *Vico: La politica e la storia* (Naples: Guida, 1981).

151. Vico, *The New Science*, par. 38.

152. Ibid., pars. 531–32. Livy, *History of Rome*, 1.8.

153. Vico, *The New Science*, par. 317.

154. Ibid., pars. 647, 653. For a brilliant reconstruction of Vico's mythological counterhistory of Rome, see Mark Lilla, *G. B. Vico: The Making of an Anti-Modern* (Cambridge, Mass.: Harvard University Press, 1993), 152–203.

155. Vico, *The New Science*, par. 537.

156. Ibid., pars. 604, 606.

157. This curious relationship is the subject of the anthology of essays *Vico and Marx: Affinities and Contrasts*, ed. G. Tagliacozzo (Atlantic Highlands, N.J.: Humanities Press, 1983).

158. See Max Horkheimer's chapter "Vico and Mythology," in *The Beginnings of the Bourgeois Philosophy of History*, in *Between Philosophy and Social Science*, by Max Horkheimer, trans. G. F. Hunter (Cambridge, Mass.: MIT Press, 1993), 375–88.

159. Vico, *The New Science*, par. 347.

160. Ibid., pars. 332–33, 360.

161. Ibid., pars. 334–37.

162. Peter Winch, "Understanding a Primitive Society," *American Philosophical Quarterly* 1 (1964): 322.

163. Vico, *The New Science*, par. 309. For a lucid elaboration of this notion, see James C. Morrison, "Vico's Doctrine of the Natural Law of the Gentes," *Journal of the History of Philosophy* 16 (1978): 47–60.

164. Wittgenstein, *Remarks on Frazer's Golden Bough*, 7.

165. Vico, *The New Science*, par. 1106.

166. Preface of 1869 to *L'histoire de France*, in Jules Michelet, *Œuvres complètes*, ed. P. Viallaneix (Paris, 1971–), 4:14, cited by Max Harold Fisch, introduction to Vico, *Autobiography*, 79. The classic account of Michelet's discovery of Vico is the first chapter in Edmund Wilson, *To the Finland Station* (New York: Farrar, Straus, Giroux, 1940). For more academic

studies, see Oscar Haac, *Les principes inspirateurs de Michelet* (New Haven, Conn.: Yale University Press, 1951); Paul Viallaneix, *La voie royale: Essai sur l'idée de peuple dans l'Œuvre de Michelet* (Paris: Flammarion, 1959), 214–38; Maria Donzelli, "La conception de l'histoire de J. B. Vico et son interprétation par J. Michelet," *Annales Historiques de la Révolution Française* 53 (1981): 633–55.

167. Cited by Fisch, introduction to Vico, *Autobiography*, 76. See also Viallaneix, *La voie royale*, 215.

168. Michelet's most significant discussion of Vico is the "Discours sur le système et la vie de Vico," written as a preface to the *Œuvres choisies de Vico* in 1835. It is reprinted in *Œuvres complètes*, 1:283–301.

169. Viallaneix, *La voie royale*, 115. See also Michelet's creative translation of this passage in *Œuvres complètes*, 1:434.

170. Michelet, *Œuvres complètes*, 2:64.

171. Michelet, "Discours sur le système et la vie de Vico," 1:288–92.

172. Jules Michelet, *Histoire de la République romaine* (1831), *Œuvres complètes*, 2:341.

173. Viallaneix, *La voie royale*, 215.

174. Michelet, cited in *Œuvres complètes*, 4:2.

175. Jules Michelet, *Introduction à l'histoire universelle*, in *Œuvres complètes*, 2:229.

176. Ibid., 2:238.

177. For a deep illumination of Michelet's own existential myths, see Lionel Gossman, "The Go-between: Jules Michelet, 1798–1874," *Modern Language Notes* 89 (1974): 503–41.

178. Jules Michelet, *Journal*, ed. P. Viallaneix (Paris: Gallimard, 1959), 1:491.

179. Michelet, *L'histoire de France*, in *Œuvres complètes*, 4:364.

180. Paul Viallaneix, "Michelet and the Legend of Joan," *Clio* 6 (1976): 193–203.

181. Michelet, *Histoire de la République romaine*, 2:341.

182. Michelet, "Discours sur le système et la vie de Vico," 1:283–84; Michelet, *Introduction à l'histoire universelle*, 2:227–58.

183. Michelet, *Journal*, 1:384.

184. François Hartog, *Le xixe siècle et l'histoire: Le cas Fustel de Coulanges* (Paris: Presses Universitaires de France, 1988).

185. Karl Marx, *The Eighteenth Brumaire of Louis Bonaparte*, in *Selected Works*, ed. V. Adoratsky (London: Lawrence and Wishart, 1970), 96.

186. Marcel Detienne, *The Creation of Mythology*, trans. M. Cook (Chicago: University of Chicago Press, 1986).

187. Edward Gibbon, *The Decline and Fall of the Roman Empire* (New York: Modern Library, n.d.), chap. 23, p. 759.

188. Karl Marx, *A Contribution to the Critique of Political Economy*, trans. N. I. Stone (New York: International Library, 1904), 310–11. Marx's own "mythology" is analyzed in the studies of Robert C. Tucker, *Philosophy and Myth in Karl Marx* (Cambridge: Cambridge University Press, 1972); and Leonard P. Wessell, *Prometheus Bound: The Mythic Structure of Karl Marx's Scientific Thinking* (Baton Rouge: Louisiana State University Press, 1984).

189. See the important observations of Michael Kammen, who also points out that American historians first discovered myth around 1870 and then, more pervasively, between 1920 and 1930—precisely the pivotal dates of my study. *Mystic Chords of Memory:*

The *Transformation of Tradition in American Culture* (New York: Knopf, 1991), 32-39, 481-514.

190. For a brief discussion of Michelet's conception of the Renaissance, see Wallace K. Ferguson, *The Renaissance in Historical Thought* (Cambridge, Mass.: H. Mifflin, 1948), 174-78.

191. Michelet, *Introduction à l'histoire universelle*, 2:237.

CHAPTER THREE

1. Burckhardt to von Preen, 24 July 1889, *The Letters of Jacob Burckhardt*, ed. and trans. A. Dru (London: Routledge and Kegan Paul, 1955), 219.

2. Werner Kaegi, *Jacob Burckhardt: Eine Biographie*, 7 vols. (Basel/Stuttgart: Schwabe, 1949-82), 1:21.

3. For a perceptive discussion of this notion in Burckhardt's life and works, see Albert Salomon, "Jacob Burckhardt: Transcending History," *Philosophy and Phenomenological Research* 6 (1946): 225-69.

4. David Friedrich Strauss, *The Life of Jesus Critically Examined*, trans. G. Eliot (London: S.C.M., 1973), 87.

5. Ibid., 258-63.

6. Ibid., 91-92.

7. Dewette typified the Gospels as "Geschichtssagen" in his *Lehrbuch der christlichen Dogmatik in ihrer historischen Entwicklung*, first published in 1818. On Dewette's mythological theory, see the fine discussion in Paul Handschin, *Wilhelm Martin Leberecht de Wette als Prediger und Schriftsteller* (Basel: Helbing und Lichtenhau, 1957), 55. For a general assessment, see John W. Rogerson, *W. M. L. De Wette: Founder of Modern Biblical Criticism: An Intellectual Biography* (Sheffield: Sheffield Academic Press, 1992).

8. Kaegi, *Jacob Burckhardt*, 1:445-81.

9. Burckhardt to Johan Riggenbach, 28 August 1838, *The Letters of Jacob Burckhardt*, 36. On Burckhardt's early religious conflicts and crises, see Ernst Walter Zeeden, "Die Auseinandersetzungen des jungen Burckhardts mit Glaube und Christentum," *Historische Zeitschrift* 178 (1954): 493-514.

10. Jacob Burckhardt, *The Civilization of the Renaissance in Italy*, trans. S. G. C. Middlemore (Vienna: Phaidon Press, n.d.), 260.

11. Burckhardt to Friedrich von Tschudi, 1 December 1839, *The Letters of Jacob Burckhardt*, 48. Felix Gilbert rightly relates Burckhardt's mature historical works to his youthful theological quest for meaning: "Jacob Burckhardt's Student Years: The Road to Cultural History," *Journal of the History of Ideas* 48 (1986): 247-74.

12. Burckhardt to Friedrich von Tschudi, 1 December 1839, *The Letters of Jacob Burckhardt*, 48.

13. Burckhardt to Willibald Beyschlag, 30 January 1844, *The Letters of Jacob Burckhardt*, 89.

14. Burckhardt to Gottfried Kinkel, 28 June 1845, *The Letters of Jacob Burckhardt*, 94.

15. Jacob Burckhardt, *Griechische Kulturgeschichte*, in *Gesamtausgabe* (Berlin/Stuttgart: Schwabe, 1929-34), 10:400. For a magisterial reconstruction of Burckhardt's *historia altera*,

see Lionel Gossman, *Basel in the Age of Burckhardt* (Chicago: University of Chicago Press, 2000), 251–346.

16. Jacob Burckhardt to Louise Burckhardt, 15 August 1840, *The Letters of Jacob Burckhardt*, 58.

17. For a brief and brilliant interpretation of Burckhardt's life and works in contradistinction to Ranke's, see Hugh Trevor-Roper, "Jacob Burckhardt," *Proceedings of the British Academy* 70 (1984): 359–78.

18. Friedrich Meinecke, "Ranke and Burckhardt," in *German History: Some New German Views*, ed. H. Kohn (Boston: Beacon Press, 1954), 142.

19. Leopold von Ranke, *Zur eigenen Lebensgeschichte*, in *Sämtliche Werke* (Leipzig: Duncker und Humblot, 1890), vol. 53 –54, pp. 61–62. See the discussion by Leonard Krieger, *Ranke: The Making of History* (Chicago: University of Chicago Press, 1977), 98.

20. Theodore H. von Laue, *Leopold Ranke: The Formative Years* (Princeton, N.J.: Princeton University Press, 1950). For a revision of Ranke's alleged "positivism," see Rudolf Vierhaus, "Historiography between Science and Art," in *Leopold von Ranke and the Shaping of the Historical Discipline*, ed. G. G. Iggers and J. M. Powel (Syracuse, N.Y.: Syracuse University Press, 1990), 61–69. See also the fine attempt at "reconciliation" by Felix Gilbert, *History: Politics or Culture? Reflections on Ranke and Burckhardt* (Princeton, N.J.: Princeton University Press, 1990).

21. Leopold von Ranke, "On the Character of Historical Science," trans. W. A. Iggers, in *The Theory and Practice of History*, ed. G. G. Iggers and K. von Moltke (Indianapolis: Bobbs-Merrill, 1973), 44–45.

22. Leopold von Ranke, *Universal History*, trans. G. W. Prothero (New York: Harper, 1884), xi.

23. Ranke acknowledges his debt and admiration for these sources in his *History of the Popes*, trans. E. Fowler (New York: Colonial Press, 1901), xvii–xxii.

24. Gino Benzoni, "Ranke's Favorite Source: The Venetian *Relazioni*: Impressions with Allusions to Later Historiography," in Iggers and Powel, *Leopold von Ranke and the Shaping of the Historical Discipline*, 53–57. See also the chapter "Renaissance Epistolarity" in John M. Najemy, *Between Friends: Discourses of Power and Desire in the Machiavelli-Vettori Letters of 1513–15* (Princeton, N.J.: Princeton University Press, 1993), 18–57.

25. Anthony Grafton, "The Footnote from De Thou to Ranke," *History and Theory*, suppl. 33 (1994): 61.

26. Donald R. Kelley, "Mythistory in the Age of Ranke," in Iggers and Powel, *Leopold Ranke and The Shaping of the Historical Discipline*, 3–20.

27. Burckhardt to von Tschudi, 16 March 1840, *The Letters of Jacob Burckhardt*, 53.

28. Ibid.

29. Kaegi, *Jacob Burckhardt*, 1:84.

30. Burckhardt to Karl Fresenius, 9 June 1842, *The Letters of Jacob Burckhardt*, 73–74. On Burckhardt's poetic vision of history and its origins (in Goethe's notion of *Anschauung*) and transformation into a total *Kulturgeschichte*, see the excellent discussion in Karl J. Weintraub's chapter on Burckhardt in his *Visions of Culture* (Chicago: University of Chicago Press, 1966), 115–60. See also Peter Gay, *Style in History* (New York: Basic Books, 1974), 176–77.

31. Jacob Burckhardt, *Reflections on History*, trans. M. D. Hottinger (Indianapolis: Liberty Fund, 1979), 107.

32. Burckhardt to Albert Brenner, 11 November 1855, *The Letters of Jacob Burckhardt*, 116.

33. Burckhardt, *The Civilization of the Renaissance in Italy*, 82.

34. Quoted by Hugh Trevor-Roper in his introduction to Jacob Burckhardt, *On History and Historians*, trans. H. Zohn (Boston: Beacon Press, 1958), xx–xxi.

35. Burckhardt, *Reflections on History*, 34.

36. Jacob Burckhardt, *The Age of Constantine the Great*, trans. M. Hadas (New York: Pantheon Books, 1949), 11.

37. Burckhardt, *Reflections on History*, 36.

38. Burckhardt, *The Age of Constantine the Great*, 214–16.

39. For a perceptive interpretation of Burckhardt's notion of religion, see Alfred von Martin, *Die Religion Jacob Burckhardts* (Munich: Erasmus, 1947).

40. As Lionel Gossman has shown, this was the common conception of history in Basel: "The Boundaries of the City: A Nineteenth-Century Essay on the Limits of Historical Knowledge," *History and Theory* 25 (1986): 33–51. The essay that Gossman introduces is the formal *Rektoratrede* of Wilhelm Vischer, given in 1877. In the guise of an apology for the scientific fallacies of history, owing to its poetic sources and methods, this essay bears a positive message: that history is valuable and can prevail as mythistory. Note, for example, its conclusion that "the historical content and significance of legend may be more important, in certain cases, than what we would gain if we had the most precise information about the same facts or events and could thus construct a so-called reliable and accredited history" (49–50).

41. Hans-Georg Gadamer, *Truth and Method* (London: Seabury Press, 1975), 12.

42. On Burckhardt's *Bildung*, see the engaging and enlightening discussion by Gossman, *Basel in the Age of Burckhardt*, 203–50.

43. Burckhardt, *The Age of Constantine the Great*, 323–24.

44. On Burckhardt's agnosticism, see David Norbrook, "Life and Death of Renaissance Man," *Raritan* 8 (1989): 89–110.

45. Alan S. Kahan, *Aristocratic Liberalism: The Social and Political Thought of Jacob Burckhardt, John Stuart Mill, and Alexis de Tocqueville* (New York: Oxford University Press, 1992).

46. Burckhardt to Gottfried Kinkel, 18 April 1845, *The Letters of Jacob Burckhardt*, 93.

47. Burckhardt to Friedrich Nietzsche, 25 February 1874, ibid., 158.

48. Burckhardt to Hermann Schauenburg, 5 March 1846, ibid., 97. For a comprehensive discussion of Burckhardt's notion of *Alteuropa*, see Wolfgang Hardtwig, *Geschichtsschreibung zwischen Alteuropa und moderner Welt: Jacob Burckhardt in seiner Zeit* (Göttingen: Vandenhoeck und Ruprecht, 1974), 273–360.

49. Henri Bergson, *Œuvres*, ed. A. Robinet (Paris: Presses Universitaires de France, 1970), 1347.

50. Burckhardt to Hermann Schauenburg, 5 March 1846, *The Letters of Jacob Burckhardt*, 97.

51. Burckhardt, *Reflections on History*, 105.

52. It begins with these lines:

Versenkt mich in Tyrrhenische Meer!
Das ist die stillste Grabesgrotte!
Dort liegt von alten Zeiten her
Manche karthagische Silberflotte.

The poet then presents himself against his *Zeitgenossen:*

Bei diesen Altertümern mag
Erminus Conservator werden;
Dann freßt euch auf, ihr Lumpenpack,
Daß wieder Stille wird auf Erden!

He concludes with these mythical visions:

Vielleicht in später, später Zeit,
Wann wieder jung die Welt geworden,
Tönt auf den Fluten weit und breit
Jubel von hohen Schiffesborden.

Auf gold'nem Deck wird Helena,
Von Paris Arm umschlungen, thronen;
Ob ihrer Schönheit fern und nah
Jauchzen die Nymphen und Tritonen.

Bekränzte Purpursegel schwellt
Ein Balsamhauch, und Lieder tönen:
Wandelt vorbei, Zeitalter der Welt!
Ewige Jugend verbleibt dem Schönen!
(Burckhardt to Hermann Schauenberg, 28 February 1847, *Briefe,* 3:57)

For a fine illumination of this poem, see Heinz Schlaffer, "Jacob Burckhardt oder das Asyl der Kulturgeschichte," in Hannelore Schlaffer und Heinz Schlaffer, *Studien zum ästhetischen Historismus* (Frankfurt am Main: Suhrkamp, 1975), 72−111.

53. Jacob Burckhardt, *Der Cicerone: Eine Anleitung zum Genuß der Kunstwerke Italiens* (Stuttgart: Kröner, 1855). For insightful discussions of this book and Burckhardt's other studies in art history, see Irmgard Siebert, *Jacob Burckhardt: Studien zur Kunst- und Kulturgeschichtsschreibung* (Basel: Schwabe, 1991).

54. On these critical intentions and reactions, see Kaegi, *Jacob Burckhardt,* 3:425−530.

55. Burckhardt to Johannes Riggenbach, 12 December 1838, *The Letters of Jacob Burckhardt,* 40.

56. Jacob Burckhardt, *The Cicerone: An Art Guide to Painting in Italy for the Use of Travelers and Students,* trans. A. H. Clough (London: T. Werner Laurie, 1873), bk. 3, p. 139.

57. Jacob Burckhardt, "Über erzählende Malerei," in *Kulturgeschichtliche Vorträge,* ed. Rudolf Marx (Stuttgart: Kröner, 1929), 195−96.

58. On Burckhardt's conception of art (*Kunst*), see Martina Sitt, *Kriterien der Kunstrkritik: Jacob Burckhardts unveröffentliche Ästhetik als Schlüssel seines Rangsystem* (Vienna: Böhlau, 1992); Gossman, *Basel in the Age of Burckhardt*, 347−410.

59. Burckhardt to Willibald Beyschlag, 14 June 1842, *The Letters of Jacob Burckhardt*, 72−73. On Burckhardt's notion of *Bild*, see Peter Ganz, "Jacob Burckhardt: Wissenschaft—Geschichte—Literatur," in *Umgang mit Jacob Burckhardt*, ed. Hans G. Guggisberg (Basel: Schwabe, 1994), 11−35.

60. Paul O. Kristeller, "Changing Views of the Intellectual History of the Renaissance since Jacob Burckhardt," in *The Renaissance: A Reconsideration of the Theories and Interpretation of the Age*, ed. T. Helton (Madison: University of Wisconsin Press, 1961), 29.

61. For a critical assessment of Burckhardt from new perspectives, see Alison Brown, introduction to *Language and Images of Renaissance Italy*, ed. A. Brown (Oxford: Clarendon Press, 1995), 7−8, and other essays in that volume.

62. Denys Hay, "Historians and the Renaissance during the Last Twenty-Five Years," in *The Renaissance: Essays in Interpretation* (London: Methuen, 1982), 1−2.

63. This is the judgment of William Kerrigan and Gordon Bragen, *The Idea of Renaissance* (Baltimore: Johns Hopkins University Press, 1989), 3−35. For a critical discussion of Burckhardt's notion of "individualism," see Hans Baron, "The Limits of the Notion of 'Renaissance Individualism': Burckhardt after a Century" (1960), in his *In Search of Florentine Civic Humanism* (Princeton, N.J.: Princeton University Press, 1988), 2:155−81. On Burckhardt's "secularism," see Timothy Verdon, "Christianity, the Renaissance, and the Study of History: Environments of Experience and Imagination," in *Christianity and the Renaissance: Image and Religious Imagination in the Quattrocento*, ed. T. Verdon and J. Handerson (Syracuse: Syracuse University Press, 1990), 1−2.

64. Johan Huizinga, "The Problem of the Renaissance," In his *Men and Ideas*, trans. J. H. Holmes and H. van Marle (New York: Meridian Books, 1959), 256. See also Kaegi's discussion in *Jacob Burckhardt*, 3:689.

65. Burckhardt's affection for Alberti as a mythmaker—primarily of himself—is evident in his sumptuous description of his character in *The Civilization of the Renaissance*, 74. On Burckhardt's admiration for Alberti, see also Kaegi, *Jacob Burckhardt*, 3:657−58; and Michael Ann Holly, "Burckhardt and the Ideology of the Past," *History of the Human Sciences* 1 (1988): 47−73, where she argues convincingly that Burckhardt in fact designed his *Civilization of the Renaissance in Italy* according to the aesthetic principles of Alberti's treatise *On Painting* (1435).

66. Eugenio Garin, *Science and Civic Life in the Italian Renaissance*, trans. P. Munz (Garden City, N.Y.: Anchor Books, 1969), 6−7.

67. Burckhardt to von Preen, 27 September 1870, *The Letters of Jacob Burckhardt*, 144; Burckhardt, *Reflections on History*, 107.

68. Eric Heller, "Burckhardt and Nietzsche," in his *Disinherited Mind* (New York: Meridian Books, 1959), 76−80.

69. Arthur Schopenhauer, *Ein Lesebuch*, ed. A. Hübscher (Wiesbaden: Brockhaus, 1980), 168.

70. Hayden White, *Metahistory: The Historical Imagination in Nineteenth-Century Europe* (Baltimore: Johns Hopkins University Press, 1973), 242.

71. Nikolaus Meier, "'Aber ist es nicht eine herrliche Sache, für ein Volk zu meisseln, daß auch das Künste für wirklich hält?' Zum Italienerlebnis Jacob Burckhardts," in *Jacob Burckhardt und Rom*, ed. H-M. von Kaenel (Zurich: Schweizerisches Institut in Rom, 1988), 33–56.

72. Burckhardt, *The Civilization of the Renaissance in Italy*, 48.

73. Ibid., 3.

74. Ibid., 12. On Burckhardt's sources for this story, see Peter Ganz, "Jacob Burckhardts *Kultur der Renaissance in Italien:* Handwerk und Methode," in Guggisberg, *Umgang mit Jacob Burckhardt*, 70–71.

75. Gilbert, *History*, 89.

76. Burckhardt, *The Civilization of the Renaissance in Italy*, 16.

77. Ibid., 17–18.

78. Eugenio Garin, introduction to the Italian translation of Burckhardt's masterpiece, *La Civiltà del Rinascimento in Italia* (Florence: G. C. Sassoni, 1955).

79. F. R. Ankersmitt, *Narrative Logic: A Semantic Analysis of the Historian's Language* (The Hague: M. Nijhoff, 1983).

80. William Bouwsma, "The Renaissance and the Drama of Western History," *American Historical Review* 94 (1979): 1–15, quotation on 8.

81. Burckhardt, *The Civilization of the Renaissance in Italy*, 42.

82. Ibid., 173.

83. Burckhardt to von Preen, 31 December 1870, *The Letters of Jacob Burckhardt*, 146. Burckhardt's preference for cultural history over political history has received much attention and many interpretations. The best intellectual reconstruction of his decision to adopt this view is Gossman, *Basel in the Age of Burckhardt*, 251–64. For a philosophical discussion of its meaning, see Karl Löwith, *Jacob Burckhardt: Der Mensch inmitten der Geschichte*, in *Sämtliche Schriften* (Stuttgart: J. B. Metzler, 1984), 7:44–90, 197–205.

84. Jacob Burckhardt, The Greeks and Greek Civilization, ed. O. Murray, trans. S. Stern (London: HarperCollins, 1998), 5. This is a partial translation of Griechische Kulturgeschichte.

85. Ibid., 6.

86. Jacob Burckhardt, "The Great Men of History," in *Reflections on History*, 290–91.

87. Translation by Alexander Dru in his introduction to *The Letters of Jacob Burckhardt*, 23.

88. Löwith, *Jacob Burckhardt*, 44–90; Edgar Salin, *Jacob Burckhardt und Nietzsche* (Heidelberg: L. Schneider, 1948); Heller, "Burckhardt and Nietzsche," 66–88.

89. Heller, "Burckhardt and Nietzsche," 80.

90. Burckhardt, *The Greeks and Greek Civilization*, 37.

91. Friedrich Nietzsche, "We Philologists," trans. J. M. Kennedy, in *The Complete Works of Friedrich Nietzsche*, ed. O. Levi (New York: Russell and Russell, 1964), 8:170.

92. Friedrich Nietzsche, *On the Utility and Liability of History for Life*, trans. R. T. Gray (Palo Alto, Calif.: Stanford University Press, 1995), 88.

93. Ibid., 116–19.

94. Ibid., 102–3.

95. Burckhardt, *The Age of Constantine the Great*, 124–62.

96. Ibid., 185.

97. Ibid., 190.

98. Jean Seznec, *The Survival of the Pagan Gods: The Mythological Tradition and Its Place in Renaissance and Art*, trans. B. F. Sessions (Princeton, N.J.: Princeton University Press, 1953), 3.

99. Burckhardt, *The Age of Constantine the Great*, 237.

100. Ibid., 240-42.

101. Ibid., 242-43, 312-13.

102. Burckhardt, *The Civilization of the Renaissance in Italy*, 292.

103. Friedrich Nietzsche, "The Antichrist," trans. A. M. Ludovici, in *Complete Works*, 16:228.

104. Friedrich Nietzsche, *Nietzsches Briefe*, in *Kritische Gesamtausgabe*, ed. G. Colli und M. Montinari (Berlin, 1977), sec. 2, 1:293-94. For a more objective evaluation, see Salin, *Jacob Burckhardt und Nietzsche*, 96-106; Kaegi, *Jacob Burckhardt*, 7:36-37.

105. Friedrich Nietzsche, *Twilight of the Idols*, trans. R. J. Hollingdale (Harmondsworth: Penguin, 1968), 108.

106. Burckhardt to Ludwig von Pastor, 13 January 1896, *The Letters of Jacob Burckhardt*, 235.

107. Burckhardt, *The Greeks and Greek Civilization*, 271.

108. Kaegi, *Jacob Burckhardt*, 7:81.

109. On Burckhardt's antiromantic conception of mythology, see Heinrich Knittermeyer, *Jacob Burckhardt: Deutung und Berufung des abendländischen Menschen* (Stuttgart: S. Hirzel, 1949), 85-86.

110. Burckhardt to von Preen, 31 December 1872, *The Letters of Jacob Burckhardt*, 157.

111. Burckhardt, *The Civilization of the Renaissance in Italy*, 167.

112. Burckhardt, *The Greeks and Greek Civilization*, 12.

113. Jacob Burckhardt, *Recollections of Rubens*, trans. Mary Hottinger (London: Phaidon Press, 1950), 23-24.

114. Julius Langbehn, *Rembrandt als Erzieher* (Leipzig: C. L. Hirschfeld, 1890).

115. Burckhardt, *Recollections of Rubens*, 116.

116. Ibid., 157.

117. Burckhardt to Wilhelm Vischer, 14 June 1863, *Briefe*, 4:130.

118. Kaegi, *Jacob Burckhardt*, 3:383-95.

119. Burckhardt, *The Civilization of the Renaissance in Italy*, 3.

120. Ibid., 124-25.

121. Ibid., 45-46.

122. Burckhardt to von Preen, 31 December 1870, *The Letters of Jacob Burckhardt*, 146.

123. Burckhardt to von Preen, 23 December 1871, Ibid., 149.

124. Burckhardt, *The Greeks and Greek Civilization*, 5.

125. Burckhardt, *Griechische Kulturgeschichte*, 9:59.

126. Ibid., 10:297.

127. Ibid., 10:283.

128. Burckhardt, *The Greeks and Greek Civilization*, 87.

129. Burckhardt, *Griechische Kulturgeschihcte*, 10:399-400.

130. Friedrich Nietzsche, *The Birth of Tragedy*, trans. W. Kaufmann (New York: Vintage Books, 1967), 135; Burckhardt, *The Greeks and Greek Civilization*, 28.

131. Löwith, *Jacob Burckhardt*, 279.

132. Burckhardt, *The Civilization of the Renaissance in Italy*, 290.

133. Burckhardt, *The Greeks and Greek Civilization*, 37.

134. Ibid., 35–6.

135. Ibid., 7.

136. Significantly, the classical scholar who revived the modernistic interpretations of Pausanias was Sir James Frazer, whose work as a translator and commentator of Pausanias's *Description of Greece* is inspired by the same recognition of myth he previously employed in *The Golden Bough*. For full information and elaboration, see Robert Ackerman, *J. G. Frazer: His life and Work* (Cambridge: Cambridge University Press, 1987), 127–42.

137. Pausanias, *Description of Greece*, trans. W. H. S. Jones (Cambridge, Mass.: Harvard University Press, 1918), 8.3.

138. Ibid., 8.33.

139. Burckhardt to Karl Fresenius, 9 June 1842, *The Letters of Jacob Burckhardt*, 74.

140. Niklaus Röthlin, "Burckhardts Stellung in der Kulturgeschichtsschreibung des 19. Jahrhunderts," in Guggisberg, *Umgang mit Jacob Burckhardt*, 117–34.

141. Meinecke, "Ranke and Burckhardt," 141–56. For a critical evaluation of this essay in Meinecke's life and works, see J. L. Herkless, "Meinecke and the Ranke-Burckhardt Problem," in *History and Theory* 9 (1970): 290–321.

142. For a recent assessment of Burckhardt's legacy in German cultural historiography, see the discussions in *Kulturgeschichte Heute*, ed. W. Hardtwig and H. U. Wehler (Göttingen: Vandenhoeck und Ruprecht, 1996).

143. Meinecke, "Ranke and Burckhardt," 142.

144. Friedrich Meinecke, "Jacob Burckhardt, die deutsche Geschichtsschreibung und der nationale Staat," *Historische Zeitschrift* 97 (1906): 557–62.

145. See the general discussion in Robert A. Pois, *Friedrich Meinecke and German Politics in the Twentieth Century* (Berkeley: University of California Press, 1972), 49–85.

146. Friedrich Meinecke, *The German Catastrophe* (1946), trans. S. B. Fay (Cambridge, Mass.: Harvard University Press, 1950), 1–2, 107–11.

147. Meinecke, "Ranke and Burckhardt," 143.

148. Ibid., 144.

149. Ibid., 154.

150. Aby Warburg, "Sandro Botticelli's *Birth of Venus* and *Spring*: An Examination of Concepts of Antiquity in the Italian Early Renaissance" (1893), in his *Renewal of Pagan Antiquity: Contributions to the Cultural History of the Renaissance*, ed. K. Forster, trans. D. Britt (Los Angeles, Calif.: Getty Research Institute for the History of Art and the Humanities, 1999), 89–156, 405–30.

151. Ibid., 125.

152. Werner Kaegi, "Das Werk Aby Warburgs: Mit einem unveröffentlichen Brief Jacob Burckhardts," *Neue Schweitzer Rundschau* 1 (1933): 283–93.

153. Aby Warburg, "The Art of Portraiture and the Florentine Bourgeoisie," in Warburg, *The Renewal of Pagan Antiquity*, 186.

CHAPTER FOUR

1. The main study of Aby Warburg's life and work is Ernst Gombrich's *Aby Warburg: An Intellectual Biography* (London: Warburg Institute, 1970). Bristling with enormous erudition and brilliant illuminations, this book is the pivotal study for our times, all the more so because it is still the source for Warburg's unpublished writings. Gombrich's documentation of Warburg's life and writings has been invaluable, but his interpretation of these sources remains disputable. For critical reactions and counterinterpretations, see the review essay of Edgar Wind, "On a Recent Biography of Warburg," in Edgar Wind, *The Eloquence of Symbols: Studies in Humanist Art*, ed. J. Anderson (Oxford: Oxford University Press, 1983), 106−13; Felix Gilbert, "From Art History to the History of Civilization: Gombrich's Biography of Aby Warburg," *Journal of Modern History* 44 (1972): 381−91; and Hans Liebeschütz, "Aby Warburg (1866−1929) as Interpreter of Civilization," in *Year Book of the Leo Baeck Institute* 10 (1971): 225−36. They all criticize Gombrich's reluctance to deal with Warburg's illness. For a moving eyewitness account of this traumatic episode, see Carl Georg Heise, *Persönliche Erinnerungen an Aby Warburg* (New York: n.p., 1947), 44−59. For a careful examination of Warburg's ordeal during and after the war, see Karl Königseder, "Aby Warburg im 'Bellevue,'" in *Aby M. Warburg: "Ekstatische Nymphe . . . trauernder Flußgott": Portrait eines Gelehrten*, ed. R. Galitz and B. Reimers (Hamburg: Dölling und Galitz, 1995), 74−98. Additional (and somewhat sensational) information is supplied by Ron Chernow, *The Warburgs: The Twentieth-Century Odyssey of a Remarkable Jewish Family* (New York: Random House, 1993), 191−206, 255−65.

2. Paul de Man, "Ludwig Binswanger and the Sublimation of the Self," in his *Blindness and Insight* (Minneapolis: University of Minnesota Press, 1983), 36−50.

3. Aby Warburg, *Images from the Region of the Pueblo Indians of North America*, trans. M. P. Steinberg (Ithaca, N.Y.: Cornell University Press, 1995). The photographs are reprinted and annotated in *Photographs at the Frontier: Aby Warburg in America, 1895−1896*, ed. B. Cestelli and N. Mann (London: Merrell Holberton, 1998). See also the interpretive essay of Ulrich Raulff in his edition of that work: *Schlangenritual: Ein Reisebericht (Bilder aus dem Gebiet der Pueblo-Indianer in Nord Amerika)* (Berlin: K. Wagenbach, 1988), 63−94.

4. Warburg, *Images from the Region of the Pueblo Indians*, 16.

5. Hans Blumenberg, *Work on Myth*, trans. R. M. Wallace (Cambridge, Mass.: MIT Press, 1985), 8.

6. Quoted by Gombrich, *Aby Warburg*, 222.

7. Ibid., 222−23.

8. Warburg, *Images from the Region of the Pueblo Indians*, 38−49.

9. On Warburg's attempt to retrieve the "animalistic" in human life and history, see the perceptive observations of Salvatore Settis, "Pathos und Ethos: Morphologie und Funktion," in *Vorträge aus dem Warburg-Haus*, ed. W. Kemp (Hamburg: Akademie Verlag, 1997), 1:31−73.

10. Warburg, *Images from the Region of the Pueblo Indians*, 53.

11. For a precise reconstruction of Warburg's journey, see Claudia Naber, "Pompei in Neu-Mexico: Aby Warburgs amerikanische Reise," in *Freibeuter* 38 (1988): 88−97.

12. Warburg, *Images from the Region of the Pueblo Indians*, 38.

13. Quoted by Gombrich, *Aby Warburg*, 226.

14. Aby Warburg, "Pagan-Antique Prophecy in Words and Images in the Age of Luther" (1920), in Aby Warburg, *The Renewal of Pagan Antiquity: Contributions to the Cultural History of the Renaissance*, ed. K. Forster, trans. D. Britt (Los Angeles, Calif.: Getty Research Institute for the History of Art and the Humanities, 1999), 599.

15. Ibid.

16. Warburg, *Images from the Region of the Pueblo Indians*, 1−2.

17. Quoted by Michael P. Steinberg, "Aby Warburg's Kreuzlingen Lecture: A Reading," in Warburg, *Images from the Region of the Pueblo Indians*, 66.

18. Fritz Saxl, "Warburg's Visit to New Mexico," in his *Lectures* (London: Warburg Institute, 1957), 1:325−30. On Warburg's contribution to modern anthropological history, see Peter Burke, "Aby Warburg as a Historical Anthropologist," in *Aby Warburg: Akten des internationalen Symposiums*, ed. H. Bredekamp, M. Diers, and C. Schoell-Glass (Weinheim: VCH, 1991), 39−44.

19. Warburg, *Images from the Region of the Pueblo Indians*, 17.

20. Edgar Wind, "Warburg's Concept of *Kulturwissenschaft* and Its Meaning for Aesthetics" (1930), in Wind, *The Eloquence of Symbols*, 21−35.

21. Wind, "Warburg's Concept of *Kulturwissenschaft*," 28.

22. Friedrich Nietzsche, *The Birth of Tragedy*, trans. W. Kaufmann (New York: Viking Press, 1967), 50.

23. Quoted by Gombrich, *Aby Warburg*, 288.

24. Kurt W. Forster, "Aby Warburg's History of Art: Collective Memory and the Social Mediation of Images," *Daedalus* 105 (1976): 170.

25. Quoted by Gombrich, *Aby Warburg*, 303.

26. For a reproduction and discussion of Warburg's lecture, see Bernd Roeck, "Aby Warburgs Seminarübungen über Jacob Burckhardt," *Idea: Jahrbuch der Hamburger Kunsthalle* 10 (1991): 65−89.

27. Quoted by Gombrich, *Aby Warburg*, 254.

28. Quoted by Steinberg, "Aby Warburg's Kreuzlingen Lecture," 74.

29. Quoted by Gertrud Bing, "Aby M. Warburg," in *Ausgewählte Schriften und Würdigungen*, by Aby Warburg, ed. D. Wuttke (Baden-Baden: V. Koerner, 1979), 464.

30. Charles Taylor, *Sources of the Self: The Making of Modern Identity* (Cambridge, Mass.: Harvard University Press, 1989).

31. See the works of Chernow, Liebeschütz, and Steinberg mentioned above. See also Charlotte Schoell-Glass, "Aby Warburg: Forced Identity and 'Cultural Science,'" in *Jewish Identity and Art History*, ed. C. M. Soussloff (Berkeley: University of California Press, 1999), 218−30; and, more generally, Bernd Roeck, *Der junge Aby Warburg* (Munich: Beck, 1997).

32. Anne Marie Meyer, "Aby Warburg in His Early Correspondence," *American Scholar* 57 (1988): 445−52.

33. Ibid., 451−52.

34. Aby Warburg to Anna Warburg, 18 November 1917, quoted by Chernow, *The Warburgs*, 195.

35. Heise, *Persönliche Erinnerungen an Aby Warburg*, 51.

36. Gilbert, "From Art History to the History of Civilization," 390.

37. Meyer, "Aby Warburg in His Early Correspondence," 452.

320 : NOTES TO PAGES 145 – 149

38. Liebeschütz, "Aby Warburg (1866–1929) as Interpreter of Civilization," 230.

39. See the letter in Claudia Naber, "'Heuernte bei Gewitter': Aby Warburg 1924–1929," in Galitz and Reimers, Aby M. Warburg, 125. See also the testimony of Ernst Cassirer, "Worte zum Beisetzung von Professor Dr. Aby M. Warburg," reprinted in Mnemosyne: Beiträge zum 50. Todestag von Aby M. Warburg, ed. S. Füssel (Göttingen: Gratia Verlag, 1979), 19–26. Significantly, it fell to another great scholar at the Warburg Institute, Frances Yates, to achieve that task in her Giordano Bruno and the Hermetic Tradition (Chicago: University of Chicago Press, 1964).

40. Aby Warburg, "The Art of Portraiture and the Florentine Bourgeoisie: Domenico Ghirlandaio in Santa Trinita: The Portraits of Lorenzo de' Medici and His Household" (1902), in Warburg, The Renewal of Pagan Antiquity, 190.

41. Steinberg, "Aby Warburg's Kreuzlingen Lecture," 76–87.

42. Michael Brenner, The Renaissance of Jewish Culture in Weimar Germany (New Haven, Conn.: Yale University Press, 1996).

43. Charlotte Schoell-Glass, Aby Warburg und der Antisemitismus: Kulturwissenschaft als Geistespolitik (Frankfurt am Main: Fischer, 1998).

44. George Mosse, German Jews beyond Judaism (Bloomington: Indiana University Press, 1985), 47.

45. Peter Gay, Weimar Culture: The Outsider as Insider (New York: Harper and Row, 1970).

46. Schoell-Glass, Aby Warburg und der Antisemitismus, 65. See also Heinrich Dilly, "Sokrates im Hamburg: Aby Warburg und seine Kulturwissenschaftliche Bibliothek," in Bredekamp, Diers, and Schoell-Glass, Aby Warburg: Akten des internationalen Symposiums, 125–40.

47. Quoted by Gombrich, Aby Warburg, 151–52.

48. Gombrich, Aby Warburg, 152.

49. Quoted by Gombrich, Aby Warburg, 153.

50. Gombrich, Aby Warburg, 130–31.

51. Fritz Schumacher, "Kämpfe um die Hamburgische Universität," in Selbstgespräche: Erinnerungen und Betrachtungen (Hamburg: A. Springer, 1949), 91–101.

52. Fritz Saxl, "The History of Warburg's Library (1886–1944)," in Gombrich, Aby Warburg, 329, 332, 334.

53. This description is based on Edgar Wind, "The Warburg Institute Classification Scheme," in Library Association Record 2, no. 4 (1930): 193–95. The current literature on the Warburg Library in Hamburg is vast. On the conception and construction of the institution, see the fundamental statements of Fritz Saxl, "Die Bibliothek Warburg und ihr Ziel," in Vorträge der Bibliothek Warburg 1921–2, ed. F. Saxl (Leipzig: B. G. Teubner, 1923), 1–10. For more comprehensive studies, see Martin Jesinghausen-Lauster, Die Suche nach der symbolishen Form: Der Kreis um die Kulturwissenschaftliche Bibliothek Warburg (Baden-Baden: V. Koerner, 1985); and Tilman von Stockhausen, Die Kulturwissenschaftliche Bibliothek: Architektur, Einrichtung und Organization (Hamburg: V. Koerner, 1992).

54. For an inspired description of the Warburg Library, see Salvatore Settis, "Warburg continuatus: Description d'une bibliothèque," in Le pouvoir des bibliothéques: La mémoire des livres en Occident, ed. M. Baratin and C. Jacob (Paris: A. Michel, 1996), 122–73.

55. On Warburg's activities during the last years of his life, see Naber, "'Heuernte bei Gewitter,'" 104–29.

56. Wolfgang Kemp, "Walter Benjamin und Aby Warburg," *Kritische Berichte* 3 (1975): 3–25.

57. Fritz Saxl, "Ernst Cassirer," in *The Philosophy of Ernst Cassirer,* ed. P. A. Schilpp (Evanston, Ill.: Library of Living Philosophers, 1949), 49. See also Ulrich Raulff, "Von der Privatbibliothek des Gelehrten zum Forschungsinstitut: Aby Warburg, Ernst Cassirer, und die neue Kulturwissenschaft," *Geschichte und Gesellschaft* 23 (1997): 28–43. On the philosophical association between Warburg and Cassirer, see Jürgen Habermas, "Die befreiende Kraft der symbolischen Formgebung: Ernst Cassirers humanistisches Erbe und die Bibliothek Warburg," in *Ernst Cassirers Werk und Wirkung: Kultur und Philosophie,* eds. D. Frede and R. Schmücker (Darmstadt: Wissenschaftliche Buchgesellschaft, 1997), 79–104.

58. Ernst Cassirer, *Die Begriffsform im mythischen Denken,* Studien der Bibliothek Warburg, vol. 1 (Leipzig: B. G. Teubner, 1922).

59. Ernst Cassirer, *The Philosophy of Symbolic Forms,* vol. 2, *Mythical Thought* (1924–25), trans. R. Manheim (New Haven, Conn.: Yale University Press, 1955), xviii.

60. Ernst Cassirer, *The Individual and the Cosmos in Renaissance Philosophy* (1926), trans. M. Domandi (New York: Harper and Row, 1963), xiii.

61. Paul Tillich, "Renaissance und Reformation: Zur Einführung in die Bibliothek Warburg" (1922), in *Gesammelte Werke,* by Paul Tillich, ed. R. Albrecht (Stuttgart: Evangelisches Verlagswerk, 1972), 13:137–40. For additional information, see Roland Kany, *Die religionsgeschichtliche Forschung an der Kulturwissenschaftlichen Bibliothek Warburg* (Bamberg: S. Wendel, 1989).

62. Ernst Cassirer, "Giovanni Pico della Mirandola," in *Renaissance Essays,* ed. P. O. Kristeller and P. P. Wiener (New York: Harper and Row, 1968), 11–60.

63. Horst Günther, "D'anima Fiorentino," in Galitz and Reimers, *Aby Warburg,* 36.

64. Warburg, "The Art of Portraiture and the Florentine Bourgeoisie," 187.

65. Quoted by Gombrich, *Aby Warburg,* 134.

66. Aby Warburg to Paul Warburg, 4 January 1904, quoted by Gombrich, *Aby Warburg,* 155–56.

67. Warburg, "The Art of Portraiture and the Florentine Bourgeoisie," 200.

68. Jacob Burckhardt, *The Civilization of the Renaissance in Italy,* trans. S. G. C. Middlemore (Vienna: Phaidon Press, n.d.), 70.

69. Warburg, "The Art of Portraiture and the Florentine Bourgeoisie," 191.

70. Ibid., 203.

71. Aby Warburg, "Francesco Sassetti's Last Injunctions to His Sons" (1907), in Warburg, *The Renewal of Pagan Antiquity,* 223–62.

72. On the emergence of this "modernistic" conception of man, see the following classic books: H. Stuart Hughes, *Consciousness and Society: The Reorientation of European Social Thought, 1890–1930* (New York: Vintage Books, 1930); Carl E. Schorske, *Fin-de-siècle Vienna: Politics and Culture* (New York: Vintage Books, 1981); Stephen Kern, *The Culture of Time and Space, 1880–1918* (Cambridge, Mass.: Harvard University Press, 1983).

73. Quoted by Gombrich, *Aby Warburg,* 142–43.

74. Johan Huizinga, "The Problem of the Renaissance," in his *Men and Ideas*, trans. J. S. Holmes and H. van Marle (New York: Meridian Books, 1959), 259-60.

75. Gombrich, *Aby Warburg*, 142.

76. Ibid., 118.

77. Henry Thode, *Franz von Assisi und die Anfänge der Kunst der Renaissance* (Leipzig: G. Grote, 1885).

78. Quoted by Gombrich, *Aby Warburg*, 111.

79. Burckhardt, *The Civilization of the Renaissance in Italy*, 89.

80. Burckhardt to Friedrich Salomon Vögelin, 17 September 1866, *Briefe*, ed. M. Burckhardt, 10 vols. (Basel: Schwabe, 1949-94), 4:227. Burckhardt's quoted phrase, "my mind drained away," is from Bellini's opera *Norma*.

81. Saxl, "Warburg's Visit to New Mexico," 327.

82. Quoted by Gombrich, *Aby Warburg*, 130.

83. Aby Warburg, "The Art of Portraiture and the Florentine Bourgeoisie," 186.

84. Gertrud Bing, "Aby M. Warburg," *Journal of the Warburg and Courtland Institutes* 28 (1965): 304-5.

85. Ibid., 305.

86. Aby Warburg, "Sandro Botticelli's *Birth of Venus* and *Spring*: An Examination of Concepts of Antiquity in the Italian Early Renaissance" (1893), in Warburg, *The Renewal of Pagan Antiquity*, 89-156, 405-30.

87. Ibid., 89.

88. Ibid., 117. For a thorough discussion of Warburg's opposition to Winckelmann's conception of the "classical," see Silvia Ferretti, *Cassirer, Panofsky, and Warburg: Symbol, Art, and History*, trans. R. Price (New Haven, Conn.: Yale University Press, 1989).

89. Ernst H. Gombrich, "Botticelli's Mythologies: A Study in Neoplatonic Symbolism of His Circle," in his *Symbolic Images: Studies in the Art of the Renaissance* (London: Phaidon Press, 1972), 37.

90. Charles Dempsey, *The Portrayal of Love: Botticelli's Primavera and Humanist Culture at the Time of Lorenzo the Magnificent* (Princeton, N.J.: Princeton University Press, 1992), 123-24.

91. For reassertions of this opposition, see, e.g., Aby Warburg, "The Gods of Antiquity and the Early Renaissance in Southern and Northern Europe" (1908); and Aby Warburg, "Pagan-Antique Prophecy in Words and Images in the Age of Luther" (1920), both in Warburg, *The Renewal of Pagan Antiquity*, 559, 598.

92. Warburg, "Sandro Botticelli's *Birth of Venus* and *Spring*," 141.

93. Friedrich Nietzsche, "The Antichrist," trans. A. M. Ludovici, in *The Complete Works of Friedrich Nietzsche*, ed. O. Levi (New York: Russell and Russell, 1964), 16:228.

94. Translation by Alexander Dru in his introduction to Jacob Burckhardt, *The Letters of Jacob Burckhardt*, ed. and trans. A. Dru (London: Routledge and Kegan Paul, 1955), 23.

95. Quoted by Gombrich, *Aby Warburg*, 255.

96. Ibid., 111.

97. Ibid., 184-85. For a critical discussion of the rationalistic interpretation imposed on Warburg's Nietzschean tendencies by Gombrich (and Panofsky), see Margaret Iversen, "Retrieving Warburg's Tradition," *Art History* 16, no. 4 (1993): 541-53.

98. Quoted by Kurt W. Forster, introduction to Warburg, *The Renewal of Pagan Antiquity*, 7.

99. Forster, introduction to Warburg, *The Renewal of Pagan Antiquity*, 55.

100. Helmut Pfotenheimer, "Das Nachleben der Antike: Aby Warburgs Auseinandersetzung mit Nietzsche," *Nietzsche-Studien* 14 (1985): 298–313.

101. Quoted by Gombrich, *Aby Warburg*, 113.

102. Ibid., 123.

103. Ibid., 124.

104. Warburg, "Francesco Sassetti's Last Injunctions to His Sons," 240, 242.

105. Ibid., 241.

106. Quoted by Gombrich, *Aby Warburg*, 190–91.

107. Gombrich, *Aby Warburg*, 247–49.

108. Quoted by Gombrich, *Aby Warburg*, 249.

109. Quoted by Gombrich, *Aby Warburg*, 137.

110. Ibid., 188.

111. Gombrich, *Aby Warburg*, 190–91.

112. Chernow, *The Warburgs*, 120.

113. Jay Winter, *Sites of Memory, Sites of Mourning: The Great War in European Cultural History* (Cambridge: Cambridge University Press, 1995).

114. William S. Heckscher, "The Genesis of Iconology," in *Stil und Überlieferung in der Kunst des Abendlandes* (Akten des XXI. Internationalen Kongress für Kunstgeschichte in Bonn, 1964) (Berlin: Gebr. Mann, 1967), 249–50.

115. Cassirer, "Worte zum Beisetzung von Professor Dr. Aby M. Warburg," 19.

116. Gombrich, *Aby Warburg*, 215.

117. Ibid., 9–10.

118. Wind, "On a Recent Biography of Warburg," 110.

119. The question whether, and to what extent, Warburg may rightly be called the founder of "iconology" has been much debated. Gombrich denies him that right, *Aby Warburg*, 313. Jan Białostocki upholds it, in "Iconography and Iconology," *Encyclopedia of World Art* (New York, 1963), 7:769–85. Michael Ann Holly regards Warburg as one of several rediscoverers of iconology in "Unwriting Iconology," in *Iconography at the Crossroads*, ed. B. Cassidy (Princeton, N.J.: Princeton University Press, 1993), 17–25. For a general discussion, see the anthology of essays *Iconographie und Iconology: Theorien, Entwicklung, Probleme*, ed. E. Kaemmerling (Cologne: DuMont, 1979).

120. Heckscher, "The Genesis of Iconology," 240.

121. Aby Warburg, "Italian Art and International Astrology in the Palazzo Schifanoia, Ferrara" (1912), in Warburg, *The Renewal of Pagan Antiquity*, 565.

122. Warburg, "Pagan-Antique Prophecy in Words and Images," 618–19.

123. Aby Warburg, "Italian Art and International Astrology," 586.

124. Ibid.

125. Ibid., 585.

126. Warburg does not refer to Vico in his published writings, but, as Roland Kany points out, he must certainly have become familiar with his work while attending Usener's *Vorlesung über Mythologie* in Bonn in the winter of 1886. Roland Kany, *Mnemosyne als*

Programm: Geschichte, Erinnerung und die Andacht zum Unbedeutenden im Werk von Usener, Warburg und Benjamin (Tübingen: Max Niemeyer, 1987), 72. On Usener's recommendation, Warburg then read Tito Vignoli's *Wissenschaft und Mythos,* which deals extensively with Vico's theory of myth. Some scholars have traced Warburg's "psychological history of human expression" to Vico's linguistic theory. Heckscher, "The Genesis of Iconology," 259; Matthew Rampley, "From Symbol to Allegory: Aby Warburg's Theory of Art," *Art Bulletin* 69 (1997): 50, 55.

127. Warburg, "Pagan-Antique Prophecy in Words and Images," 598, 599.

128. Gilbert, "From Art History to the History of Civilization," 385.

129. Steinberg, "Aby Warburg's Kreuzlingen Lecture," 67−68.

130. Salvatore Settis, "Kunstgeschichte als vergleichende Kulturwissenschaft: Aby Warburg, die Pueblo-Indianer und das Nachleben der Antike," in *Künstlerischer Austausch,* ed. T. W. Gaethgens (Berlin: Akademie Verlag, 1993), 1 : 139−58.

131. Quoted by Gombrich, *Aby Warburg,* 88−89.

132. For a comprehensive discussion, see Gombrich, *Aby Warburg,* 239−54. On Warburg's social theory and history of art, see also the important observations of Carlo Ginzburg, "From Aby Warburg to E. H. Gombrich," in his *Myths, Emblems, Clues,* trans. J. Tedeschi and A. Tedeschi (Baltimore: Johns Hopkins University Press, 1990), 17−59; and Martin Warnke, "Der Leidenschatz der Menschheit wird humaner Besitz," in *Die Menschenrechte des Auges,* ed. W. Hofmann, G. Syamken, M. Warnke (Frankfurt am Main: Europäische Verlagsanstalt, 1980), 113−86.

133. Quoted by Gombrich, *Aby Warburg,* 248.

134. Ibid., 250.

135. On this project, see Aby Warburg, "Einleitung zum Mnemosyne-Atlas," in *Die Beredsamkeit des Leibes: Zur Körpersprache in der Kunst,* ed. I. Barta Fliedl and C. Geissner (Salzburg: Residenz Verlag, 1992), 171−73; the discussions in Gombrich, *Aby Warburg,* 283−306; and Peter van Huisstede, "Der Mnemosyne-Atlas: Ein Laboratorium der Bildgeschichte," in Galitz and Reimers, *Aby Warburg,* 130−71.

136. Rampley, "From Symbol to Allegory," 53.

137. See the discussion in Gombrich, *Aby Warburg,* 235−38.

138. Quoted by Gombrich, *Aby Warburg,* 238.

139. The full text of Warburg's lecture is appended to Roeck's essay "Aby Warburgs Seminarübungen über Jacob Burckhardt," 86−89. I use it to augment Gombrich's incomplete translation in *Aby Warburg,* 254−58.

140. Goethe, *Faust,* trans. W. H. Bruford (London: J. M. Dent, 1954), part 2, act 5, sc. 4, p. 391.

141. Quoted by Gombrich, *Aby Warburg,* 254−55.

142. Ibid., 256.

143. Quoted by Roeck, "Aby Warburgs Seminarübungen über Jacob Burckhardt," 87.

144. Quoted by Gombrich, *Aby Warburg,* 257.

145. Ibid., 258.

146. Ibid., 257−58.

147. Quoted by Kany, *Mnemosyne als Programm,* 185.

148. Quoted by Gombrich, *Aby Warburg,* 258.

149. Cassirer, *The Philosophy of Symbolic Forms*, vol. 2, *Mythical Thought*, 147–48. For a thorough examination of the origins and ramifications of *Gelehrtenpolitik*, see Fritz Ringer, *The Decline of the German Mandarins* (Cambridge, Mass.: Harvard University Press, 1969).

150. Charlotte Schoell-Glass, "Aby Warburg's Late Comments on Symbol and Ritual," *Science in Context* 12 (1999): 621–42.

151. Quoted by Gombrich, *Aby Warburg*, 281.

152. On the political mythology in Italian fascism, see Emilio Gentile, *The Sacralization of Politics in Fascist Italy*, trans. K. Botsford (Cambridge, Mass.: Harvard University Press, 1996).

153. Alfred Rosenberg, *Der Mythus des zwanzigsten Jahrhunderts* (Munich: Hoheneichen, 1930). On Rosenberg's notion of *Mythus*, see the interpretation of his fellow Nazi ideologist Alfred Baeumler, *Alfred Rosenberg und der Mythus des 20. Jahrhunderts* (Munich: Hoheneichen, 1943), 71.

154. Rosenberg, *Der Mythus des zwanzigsten Jahrhunderts*, 700.

CHAPTER FIVE

1. Ernst Cassirer, *The Myth of the State* (New Haven, Conn.: Yale University Press, 1946), 1.

2. Henry Tudor, *Political Myth* (London: Macmillan, 1972), 31–35.

3. Ibid., 35–36.

4. Cassirer, *The Myth of the State*, 286.

5. Ernst Cassirer, *The Philosophy of Symbolic Forms*, vol. 2, *Mythical Thought*, trans. R. Manheim (New Haven, Conn.: Yale University Press, 1955), 147–48.

6. Ernst Cassirer, "Judaism and the Modern Political Myths," in *Contemporary Jewish Records* 7 (1944): 115–26.

7. Although Cassirer does not mention Rosenberg in *The Myth of the State*, the title of part 3 of the book, "The Myth of the Twentieth Century," betrays Cassirer's acute attention to Rosenberg's work.

8. Martin Buber, *On Judaism*, ed. N. N. Glatzer, trans. R. Manheim (New York: Schocken Books, 1967), 95–107. Scholem elaborates his theory in "Kabbalah and Myth," in his *On the Kabbalah and Its Symbolism*, trans. R. Manheim (New York: Schocken Books, 1965), 87–117.

9. See, e.g., the recent studies of Nachman Ben Yehuda, *The Masada Myth: Collective Memory and Mythmaking in Israel* (Madison: University of Wisconsin Press, 1995); and Yael Zerubavel, *Recovered Roots: Collective Memory and the Making of Israeli National Tradition* (Chicago: University of Chicago Press, 1995).

10. On Scholem's theory of myth and its impact on his conception of Jewish religion and history, see David Biale, *Gershom Scholem: Kabbalah and Counter-History* (Cambridge, Mass.: Harvard University Press, 1979).

11. On the intellectual and historical origins of Cassirer's theory of myth, see Ivan Strenski, "Ernst Cassirer's *Mythical Thought* in Weimar Culture," *History of European Ideas* 5 (1984): 363–85.

12. Cassirer, *The Myth of the State*, 296.

13. Ibid. For a full account of Cassirer's political engagement in Weimar Germany, see David P. Lipton, *Ernst Cassirer: The Dilemma of a Liberal Intellectual in Germany, 1914–1933* (Toronto: University of Toronto Press, 1978).

14. Tudor, *Political Myth*, 31.

15. Hans Kohn, review of *The Myth of the State*, by Cassirer, *Commentary* 4 (1947): 80–82.

16. Leo Strauss, review of *The Myth of the State*, by Cassirer, *Social Research* 14 (1947): 125–28.

17. Cassirer, *The Myth of the State*, 282; Cassirer, *The Philosophy of Symbolic Forms*, vol. 2, *Mythical Thought*, 11–12.

18. Peter Gay, "The Social History of Ideas: Ernst Cassirer and After," in *The Critical Spirit: Essays in Honor of Herbert Marcuse*, ed. K. H. Wolff and Barrington Moore Jr. (Boston: Beacon Press, 1967), 106–20.

19. Max Weber, "Science as a Vocation," in *From Max Weber*, by Max Weber, trans. H. H. Gerth and C. Wright Mills (London: Routledge and Kegan Paul, 1974), 155. On Weber's theory of modernity, see Detlef Peukert, *Max Webers Diagnose der Moderne* (Göttingen: Vandenhoeck und Ruprecht, 1989).

20. On Weber and Stefan George, see Wolf Lepenies, *Between Science and Literature*, trans. R. Hollingdale (Cambridge: Cambridge University Press, 1988), 258–96.

21. Weber, "Science as a Vocation," 148–49.

22. The renascence of myth in German historiography between the wars has not yet received the attention it deserves, mainly, it seems, because most of it was brought about by nationalistic ideologists and propagandists and might still be abused by contemporary revisionists. For some recent attempts to reassess the innovative methodology of this conservative ideology, see Willi Oberkrome, *Volksgeschichte: Methodische Innovation und völkische Ideologisierung in der deutschen Geschichtswissenschaft 1918–1945* (Göttingen: Vandenhoeck und Ruprecht, 1993); and Ursula Wolf, *Litteris und Patriae: Das Janusgesicht der Historie* (Stuttgart: F. Steiner, 1996).

23. Karl Löwith, *Mein Leben in Deutschland vor und nach 1933: Ein Bericht* (Stuttgart: J. B. Metzler, 1986), 16–17. See also Marianne Weber, *Max Weber: Ein Lebensbild* (Tübingen: J. C. B. Mohr, 1926), 683.

24. Weber, "Politics as a Vocation," 77–128.

25. Ibid., 125–26.

26. Ibid., 126.

27. Erich von Kahler, *Der Beruf der Wissenschaft* (Berlin: G. Bondi, 1921).

28. Two comprehensive volumes of essays were published on the centennial of Kantorowicz's birth: *Ernst H. Kantorowicz: Erträge der Doppeltagung Institute for Advanced Study, Princeton, Johann Wolfgang Goethe-Universität, Frankfurt*, ed. J. Fried and R. Benson (Stuttgart: F. Steiner, 1997); and *Geschichtskörper: Zur Aktualität von Ernst H. Kantorowicz*, ed. W. Ernst and C. Vismann (Munich: Wilhelm Fink, 1998).

29. Adam S. Labuda, "Ein Posener Itinerar zu Kantorowicz," in Ernst and Vismann, *Geschichtskörper*, 73–91; Eckhart Grünewald, *Ernst Kantorowicz und Stefan George: Beiträge zur Biographie des Historikers bis zum Jahre 1938 und zu seinem Jugendwerk "Kaiser Friedrich der Zweite"* (Wiesbaden: F. Steiner, 1982), 27–30.

30. Ernst H. Kantorowicz, *Kaiser Friedrich der Zweite* (Hauptband, Berlin: G. Bondi,

1927; Ergänzungsband, Berlin: G. Bondi, 1931). I quote from the English translation: *Frederick the Second, 1194-1250*, trans. E. O. Lorimer (London: Constable, 1931).

31. Albert Brackmann, "Kaiser Friedrich der Zweite in 'mythischer Schau,'" *Historische Zeitschrift* 140 (1929): 534-49; Ernst H. Kantorowicz, "'Mythenschau': Eine Erwiderung,'" *Historische Zeitschrift* 141 (1930): 457-71, both reprinted in *Stupor Mundi: Zur Geschichte Friedrich II. von Hohenstaufen*, ed. G. Wolf (Darmstadt: Wissenschaftliche Buchgesellschaft, 1966), 5-40. On the controversy, see Joseph Mali, "Ernst H. Kantorowicz: History as Mythenschau," *History of Political Thought* 18 (1997): 579-603. On the specific meanings of *Mythenschau*, see also the comments of Edgar Salin, "Ernst H. Kantorowicz, 1895-1963," *Historische Zeitschrift* 199 (1964): 551-57; and Yakov Malkiel, "Ernst H. Kantorowicz," *Romance Philology* 18 (1964-65): 6-8.

32. Ernst H. Kantorowicz, *The King's Two Bodies: A Study in Medieval Political Theology* (Princeton, N.J.: Princeton University Press, 1957).

33. On Kantorowicz's life and works in Germany, see Grünewald, *Ernst Kantorowicz und Stefan George*. On Kantorowicz's life and works after his emigration to the United States, see Ralph E. Giesey, "Ernst H. Kantorowicz: Scholarly Triumphs and Academic Travails in Weimar Germany and the United States," *Leo Baeck Institute Year Book* 30 (1985): 191-202; and Robert E. Lerner, "Ernst H. Kantorowicz (1895-1963)," in *Medieval Scholarship: Biographical Studies in the Formation of a Discourse*, vol. 1, *History*, ed. H. Damico and J. B. Zavadil (New York: Garland, 1995), 263-75. Kantorowicz's major essays are reprinted in *Selected Studies*, ed. M. Cherniavsky and R. Giesey (Locust Valley, N.Y.: J. J. Augustin, 1965).

34. Felix Gilbert, *A European Past: Memoires, 1905-1945* (New York: Norton, 1988), 106-7.

35. On the reception of Kantorowicz's work, see Eckhart Grünewald, "'Not Only in Learned Circles': The Reception of *Frederick the Second* in Germany before the Second World War," in Fried and Benson, *Ernst H. Kantorowicz*, 162-79.

36. Eckart Kehr, "Der neue Plutarch: Die 'historische Belletristik,' die Universität und die Demokratie," reprinted in *Der Primat der Innenpolitik: Gesammelte Aufsätze zur preussischdeutschen Sozialgeschichte im 19. und 20. Jahrhundert*, ed. H. U. Wehler (Berlin: de Gruyter, 1965), 269-78. Kehr's targets were Friedrich Gundolf and Emil Ludwig. See, however, the attack on Kantorowicz in Christoph Gradmann, *Historische Belletristik: Populäre historische Biographien in der Weimarer Republik* (Frankfurt am Main: Campus Verlag, 1993), 176-80.

37. Kantorowicz, *Frederick the Second*, 3.

38. Ibid., 5.

39. Ibid., 689.

40. On the pervasive antidemocratic and autocratic tendencies among German historians in the Weimar Republic, see Bernd Faulenbach, *Ideologie des deutschen Weges: Die deutsche Historiographie zwischen Kaiserreich und Nazionalsozialismus* (Munich: Beck, 1980), 248-316.

41. Peter Gay, *Weimar Culture: The Outsider as Insider* (New York: Harper and Row, 1970), 50-51. Norman F. Cantor is even harsher in his judgment of "that wonderful book, the most brilliant and fortunate piece of propaganda that Hitler's cloddish and violent followers could imagine, as Kantorowicz expatiated on 'German world rule and world greatness, resting on the qualities of a single man and not upon the people.'" Norman F. Cantor, *Inventing the Middle Ages: The Lives, Works, and Ideas of the Great Medievalists of the Twentieth Century* (New York: W. Morrow, 1990), 96. In the same virulent vein, Steven

Rowan refers to the book as a "fascist classic." See his "Comment: Otto Brunner," in *Paths of Continuity: Central European Historiography from the 1930s to the 1950s*, ed. H. Lehmann and J. Van Horn Melton (Cambridge: Cambridge University Press, 1994), 296.

42. Kantorowicz to Ursula Küpper, 12 June 1960, in Grünewald, *Ernst Kantorowicz und Stefan George*, 160.

43. Ibid., 164–65. Speidel's words notwithstanding, the figure of Frederick II was not as important for Nazi historiography as those of Friedrich Barbarossa and Karl the Great, who were better suited for the role of "pure" Aryan German emperors. See the interesting comments of Karen Schönwälder, *Historiker und Politik: Geschichtswissenschaft im National-sozialismus* (Frankfurt am Main: Campus Verlag, 1992), 76.

44. Quoted by Grünewald, *Ernst Kantorowicz und Stefan George*, 165.

45. For modern assessments of *Frederick the Second*, see Karl Leyser, "The Emperor Frederick II," in his *Medieval Germany and Its Neighbours* (London: Hambledon Press, 1982), 269–76; David Abulafia, "Kantorowicz and Frederick II," *History* 62 (1977): 193–210. In his book *Frederick II: A Medieval Emperor* (London: Allen Lane, 1988), Abulafia accentuates, against Kantorowicz, the distinctly medieval characteristics of the emperor, but he reaffirms Kantorowicz's book as a modern classic of medieval historiography (441–42).

46. Robert E. Lerner: "Ernst Kantorowicz and Theodor E. Mommsen," in *An Interrupted Past: German-Speaking Historians in the United-States after 1933*, ed. H. Lehmann and J. J. Sheehan (Cambridge: Cambridge University Press, 1991), 197. For similar views, see also Josef Fleckenstein, "Ernst Kantorowicz zum Gedächtnis," *Frankfurter Universitätsreden*, 34 (1964): 11–27.

47. Richard W. Southern, review of *The King's Two Bodies*, by Ernst H. Kantorowicz, *Journal of Ecclesiastical History* 10 (1959): 106.

48. Karl Hampe, "Das neueste Lebensbild Kaiser Friedrich II," *Historische Zeitschrift* 146 (1932): 441–75, quoted from Wolf, *Stupor Mundi*, 70–71. On this problem in Kantorowicz's book, see the illuminating discussion of Walther Lammers, "Bild und Urteil in der Geschichtsschreibung," in his *Vestigia Mediaevlia* (Wiesbaden: F. Steiner, 1977), 109–23.

49. Hampe, "Das neueste Lebensbild Kaiser Friedrich II," in Wolf, *Stupor Mundi*, 67–68.

50. Ibid., 72–73.

51. Kantorowicz, *Frederick the Second*, 202–3.

52. Albert Brackmann, "Kaiser Friedrich II. in 'mythischer Schau,'" in Wolf, *Stupor Mundi*, 7–12.

53. Kantorowicz, *Frederick the Second*, 522. See also Ernst Kantorowicz's essay "Petrus de Vinea in England" (1937), reprinted in Cherniavsky and Giesey, *Selected Studies*, 213–46, where he shows how this first *Kanzler* shaped the rhetorical-political style of all his modern followers.

54. Kantorowicz, *Frederick the Second*, 447.

55. Ernst Kantorowicz, "The Problem of Medieval World Unity" (1942), in Cherniavsky and Giesey, *Selected Studies*, 76–81.

56. Ibid., 78.

57. Kantorowicz, *Frederick the Second*, 668.

58. Cecil M. Bowra, *Memoires, 1898–1939* (Cambridge, Mass.: Harvard University Press, 1967), 294.

59. Kantorowicz, *Frederick the Second*, 245, 669.

60. For a lucid elaboration of this argument, see Marine Valensise, "Ernst Kantorowicz," *Rivista Storica Italiana* 101 (1989): 194–221.

61. Kantorowicz, *Frederick the Second*, 669.

62. Ibid., 443–45.

63. Horst Rüdiger, "Der dritte Humanismus," in *Humanismus*, ed. H. Oppermann (Darmstadt: Wissenschaftliche Buchgesellschaft, 1970), 206–23.

64. Kantorowicz, *Frederick the Second*, 447.

65. Ibid., 444.

66. Percy Ernst Schramm, *Kaiser, Rom und Renovatio: Studien zur Geschichte des romanischen Erneuerungsgedankens vom Ende des karolingischen Reiches bis zum Investiturstreit*, 2 vols. (Leipzig: B. G. Teubner, 1929). On Schramm's life and work, see János Bak, "Percy Ernst Schramm (1894–1970)," in Damico and Zavadil, *Medieval Scholarship*, 247–61.

67. Kantorowicz, *Frederick the Second*, 456.

68. Ibid., 293–368.

69. Ibid., 669.

70. Jacob Burckhardt, *The Civilization of the Renaissance in Italy*, trans. S. G. C. Middlemore (Vienna: Phaidon Press, n.d.), 2.

71. Wallace K. Ferguson, *The Renaissance in Historical Thought* (Cambridge, Mass.: H. Mifflin, 1948), 330–85.

72. Charles H. Haskins, *The Renaissance of the Twelfth Century* (Cambridge, Mass.: Harvard University Press, 1927), v–vi.

73. Kantorowicz, *Frederick the Second*, 160–63, 202–3, 239.

74. *Purgatorio*, 27.139–42 (Singleton's translation). And see the discussion in Charles Davis, "Kantorowicz and Dante," in Fried and Benson, *Ernst H. Kantorowicz*, 240–64.

75. Kantorowicz, *Frederick the Second*, 260.

76. On the conflation of Dante and George in Kantorowicz's life and works, see the fine essay by Kay E. Schiller, "Dante and Kantorowicz: Medieval History as Art and Autobiography," *Annali Italianistica* 8 (1990): 396–411.

77. Karl Hampe, "Das neueste Lebensbild Kaiser Friedrichs II," in Wolf, *Stupor Mundi*, 68–71. Hampe duly mentions the works of Schramm and his fellow scholars at the Warburg Library in Hamburg as pertinent to that new scholarship. Schramm's *Kaiser, Rom und Renovatio* appeared in the series Studien der Bibliothek Warburg. Although as a member of the George *Kreis*, Kantorowicz was rather alien to the Warburg *Kreis*, his *Frederick the Second* exercised a profound impression on its members, as can be gleaned from Fritz Saxl's letter to Hans Meier, quoted by Silvia Ferretti, *Cassirer, Panofsky, and Warburg: Symbol, Art, and History*, trans. R. Pierce (New Haven, Conn.: Yale University Press, 1989), xi. Kantorowicz's association with the Warburg Institute intensified after his emigration from Germany. Between 1939 and 1942, he published two major essays in the *Journal of the Warburg and Courtland Institutes*. During the 1940s he formed a close personal and professional relationship with Erwin Panofsky, who eventually arranged for Kantorowicz's fellowship at the Institute for Advanced Studies in Princeton.

78. Friedrich Nietzsche, *On the Utility and Liability of History for Life*, trans. R. T. Gray (Palo Alto, Calif.: Stanford University Press, 1995), 163. For a perceptive interpretation of Nietzsche's notion of the "suprahistorical," see Peter Berkowitz, *Nietzsche: The Ethics of an Immoralist* (Cambridge, Mass.: Harvard University Press, 1995), 27–32.

79. Friedrich Nietzsche, *The Birth of Tragedy*, trans. W. Kaufmann (New York: Vintage Books, 1967), 42. On Nietzsche's theory of myth, see the excellent essay of Benjamin Bennett, "Nietzsche's Idea of Myth: The Birth of Tragedy out of the Spirit of Eighteenth-Century Aesthetics," *PMLA* 94 (1979): 420–33. See also Allan Megill's discussion in *Prophets of Extremity* (Berkeley: University of California Press, 1985), 65–102.

80. Nietzsche, *The Birth of Tragedy*, 59.

81. Nietzsche, *On the Utility and Liability of History*, 128.

82. Ibid., 129.

83. Ibid., 142.

84. Heinz Raschel, *Das Nietzsche-Bild im George-Kreis: Ein Beitrag zur Geschichte der deutschen Mythologie* (Berlin: de Gruyter, 1984).

85. Steven E. Aschheim, *The Nietzsche Legacy in Germany, 1890–1990* (Berkeley: University of California Press, 1992), 71–84.

86. Friedrich Nietzsche, *Human All Too Human*, trans. R. J. Hollingdale (Cambridge: Cambridge University Press, 1986), 235.

87. Ernst Troeltsch, *Der Historismus und seine Probleme* (Tübingen: J. C. B. Mohr, 1922).

88. Friedrich Gundolf, *George* (Berlin: G. Bondi, 1921), 10. English translation quoted from Lepenies, *Between Science and Literature*, 274. On Gundolf's theory of history, see Ulrich Raulff, "Der Bildungshistoriker Friedrich Gundolf," in Friedrich Gundolf, *Anfänge deutscher Geschichtsschreibung von Tschudi bis Winckelmann*, ed. E. Wind (Frankfurt am Main: Fischer, 1992), 115–54. For general assessment of the notion of *Bildung* in German historiography, see Aleida Assmann, *Arbeit am nationalen Gedächtnis: Eine kurze Geschichte der deutschen Bildungsidee* (Frankfurt am Main: Campus Verlag, 1993).

89. For a positive evaluation of George's notions of myth in the academic community in Heidelberg, see the pertinent recollections of Hans-Georg Gadamer, "Stefan George (1868–1933)," in *Die Wirkung Stefan George auf die Wissenschaft*, ed. H.-J. Zimmermann (Heidelberg: C. Winter, 1985), 43–47. For a general assessment of George and his circle, see Stefen Breuer, *Ästhetischer Fundamentalismus: Stefan George und der deutsche Antimodernismus* (Darmstadt: Wissenschaftliche Buchgesellschaft, 1995).

90. *The Works of Stefan George*, trans. O. Marx and E. Morwitz (Chapel Hill: University of North Carolina Press, 1974), 224. For a political-historical interpretation of George's poetry, see Klaus Landfried, *Stefan George—Politik des Unpolitischen* (Heidelberg: L. Stiehm, 1975).

91. Ernst Bertram, *Nietzsche: Versuch einer Mythologie* (Berlin: G. Bondi, 1918).

92. Friedrich Gundolf, *Caesar: Geschichte seines Ruhms* (Berlin: G. Bondi, 1924), 91.

93. Kantorowicz, "'Mythenschau,'" in Wolf, *Stupor Mundi*, 40.

94. Kahler, *Der Beruf der Wissenschaft*, 9. See also von Kahler's essay "Das Fortleben des Mythos," in his *Die Verantwortung des Geistes* (Frankfurt am Main: Fischer, 1952), 202–12.

95. According to Karl Ferdinand Werner, most German historians during that period conceived of their task in these pedagogical-demagogic terms, as teachers of the right "national" sentiments and opinions. "Machtstaat und nationale Dynamik in der Konzeption

der deutschen Historiographie 1933–1940," in *Machtbewußtsein in Deutschland am Vorabend des Zweiten Weltkrieges*, ed. F. Knippig (Paderborn: Schnönigh, 1984), 332–33.

96. Otto Gerhard Oexle, "German Malaise of Modernity: Ernst H. Kantorowicz and his 'Kaiser Friedrich der Zweite,'" in Fried and Benson, *Ernst H. Kantorowicz*, 33–56.

97. Eckhardt Grünewald, "'Übt an uns Mord und reicher blüht was blüht!': Ernst Kantorowicz spricht am 14. November 1933 über das 'Geheime Deutschland,'" in Fried and Benson, *Ernst H. Kantorowicz*, 57–76.

98. For general discussion, see Faulenbach, *Ideologie des deutschen Weges*, 248–89, 309–16.

99. Helmut Scheuer, *Biographie: Studien zur Funktion und zum Wandel einer literarischen Gattung vom. 18 Jahrhundert bis zur Gegenwart* (Stuttgart: J. B. Metzler, 1979), 131.

100. On Brackmann's role as the director of the notorious "Nord- und Ostdeutschen Forschungsgemeinschaft," see Michael Burleigh, *Germany Turns Eastward, A Study of "Ostforschung" in the Third Reich* (Cambridge: Cambridge University Press, 1988); and Schönwälder, *Historiker und Politik*. The standard work on German historiography under Nazism is still Karl Ferdinand Werner, *Das NS Geschichtsbild und die deutsche Geschichtswissenschaft* (Stuttgart: Kohlhammer, 1967).

101. Johannes Fried, "Ernst H. Kantorowicz and Postwar Historiography: German and European Perspectives," in Fried and Benson, *Ernst H. Kantorowicz*, 186.

102. Ernst Kantorowicz, "Grenzen, Möglichkeiten und Aufgaben der Darstellung mittelalterlicher Geschichte," ed. E. Grünewald, *Deutsches Archiv für Erforschung des Mittelalters* 50 (1994): 104–25.

103. Kantorowicz, *Frederick the Second*, 367–68.

104. Ibid., 203.

105. Ibid., 688–89.

106. Friedrich Hebbel, quoted by Grünewald, *Ernst Kantorowicz und Stefan George*, 79–80.

107. Kantorowicz, prefatory note to *Frederick the Second*. On the whole affair, see Grünewald, *Ernst Kantorowicz und Stefan George*, 65–76.

108. Brackmann, "Kaiser Friedrich der Zweite in 'mythischer Schau,'" in Wolf, *Stupor Mundi*, 22.

109. Kantorowicz, "'Mythenschau,'" in Wolf, *Stupor Mundi*, 24.

110. Ibid., 38–39, referring to Brackmann, "Kaiser Friedrich der Zweite in 'mythischer Schau,'" in Wolf, *Stupor Mundi*, 24.

111. Ibid., 23.

112. Ibid., 35–37.

113. Albert Brackmann, "Nachwort: Anmerkung zu Kantorowicz' Erwiderung," *Historische Zeitschrift* 141 (1930): 478.

114. Cited from Hans Belting, "Images in History and Images of History," in Fried and Benson, *Ernst H. Kantorowicz*, 96.

115. On Kantorowicz's studies in Heidelberg, see Grünewald, *Ernst Kantorowicz und Stefan George*, 43–53. On the "Heidelberg School" in medieval studies, see Herman Jakobs, "Die Mediavistik bis zum Ende der Weimarer Republik," in *Geschichte in Heidelberg*, ed. J. Miethke (Heidelberg: Springer Verlag, 1992), 39–66.

116. Eberhard Gothein, *Die Aufgaben der Kulturgeschichte* (Leipzig: Duncker und Humblot, 1889).

117. Lionel Gossman, *Orpheus Philologus: Bachofen versus Mommsen on the Study of Antiquity* (Philadelphia: American Philosophical Society, 1983). On Kantorowicz's association with this school, see the insightful comments of Roberto delle Donne, afterword to Alain Bureau, *Kantorowicz* (Frankfurt am Main: Klett-Cotta, 1990), 168.

118. Löwith, *Mein Leben in Deutschland vor und nach 1933*, 24.

119. Ernst Kantorowicz, *Laudes Regiae: A Study in Liturgical Acclamations and Medieval Ruler Worship* (Berkeley: University of California Press, 1946), 186.

120. Reprinted in Grünewald, *Ernst Kantorowicz und Stefan George*, 158-67.

121. For a fine elaboration of this transformation, see Ulrich Raulff, "Der letzte Abend des Ernst Kantorowicz: Von der Würde, die nicht stirbt: Lebensfragen eines Historikers," *Rechtshistorisches Journal* 18 (1999): 167-91.

122. Kantorowicz, *The King's Two Bodies*, ix. Cassirer refers to Kantorowicz in *The Myth of the State*, 137.

123. Kantorowicz, *The King's Two Bodies*, vii.

124. On Kantorowicz's role in the controversy, see David P. Gardner, *The California Oath Controversy* (Berkeley: University of California Press, 1967), 120-21.

125. Kantorowicz, *The King's Two Bodies*, viii.

126. Ibid., ix.

127. Cassirer, *The Myth of the State*, 3, 296.

128. Ernst H. Kantorowicz, "*Pro patria mori* in Medieval Political Theology," *American Historical Review* 56 (1951): 472-92.

129. Ibid., 490-91.

130. Ibid., 491.

131. On the meaning and history of this notion, see Josef Chytry, *The Aesthetic State: A Quest in Modern German Thought* (Berkeley: University of California Press, 1989).

132. Quoted by Grünewald in his "Biographisches Nachwort" to a new edition of Kantorowicz's *Friedrich der Zweite* (Stuttgart: Klett-Cotta, 1998), 548.

133. Kantorowicz, *The King's Two Bodies*, 26.

134. Ibid., 291-313.

135. Ibid., 495.

136. Ibid., 465. On Dante's distinctly mythological conception of life and history, see Patrick Boyde, *Dante Philomythes and Philosopher* (Cambridge: Cambridge University Press, 1981).

137. Kantorowicz, *The King's Two Bodies*, 474.

138. Ernst Kantorowicz, "The Problem of Medieval World Unity," *Annual Report of the American Historical Association for 1942* 3 (1944): 31-37, reprinted in Cherniavsky and Giesey, *Selected Studies*, 76-81.

139. Thomas Mann, *The Theme of the Joseph Novels* (Washington, D.C.: U.S. G.P.O., 1943), 21.

140. The best account is Peter Hoffmann, *Stauffenberg: A Family History, 1905-1944* (Cambridge: Cambridge University Press, 1995).

141. Peter Hoffmann, "Claus Graf Stauffenberg und Stefan George: Der Weg zur Tat," *Jahrbuch der Deutschen Schillergesellschaft* 12 (1968): 52-54.

142. Hoffmann, *Stauffenberg*, 30.

143. Grünewald, *Ernst Kantorowicz und Stefan George*, 75.

144. Hoffmann, *Stauffenberg*, 240–46.

145. Ibid., 246–47.

146. Ibid., 277, 353 n. 86. According to other sources, Stauffenberg's last call was not to the "secret [*geheime*]" but rather to the "sacred [*geheiligte*]" Germany.

147. Ibid., 282, 285.

148. Quoted from Giesey, "Ernst H. Kantorowicz," 198. For a critical examination of this letter, see Saul Friedländer, "Zwei jüdische Historiker in extremis: Ernst Kantorowicz und Marc Bloch angesichts des Nazismus und der Kollaboration," in *Bruchlinien: Tendenzen der Holocaustforschung*, ed. G. Koch (Cologne: Böhlau, 1999), 107–24.

149. Ernst H. Kantorowicz, "Das Geheime Deutschland: Vorlesung, gehalten bei Wiederaufnahme der Lehrtätigkeit am 14. November 1933," ed. E. Grünewald, in Fried and Benson, *Ernst H. Kantorowicz*, 77–93.

150. Grünewald, *Ernst Kantorowicz und Stefan George*, 127.

151. Kantorowicz, "Das Geheime Deutschland," 80.

152. Ibid., 81.

153. Ibid.

154. Max Kommerell, *Der Dichter als Führer in der deutschen Klassik* (Berlin: G. Bondi, 1928), 474.

155. Kantorowicz, "Das Geheime Deutschland," 87.

156. Ernst H. Kantorowicz, "Deutsches Papsttum," *Castrum Peregrini* 12 (1963): 7–24. See the discussion in Grünewald, *Ernst Kantorowicz und Stefan George*, 130–35.

157. Kantorowicz, "Deutsches Papsttum," 19–20, 23–4.

158. Ibid., 8.

159. For a comprehensive discussion of the Phoenix myth, see Kantorowicz, *The King's Two Bodies*, 388–401.

160. Ibid., 451.

161. Ibid., 5.

162. Clifford Geertz, "Centers, Kings, and Charisma," in *Rites of Power: Symbolism, Ritual and Politics since the Middle Ages*, ed. S. Wilentz (Philadelphia: University of Pennsylvania Press, 1985), 14–15, 34.

163. *Rituals of Royalty*, ed. D. Cannadine and S. Price (Oxford: Oxford University Press, 1987), 7.

164. Peter Schöttler, "Ernst Kantorowicz in Frankreich," in Fried and Benson, *Ernst H. Kantorowicz*, 144–61.

CHAPTER SIX

1. Ernst Bloch, "Recollections of Walter Benjamin," in *On Walter Benjamin: Critical Essays and Recollections*, ed. G. Smith (Cambridge, Mass.: MIT Press, 1988), 341.

2. Karola Bloch, *Aus meinem Leben* (Pfullingen: Neske, 1981), 53.

3. Theodor W. Adorno, "A Portrait of Walter Benjamin," in his *Prisms*, trans. S. Weber (London: Spearman, 1967), 231.

4. Gershom Scholem, "Walter Benjamin," in his *On Jews and Judaism in Crisis: Selected Essays*, ed. W. J. Dannhauser (New York: Schocken Books, 1976), 176–77.

5. Benjamin to Gershom Scholem, 9 August 1935, *The Correspondence of Walter Benjamin*,

ed. G. Scholem and T. Adorno, trans. M. R. Jacobson and E. M. Jacobson (Chicago: University of Chicago Press, 1994), 505.

6. Walter Benjamin, *Berliner Kindheit um Neunzehnhundert,* in *Gesammelte Schriften,* ed. R. Tiedemann and H. Schweppenhäuser, 8 vols. (Frankfurt am Main: Suhrkamp, 1972–88), 4:236.

7. Gershom Scholem, *Walter Benjamin: The Story of a Friendship,* trans. H. Zohn (Philadelphia: Jewish Publication Society of America, 1981), 190.

8. Ibid., 242.

9. Aristotle, *Metaphysics,* in *The Works of Aristotle,* trans. W. D. Ross (Oxford: Oxford University Press, 1928), 982b, 13–19.

10. Scholem, "Walter Benjamin," 178.

11. Ibid.

12. Scholem, *Walter Benjamin,* 57–58.

13. On the significance of Lehmann and his circle for Benjamin's intellectual development, see John McCole, *Walter Benjamin and the Antinomies of Tradition* (Ithaca, N.Y.: Cornell University Press, 1993), 73–79.

14. Scholem, *Walter Benjamin,* 22.

15. Gershom Scholem, "Walter Benjamin und Felix Noeggerath," *Merkur* 35 (1981): 134–69.

16. Scholem, *Walter Benjamin,* 31.

17. Ibid., 32. The entire discussion is published in Gershom Scholem, *Tagebücher 1913–1917,* ed. K. Gründer and F. Niewöhner (Frankfurt am Main: Jüdischer Verlag, 1995), 388–91.

18. Scholem, *Walter Benjamin,* 31.

19. Ibid., 61.

20. Walter Benjamin, *The Arcades Project,* trans. H. Eiland and K. McLaughlin (Cambridge, Mass.: Harvard University Press, 1999), 831–34.

21. Ibid., 461.

22. McCole, *Walter Benjamin and the Antinomies of Tradition,* 74 n. 8. See, however, the preliminary study of Winfried Menninghaus, *Schwellenkunde: Walter Benjamins Passage des Mythos* (Frankfurt am Main: Suhrkamp, 1986).

23. See, e.g., Rolf-Peter Janz, "Mythos und Moderne bei Walter Benjamin," in *Mythos und Moderne,* ed. K.-H. Bohrer (Frankfurt am Main: Suhrkamp, 1983), 363–81.

24. Jürgen Habermas, "Consciousness-Raising or Redemptive Criticism—The Contemporaneity of Walter Benjamin," trans. P. Brewster and C. H. Buchner, *New German Critique* 17 (1979): 47.

25. Ibid., 50.

26. Walter Benjamin, "Paris, the Capital of the Nineteenth Century," in Benjamin, *The Arcades Project,* 10.

27. Walter Benjamin, "The Work of Art in the Age of Mechanical Reproduction," in his *Illuminations,* ed. and with an introduction by H. Arendt, trans. H. Zohn (London: Fontana, 1973), 224–25.

28. Walter Benjamin, "One-Way Street," trans. E. Jephcott, in *Selected Writings,* vol. 1, *1913–1926,* ed. M. Bullock and M. W. Jennings (Cambridge, Mass.: Harvard University Press, 1996), 486. For a sensitive and positive interpretation of Benjamin's conception of the

"auratic," see Marlene Stoessel, *Aura: Das vergessene Menschliche: Zu Sprache und Erfahrung bei Walter Benjamin* (Munich: C. Hanser, 1983).

29. McCole, *Walter Benjamin and the Antinomies of Tradition,* 5.

30. Benjamin, "One-Way Street," 486.

31. Walter Benjamin, "Theories of German Fascism," trans. R. Livingstone, in *Selected Writings,* vol. 2, *1927–1934,* ed. M. W. Jennings, H. Eilland, and G. Smith (Cambridge, Mass.: Harvard University Press, 1999), 312–21.

32. Walter Benjamin, "On Some Motifs in Baudelaire," in *Illuminations,* 182. For a sensitive interpretation of Benjamin's later theory of experience, see Richard Wolin, *Walter Benjamin: An Aesthetic of Redemption* (New York: Columbia University Press, 1982), 226–49.

33. Benjamin, "On Some Motifs in Baudelaire," 184–85.

34. Ibid., 187.

35. Ibid., 183.

36. Walter Benjamin, "Oedipus, or Rational Myth," trans. R. Livingstone, in *Selected Writings,* 2:578.

37. Ibid., 580, quoting André Gide, *Incidences* (Paris: Nouvelle Revue Française, 1924), 81.

38. Walter Benjamin, *The Origin of German Tragic Drama,* trans. J. Osborn (London: NLB, 1977), 109.

39. Rolf Tiedemann, *Studien zur Philosophie Walter Benjamins* (Frankfurt am Main: Suhrkamp, 1973), 98–99.

40. Walter Benjamin, "Socrates" (1916), trans. T. Levin, in *Selected Writings,* 1:52.

41. Walter Benjamin, "Goethe's Elective Affinities," trans. S. Corngold, in *Selected Writings,* 1:310. See also the perceptive essay of Burckhardt Lindner, "Goethes 'Wahlverwandschaften' und die Kritik der mythischen Verfassung der bürgerlichen Gesellschaft," in *Goethes "Wahlverwandschaften": Kritische Modelle und Diskursanalysen zum Mythos Literatur,* ed. N. Bolz (Hildesheim: Gerstenberg, 1981), 23–44.

42. Benjamin, "Goethe's Elective Affinities," 1:326.

43. Ibid., 1:327.

44. Benjamin, *The Origin of German Tragic Drama,* 102.

45. Benjamin to Hugo von Hofmannstahl, 28 December 1925, *The Correspondence of Walter Benjamin,* 287.

46. Benjamin, "Paris, the Capital of the Nineteenth Century," 10.

47. Benjamin, "Goethe's Elective Affinities," 1:325–26.

48. I borrow the term from Irving Wohlfarth, "Re-fusing Theology: Some First Responses to Walter Benjamin's Arcades Project," *New German Critique* 39 (1986): 3–24.

49. On the controversy concerning this translation, see Martin Jay, "Politics of Translation: Sigfried Kracauer and Walter Benjamin on the Buber-Rosenzweig Bible," *Leo Baeck Institute Yearbook* 21 (1976): 3–24. For Benjamin's general theory of translation, see his essay "The Task of the Translator," in *Illuminations,* 69–82. For a discussion, see Winfried Menninghaus, *Walter Benjamins Theorie der Sprachmagie* (Frankfurt am Main: Suhrkamp, 1980).

50. Franz Kafka, "The Silence of the Sirens," trans. W. Muir and E. Muir, in *The Complete Stories,* by Franz Kafka, ed. N. N. Glatzer (New York: Schocken Books, 1971),

430–32. Benjamin comments on this parable in his essay "Franz Kafka," in *Illuminations*, 117–18.

51. Benjamin, "Franz Kafka," 117.

52. Max Horkheimer and Theodor Adorno discuss this episode in *The Dialectic of Enlightenment*, trans. J. Cummings (New York: Seabury Press, 1972), 33–36.

53. Benjamin, "Franz Kafka," 118.

54. Benjamin to Theodor Adorno, 31 May 1935, *The Correspondence of Walter Benjamin*, 488.

55. Louis Aragon, *Paris Peasant*, trans. S. Watson Taylor (London: Cape, 1980), 24, 28. On the reception of Aragon's novel in Germany, see Hans Freier, "Odyssee eines Pariser Bauern: Aragons 'mythologie moderne' und der deutsche Idealismus,' in Bohrer, *Mythos und Moderne*, 157–93.

56. Aragon, *Paris Peasant*, 130.

57. Walter Benjamin, "Surrealism," trans. E. Jephcott, in *Selected Writings*, 2:208.

58. Walter Benjamin, "On the Program of the Coming Philosophy," trans. M. Ritter, in *Selected Writings*, 1:100–110.

59. Benjamin, "Surrealism," 2:215.

60. Ibid., 2:209.

61. Ultimately, however, Benjamin was very disappointed with his experiments with hashish. "Main Features of My Second Impression of Hashish," trans. R. Livingstone, *Selected Writings*, 2:88.

62. Hannah Arendt, "Introduction: Walter Benjamin: 1892–1940," *Illuminations*, 7.

63. Walter Benjamin, "The Image of Proust," in *Illuminations*, 212–13.

64. Scholem, *Walter Benjamin*, 61.

65. Walter Benjamin, "On the Mimetic Faculty," trans. R. Livingstone, in *Selected Writings*, 2:720–22.

66. Walter Benjamin, "Theses on the Philosophy of History," in *Illuminations*, 263.

67. Benjamin, "On Some Motifs in Baudelaire," 160 (translation revised).

68. Benjamin, "The Image of Proust," 213.

69. Benjamin, "On Some Motifs in Baudelaire," 161–62.

70. Walter Benjamin, "The Storyteller," in *Illuminations*, 84, repeating the text of "Experience and Poverty," trans. R. Livingstone, in *Selected Writings*, 2:731–32.

71. Benjamin, "The Storyteller," 83.

72. Scholem, *Walter Benjamin*, 80. See also Wolin, *Walter Benjamin*, 15–27.

73. Benjamin, "The Storyteller," 99.

74. Benjamin, *The Origin of German Tragic Drama*, 232–33.

75. Benjamin, *The Arcades Project*, 268.

76. Benjamin, "Paris, the Capital of the Nineteenth Century," 11.

77. Charles Baudelaire, "The Painter of Modern Life," in his *Painter of Modern Life and Other Essays*, ed. and trans. J. Mayne (London: Phaidon, 1964), 12.

78. Benjamin, *The Arcades Project*, 367, referring to Friedrich von Bezold, *Das Fortleben der antiken Götter in mittelalterlichen Humanismus* (Leipzig: K. Schroeder, 1922).

79. Walter Benjamin, "Zu einer Arbeit über die Idee der Schönheit," *Gesammelte Schriften*, 6:128.

80. Ibid. On Benjamin's aesthetic theory, see Rainer Rochlitz, *The Disenchantment of Art: The Philosophy of Walter Benjamin*, trans. J. M. Todd (New York: Guilford Press, 1996).

81. Adorno, "A Portrait of Walter Benjamin," 234.

82. Jürgen Habermas, "The Entwinement of Myth and Enlightenment: Max Horkheimer and Theodor Adorno," in his *Philosophical Discourse of Modernity*, trans. F. Lawrence (Cambridge, Mass.: MIT Press, 1987), 106–30.

83. Walter Benjamin, "Johann Jakob Bachofen," in *Gesammelte Schriften*, 2:219–33. For full biographical and bibliographical background, see the editors' commentary, 2:963–76. On the intellectual background of Benjamin's essay, see Gerhard Plumpe, "Die Entdeckung der Vorwelt: Erläuterungen zu Benjamins Bachofenlektüre," *Text und Kritik* 31–32 (1971): 19–27.

84. Benjamin to Max Horkheimer, 8 April 1935, *The Correspondence of Walter Benjamin*, 481.

85. Scholem to Peter Szondi, 28 November 1961, in Gershom Scholem, *Briefe*, vol. 2 (1948–1970), ed. T. Sparr (Munich: C. H. Beck, 1995), 83.

86. Benjamin to Scholem, 20 July 1934, *The Correspondence of Walter Benjamin*, 450. However, contrary to Benjamin's claim, and according to his own testimony in a previous letter to Scholem on 11 October 1922, he had read at least some parts ("The Introduction," the chapter on Lesbos) of Bachofen's *Mutterrecht* before.

87. Scholem, *Walter Benjamin*, 31.

88. Werner Fuld, "Walter Benjamins Beziehung zu Ludwig Klages," *Akzente* 28 (1991): 274–87.

89. As late as 1930, Benjamin could still say of Klages's *Der Geist als Widersacher der Seele* that "it is without doubt a great philosophical work, regardless of the context in which the author may be and remain suspect." Benjamin to Scholem, 15 August 1930, *The Correspondence of Walter Benjamin*, 366.

90. Benjamin to Scholem, 14 January 1926, ibid., 288.

91. Alfred Baeumler, *Der Mythus von Orient und Occident: Eine Metaphysik der alten Welt, aus den Werken von J. J. Bachofen* (Munich: Beck, 1926).

92. Lionel Gossman, *Orpheus Philologus: Bachofen versus Mommsen on the Study of Antiquity* (Philadelphia: American Philosophical Society, 1983), 7.

93. Mann elaborates this notion in his essay "Freud and the Future," in *Essays by Thomas Mann*, trans. H. T. Lowe-Porter (New York: Vintage Books, 1957), 316–19.

94. Elisabeth Galvan, *Zur Bachofen-Rezeption in Thomas Manns Joseph-Roman* (Frankfurt am Main: Klostermann, 1996). On the wider intellectual background to Mann's work, see *Mythology and Humanism: The Correspondence of Thomas Mann and Karl Kerényi*, trans. A. Gelley (Ithaca, N.Y.: Cornell University Press, 1975).

95. Thomas Mann, *The Theme of the Joseph Novels* (Washington, D.C., 1943), 21–22. On Mann's opposition to Nazi mythology, see the discussion by Willy R. Berger, *Die mythologischen Motive in Thomas Manns Roman "Joseph und seine Brüder"* (Vienna: Böhlau, 1971), 22–26.

96. Benjamin to Theodor Adorno, 7 May 1940, *The Correspondence of Walter Benjamin*, 632.

97. Benjamin, "Johann Jakob Bachofen," 2:219–20.

98. Benjamin, "Franz Kafka," 117.

99. Ibid., 130.

100. For an excellent discussion of Benjamin, Proust, and the new art of remembrance, see McCole, *Walter Benjamin and the Antinomies of Tradition*, 253–79.

101. Benjamin, "The Image of Proust," 204.

102. Ibid., 216.

103. Ibid., 205–6.

104. Benjamin, *Berliner Kindheit*, 4:237.

105. Benjamin, *Berliner Kindheit*, introduction to the revised version, in *Gesammelte Schriften*, 7:1, 385. For a sensitive elaboration of this notion, see Peter Szondi, "Hope in the Past: On Walter Benjamin," trans. H. Mendelsohn, *Critical Inquiry* 4 (1978): 491–506.

106. Benjamin, *Berliner Kindheit*, 4:239.

107. Ibid., 4:238. See also Marianne Muthesius, *Mythos, Sprache, Erinnerung: Untersuchungen zu Walter Benjamins "Berliner Kindheit um Neunzehnhundert"* (Basel: Stromfeld, 1996).

108. For a luminous interpretation of this dimension in Benjamin's work, see Bernd Witte, *Walter Benjamin: An Intellectual Biography*, trans. J. Rolleston (Detroit: Wayne State University Press, 1991), 142–50. See also Burkhardt Lindner, "The *Passagen-Werk*, the *Berliner Kindheit*, and the Archaeology of the Recent Past," *New German Critique* 39 (1986): 25–46.

109. Benjamin, "The Storyteller," 86–87.

110. Benjamin, *Berliner Kindheit*, 4:250.

111. Ibid., 4:253.

112. Ibid., 4:248.

113. Benjamin, "Franz Kafka," 131.

114. Benjamin, "Theses on the Philosophy of History," 256.

115. Benjamin, "Franz Kafka," 117. On the proliferation of such "messianic" theories among German Jewish intellectuals at the time, see Anson Rabinbach, "Between Enlightenment and Apocalypse: Benjamin, Bloch, and Modern German Jewish Messianism," *New German Critique* 34 (1985): 78–124.

116. Benjamin, *Berliner Kindheit*, 4:270. Benjamin detects the same pattern in the life and works of Nikolai Leskov. "The Storyteller," 103.

117. Benjamin, *Berliner Kindheit*, 4:271.

118. Ibid., 4:272.

119. Ibid., 4:275.

120. Benjamin, "Franz Kafka," 130. On the "archaic" structure of Benjamin's worldview, see the groundbreaking study of Beatrice Hanssen, *Walter Benjamin's Other History: Of Stones, Animals, Human Beings, and Angels* (Berkeley: University of California Press, 1998).

121. Benjamin, "Franz Kafka," 130–31.

122. Walter Benjamin, "Max Brod's Book on Kafka: And Some of My Own Reflections," *Illuminations*, 144, 146. For a masterful illumination of this letter as a key to Benjamin's life and works, see Arendt, "Introduction: Walter Benjamin," 38–51.

123. Benjamin, "Franz Kafka," 128.

124. "Dialectical enchantment" is McCole's rendering of Benjamin's "dialektische

Feerie," literally "dialectical fairyland." *Walter Benjamin and the Antinomies of Tradition,* 229, 240–52. See the translation of this text in *The Arcades Project,* 873–84.

125. Benjamin, *The Arcades Project,* 874.

126. The standard architectural and cultural study of the arcades is Johann Friedrich Geist, *Arcades: The History of Building Type* (Cambridge, Mass.: MIT Press, 1983). For a useful collection of studies on Benjamin's project, see *Walter Benjamin et Paris,* ed. H. Wisman (Paris: Cerf, 1983).

127. Benjamin, *The Aracdes Project,* 875, 84.

128. Ibid., 85.

129. See, e.g., the description of Moscow in *Selected Writings,* 2:23–24. For a stimulating reading, see Peter Szondi, "Walter Benjamin's 'City Portraits,'" trans. H. Mendelsohn, in *On Textual Understanding and Other Essays,* by Peter Szondi (Minneapolis: University of Minnesota Press, 1986), 133–44.

130. Benjamin, *The Arcades Project,* 83.

131. David Frisby, *Fragments of Modernity: Theories of Modernity in the Work of Simmel, Kracauer, and Benjamin* (Cambridge, Mass.: MIT Press, 1986), 232–33.

132. Benjamin, *The Arcades Project,* 851.

133. Ibid., 461.

134. Susan Buck-Morss, *The Dialectics of Seeing: Walter Benjamin and the Arcades Project* (Cambridge, Mass.: MIT Press, 1988), 97–107.

135. Aragon, *Paris Peasant,* 27.

136. Ibid., 28–29.

137. Walter Benjamin, *The Arcades Project,* 458.

138. Aragon, *Paris Peasant,* 28–29, quoted in *The Arcades Project,* 87.

139. Walter Benjamin, "Karl Kraus" (1931), trans. E. Jephcott, in *Selected Writings,* 2:455.

140. Benjamin, *The Arcades Project,* 400.

141. Benjamin, "On Some Motifs in Baudelaire," 176.

142. Benjamin, *The Arcades Project,* 464.

143. Winfried Menninghaus, "Walter Benjamin's Theory of Myth," in Smith, *On Walter Benjamin,* 314–15.

144. Benjamin, "Paris, the Capital of the Nineteenth Century," in *The Arcades Project,* 4–5. For a perceptive discussion of Benjamin's dialectical appropriation of Michelet and romantic historiography, see Irving Wohlfarth, "Et cetera? The Historian as Chiffonier," *New German Critique* 39 (1986): 143–68.

145. August K. Wiedmann, *The German Quest for Primal Origins in Art, Culture, and Politics, 1900–1933* (Lewiston, N.Y.: Edwin Mellen Press, 1995), 113–14.

146. Scholem, "Walter Benjamin," 195. Benjamin's modern admirers have largely, and all too easily, ignored his dangerous liaison with conservative-reactionary thinkers like Klages and Schmitt. For a corrective assessment, see Richard Wolin's introduction to the revised edition of his *Walter Benjamin: An Aesthetic of Redemption* (New York: Columbia University Press, 1994), xxix–xl.

147. Erich Fromm, "Die sozialpsychologische Bedeutung der Mutterrechtstheorie," *Zeitschrift für Sozialforschung* 3 (1934): 196–227.

148. Benjamin, "Johann Jakob Bachofen," 2:230.

149. Ibid.

150. On this controversy, see Gossman, *Orpheus Philologus*, 21–41.

151. Johann Jakob Bachofen, *Beilage zu der Schrift Die Sage von Tanaquil: Theodor Mommsens Kritik der Erzählung von Ch. Marcius Coriolanus* (Heidelberg: J. C. B. Mohr, 1870).

152. J. J. Bachofen, *Myth, Religion, and Mother Right*, trans. R. Manheim (Princeton, N.J.: Princeton University Press, 1967), 72.

153. Benjamin, "Johann Jakob Bachofen," 2:224–25, recalling Friedrich Nietzsche, *The Birth of Tragedy*, trans. W. Kaufmann (New York: Vintage Books, 1967), 136.

154. Benjamin, "Theses on the Philosophy of History," 259

155. Ibid., 255, 266. For a wonderful illumination of this much-cited text, see Irving Wohlfarth, "'Männer aus der Fremde': Walter Benjamin and the German-Jewish Parnassus," *New German Critique* 70 (1997): 3–86.

156. Rolf Tiedemann, "Historical Materialism or Political Messianism? An Interpretation of the Theses on the Philosophy of History," trans. B. Byg, *Philosophical Forum* 15 (1983–84): 71–104.

157. Ibid., 98.

158. Walter Benjamin, "*Die Rückschritte der Poesie* bei Carl Gustav Jochmann: Einleitung," in *Gesammelte Schriften*, 2:572–85.

159. Werner Kraft, *Carl Gustav Jochmann und sein Kreis* (Munich: Beck, 1972).

160. Ibid., 577–78. On Benjamin's reception of Jochmann, see O. K. Werckmeister, "Walter Benjamin's Angel of History, or the Transfiguration of the Revolutionary into the Historian," *Critical Inquiry* 22 (1996): 239–67.

161. Benjamin, "*Die Rückschritte der Poesie* bei Carl Gustav Jochmann," 2:583.

162. Ibid., 2:579.

163. Ibid., 2:581–82.

164. Ibid., 2:583–84. See also my essay, "Retrospective Prophets: Vico, Benjamin, and Other German Mythologists," *Clio* 26 (1997): 427–48.

165. On the reception of Vico in Germany, see Max Harold Fisch, introduction to *The Autobiography of Giambattista Vico*, trans. T. G. Bergin and M. H. Fisch (Ithaca, N.Y.: Cornell University Press, 1963), 67–72.

166. Edmund Wilson, *To the Finland Station* (New York: Farrar, Straus, Giroux, 1972), 3–6.

167. *The College of Sociology (1937–39)*, ed. D. Hollier, trans. B. Wing (Minneapolis: University of Minnesota Press, 1988). On Benjamin's intellectual association with this group, see Chryssoula Kambas, *Walter Benjamin im Exil: Zum Verhältnis von Literaturpolitik und Ästhetik* (Tübingen: Niemeyer, 1983), 178–81.

168. Roger Caillois, introduction to *The College of Sociology*, 10.

169. Georges Bataille, "The Sorcerer's Apprentice," in *The College of Sociology*, 22.

170. *The College of Sociology*, 219.

171. Ibid., 389. See also the discussion in Buck-Morss, *The Dialectics of Seeing*, 117–18.

172. Benjamin, "Theses on the Philosophy of History," 261.

173. Ibid., 259–60.

174. Gershom Scholem, "Walter Benjamin and His Angel," trans. W. J. Dannhauser, in Scholem, *On Jews and Judaism in Crisis*, 232.

175. Benjamin, *The Arcades Project*, 463.
176. Benjamin, "Theses on the Philosophy of History," 257.
177. Ibid., 263.
178. Ibid., 262.
179. Benjamin, *The Arcades Project*, 461.
180. Ibid., 476.
181. Benjamin, "Theses on the Philosophy of History," 257.
182. Ibid., 259.
183. Benjamin, *The Arcades Project*, 486, quoting Pierre-Maxime Schuhl, *Machinisme et philosophie* (Paris: F. Alcan, 1938), 7, 35.

CHAPTER SEVEN

1. Samuel L. Goldberg, *The Classical Temper* (London: Chatto and Windus, 1961), 146. See also Eric Gould, *Mythical Intentions in Modern Literature* (Princeton, N.J.: Princeton University Press, 1981), 141–43.

2. Alasdair MacIntyre, *After Virtue: A Study in Moral Theory* (London: Duckworth, 1985).

3. On Joyce and Vico, see the informative essay of Walton A. Litz, "Vico and Joyce," in *Giambattista Vico: An International Symposium,* ed. G. Tagliacozzo and H. White (Baltimore: Johns Hopkins University Press, 1969), 245–55, and the various interpretive essays in *Vico & Joyce,* ed. D. P. Verene (New York: State University of New York Press, 1987).

4. For an insightful interpretation in that direction, see Michael Seidel's discussion of Vico's "poetic geography" in *Epic Geography: James Joyce's "Ulysses"* (Princeton, N.J.: Princeton University Press, 1976), 41–50.

5. Goldberg, *The Classical Temper,* 202–3.

6. Richard Ellmann, *James Joyce* (Oxford: Oxford University Press, 1983), 693.

7. Joyce to Carlo Linati, 21 September 1920, in *The Letters of James Joyce,* ed. S. Gilbert (New York: Viking Press, 1966), 1:147.

8. Fredric Jameson, "'Ulysses' in History," in *James Joyce and Modern Literature,* ed. W. J. McCormack and A. Stead (London: Routledge and Kegan Paul, 1982), 128.

9. Martha C. Nussbaum, *Love's Knowledge: Essays on Philosophy and Literature* (Oxford: Oxford University Press, 1990), 5; Stanley Cavell, *In Quest of the Ordinary: Lines of Scepticism and Romanticism* (Chicago: University of Chicago Press, 1988); Richard Rorty, *Contingency, Irony, and Solidarity* (Cambridge: Cambridge University Press, 1989). See also the excellent study by the literary scholar Wayne C. Booth, *The Company We Keep: An Ethics of Fiction* (Berkeley: University of California Press, 1988).

10. Goldberg, *The Classical Temper,* 203.

11. Much has been written on Joyce's conception of history. Two valuable recent studies are James Fairhall, *James Joyce and the Question of History* (Cambridge: Cambridge University Press, 1993); and Robert Spoo, *James Joyce and the Language of History: Dedalus's Nightmare* (New York: Oxford University Press, 1994). See also Edmund L. Epstein's discussion of the "Nestor" chapter in *James Joyce's "Ulysses,"* ed. C. Hart and D. Hayman (Berkeley: University of California Press, 1974), 17–28.

12. On Joyce's notion and descriptions of "epiphanies," see James Joyce, *Epiphanies*, ed. O. A. Silverman (Norwood, Pa.: Norwood Editions, 1978).

13. James Joyce, *Ulysses* (New York: Modern Library, 1961), 24.

14. Ibid.

15. Ibid., 25.

16. On the actual circumstances and significance of this description, see Robert E. Spoo, "'Nestor' and the Nightmare: The Presence of the Great War in *Ulysses*," *Twentieth-Century Literature* 32 (1986): 137–54.

17. Joyce, *Ulysses*, 25. Stephen's meditations invoke Aristotle's definition of motion in *Physics*, 3.1. On Joyce and Aristotle, see Richard Ellmann, *Ulysses on the Liffey* (London: Faber and Faber, 1972), 1–23.

18. Joyce, *Ulysses*, 24–25.

19. Ibid., 25–26.

20. Ibid., 26.

21. Homer, *Odyssey*, 3.36–35.

22. Joyce, *Ulysses*, 29.

23. On Deasy's historical fallacies, see Robert M. Adams, *Surface and Symbol: The Consistency of James Joyce's "Ulysses,"* (New York: Oxford University Press, 1962), 20–24.

24. Joyce, *Ulysses*, 31, 33, 34–35.

25. Giambattista Vico, *The New Science*, trans. T. Bergin and M. H. Fisch (Ithaca, N.Y.: Cornell University Press, 1968), par. 149. For an insightful elaboration of Joyce's mythopoeic conception of history in the "Proteus" chapter, see Spoo, *James Joyce and the Language of History*, 107–12.

26. James Joyce, *Finnegans Wake* (London: Viking Press, 1939), 255, 262. Norman O. Brown uses the mythopoeic perceptions of Vico and Joyce in his daring theory of poetic history, *Closing Time* (New York: Random House, 1973). See also the brilliant review essay on this book by Stuart Hampshire, "Joyce and Vico: The Middle Way," in *Giambattista Vico's Science of Humanity*, ed. G. Tagliacozzo and D. P. Verne (Baltimore: Johns Hopkins University Press, 1976), 321–32.

27. Joyce, *Finnegans Wake*, 452.

Index

Achilles, 55, 76, 89, 127, 142
Adorno, Theodor, 177, 179, 228, 232, 252, 255, 271
Aeschylus, 19
Alberti, Leon Battista, 109–10, 164
Alexander the Great, 55, 213
Ammianus Marcelinus, 101
Anderson, Benedict, 7–8
Annales, 3, 20–21
anti-Semitism, 33–34, 144, 146, 171, 179, 189, 253
Apollo, 79, 80, 120, 131
Aragon, Louis, 246, 271; *Paris Peasant*, Benjamin on, 241–42, 265–68
Arcadia, 128
Aretino, Leonardo, 114
Aristotle, 42, 60, 149, 167; on "lover of myths," 229–30; Joyce on theory of history and poetry of, 289
Arminius the Cheruscan, 7
Arnauld, Antoine, 82
art history and theory: Benjamin on, 251–52; Burckhardt's contribution to, 105–8; modernistic aspects of, 12–13; neoromantic aestheticism in, 159–60, 163, 178; Schorske on, 17–18; F. T. Vischer on, 141–42; Warburg's contribution to, 135–37, 145–50, 152–58, 168–69, 172–75
Aschheim, Steven, 34, 206
Asclepius, 135
astrology, 12, 118, 149; Warburg on, 171–75

Atalanta, 80
Auerbach, Erich, 74
aura: Benjamin's conception of, 233–35; in Baudelaire's poetry, 234–35, 242
authority: Benjamin on mythic norms and forms of, 236–41, 247, 261, 272–73; Kantorowicz on Emperor's, 197–99; Livy on Roman, 41; Machiavelli on meanings and means of, 45–48, 56–57; Vico on mythopoeic origins of, 72–73, 80

Baader, Franz von, 230, 238
Bachofen, Johann Jacob, 3, 9, 161, 214, 236; animosity to Mommsen, 273–74; on archaic society, 255–56; Benjamin on, 252–62, 265, 271–74; exploitation by Fascists, 255; on prehistoric legacies in Western Civilization, 261–64; theory of matriarchy, 258–60, 272–73
Bacon, Francis, *Wisdom of the Ancients*, Vico on, 67, 70–72
Baeck, Leo, 146
Baethgen, Friedrich, 194
Baeumler, Alfred, 253–54, 272
Baglione, Astore and Simonetto, 112–13
Balzac, Honoré de, 233; Benjamin on, 264
Baron, Hans, 49
baroque: Benjamin on German tragic drama of, 251–52; Burckhardt disproves art of, 107, 165; Warburg on, 179–80

343